THE *LEMONADE* READER

D1598892

The Lemonade Reader is an interdisciplinary collection that explores the nuances of Beyoncé's 2016 visual album, *Lemonade*. These essays and editorials present fresh, cutting-edge scholarship fueled by contemporary thoughts on film, material culture, religion, and black feminism.

Envisioned as an educational tool to support and guide discussions of the visual album at post-graduate and undergraduate levels, *The Lemonade Reader* critiques *Lemonade*'s multiple Afrodias-poric influences, visual aesthetics, narrative arc of grief and healing, and ethnomusicological reach. The essays, written by both scholars and popular bloggers, reflect a broad yet uniquely specific black feminist investigation into constructions of race, gender, spirituality, and southern identity.

The Lemonade Reader gathers a newer generation of black feminist scholars to engage in intellectual discourse and confront the emotional labor around the *Lemonade* phenomenon. It is the premier source for examining *Lemonade*, a text that will continue to have a lasting impact on black women's studies and popular culture.

Kinitra D. Brooks is the Audrey and John Leslie Endowed Chair in Literary Studies in the Department of English at Michigan State University, USA. Dr. Brooks specializes in the study of black women, genre fiction, and popular culture. She currently has two books in print: *Searching for Sycorax: Black Women's Hauntings of Contemporary Horror* (2017), a critical treatment of black women in science fiction, fantasy, and horror; and *Sycorax's Daughters* (2017), an edited volume of short horror fiction written by black women. Her current research focuses on portrayals of the conjure woman in popular culture. Dr. Brooks is serving as the Advancing Equity Through Research Fellow at the Hutchins Center for African & African American Research at Harvard University for the 2018–2019 academic year.

Kameelah L. Martin is Professor of African American Studies and English at the College of Charleston in South Carolina, USA, where she is also Director of the African American Studies Program. Dr. Martin's research explores the lore cycle of the conjure woman as an archetype in literature and visual texts. She is author of two monographs: *Conjuring Moments* *in African American Literature: Women, Spirit Work, and Other Such Hoodoo* (2013) and *Envisioning Black Feminist Voodoo Aesthetics: African Spirituality in American Cinema* (2016). She is the Assistant Editor of the *College Language Association Journal* and has published in *Studies in the Literary Imagination*; *Black Women, Gender, and Families*; and the *African American National Biography*. She has edited special issues of *Genealogy* and *South Atlantic Review*, and co-edited a section of *The Routledge Anthology of African American Rhetoric* (2018).

THE *LEMONADE* READER

Edited by Kinitra D. Brooks and Kameelah L. Martin

Routledge
Taylor & Francis Group

LONDON AND NEW YORK

First published 2019
by Routledge
2 Park Square, Milton Park, Abingdon, Oxon OX14 4RN

and by Routledge
52 Vanderbilt Avenue, New York, NY 10017

Routledge is an imprint of the Taylor & Francis Group, an informa business

British Library Cataloguing in Publication Data
A catalogue record for this book is available from the British Library

Library of Congress Cataloging-in-Publication Data
Names: Brooks, Kinitra Dechaun. | Martin, Kameelah L., 1978-
Title: The Lemonade reader / edited by Kinitra D. Brooks and Kameelah L. Martin.
Description: London ; New York : Routledge, 2019.
Identifiers: LCCN 2018059235 | ISBN 9781138596771 (hardback : alk. paper) | ISBN 9781138596788 (pbk. : alk. paper) | ISBN 9780429487453 (ebook)
Subjects: LCSH: Beyoncâe, 1981---Criticism and interpretation. | Beyoncâe, 1981-. Lemonade. | Popular music--History and criticism. | Sex in music. | Feminism and music. | Womanism | Orishas.
Classification: LCC ML420.K675 L46 2019 | DDC 782.42164092--dc23
LC record available at https://lccn.loc.gov/2018059235

ISBN: 978-1-138-59677-1 (hbk)
ISBN: 978-1-138-59678-8 (pbk)
ISBN: 978-0-429-48745-3 (ebk)

Typeset in Bembo
by Taylor & Francis Books

To my NOLA folks, on this plane and the next. And to Cincia, this one is all you.—kdb.

To my warriors, seen and unseen. For my moon flower, Indigo Amelia-Marie, who was conjured during this creative process.—klm.

CONTENTS

List of illustrations   x

List of contributors   xii

Foreword by Candice Benbow   xx

Preface by T. Denean Sharpley-Whiting   xxiii

Acknowledgments   xxvi

Introduction: Beyoncé's *Lemonade* lexicon – Black feminism and
spirituality in theory and practice   1
Kinitra D. Brooks and Kameelah L. Martin

Interlude A: What do we want from Beyoncé?   5
Maiysha Kai

Interlude B: Bittersweet like me – When the lemonade ain't made
for Black fat femmes and women   9
Ashleigh Shackelford

PART I
Some shit is just for us   **15**

1 Some shit is just for us: Introduction   17
   Cheryl Finley and Deborah Willis

2 Something akin to freedom: Sexual love, political agency, and
   Lemonade   19
   Lindsey Stewart

3 Getting to the roots of "Becky with the good hair" in
  Beyoncé's *Lemonade*   31
  Janell Hobson

4 Pull the sorrow from between my legs: *Lemonade* as rumination
  on reproduction and loss   42
  LaKisha M. Simmons

5 The language of *Lemonade*: The sociolinguistic and rhetorical
  strategies of Beyoncé's *Lemonade*   55
  Alexis McGee

Interlude C: How not to listen to *Lemonade*: Music criticism and
epistemic violence   69
Robin James

Interlude D: Women like her cannot be contained: Warsan Shire
and poetic potential in *Lemonade*   77
Shauna M. Morgan

PART II
Of her spiritual strivings   **83**

6 Looking for Beyoncé's spiritual longing: The power of visual/
  sonic meaning-making   85
  Valerie Bridgeman

7 Beyoncé's *Lemonade* folklore: Feminine reverberations of *odú*
  and Afro-Cuban *orisha* iconography   88
  Nicholas R. Jones

8 The *slay* factor: Beyoncé unleashing the Black Feminine Divine
  in a blaze of glory   98
  Melanie C. Jones

9 Beyoncé's diaspora heritage and ancestry in *Lemonade*   111
  Patricia Coloma Peñate

10 Signifying waters: The magnetic and poetic magic of Oshún as
   reflected in Beyoncé's *Lemonade*   123
   Martin A. Tsang

11 Beyoncé reborn: *Lemonade* as spiritual enlightenment   133
   Lauren V. Highsmith

Interlude E: From Destiny's Child to Coachella – On embracing
then resisting others' respectability politics 144
L. Michael Gipson

Interlude F: "Formation" and the Black-ass truth about Beyoncé
and capitalism 155
Tamara Winfrey Harris

PART III
The lady sings her legacy **159**

12 The lady sings her legacy: Introduction 161
Daphne A. Brooks

13 To feel like a "natural woman": Aretha Franklin, Beyoncé and
the ecological spirituality of *Lemonade* 166
Michele Prettyman Beverly

14 Beyoncé's western South serenade 183
Tyina Steptoe

15 Beysthetics: "Formation" and the politics of style 192
Tanisha C. Ford

16 "I used to be your sweet Mama": Beyoncé at the crossroads of
blues and conjure in *Lemonade* 202
Kinitra D. Brooks and Kameelah L. Martin

17 Beyoncé's *Lemonade* and the black swan effect 215
Kyra D. Gaunt

18 She gave you *Lemonade*, stop trying to say it's Tang: Calling out
how race-gender bias obscures Black women's achievements in
pop music 234
Birgitta J. Johnson

Interlude G: Erasing shame – Beyoncé's *Lemonade* and the Black
woman's narrative in cinema 246
Aramide Tinubu

Afterword by Regina N. Bradley 250
Index 253

ILLUSTRATIONS

Figures

B.1	Video still of Serena Williams twerking for King Bey from "Sorry." *Lemonade*, Parkwood Entertainment, 2016	12
2.1	Video still from "Formation." *Lemonade*, Parkwood Entertainment, 2016	26
3.1	Video still from "Sorry." *Lemonade*, Parkwood Entertainment, 2016	39
4.1	Women seated and leaning, adorned with *Sacred Art of the Ori* by Laolu Senbanjo from "Sorry." *Lemonade*, Parkwood Entertainment, 2016	46
4.2	Video still from "6 Inch." *Lemonade*, Parkwood Entertainment, 2016	47
4.3	Video still of the title card for the chapter titled "Loss." *Lemonade*, Parkwood Entertainment, 2016	48
4.4	Video still of Lezley McSpadden. *Lemonade*, Parkwood Entertainment, 2016	50
C.1	Video still of Beyoncé singing while composing on the piano from "Sandcastles." *Lemonade*, Parkwood Entertainment, 2016	73
D.1	Video still of women seated and leaning, adorned with *Sacred Art of the Ori* by Laolu Senbanjo from "Sorry." *Lemonade*, Parkwood Entertainment, 2016	78
9.1	Video still "Don't Hurt Yourself." *Lemonade*, Parkwood Entertainment, 2016	117

10.1 Painting of Oshún incorporating many of her symbols and
flowing water. Titled *Iyalode Oxum* (2018), by André Hora.
With permission of the artist   124
 F.1 Video still of Beyoncé referencing "paper" from "Formation."
Lemonade, Parkwood Entertainment, 2016   156
13.1 Video still from "Pray You Catch Me." *Lemonade*, Parkwood
Entertainment, 2016   178
15.1 Video still of Beyoncé dancing in a hallway from
"Formation." *Lemonade*, Parkwood Entertainment, 2016   196
17.1 Video still of Beyoncé walking down a street with both hands
held high in a yellow dress from "Hold Up." *Lemonade*,
Parkwood Entertainment, 2016   228
17.2 Video still of Beyoncé opening double doors as water rushes
from behind her from "Hold Up." *Lemonade*, Parkwood
Entertainment, 2016   229
 G.1 Beyoncé Knowles-Carter sits pensively in a tub. Her face is
turned downward and she's cast in hues of blue and green   248

Tables

5.1 Language Feature Frequency in *Lemonade* tracks, actual
[potential]   64
5.2 Feature Frequency Comparison (%)   65

CONTRIBUTORS

Candice Benbow is a writer and educator. She has appeared on Huff Post Live and is a columnist with *Urban Cusp Magazine*. In addition to her own blog, her work has appeared in *ShePreaches Magazine*, Ebony.com, For Harriet, and Patheos. Candice is a native of Winston-Salem, North Carolina, and a graduate of Tennessee State University. Currently, she is a doctoral student in Religion and Society at Princeton Theological Seminary and a Lecturer in Women's and Gender Studies at Rutgers University. Her work lies at the intersections of Black feminist theory, womanist theology and doctrines of creation. She is the founder of "Red Lip Theology," a movement to encourage young Black Christian women to embrace their whole selves as good creation.

Michele Prettyman Beverly is a scholar of film, media, and African American visual culture, and an Assistant Professor of Media Studies at Mercer University. Her work explores black independent cinema, hip hop visual culture, Southern film and iconography, and how spirituality is mediated through film, imagery, and culture. Michele is co-editor of a forthcoming "Close-Up" in *Black Camera* on the New York "scene" of black independent filmmakers. She is also an advisory board member of liquid blackness: a research project on blackness and aesthetics. Her work has been presented at diverse forums including the Collegium of Black Women Philosophers, the Society for Cinema and Media Studies, the Association for the Study of the Arts of the Present (ASAP), and the World Picture Conference.

Regina N. Bradley is a writer and researcher of African American life and culture. She is an alumna Nasir Jones HipHop Fellow (2016) and is Assistant Professor of English and African Diaspora Studies at Kennesaw State University in Georgia. Dr. Bradley's expertise and research interests include twentiethth- and twenty-first-century African American literature, hip hop culture, race and the contemporary U.S. South, and sound studies. Her current book-length project, *Chronicling Stankonia: OutKast and the Rise of the Hip Hop South* (under contract), explores how Atlanta, GA hip hop duo OutKast influences renderings of the Black American South after the Civil Rights Movement.

Valerie Bridgeman is Dean and Vice President for Academic Affairs and Associate Professor of Homiletics and Hebrew Bible at Methodist Theological School in Ohio. She is also Founder and CEO of WomanPreach! Inc.

Daphne A. Brooks is Professor of African American Studies, Theater Studies, American Studies, and Women's, Gender, and Sexuality Studies at Yale University. She is the author of two books: *Bodies in Dissent: Spectacular Performances of Race and Freedom, 1850–1910* (2006), winner of The Errol Hill Award for Outstanding Scholarship on African American Performance from the American Society for Theatre Research (ASTR); and *Jeff Buckley's Grace* (2005). Brooks is currently working on a three-volume study of black women and popular music culture entitled *Subterranean Blues: Black Women Sound Modernity*. The first volume in the trilogy, *Liner Notes for the Revolution: The Archive, the Critic, and Black Women's Sound Cultures*, is forthcoming from Harvard University Press. Brooks has also authored numerous articles on race, gender, performance, and popular music culture.

Kinitra D. Brooks is the Audrey and John Leslie Endowed Chair in Literary Studies in the Department of English at Michigan State University. Dr. Brooks specializes in the study of black women, genre fiction, and popular culture. She currently has two books in print: *Searching for Sycorax: Black Women's Hauntings of Contemporary Horror* (2017), a critical treatment of black women in science fiction, fantasy, and horror; and *Sycorax's Daughters* (2017), an edited volume of short horror fiction written by black women. Her current research focuses on portrayals of the conjure woman in popular culture. Dr. Brooks will serve as the Advancing Equity Through Research Fellow at the Hutchins Center for African & African American Research at Harvard University for the 2018–2019 academic year.

Cheryl Finley is an art historian, curator, and contemporary art critic. She has contributed essays and reviews to *Aperture, Nka: Journal of Contemporary African Art, American Quarterly*, and *Art Forum*. Dr. Finley is Associate Professor of Art History at Cornell University, and is the author of *Committed to Memory: The Art of the Slave Ship Icon*. Her prolific critical attention to photography has produced co-authored publications such as *Teenie Harris, Photographer: An American Story, Harlem: A Century in Images*, and numerous catalog essays and journal articles on artists such as Lorna Simpson, Hank Willis Thomas, Walker Evans, Joy Gregory, Carrie Mae Weems, Roshini Kempadoo, and Berenice Abbott.

Tanisha C. Ford is an award-winning writer and cultural critic, and Associate Professor of Africana Studies and History at the University of Delaware. She is the author of *Liberated Threads: Black Women, Style, and the Global Politics of Soul* (2015), which narrates the powerful intertwining histories of the Black Freedom movement and the rise of the global fashion industry. *Liberated Threads* won the 2016 Organization of American Historians' Liberty Legacy Foundation Award for best book on civil rights history. She is a co-founder of TEXTURES, a pop-up material culture lab, creating and curating content on fashion and the built environment. Tanisha's work centers on social movement history, feminist issues, material culture, the built environment, black life in the Rust Belt, girlhood studies, and fashion, beauty, and body politics. Her public writing and cultural commentary have been featured in diverse media outlets and publications including *ELLE, The Atlantic, The Root, Aperture, The Feminist Wire, Cognoscenti, The New York Times, The New Yorker, Ebony, NPR: Code Switch, Fusion, News One, New York Magazine: The Cut, Yahoo! Style, Vibe Vixen,* and New York City's HOT 97. Her scholarly research has been published in the *Journal of Southern History, NKA: Journal of Contemporary African Art, The Black Scholar,* and *Qed.*

Kyra D. Gaunt is an Assistant Professor in the Music Department at the University at Albany. She is an ethnomusicologist and a social media researcher, and has taught both undergraduate and graduate courses using a multi-disciplinary approach to black music studies that incorporates sociology, anthropology, political sociology, race/racism studies, gender and feminist studies, digital humanities, and new media studies. In 2007, her radical counter-history *The Games Black Girls Play: Learning the Ropes from Double-Dutch to Hip-Hop* (New York University Press) won the Alan Merriam Book Prize for most outstanding English-language monograph awarded by the Society for Ethnomusicology. Among other significant publications, her peer-reviewed articles appear in *Musical Quarterly, Parcours anthropologiques,* and *Journal for Popular Music Studies.* Dr. Gaunt's scholarship has been funded by the Mellon Foundation, the National Endowment for the Humanities and the Ford Foundation. Her research focuses on the critical study and hidden musicianship in black girls' musical play at the intersections of race, gender, and the body in the age of hip hop. Her current research involves the critical study of the unintended consequences of race, gender, and technology from YouTube to Wikipedia.

L. Michael Gipson is an award-winning writer, public health, and youth advocate who has worked on HIV/AIDS, youth, and community development programming on the local, state and national level for 20 years. As an author, his short stories, speeches, public health, and socio-political essays have also been published in three recent anthologies: *Poverty and Race in America: The Emerging Agendas; Health Issues Confronting Minority Men Who Have Sex with Men;* and *Mighty Real: Anthological Works by African American SGLBT People.* Two future anthologies will also boast his personal narrative essay contributions, including Keith Boykin's *For Colored Boys* and Kevin Harewood's *From Us to You with Love: Black Men Writing About The Black Women They Love.*

Tamara Winfrey Harris is a writer who specializes in the ever-evolving space where current events, politics, and pop culture intersect with race and gender. Well versed on a range of topics—including Beyoncé's feminism, Rachel Dolezal's white privilege, and the black church and female sexuality—Tamara has been published in media outlets including *The New York Times, Cosmopolitan, New York, Ebony, The American Prospect*, and *Ms.* She pens a regular column, "Some of Us Are Brave," for *Bitch* magazine. Her work, including "No Disrespect: Black Women and the Burden of Respectability," which first appeared in *Bitch*, has been republished in textbooks such as *The Arlington Reader* (2013). Tamara has also been called to share her analysis on media outlets including NPR's *Weekend Edition* and Janet Mock's *So Popular* on MSNBC.com, as well as university campuses nationwide, including Princeton University, Purdue University, and Ohio State University. Tamara's first book, *The Sisters Are Alright: Changing the Broken Narrative of Black Women in America* was published in 2015 by Berrett-Koehler.

Lauren V. Highsmith is a scholar-artist pursuing her English PhD at Emory University. Her interdisciplinary research explores issues, concepts, and phenomena of (Black) popular American culture; intersections between literature and music; ethics; and (African) American literature. As a musician and academic, Highsmith endeavors to continue researching projects themed around deconstructing popular music. Her broader interests include African American Studies, Performance Studies, Black Feminism, Critical Philosophy of Race, Popular Culture Studies, and Media Studies. Highsmith is also invested in public scholarship, and works to create spaces to bridge the gap between the academy and the community, with artists as the intermediaries.

Janell Hobson is Professor of Women's, Gender, and Sexuality Studies at the University at Albany. She is the author of two books—*Venus in the Dark: Blackness and Beauty in Popular Culture* (Routledge, 2005, 2nd edition 2018) and *Body as Evidence: Mediating Race, Globalizing Gender* (2012)—and the *Ms.* cover story "Beyoncé's Fierce Feminism" (2013). She is the editor of the special issue, "Harriet Tubman: A Legacy of Resistance," for the refereed journal *Meridians: Feminism, Race, Transnationalism* and the volume *Are All the Women Still White? Rethinking Race, Expanding Feminisms* (2016). Hobson is at work on projects addressing the intersections of black women's histories and popular culture.

Robin James is Associate Professor of Philosophy and Women's and Gender Studies at the University of North Carolina Charlotte. Her research and teaching focus mainly on sound and music, theories of gender/race/sexuality, feminist philosophy, continental philosophy, and political philosophy. She is especially interested in the ways neoliberalism and biopolitics impact gender norms, race relations, and pop music aesthetics, and in the ways women and gender non-conforming musicians and fans write, perform, and listen to music to mitigate the negative effects of cisheterosexism and racism. She is the author of three books: *The Sonic Episteme* (under contract with

Duke University Press); *Resilience and Melancholy: Pop Music, Feminism, Neoliberalism* (2015); and *The Conjectural Body: Gender, Race, and the Philosophy of Music* (2010).

Birgitta J. Johnson teaches undergraduate and graduate courses in world music, African American music, African music, and ethnomusicology at the University of South Carolina, where she is Associate Professor. She received her Bachelor of Arts in Music from Agnes Scott College, where she played piano (major), violin (principal second), and Ghanaian drums, and sang in the Joyful Noise gospel choir. Johnson received her Masters and Doctorate degrees in Ethnomusicology from the University of California, Los Angeles, where she worked with Jacqueline Cogdell DjeDje, Cheryl L. Keyes, and Francisco Aguabella in African American and African music and Afro-Cuban music, drumming, and dance. Dr. Johnson's research interests include: ethnomusicology; world music; African American and African music; music and worship in African American churches; musical change and identity in black popular music; music in African American megachurches; sacred music in the African Diaspora, and community archiving. Specific genres: gospel music, praise and worship, blues, hip-hop, rhythm and blues, soul, and neo-soul.

Melanie C. Jones is 2018–19 Crump Visiting Professor and Black Religious Scholar-in-Residence at Seminary of the Southwest in Austin, TX. She has lectured at Brite Divinity School in Fort Worth, TX, American Baptist College in Nashville, TN, Chicago Theological Seminary and The Illinois Institute of Technology in Chicago, teaching introductory and upper-level face-to-face and online courses in humanities, theology, ethics, gender/sexuality studies, and writing. She earned a BA in Economics and Political Science from Howard University and a Master of Divinity with a certificate in Black Church Studies from Vanderbilt University Divinity School. She is a womanist ethicist, millennial preacher, and intellectual activist. As a third-generation Baptist preacher, Rev. Melanie was ordained as the youngest clergywoman in its 49-year history, at South Suburban Missionary Baptist Church of Harvey, Illinois.

Nicholas R. Jones specializes in race, gender, and sexuality in early modern Iberia and the early Atlantic world. With particular interest in material and visual cultures, his research examines the articulation of agency, subjectivity, and the performance of black diasporic identity-formation in early modern Spain and Portugal as well as their colonial kingdoms. His most recent publications include "Cosmetic Ontologies, Cosmetic Subversions: Articulating Black Beauty and Humanity in Luis de Góngora's 'En la fiesta del Santísimo Sacramento'" published in the 2015 Winter issue of *Journal for Early Modern Cultural Studies* and a forthcoming monograph, *"Black Talk": Transoceanic Blackness and the Performance of Black Diasporic Identity in Imperial Iberia*, and he is working on a second book project that analyzes archival and literary representations of black women as celebrity figures in transatlantic early modernity. He is Assistant Professor of Spanish at Bucknell University.

Maiysha Kai is managing editor of the "The Glow Up," the beauty, fashion, and women's empowerment vertical of premier African American news site TheRoot. com. Her commentary on social and cultural issues has been cited by major outlets such as *The New York Times* and CNN. Prior to becoming a journalist, Maiysha enjoyed a successful career as a model and voiceover and commercial actress, represented by some of the top agencies in the world. In addition, she is a critically acclaimed singer/songwriter whose debut single, "Wanna Be" from her first album *This Much Is True*, was nominated for a 2009 Grammy.

Kameelah L. Martin is Professor of African American Studies and English at the College of Charleston in South Carolina, where she is also Director of the African American Studies Program. Dr. Martin's research explores the lore cycle of the conjure woman as an archetype in literature and visual texts. She is the author of two monographs: *Conjuring Moments in African American Literature: Women, Spirit Work, and Other Such Hoodoo* (2013) and *Envisioning Black Feminist Voodoo Aesthetics: African Spirituality in American Cinema* (2016). She is the Assistant Editor of the *College Language Association Journal* and has published in *Studies in the Literary Imagination* and *Black Women, Gender, and Families*, as well as *The African American National Biography*. She has also edited special issues of *Genealogy* and *South Atlantic Review*, and co-edited a section of the *Routledge Anthology of African American Rhetoric* (2018).

Alexis McGee received her PhD from the University of Texas at San Antonio, where she also received two certificates of concentration in Linguistics and Rhetoric and Composition. Her research focuses on Black feminist theory, African American language, literacies, and rhetorics as well as rhetorical theory and composition pedagogy. Dr. McGee has published in *Pedagogy* and *Obsidian*, as well as *Computers and Composition*. She is Assistant Professor in the Department of English at the University of Alabama.

Shauna M. Morgan, the author of *Fear of Dogs and Other Animals*, is a poet and scholar who springs from a rural district in Clarendon, Jamaica and holds an enduring love for the Diaspora about which she writes. She teaches creative writing and literature of the African Diaspora at Howard University in Washington, D.C., and her current research focuses on representations of black womanhood in twenty-first-century literature. Her poems were shortlisted for the 2011 Small Axe literary prize and recently won Interviewing the Caribbean's 2016 Catherine James Palmer Prize. She has published poetry in *A Gathering Together, ProudFlesh: New Afrikan Journal of Culture, Politics & Consciousness, Pluck! The Journal of Affrilachian Arts & Culture, The Pierian, Illuminations*, and elsewhere. Her critical work has appeared in the *College Language Association Journal, ARIEL, Bulletin of the School of Oriental and African Studies, Journal of Postcolonial Writing*, and *South Atlantic Review*.

Patricia Coloma Peñate is a native of Madrid, Spain. Patricia earned a PhD in Literary Studies at Georgia State University (2012), where she gained expertise in

African American and Afro-Hispanic Literature and folklore. She taught Spanish, African American, and Afro-Hispanic literature at the University of Alabama Birmingham before returning to Spain, where she currently serves on the faculty at San Antonio Catholic University of Murcia (UCAM). Her research focuses on ethnography, women's studies, and transatlantic modernism. She has published in *Callaloo, Black Magnolias: A Literary Journal*, and *College Language Association Journal*.

Ashleigh Shackelford is a Black fat cultural producer, multidisciplinary artist, nonbinary shapeshifter, and data futurist based in Atlanta, Georgia, with roots in Richmond, Virginia. She is the creator and director of a Southern body liberation organization, Free Figure Revolution, which focuses on decolonizing antiblack body violence. She is also the project director and creator of "The Fat Census" and the "Queer Domestic Violence & Sexual Assault Survey." Ashleigh is just a regular degular bad bitch that illustrates the relationship between Blackness, fatness, desire politics, gender deviance, queerness, and technology through art, writing, and community organizing.

T. Denean Sharpley-Whiting is the Gertrude Conaway Vanderbilt Distinguished Professor of Humanities (African American and Diaspora Studies and French) at Vanderbilt University, where she is also Chair of the Department of African American and Diaspora Studies and Director of the Callie House Research Center for the Study of Global Black Cultures and Politics. She is author/editor of 14 books and 3 novels, of which the latest academic volume is *La Vénus hottentote: écrits, 1810 à 1814, suivi des textes inédits* (Paris: L'Harmattan, 2018).

LaKisha M. Simmons is the author of *Crescent City Girls: The Lives of Young Black Women in Segregated New Orleans* (2015), which won the SAWH Julia Cherry Spruill Prize for best book on southern women's history and received Honorable Mention for the ABWH Letitia Woods Brown Memorial Book Award for the best book on African American women's history. Simmons has written about black girlhood and historical method in the *Journal of the History of Childhood and Youth*; about black college students and sexual cultures in the 1930s for *Gender & History*; has a forthcoming article on southern black girl writers in *Tulsa Studies in Women's Literature*; and is working on an article on the ways in which Beyoncé's *Lemonade* remembers Louisiana's sugar plantations. She is also the co-organizer and co-creator of the Global History of Black Girlhood Conference, which first convened at the University of Virginia (UVA) in 2017.

Tyina Steptoe is an Associate Professor of History at the University of Arizona. Her writing has appeared in the *American Quarterly, Journal of African American History, Oxford American, Houston Chronicle*, and *TIME*. Her book, *Houston Bound: Culture and Color in a Jim Crow City*, examines how the migration of black East Texans, Creoles of color, and ethnic Mexicans complicated notions of race in Houston between the 1920s and 1960s. *Houston Bound* won the Kenneth Jackson

Award for Best Book (North American) from the Urban History Association and the W. Turrentine Jackson Book Prize from the Western History Association.

Lindsey Stewart joined the Department of Philosophy at the University of Memphis as Assistant Professor in 2017. Previously, she was a Postdoctoral Mellon Fellow at Wellesley College. Her teaching and research interests are in black feminism, African American philosophy, and social and political philosophy. Being a native Southerner (born and raised in Louisiana), her approach to research and teaching is particularly informed by an attentiveness to regional dynamics in the U.S. Her research focuses on developing black feminist conceptions of political agency, with special attention to the intersection of sexuality, region, religion, and class.

Aramide Tinubu is a film critic and entertainment writer. Her work has been published in *EBONY, JET, ESSENCE*, Bustle, the *Daily Mail*, IndieWire, and Blavity. She wrote her master's thesis on Black Girlhood and Parental Loss in Contemporary Black American Cinema. She is a cinephile and NYU + Columbia University alum.

Martin A. Tsang is the Cuban Heritage Collection Librarian and Curator of Latin American Collections at the University of Miami. He is a cultural anthropologist whose work explores Afro-Asian religiosity in Cuba as well as issues concerning HIV in the wider Caribbean. Martin is a Junior Fellow in the Andrew W. Mellon Society of Fellows in Critical Bibliography at the Rare Book School, and he is interested in print and material cultures of the circum-Atlantic.

Deborah Willis, PhD, is University Professor and Chair of the Department of Photography & Imaging at the Tisch School of the Arts at New York University (NYU). She is also affiliated to NYU's Department of Social & Cultural Analysis, Africana Studies, where she teaches courses on iconicity, and cultural histories visualizing the black body, women, and gender. She received a MacArthur Fellowship and a Guggenheim Fellowship. Dr. Willis is the author of *Posing Beauty: African American Images from the 1890s to the Present* and co-author of *The Black Female Body: A Photographic History; Envisioning Emancipation: Black Americans and the End of Slavery*; and *Michelle Obama: The First Lady in Photographs*.

FOREWORD

Undeniable is the love Black women have for Beyoncé Giselle Knowles-Carter. For many, it was instant. From the moment she stepped on the scene with Destiny's Child, we felt drawn to her. She had the look and she could sing. It seemed that every generation had that one Black female superstar, and Beyoncé filled that void for mine. We grew up with her. We knew the bugaboos she was singing about because we were dating them, too. She embodied everything about our experience as young Black women growing up at the turn of the century because she was us. We knew her. And we loved her.

For many, the adoration came much later. As Beyoncé matured, so did her sound. And while the *B'Day* album catapulted her into that international superstardom stratosphere, it was the *IV* album that took many from simply loving Bey to actually seeing her. Breaking ranks with her father's management company and taking the reins of her career, *IV* introduced us to a woman navigating newfound freedom and a love that was testing its limits and her boundaries. There was a depth and a darkness to those songs that we'd never heard from the Queen before. She sang, at times, with an assured uncertainty that reflected the chaos in our own lives. She knew us. And she loved us enough to sing about it.

Just as we all were settling into Mrs. Knowles-Carter's newfound ownership of herself, out of nowhere, she gave us a Black feminist manifesto for the ages. The surprise self-titled album kicked in the door and made way for a Beyoncé that was unapologetically Black, unapologetically sexual, and unapologetically free. Pushing past the limits of the girl-next-door persona in her alter ego "Sasha Fierce" that many came to love, Bey showed our generation that it is possible for all of these aspects of our identities to find synergy. We can embrace the erotic and be educated at the same time. Sex and Spirit can dwell together. Though many of us may have been ready, all of us were not. Yet, leaning into her own liberation, Beyoncé taught us that we don't have to wait for others if we are ready to be free.

And it was that freedom, that love of self and Black women that permeated *Lemonade*. This was not just another album; she'd already given us those. It wasn't just another visual project, either. We'd come to expect powerful imagery from Beyoncé. This was so much more. This was a sonnet to all Black women who had ever believed in a love that failed them. It was a love letter to sisters who didn't think it was possible to live beyond betrayal. It was a meal from Grandma's kitchen, reminding us that we've been here before and everything is going to be alright. Situating her personal experience of betrayal within the trajectory of Black women's lived trauma and resilience, *Lemonade* forced us to question why broken hearts are considered a rite of passage, and pushed us to reimagine what healing and wholeness can look like for ourselves.

Those questions and answers catapulted me into creating the Lemonade Syllabus. When the *Lemonade* visual album premiered on HBO in 2016, I and so many other sisters were struck by how deeply it drew from the Black feminist and womanist wells. Many of us were on social media, quoting passages from popular and academic works that were foreign to many. We knew where she was coming from, even if everyone else did not. After several women asked me to explain what we meant when we proclaimed that *Lemonade* was another treatise on Black female life in America, the Syllabus came to life. With submissions from over 70 Black women, the Lemonade Syllabus is a collection of over 250 works that center Black womanhood in its historical and contemporary contexts. This free resource has been downloaded over 600,000 times and has been used to create new undergraduate courses and "lemonade stands" in public libraries across the United States and the UK.

Creating the Lemonade Syllabus taught me several things. First, as Black women with access to a wealth of academic information, we often take for granted that the conversations we're having are universal. It's nothing for my friends and I to discuss Bey's latest project—or any Black cultural production—using the tools we learned in grad school. That's not everyone's experience, and I'm sure it's not Bey's desire that any conversation concerning her art be exclusionary. She has always been here for all of us. In many ways, the Lemonade Syllabus was my attempt at breaking down the barriers that keep access a privilege denied to many simply because they can't afford it. Not only that: The Lemonade Syllabus proved many who hold their educations to be sacrosanct wrong in their estimations that Bey "just isn't that smart." We've long heard the critiques of Beyoncé's intelligence, as if she could not be an iconic pop star and read. What many learned is that not only does Bey read, but she was also raised on the same Black feminist sheroes that we were. It was not a fluke that, when watching *Lemonade*, we could see Zora, Maya, Toni, and June. The imprint of Black women creators and thinkers is as much on her as it is on us. They loved us all that much.

It's that love that brings us to this *Lemonade Reader*. I am excited about the opportunity to discuss this visual album as an intellectual production worthy of inquiry. For far too long Black feminist work and art has been viewed as niche theoretical work that only applies to a select few. As Black feminist and womanist thinkers continue to dominate in academic, political, entertainment, and cultural spheres, those who seek to diminish our work will have to reckon with the fact that it is everywhere. It is not going anywhere, and we will continue to use it to best articulate the experiences of Black people nationally and abroad. That *Lemonade* is rightly discussed as a point of entry into broader conversations concerning intersectional violence, structural oppression, and the survival strategies of Black women, that Beyoncé Knowles-Carter's work can be placed in conversation with the work of Kimberlé Crenshaw, Patricia Hill Collins, and Delores Williams only speaks to Black feminism's legacy of informed art. We have always worked with us, on behalf of us, to think and create a way forward. It will never be held hostage to non-Black modes of inquiry or life.

Assembled in this reader are scholars and thinkers who, first and foremost, love Black people. Any substantive conversation about Black art and artists can only include those who love the totality of Black people and know what it takes to make healing art in an anti-Black world. And, if anyone knows how viciously Beyoncé has been picked apart by White standards of beauty and Black respectability politics, it's Black women. These essays look at the person and work Beyoncé through a lens of love. Pushing us to think critically about sexuality, race, religion, and gender, the work of these theorists and thought leaders center an affection for the woman who has given us work from the depths of her heart. That affection also opens up the room for a loving critique of the erasure of other Black women's narratives and the reinforcement of capitalism that also happens in some of Bey's work. Only those who love you well and want you to be your best self get the space to hold you accountable. Through the power of *Lemonade*, these essays will cause us to become self-reflexive and do the work to check where we may have, even ever so slightly, leaned into death-dealing systems that work overtime to oppress the vulnerable and marginalized.

Because the question remains: If we aren't doing this work to free ourselves and our people, what are we doing? Beyoncé didn't give us *Lemonade* so that we might discuss it with those who have created and contributed to the structures of our oppression that they might become fascinated with how intelligent and astute we are. She offered it to us that we might become free. We have not scratched the surface of all of *Lemonade*'s themes and meanings. We will be sitting with it for quite some time. It haunts us as much as it heals us. That is a hard truth. But using ingredients the master could not grow or sustain himself yet thought belonged to him, she mixed a concoction that honored the past, told the truth about the present, and welcomes a future of our making. She knew what we needed. That's real love.

Candice Benbow

PREFACE

That Beyoncé Knowles-Carter's *Lemonade* was as sonically pleasing as it was visually stunning is the stuff of countless music reviews and blogs. Situated at a generational crossroads with respect to the thespian—that is, I am too young to be her mother but too old for her to be an aspirational muse or feminist influencer—*Lemonade* nonetheless struck me in the way it has the writers in the present volume: as complicated, complex, and even purposefully contradictory. Its *Daughters of the Dust* (1991)-like cinematic quality is owing to both Julie Dash and Arthur Jafa with an undeniable nod to photographer Carrie Mae Weems's *Louisiana Project* (2003), while its haunting poetic lyricism, outside of song, is that of British-Somali poet Warsan Shire. Beyoncé herself neither terrorizes or puzzles me as an artist; but her skilled blend of artistry, capitalism, and the personal does intrigue, at least in her latest iteration that is *Lemonade*: seeming invulnerability made vulnerable, therefore relatable, accessible, and certainly marketable—for an instant—alongside that of her husband's Rousseau-like *Confessions* in *4:44*.

Tapping into a fountainhead of pain to author creativity parallels the experiences of New World Africans. If slavery was social death, as sociologist Orlando Patterson argues, it was also "life"—life that produced and sustained "families, churches, and associations of all kinds," in the words of historian Ira Berlin, that forged "new languages, aesthetics, and philosophies as expressed in stories, music, dance, and cuisine."[1] My turn to slavery and New World Africans is not accidental, for Beyoncé has drawn different, but no less interesting, inspirations from American slavery in her conception of *Lemonade*. According to Melina Matsoukas, *Lemonade*'s director: "She wanted to show the historical impact of slavery on black love, and what it has done to the black family. And black men and women—how we're almost socialized not to be together."[2] Slavery as the inexorable *bête noire* to the black family and black love populates

American cultural memory; it engendered the controversial Moynihan Report on the Negro Family, which turns up like the clichéd bad penny in *Lemonade*, despite ample historical evidence by John Blassingame, Eugene Genovese, and Herbert Gutman to the contrary. This historically revisionist employment is fascinatingly put to work by a feminist artist to interrogate boorish male behavior. And, in so doing, patriarchy and black male entitlement receive a version of *ego te absolve*, but not quite, as one can legitimately argue, *Lemonade* still centers black women's pain and becoming whole. Quite plainly, this is the stuff that drives feminists *d'un certain âge* and era to distraction.

And yet it is precisely *Lemonade*'s exploration of an age-old problem with an admittedly highly flawed origin story, its daring to plumb a personal yet collective pain so deep in its 11 chapters that the hauntingly unspeakable is spoken, that reminded me of Haitian writer Marie Vieux-Chauvet's 1968 triptych, *Love, Anger, and Madness* (*Amour, Colère et Folie*). The thematic spines in Vieux-Chauvet's three novellas are fear, longing, loss, and repression against the backdrop of Haiti's history under the Duvalier (Papa Doc) regime and American economic imperialism. Our narrator of *Love*, Claire, writes in her diary:

All private lives are alike. Why would you be different from me? Suffocating fear makes freaks of all of us. That's why we take shelter behind a façade. When the façade crumbles, we are handed over to merciless judges worse than we are.

Commercially branded, marketed, shielded, and sheltered, Beyoncé allows a nearly 46-minute glimpse behind the façade by handing the "merciless judges" the carefully curated *Lemonade*. Repressive ideals of femininity accompanied by longing and fear of marital loss to those unattainable ideals, maternal loss (miscarriages), infertility, and the enduring and bedeviling forms of state-sanctioned violence and neglect directed towards black (women's) lives and emotional well-being linked to the traumas of racism, sexism, and slavery animate *Lemonade* and function like Vieux-Chauvet's brutally, nightmarish Tonton Macoutes and French slavery and colonialism's afterlives. Art is succor; lemonade is made from the lemons of racism, sexism, colorism, classism, faithless lovers, murdered children, never-born children, black maternal health-care disparities allotted to black women the world over. Beyoncé, like Claire of Vieux-Chauvet's *Love*, channels her fire and fury into redemptive possibilities.

The appealing perfectness that is Beyoncé—tall, wealthy, blonde-tressed, red-boned, hour-glassed—is contrasted with the appealing ordinariness of most every black woman's story given flight in *Lemonade*. The essays contained therein collectively think around and through these tensions in a push and pull fashion. It is after all what art—and *Lemonade* is undeniably art—forces us to do.

T. Denean Sharpley-Whiting
Nashville, TN, 2018

Notes

1 Ira Berlin, "Coming to Terms with Slavery in Twenty-First-Century America," in James Oliver Horton and Lois E. Horton, *Slavery and Public History: The Tough Stuff of American Memory*, University of North Carolina Press, 2008, 6.
2 Anupa Mistry, "Matsoukas: Beyoncé Wanted to Show the Historical Impact of Slavery on Black Love," February 27, 2017, https://www.thefader.com/2017/02/27/beyonce-paid-lemonade-visuals.

ACKNOWLEDGMENTS

Getting to this point has been an absolute whirlwind of blessings and goodwill from so many folks in our lives. A huge thank you to all our contributors for their time, words, goodwill, and flexibility.

We would like to thank the Institute for Research on Women at the University of Michigan for awarding us their Feminist Research Seminar grant which gave us our first opportunity to work with many of the scholars whose work appears in this very volume. Fondly remembered as The *Lemonade* Seminar we had an amazing weekend of black woman bonding that included our sister in Bey, Omise'eke Tinsley, whose work precedes this volume. We would especially like to thank Heidi Bennett, who catered to our every need, and Jocelyn Stitt, who invited us to apply.

Thank you, John Jennings, for an awesome book cover. We love it!

We would also like to thank the Hutchins Center for African & African American Research at Harvard University for their administrative support. The community at the Hutchins Center provided us with our amazing Editorial Assistant, Kyra March, who became crucial in our organization and communication of the volume in its last few months of coming together. Thank you to the Fall 2018 class of Hutchins Fellows for their feedback and enthusiasm. And a final thank you to Drs. Krishna Lewis and Abby Wolf, and Professor Henry Louis Gates, Jr.

Finally, we would like to thank our family, friends, and valued colleagues for their continued love and support. Without you, we would not be here.

INTRODUCTION: BEYONCÉ'S *LEMONADE* LEXICON

Black feminism and spirituality in theory and practice

Kinitra D. Brooks and Kameelah L. Martin

bell hooks's critique of *Lemonade* created a firestorm of responses from myriad scholars, artists, writers, and others who self-identify as black and feminist. Many black feminists, including those of her own generation, read her words to be symptomatic of a second-wave feminism that is unable to account for those women that employ their sexuality as power, particularly in high femme performance. The hooks blog debate signaled, if nothing more, that there is much left to be said and understood about Beyoncé's recent creative endeavor. The overwhelming response to *Lemonade* by black women of all ethnicities, classes, and creeds is a testament to the undeniable, though often unrecognized, power of black women's lived experiences. Black women—as mothers, daughters, wives, and as their own, self-actualized beings—have to negotiate multiple identities and forms of oppression. The visual album gave voice to how black women maneuver through the triple jeopardy of race, class, and gender in the twenty-first century. Beyoncé's body of work engages with black feminist ethos in ways that are still yet to be explored. The global platform on which Beyoncé stands is incomparable to anything black feminists saw in their generation or since. The urgency of the moment—the multivalent dialogues about black women's emotional labor, joy, and healing in love relationships—propels us toward developing a single volume that offers just a sample of the numerous paths along black feminism that one might take when viewing and studying *Lemonade*. It is a trailblazing visual text that is forcing the academy to reconsider how black feminists engage in the popular world and scholarship simultaneously.

With the slew of editorials, blogs, podcasts, and other media coverage and conversations about the impact of Beyoncé's latest visual album, we were drawn by the alluring combination of *Lemonade* being hyper-contemporary and the urgency to seize the opportunity to critique such a rich text while it still lingers in the popular culture mind. In that vein, we offer you *The Lemonade Reader*—an interdisciplinary text that initiates a theoretical and critical dialogue among diverse voices. *The Lemonade Reader* is a collection of essays in which multiple generations of black feminist scholars and thinkers engage in intellectual discourse and confront the emotional labor around the *Lemonade* phenomenon. When we first undertook this endeavor, only a few scholarly journals proposed special issues around Beyoncé as a media and pop culture icon in general, and a couple of books had attempted to conquer the mystic of Queen Bey.

There is currently no definitive ur-text on Beyoncé's *Lemonade* that is scholarly in nature. There is The Lemonade Syllabus and the blog post collected and aggregated by Janell Hobson and Jessica Marie Johnson on African American Intellectual History Society's website. McFarland Press recently published *The Beyoncé Effect: Essays on Sexuality, Race, and Feminism* (2016), edited by Adrienne Trier-Bieniek, which treats the criticism and praise of her trajectory from girl group to solo artist. While this is one of few scholarly books on the star, it does not include any discussion of the *Lemonade* visual album. More recently there is Omise'eke Tinsley's *Beyoncé in Formation: Remixing Black Feminism* (University of Texas Press, 2018) and *Queen Bey: A Celebration of Power and Creativity of Beyoncé Knowles-Carter*, edited by Veronica Chambers (St. Martin's Press, 2019). There are disparate scholarly works in various journals. There is also the special issue of *Black Camera* on Beyoncé as visual icon in general, but not specifically on the phenomenon of *Lemonade*. Many well-known blogs have long considered Beyoncé a subject of scholarly inquiry, such as The Crunk Feminist Collective and The Feminist Wire. There are a growing number of blogs and think pieces by credible scholars that take up myriad interpretations of *Lemonade*, yet none have attempted to collect the intellectual discourse around the visual album in a single, coherent collection of essays.

We have created an intellectual community that has come together collectively to produce in-depth, theoretical treatments of *Lemonade* in plain language steeped in scholarly rigor through the specific lenses of black feminist criticism and black spectatorship. We are proudly intergenerational as we reject the simplistic paradigms of hooks's rhetoric—reflective of both the best of her theorizations of the popular and new thinking in the field. As a community of Bey-thinkers, we examine *Lemonade*'s multiple Afrodiasporic influences, visual aesthetics, narrative arc of grief and healing, and ethnomusicological reach; our collection reflects the broad, yet uniquely specific black feminist investigation into constructions of gender, spirituality, black southern identity, and the presences of the Ancestors. Our interests lie in deciphering Beyoncé's choice to invoke her conjuring Creole ancestors, to embody the Afro-feminine divine, and to embed resistance in her fashion choices such as wearing a nineteenth-century tignon, Kente cloth, and Yoruba body art. Likewise, we are invested in uncovering the spiritual implications of returning to the liminal space of the Louisiana bayou and slave quarters for black women who inherit the role of cultural bearers in their families and communities. How does understanding African spiritual traditions allow the south to be a site of horror and a safe space simultaneously? What can we learn from the film about the womanist practice of black female communal healing?

In centering the audiovisual film as the topic of our anthology, we advance the theory and practice of what co-editor Kameelah Martin has termed black feminist voodoo aesthetics. Black feminist voodoo aesthetics, or

> the inscription of African ritual cosmologies on the black female body ... has been deployed in visual media for varying purposes. Voodoo aesthetics become manifest in the performance of ceremony, the inclusion of sacred objects or accoutrements on the body, the use of the body as a vessel for Spirit, and various other associations between persons of African descent and African religious iconography.[1]

Citing Julie Dash's *Daughters of the Dust* (1991) as an exemplary film that engages this aesthetic, *Lemonade*, with its allusions to Dash's iconic film, is situated as the most recent iteration of black women's sacred traditions in visual media. Within these pages, we have produced fresh, cutting-edge scholarship fueled by contemporary thoughts about film, material culture, religion, and black feminism.

We ruminate on the blueprint for healing Beyoncé has provided for black women when their worlds fall apart. We move beyond the intimacies of romantic betrayal as *Lemonade* attempts to break the cycles of emotional violence in black heterosexual relationships. The audiovisual album also portrays the potential for Black women's worlds to fall apart through the experience of child loss, be it through miscarriage or state violence. Beyoncé's blueprint for healing encourages black women to 1) Go home—as we see her return to her Louisiana roots, to her mother's people; 2) Go to water—we see this in the latter half as Beyoncé returns to the natural world, pays homage to Ibo landing, and chooses the swamp to create a maroon colony of black women; 3) Heal with other women—the end of *Lemonade* shows Beyoncé recovering her freedom in the midst of generations of black women, both living and on the ancestral plane. Beyoncé presents us with a liberatory feminist practice that "is rooted in an ethical commitment to undoing [racially] gendered domination."[2]

We bring together a cadre of contributors that reaches across disciplinary boundaries, yet shares an expertise in African Diaspora histories and culture. These include ethnomusicologists, religious practitioners, literary scholars, pop culture critics, historians, philosophers, bloggers, and Religious Studies scholars. These contributors read and interpret *Lemonade* from various disciplines and positionalities, offering the unique opportunity to address transdisciplinary quandaries about the theoretical, pedagogical, cultural, and racial complexities of Beyoncé's *Lemonade*. Everyone is writing at a level that is open and approachable, and we encourage you to make this book your own. Those readers that prefer a lighter treatment are encouraged to read the Interludes. You can get a wonderful sense of the in-depth work being done on *Lemonade* by reading the Interludes as they are shorter and lack academic jargon. We ultimately see the reader as an integrated volume that joins together the best of in-depth research by top scholars in their respective fields and cultural critics. We are pleased to have both Candice Benbow and Janell

Hobson, scholars who authored the most popular and cohesive online sources about *Lemonade* that are currently accessible. We want this piece to be the premier source for examining *Lemonade*, a text that will continue to have a lasting impact on black women's studies and popular culture.

Our aspiration for *The Lemonade Reader* is for it to be the leading, foundational work in Beyoncé studies. Beyoncé Knowles's musical and visual/performing artistry has the breadth (already spanning twenty years) to diversify and problematize conversations about popular culture studies centered on specific larger-than-life figures such as Sarah Baartman, Josephine Baker, and Billie Holliday. Her feminist and political sensibilities continue to evolve, and *The Lemonade Reader* seeks to capture and reflect a foundational moment in that trajectory of what promises to be a lifelong career.

Notes

1 Martin, Kameelah L. 2016. *Envisioning Black Feminist Voodoo Aesthetics: African Spirituality in American Cinema.* Lanham, MD: Lexington Books, xi.
2 Perry, Imani. 2018. *Vexy Thing: On Gender and Liberation.* Durham, NC: Duke University Press, 7.

INTERLUDE A: WHAT DO WE WANT FROM BEYONCÉ?

Maiysha Kai

I find myself asking that question more often than I'd expect, given that I've never been a card-carrying member of the "Hive." Not that I dislike Beyoncé—I appreciate her, admire her talent, tenacity, and good works. I critique and defend her at equal turns, and enthusiastically applaud, when the spirit moves me. But if asked about my feelings for the mononymous megastar, they are best described as blessedly neutral. Because blessed are those who are neutral on the topic of Beyoncé. That might seem an odd statement, especially in a book devoted to an exploration of her seminal work, *Lemonade*. One might even ask: Why, then, am I writing about Beyoncé? Well, I write for and about black women for a living—all types of black women, but most often, famous ones. Therefore, it's probably safe to say that despite any personal ambivalence, I have spent a significant amount of my professional life meditating on the movements and enduring mystique of the famous black woman we know as Beyoncé. Strikingly, of the handful of black women who have achieved her level of fame, few are as polarizing. In fact, a widely publicized 2018 poll declared Beyoncé "the most politically divisive entertainer on the Forbes 100 list."[1] It was a dubious distinction that prompted even this blessedly neutral journalist to ask, "Why?"

Obvious signs point to 2016. It was a pivotal year for America, and an equally pivotal one for Beyoncé. After years of sustaining her own seemingly blessed neutrality (save a close relationship with the Obamas), the debut of her *Formation* video—and subsequent Black Panther-inspired Super Bowl performance—displayed an unexpected streak of activism in a woman better known for her performances than her politics. As 2016 exposed more of the darkness lurking just beneath the surface of our country's well-polished veneer, so did Beyoncé. The release of her *Lemonade* album revealed a woman as fractured as she is famous, and seemingly, as socially concerned as successful.

And yet, even as she pulled back the curtain on her famously private life with a work more personal than any she'd ever offered before, there was suspicion that it was just another layer of the façade. Were her politics performative? Her confessions another bit of choreography? For black women, in particular, our perception of Beyoncé is far more than political; it's personal. Her presence—as icon, instigator, archetype—at times feels as visceral and conflicted as the crossroads of intersectionality itself. For instance, if I were to ask any of the myriad brilliant black women I know, observe, and write about how they feel about Beyoncé, their answers might range from "certified stan" to "that woman," as one friend has inexplicably done for years, refusing to refer to her as anything but. So provocative is Beyoncé's presence that even I, as indifferent as I claim to be, once bristled unexpectedly during an otherwise entertaining television performance, when my lover at the time blithely praised Beyoncé as "the paragon of womanhood."

How could I ever hope to live up to that?

Even intellectual discourse on Beyoncé is fraught with conflict: In her memoir, *Eloquent Rage*, feminist scholar and author Brittney Cooper refers to her as both a "victim" and "feminist muse."[2] Beyoncé-endorsed writer and feminist thinker Chimamanda Ngozi Adichie once distanced herself from the entertainer, declaring "her type of feminism is not mine," yet just as quickly conceding that she had "nothing but the best intentions."[3] Black feminist icon bell hooks has, at intervals, infamously labeled Beyoncé a "terrorist"[4] who "positively exploits images of black female bodies"[5]—presumably, including her own. That assessment prompted activist and author Janet Mock to defend the superstar against what she considered "femmephobia."[6] So, which is it? Perhaps all of the above, though few will give Beyoncé credit for such layered complexity. But what is undeniable is that the person, the persona, and our collective response to the cultural phenomenon we call Beyoncé remain a study in contrasts.

We admire her—and resent her. We laud her as a beacon of black excellence; yet we doubt her capacity to fully love and understand our blackness. We criticize her well-curated image; yet, when she reveals herself, we question what we see, because her pain too closely resembles our own. We do not trust that, most of all. We don't trust that Beyoncé's blues could, in any way, resemble our own. We do not trust her blondeness, her bronze-ness, her beauty, or her well-guarded boundaries. We don't trust her talent or her testimony. We don't trust her access— to fame, to love, or to happiness. We don't trust that her privilege could allow her to comprehend our pain. And we certainly don't trust her feminism; it's too sexual, too splashy, too sudden. Plus, it looks too much like forgiveness—and we struggle to give that, even to ourselves.

In short, we don't trust Beyoncé to enlighten us, only to entertain us. Hell, some of us don't even trust her to enlighten herself. We want her art, not her agency. So, what do we want from Beyoncé? As Brittney Cooper would likely note, even if many of us idealize her, we certainly don't want her to "have it all." Those of us who reside at the intersection of blackness and womanhood are often expected to make a choice between the two. It is never presumed that we can have both—or more—in full. There is always a sacrifice, a devil's debt to be paid. And yet, here is Beyoncé, publicly pushing the limits of what black womanhood can be—on stage and in her own life as muse, musician, mogul, mother, martyr. To the casual observer, even the well-documented chinks in her armor (infidelity, infertility) seem like plot points en route to an inevitably happy ending—an ending that continues to elude most of us.

For the sake of our own egos, it's better that we set her apart, make her different than us. So we reduce "Beyoncé" to a symbol, and for the sake of our own edification, prefer to think her a simpleton. Anything more—especially granting her the intellectual prowess and self-awareness to be the architect of her own evolution— would overwhelm, and often does. Reflecting on the political posture of iconic entertainer and legendary beauty Lena Horne, her granddaughter, screenwriter Jenny Lumet, shared the following with me during an interview:

> She knew that her beauty was political. She had a complex relationship with her beauty. It wasn't enough for her to just step on a stage. And she did indeed walk the walk and she was indeed at the March on Washington, where she said one word: "Freedom" … She was a very particular soul in a very particular package.[7]

But for a few historical details, couldn't those words also apply to Beyoncé? Hasn't she also said—no, sung—"Freedom"? Or are we incapable of seeing her as a free black woman because she comes in such a very particular package?

What do we want from Beyoncé?

I'd argue that we—her devotees, her detractors, and even those of us who are decidedly neutral—want the same things from Beyoncé the world has historically wanted from every woman, and especially black women. We want her to be both madonna and whore. We want her to remain abstract; an object upon which we can project our fantasies, our needs, our hopes, and our resentments. We want her to both "run the world" and be its mule. And while we don't want her to have it all, we still want her to be all things—so that we can then tell her it's too much, or not enough. What do we want from Beyoncé? We want her to be everything we're not—but not everything we are.

Notes

1 *The Morning Consult site*. (2018, October 15). Retrieved October 15, 2018, from http s://morningconsult.com/2018/10/15/beyonce-sean-hannity-and-lebron-james-am ong-most-politically-divisive-entertainers/.

2 Cooper, Brittney. 2018. *Eloquent Rage: A Black Feminist Discovers Her Superpower*. New York: St. Martin's Press.

3 *The Fader site*. (2016, October 7). Retrieved July 20, 2018, from https://www.thefader. com/2016/10/07/chimamanda-ngozi-adichie-beyoncs-feminism-comment.

4 *YouTube video*. (2014, August 18). Retrieved July 20, 2018, from https://www.youtube. com/watch?v=FS6LNpeJPbw.

5 *The bell hooks Institute blog.* (2016, May 9). Retrieved July 20, 2018, from http://www.bellhooksinstitute.com/blog/2016/5/9/moving-beyond-pain.

6 *YouTube video.* (2014, June 26). Retrieved July 20, 2018, from https://www.youtube.com/watch?v=P2Jr9P01ESs.

7 *The Glow Up vertical on The Root* site. (2018, March 23). Retrieved from https://theglowup.theroot.com/a-legends-legacy-jenny-lumet-remembers-life-with-lena-1824012157.

INTERLUDE B: BITTERSWEET LIKE ME

When the lemonade ain't made for Black fat femmes and women

Ashleigh Shackelford

I watched the beautiful and amazing *Lemonade* visual album that Saturday, centered and very open to the generosity of Bey's art. I was floored and enamored. It was lit as fuck, y'all! I was so proud to experience such an artistic, well-designed, politically important, empowering, and intentionally creative piece by a Black woman who is, hands down, one of the greatest artists of all time. Literally: what a time to be alive for Black women and femmes.

As I watched it again, however, to further explore the nuance and political layers, I discovered something was missing. I discovered I was missing from *Lemonade*. Which is to say, the lemons that white supremacy and the world have given me are not in Beyoncé's pitcher. The trauma and empowerment of the Black women and femmes in the video did not resonate with me or represent me, either personally or politically. The only representation of Black fat women/femmes portrayed them as references to poverty (i.e. New Orleans video stills) or desexualized, grieving mothers (note: they weren't even fat, but they were the only bigger bodied/non-sexualized bodies within the entire visual album).

When I brought up the lack of representation to other Black women and femmes, the first responses were:

- You just hate Beyoncé.
- Why don't you critique Rihanna and everyone else who's not Beyoncé?
- Beyoncé can't do it all!
- Why do you need to see yourself in something that's about Beyoncé's experiences?

This hyper-responsive clapback is what I always expect when it comes to Queen Bey. The lack of understanding around why fatness is important (and a fundamental requirement, TBH) in a conversation with another Black femme around the portrayal of Black girl magic and Black femme supremacy is absolutely disheartening.

I felt empty when I didn't see anyone centered and celebrated with a body like mine in such an iconic piece of art that has been hailed as a visual anthem for Black womanhood and femmehood. Instead of assuming that my perspective and opinion on Beyoncé's current work and her role in creating this powerful art are based in vitriol, can we make room for other Black femmes to talk about representation in something that should inherently include them? Is it possible that Black femmes and women who value Beyoncé can also give necessary thought to her work and platform? Will it ever be valid to demand revision to ahistorical storytelling about our ongoing trauma and pain, especially set in the Deep South?

Is it really too much to ask that Beyoncé include one or two cameos from Black fat women or femmes that are not desexualized, grieving mothers? Is it really too much to see Black fat women and femmes in the Deep South slaying the game ('cause we been here) incorporated in this powerful piece of art? Was it too much to give Gabby Sidibe a call real quick to channel that Southern Black femme gothic vibe she was servin' in *American Horror Story*? Is it ludicrous to think that Amber Riley could've popped her pussy for real niggas somewhere in between "Hold Up" and "6 Inch?" She couldn't do a feature with Jazmine Sullivan and get these Black fat thighs sanctified too?

Lemonade has themes of Southern Gothic, Black femme supremacy, Black magic, Black transcendence, Black religion and spirituality, betrayal and abuse, and survival and resistance. In all of the beautiful visuals, poetry (written and adapted by Warsan Shire), and storylines, complexity and humanity were never reflected in a Black fat body. The limited representation in *Lemonade* could easily be quantified as accessory trauma tropes—in which we never see Black fat femmes and women incorporated into a deep truth-telling experience like Beyoncé and her thinner and lighter-skinned cameos, but rather as a tragedy in the background for effect.

Southern Blackness is inextricably linked to Black fat femme and women's bodies, especially dark and brown skinned. Our bodies symbolize the birthright of Black struggle while also representing the lineage to white plantation/white supremacist functionality. The rich history of the Deep South and the violence around troping, codifying, and oppressing Black women and femmes is centered on mammification, sexual violence excused through hypersexual mythologies, denial of beauty, animalizing our humanity, and utilizing our bodies as literal and symbolic vessels for the continuation of slavery and subordination.

The references to mammification (caretaking, being everyone's keeper) within *Lemonade*'s visuals, poetry, and lyrics speak to a violence that is inherently constructed around fatness, dark-skinned-ness, womanhood, and femmehood. I imagine the Fannie Lou Hamers who have always been maternal figures to everyone around them, expected and praised for being that nigga for all the people in their lives but never receiving love and protection in return. I think about the Big Mama Thorntons singing their pain, creating innovative magic through fat, queer resilience but getting their legacy and craft appropriated and snatched. Black fat women and femmes are always expected to play support systems to everyone in the world (even to other Black women and femmes) while being politically denied healthy access to sexuality/sexualization, gender conformity, and humanity.

Blackness and fatness operate in a strange, violent place of oxymoronic visible erasure. We're hypervisible to the thinner and lighter bodies we take space from, but invisible to humanity, body autonomy, and sexual agency. Queerness is often denied to us because we're read as non-sexual beings because we're seen as undesirable and inhuman. And if we are unapologetically femme in our bodies, it reaffirms that if we do perform femininity—that if we're going to be sexualized or in service for anyone—it could only be for the consumption and pandering of the patriarchal cis-heteronormative gaze.

In "Hold Up," Beyoncé says, "I don't want to lose my pride, but I'ma fuck me up a bitch." Anger codified upon Black women and femme bodies is constructed as a disparaging, limited identity that seemingly invalidates our humanity and our ability to be logical, emotional, and multifaceted. This trope becomes very different when fatness is incorporated, and we are looking at a completely different type of violence. Angry Black fat women/femmes are not given space to be rightful in their anger—or even human in their feelings. We're coded as angry inherently because ugliness (through fatness AND Blackness) denies us the pride Beyoncé is referring to. Complicated and amplified by colorism, ableism, and queerphobia, anger is ultimately inaccessible to some of us as a performance narrative regardless of its righteousness. Beyoncé's prettiness (constructed through thinness, smaller features, and light skin), which hurts so badly, is also a privilege that allows her to be worthy of anger when a man betrays her.

This concept of denying Black fat femmes and women respect, fidelity, and loyalty is also where the popular line, "And I can't even get a text back" comes from. It is often used as a disparaging response when Black fat women and femmes, deemed too ugly for happiness and love, post pictures about their relationships. In response, voyeurs repost or engage with these pictures as reference for the humor in why their intimate relationships or access to desire isn't following the rules of white supremacist humanity standards. The expectation within our westernized antiblack society is that thinness is desire capital that is directly rewarded with love, happiness, wealth, and societal praise. When thin people fail to receive these things, they lash out against those of us who fail beauty standards and still find the happiness and resources we're seemingly denied.

How different would it have been if a Black fat femme had been incorporated into the *Lemonade* visual? Could our view of beauty and love for Black women and femmes grow more complex if we saw a range of body types and sizes in addition to a range of deeper, darker skin tones? What would this say about misogyny and betrayal from niggas (read: cis-het men or masculine folks) if we saw a spectrum and assortment of different Black femmes and women claiming the right to be angry and burn everything down when they are fucked over? How would desire politics be reshaped if we saw a Black fat woman claiming autonomy and respect?

In "Sorry," Beyoncé says, "Middle fingers up, put them hands high/ Wave it in his face, tell him boy, bye." All the while, Beyoncé and Serena Williams are fucking it up (read: twerking, being bad AF, Black femme supremacy). Imagine if a Black fat femme was twerking and fucking it up with them. Imagine if they were putting their middle fingers up and weren't sorry, because fuck these niggas!

Additionally, Serena Williams being a cameo in *Lemonade* was powerful. Her presence is beautiful, necessary, yet complicated. Serena experiences colorist, fatphobic, transphobic, and antiblack voyeurism and violence around her body that deeply aligns with the same issues named in this essay. Being one of the world's greatest athletes, Serena is situated within a Venn diagram of violence and fetishization. Within this context, she is positioned as someone who abides by the expectations of healthism and white supremacist able-bodied-ness enough to still be seen as an exception to how her body fails antiblack humanity standards. This doesn't anoint her with humanity, but rather a different engagement with fatphobic violence that still allows her to be seen as "good" and "worthy" because she is able to perform athletic-ness publicly. If bigger-bodied, or perceived bigger-bodied, Black women and femmes cannot be sloppy, sedentary, unhealthy, disabled, and fail expectation of performance, then it's not truly inclusive, radical, or humanizing.

Since Black fat femmes and women are always portrayed as unlovable, unworthy, ugly, angry, one-dimensional, and animalistic, the presence of our existence would call the entire song into question. How could ugly Black fat bitches[1] be unbothered and unbossed about ain't-shit niggas? How are they desired and fucked enough to even have the relationship problems Beyoncé and Serena have? And that's exactly the point. Black fat bitches been here, been getting love, been fucking, been hustling, been getting fucked over, been resilient, and have been churning out pitchers of lemonade. We are powerful, worthy, beautiful, and have autonomy to control who we give our labor, time, and bodies to. We deserve to put our middle fingers high and tell that boy, BYE.

In the same song, she also sings the infamous line: "Better call Becky with the good hair." There is a deep history of Black women and femmes being compared to the purity, beauty, and humanity of white women. As we've seen in numerous popular culture references—from songs, movies, and advertising—degrading Black

FIGURE B.1 Video still of Serena Williams twerking for King Bey from "Sorry." *Lemonade*, Parkwood Entertainment, 2016

women and femmes to uplift and justify dating (and/or having sex with) white women is a nuanced and violent reality. We've seen that Black men constantly praise dating non-Black women, specifically white women, as the ultimate achievement. In Tyler the Creator's song "French," his opening line is "Got all the Black bitches mad cause my main bitch vanilla."

However, there is a difference in how Beyoncé is able to address white women with conformity in ways other Black women and femmes cannot. Beyoncé can drag Beckys (read: white girls) to hell, but thinness (or proximity to acceptable body types), colorism, ableism, and gender contribute to her ability to do this without the same level of critique. Beyoncé has mad beauty privilege. Nonetheless, when Bey reads white girls, it's praised and relatable because she is on a beauty pedestal for being exoticized. If a Black fat bitch was next to her when she said that, would niggas still understand why Becky needs to be dragged?

Blackness + fatness denies us beauty proximity through the constructions of whiteness in ways Beyoncé and her *Lemonade* guests wouldn't get shitted on for in the same capacity. It's necessary to recognize that Black women's and femmes' pain is rooted in the policing of bigger bodies. We're denied even the thought of sustainable and healthy love in any regard. Our clapback at white women would seemingly be read as a joke because we're the literal opposite and failure of white femininity (the most noted type of physical beauty). That's why Black fat women and femmes' pain and navigation of love have to be symbolized somewhere in this visual to really get this lemonade sweet.

We live in a world where body terrorism, beauty standard hierarchies, and white supremacist patriarchy operate together to destroy access to humanity for deviant bodies in any capacity. These sociopolitical contexts shape an environment in which deviancy in beauty and humanity—Black bodies, fat bodies, disabled bodies, dark-skinned bodies, gender nonconforming bodies, trans bodies, gender-oppressed bodies, etc.—allow for the violence that those bodies should be erased, ignored, publicly and privately mocked, interrogated, and assaulted because they're not seen as human. If we're not fitting within society's beauty and humanity standards, we don't matter. When we aren't included, centered, or humanized publicly, we are perpetuating the same systems of violence we're all fighting.

As we continue to examine and enjoy *Lemonade*, I search for the stories of Black fat femmes and women who have been raped, sexually exploited, beaten, and politically ignored, and are expected to remain strong, resilient—and silent—in their pain and experiences. I continue to search for the Black fat girls who are always the shoulder to cry on for the Beyoncés of the world. I continue to question where the Aunt Jemimas (read: dark-skinned Black fat women/femmes in servitude) are—the Black fat women and femmes who are tired of servin' everybody, feeling like it's them vs. everybody, feelin' overwhelmed with people needing them and draining them. I wonder where the Sheilas (Jill Scott's character in *Why Did I Get Married?*) are—the Black fat women who are married to ain't-shit-ass niggas who continue to drain you of love and apologies while leaving you with nothing but self-hate in return. I wonder where the Big Mamas are at—the grandmas and nanas who defy gravity and able-bodied-ness to make Sunday dinner, who are berated for their physical health but never get asked about their mental health and grief in a world that was never created for their survival. I wonder where the little Black fat girls are who get told no one will ever love them, hold them, or adore them—the Preciouses of the world who have experienced more trauma than care.

My love for Beyoncé doesn't come with silence or complacency. My critique of her doesn't only happen when she's dropping an album. The space I hold for her is not conditional, but rather intentional. I love Bey. I love her cultural power and political growth. I also hope to see Black fat femmes like me in her work centered on Black femme rage and Black girl magic—specifically because there is no story of Black pain deeper than that of Black fat women and femmes.

There is no *Lemonade* for Beyoncé without the bitter violence against Black fat femmes and women. There can be no *Lemonade* for any Black woman or femme without the sweet resilience, complicated experiences, beauty, and existence of Black fat bitches.

Note

1 Gender expansive for women, femmes, and nonbinary folks.

PART I

Some shit is just for us

1

SOME SHIT IS JUST FOR US

Introduction

Cheryl Finley and Deborah Willis

Beyoncé's 2017 Grammy Awards performance relied heavily on visual references to the Yoruba river/love goddess Oshún, who is associated with sweetness, acts of kindness and generosity, calmness, and bountiful love. Beyoncé is deeply committed to changing visual narratives about being black and female. She is dedicated to researching historical narratives from fashion, beauty, religion, and the everyday—from fifteenth-century art history paintings to the black power movement of the twentieth century to black lives matter protests of the twenty-first century. Her artistry explores unique and distinctive moments in history that focus on today while harkening aesthetics of the past. Beyoncé converges the politics of beauty to political moments that transform memory.

For example, she referenced Oshún, who is one of the seven major Yoruba (Nigerian ethnic group) gods or deities incorporated into Santería, a creolized religion combining elements of Catholicism, brought to the Americas through the transatlantic slave trade hundreds of years ago. Oshún bore twins to Shangó, the thunder deity, with whom she ruled from his expansive brass palace. Hence, the brassy/gold hue of Beyoncé's elaborate crown and regal robe reference the wealth of brass objects—bracelets, fans, earrings, staffs, and swords—accumulated by Oshún as the mother of Yoruba twins. Known for her powerful maternal instinct, Oshún is a fierce, loving goddess who is charged with protecting not only her existing children, but also her unborn children and, by extension, future genera-tions. We see this in Beyoncé's performance with the participation of her own mother, Tina Knowles, and then her daughter, Blue Ivy. Of course, we are now aware that she birthed twins shortly after this performance. The contemporary relevance and power of this transgenerational visual/spiritual reference is one that, to our mind, also references the political necessity of conscious musicians and recording artists like Beyoncé, who have taken on the responsibility of motivating, empowering, and mobilizing African Americans through visual and aural reference to historical and contemporary shared experiences. This is especially evident in *Lemonade*—in its imagery and in the titles and lyrics of the songs—which seek to link African American history with the contemporary moment. At times, the chorus of women dancers referenced Oshún's watery, river goddess origins, and sometimes reflected the other goddesses that made up the multifaceted uber-goddess enacted by Beyoncé, including the African river goddess Mami Wata and the multi-armed Hindu goddess Kali (when she's wearing the beaded bikini and flowing drape) associated with love, death, and sexuality.

In addition to her association with maternity, power, and protection, Oshún's connection to love and to the golden color of brass and its durable quality are also evident in Beyoncé's performance—from the radiating, flowered crown to the reflective, brass/yellow/golden robe to the oversized throne, which in its tilting motion faces toward the sun, again projecting her connection to the heavens, as a powerful goddess. The flowers onstage and in her hair send a shout out to the Roman goddess Venus, the goddess of love, fertility, and beauty. Oshún is also associated with extreme beauty and that beauty—the beauty of black people, black women, girls, men, and boys—is a quality that Beyoncé not only exudes, but always has been keen on representing, projecting, and teaching to her own family and to her larger public family and fan base.

This first section, "Some Shit is Just for Us," frames a black interior through the writings of Lindsey Stewart, Janell Hobson, LaKisha Simmons, and Alexis McGee. Stewart introduces Beyoncé as an interlocutor reimagining freedom, connecting the notion to love and agency in *Lemonade*. Hobson engages Beyoncé through feminist critique such as bell hooks on hypervisibility, beauty, and the politics of hair. Simmons locates stories of renewal in the work of Beyoncé by linking the historical with the present. It is a haunting reflection on loss and motherhood. McGee explores the impact of Beyoncé's *oeuvre* through performance and narration. Hybridity is explored through identity, representation, and spectacle. This section explores the commonalities found in Beyoncé's use of historical accounts in her reenactments with detailed content of the everyday of black womanhood which invites us to explore fantasy, hope, loss, and possibility.

2

SOMETHING AKIN TO FREEDOM

Sexual love, political agency, and *Lemonade*

Lindsey Stewart

There is "something akin to freedom," Harriet Jacobs writes in *Incidents in the Life of a Slave Girl*, within voluntary sexual love under slavery (Jacobs 2001, 48). This insight, the kinship of sexual love and freedom, can be seen in many black cultural productions, from literature such as Zora Neale Hurston's *Their Eyes Were Watching God* (1937 [2006]) to visual albums such as Beyoncé Knowles's *Lemonade* (2016). In this essay, I develop the role of black spiritual traditions in the kinship formed between sexual love and freedom. I pair *Their Eyes Were Watching God* and *Lemonade* because the controversy they have sparked bear striking similarities that underscore how our conceptions of political agency still require improvement. That is, grasping the emancipatory effects of this kinship requires that we expand our notions of political agency beyond protest. For instance, Richard Wright thought Hurston's emphasis on sexual love indicated that her novel was not "serious fiction" (Wright 1994, 25). Similarly, *Lemonade*'s emphasis on love (both self and familial) rings hollow to bell hooks without accompanying calls "for an end to patriarchal domination" (hooks 2016).

Indeed, upon reading hooks's "Moving Beyond Pain," a critique of *Lemonade*, I was struck by how much it resonates with Wright's "Between Laughter and Tears," a critique of *Their Eyes Watching God*. Both argue that the artists in question are not *really* producing art for black people's benefits; rather, they are exploiting aspects of black culture for their own personal profit.[1] Both can appreciate various aesthetic aspects of the pieces reviewed, yet they conclude that these works of art are underdeveloped in their portraits of black life. For example, Wright claims that Hurston's characters "swing like a pendulum eternally in that safe and narrow orbit in which America likes to see the Negro live: between laughter and tears" (Wright 1937, 25). Likewise, hook argues that Beyoncé's album "stays within a conventional stereotypical framework, where the black woman is always a victim."

Both then and now, these critiques may strike us as missing fundamental aspects of the pieces reviewed. Why, for instance, do they ultimately miss the themes of the pieces reviewed?[2] A significant clue is their lack of attention to the role of black spiritual traditions in their artistic appraisals, due to their narrow focus on protest. As Angela Davis argues in *Blues Legacies and Black Feminism*, "[t]he articulation of a specifically black aesthetic ... cannot locate itself in the living tradition of African-American culture without taking seriously the practices variously called conjure, voodoo, and hoodoo" (Davis 1998, 159). In this essay, I argue that exploring sexual love within the context of black spiritual traditions offers a different conception of political agency that both Wright and hooks miss.

Hurston's missing theme

One way to contextualize Wright's critique of Hurston is to consider his "Blueprint for Negro Writing," originally written in the same year as "Between Laughter and Tears." In this essay, Wright specifies guidelines for black writers, notably their use of black folklore, as a way to develop their political responsibilities to black folk. While folklore is a term that has long fallen out of fashion, it can often serve as a divining rod of classed, gendered, and regional influences within black political thought. How a thinker delimits folklore, those traditions they emphasize as defining "the black experience," can tell us a lot about their politics. And it can diagnose how class, gender, and regional identity inform a thinker's definition of political agency.

Wright opens the essay with a critique of a current trend of black writing. He argues that black intellectuals were trying to "plead with white America for justice" (Wright 1994, 97–8)—which means they ceased to write works *for black folk*. Raising an implicit critique of the Harlem renaissance's attraction to the class-based, racial-uplift program, Wright urges black writers to return to our folklore for source material. For folklore, on Wright's account, is an element of black culture that is "addressed to him; a culture which has, for good or ill, helped to clarify his consciousness and create emotional attitudes which are conducive to action" (Wright 1937, 99). That is, folklore is the "most indigenous and complete expression" of black life, carrying "the collective sense of Negro life in America" (Wright 1994, 99). This is because folklore "rose out of a unified sense of common life and a common fate" (Wright 1994, 100). As a result, black folk traditions "embod[y] the memories and hopes of [our] struggle for freedom" (Wright 1994, 100)—which makes black folklore an important tool for liberation.

It is important to highlight Wright's central example of black folklore. He writes:

> Not yet caught in paint or stone, and as yet but feebly depicted in the poem and novel, the Negroes' most powerful images of hope and despair still remains in the fluid state of daily speech. How many John Henrys have lived and died on the lips of these black people? (Wright 1994, 100)

Lawrence Levine argues that John Henry is *the* central black folklore figure. A "steel-driving-man," John Henry worked to clear the way for the tracks of the Chesapeake and Ohio Railways. With his natural strength alone, he bore into mountain rock, beating pace of the steam-powered hammer of the white man. There are many endings to the story, including death from his heart giving out to third-day resurrections. His legend symbolizes not only the brutal work that many African American men faced, often involuntarily through chain gangs, but it also symbolizes the tension wrought by industrialization's creep upon manual labor. And he is beloved because he beat the white man (industrialization) at his *own* game (Levine 1977, 420).

John Henry draws up a number of things about Wright's politics. For instance, John Henry's power (his hammer) is also sexualized.[3] As a result, the stakes in this fight against the white man *include* the restoration of the black man's sexuality—a theme that, Hurston claims, preoccupies Wright in *Uncle Tom's Children.*[4] Folklore, for Wright, is formed in the "absences of fixed and nourishing forms of culture" (Wright 1994, 99). Through this figure, Wright emphasizes our being violently ripped from Africa, and he disavows any lingering cultural connections. It is also important to note that this includes black spiritual traditions, which Wright separates very early in "Blueprint" from black folk traditions (Wright 1994, 99).[5] As a result, John Henry is alone: cut off from ancestors both physically (being ripped from Africa) and culturally (being stripped of their tradition). Finally, John Henry signifies open, direct, honest protest against whites. Levine writes, "[John Henry] defeat[s] rivals … directly and publicly," being "contemptuous of guile and indirection" (Levine 1977, 426). By examining Wright's pick of folk heroes, we find that the "collective sense" of black life in America is defined, for Wright, by tragic struggle, heroic strife, and direct confrontation with whites. As such, protest is the privileged mode of black political agency for Wright. Black life is consumed with our struggle against race and class oppression, as exemplified in the folk-hero "John Henry."

As June Jordan's insightful essay, "Notes Toward a Black Balancing of Love and Hatred," demonstrates, privileging protest in our assessment of political agency can cause us to miss other modes of agency (such as "self-affirmation" or love).[6] I argue that Wright's preference for protest hinders him from seeing the politics at work in *Their Eyes Were Watching God.* His claim that Hurston had "no basic idea or theme"(Wright 1937, 25), was, really, that she did not have a theme that *he* recognized as valid for black folkloric writing. For Hurston chose to de-emphasize racial oppression or conflict. In fact, Hurston's novel proceeds as if "there were not white people in the world" (Hurston 1999, 144).

What (really) happens when our eyes watch God?

There is, however, another folk-hero that "runs all through our folk-lore," presenting a very different depiction of black life (Hurston 2003, 489). In "High John de Conquer," Hurston presents a folk figure who *also* embodies the hope[7] and struggles[8]of black folk in striking contrast to Wright's John Henry. Similar to Brer Rabbit, John de Conquer is a beloved trickster figure, full of guile and lofty indirection.[9] As a folk figure, John de Conquer emphasizes both our connections to Africa[10] and our spiritual traditions that stem from there.[11] And not only does John de Conquer contest a sorrowful, tragic depiction of black life,[12] but also the struggle that he signifies is fundamentally different than that of John Henry. Instead of protest against whites, John de Conquer is concerned with "[f]ighting a mighty battle without outside-side showing force, and winning his war within". Instead of seeking recognition from the oppressor, at stake in this war is "[r]eally winning in a permanent way, for he was winning with the soul of the black man whole and free" (Hurston 1995b, 924). That is, through her focus on John de Conquer, Hurston shines a spotlight on modes of agency beyond protest against whites, such as self-definition, for he provided the ex-slaves with "an inside thing to live by" that helped them "endure" slavery with dignity (Hurston 1995b, 922). It also helped them fashion a sense of themselves that slavery "sought to extinguish" (Davis 1998, 155),[13] for this "inside thing to live by" attuned them to the *inner* struggle for freedom, which had important effects in both epistemology[14] and affect.[15]

Hurston's choice of John de Conquer also draws up much about her politics. Namely, it highlights what I call the *politics of joy*—her deliberate emphasis on "joy," as Toni Morrison defines it, that "part of our lives that was spent neither on our knees nor hanging from trees" (Morrison 2008, 54). Similar to "Blueprint for Negro Writing," Hurston also lays down guidelines for black artists in her essay "Art and Such." Here, she argues that the black artist is often under pressure to reduce black life to tragedy and sorrow. "The one subject for a Negro is the Race and its sufferings," Hurston writes, "so the song of morning must be choked back"—even though we "love and hate and fight and play and strive and travel and have a thousand and one interests in life" (Hurston 1999, 142). Hurston traces the source of this trend to a group she calls "Race Champions," and, in a nearly intersectional analysis, she highlights how gender (male), region (Northeast), and class (Ivy League education) interact to produce a particular style of leadership[16]— one that privileges a sorrow-ridden, tragic depiction of black life.[17] In contrast, with John de Conquer, Hurston calls attention to other affects and modes of agency, such as self-definition through joy, that can define black life.

Within *Their Eyes Were Watching God*, black spiritual traditions inform Janie's struggle for self-definition. And sexuality is enmeshed with these spiritual traditions. For instance, the language depicting the "awakening" of Janie's self-conscious is not only sexual but also deeply spiritual, for her awakening is similar to that of a spiritual conversion.[18] She was "called" by the sacred tree, which:

> summoned her to behold a revelation [and] followed her through all her waking moments and caressed her in her sleep. It connected itself with other vaguely felt matters that had struck her outside observation and buried

themselves in her flesh. Now they emerged and quested about her consciousness. (Hurston 2006, 10–11)

That is, she was being prepared for the "vision" of sexual blooming that was to come three days later. And the number of days here also signals the conversion and vision experience.[19] After the vision, Janie "felt a pain remorseless sweet that left her limp and languid," (Hurston 2006, 11), almost as if she had been temporarily possessed or "mounted" by a spirit, her own consciousness "driven out" for involuntary sexual expression.[20] From then on, she sought "confirmation of the voice and vision," an answer that was, in fact, "seeking her" (Hurston 2006, 11).[21]

Through the blooming vision, Janie was given a revelation about love—one that enabled her to distinguish between her grandmother's definition of freedom and her own. Janie's grandmother sought to establish Janie's safety and security through a forced marriage to an older man of decent wealth. However, her grandmother's plan, Janie discloses to her friend Pheoby, was over-determined by its opposition to slave life. "[Her grandmother] was borned in slavery time," Janie asserts, "when folks ... didn't sit down anytime dey felt like it." As a result, her grandmother desired that Janie be able to "sit on porches lak de white madam ... git up on uh high chair and sit dere" (Hurston 2006, 114). But in her grandmother's freedom dream's very opposition to slavery, it reproduced very similar effects: "[s]o Ah got up on de high stool lak she told me, but Phoeby, Ah done nearly languished tuh death up there" (Hurston 2006, 114). This is because her grandmother's notion of freedom lacked self-definition, as she "didn't have time tuh think what tuh do after you got up on de stool uh do nothin'." Her only concern had been freedom; she had not considered how to "use [her soul] afterwards" (Hurston 2006, 114, 924).

In contrast, Janie's vision provided an "inside thing to live by," a "freedom feeling" that guided her own self-definition throughout her life (Hurston 2006, 90). At various points in the novel, it is the vision of the tree, the effect it produced, that caused Janie to reflect and assess where her life was going.[22] So when Pheoby tries to cajole Janie into her grandmother's freedom dream, Janie retorts that "Ah done lived Grandma's way, now I means tuh live mine." And the difference marks the shift in struggles, from a respectability politics that seeks recognition from whites to a self-definition through sexual love. "Dis ain't no business proposition, and no race after property and titles," Janie asserts. "Dis is uh love game" (Hurston 2006, 114).

Hooks's "Hold Up"

Similar to Wright, bell hooks's 2016 critique of *Lemonade* also hinges upon a narrow conception of political agency ("challeng[ing] and chang[ing] systems of domination")—one that reduces the protagonist's power to "pure fantasy." While hooks recognizes the importance of black love, and black joy,[23] she cannot work out how the hurt and anger that introduces *Lemonade* is resolved by its assertions of love at the end.[24] This is because, for hooks, the "central messages" that *Lemonade* seeks to express are consistently undercut. For instance, hooks argues that *Lemonade's* attempt to "to challenge the ongoing present day devaluation and dehumanization of the black female body" is undercut by Beyoncé's participation in a global commodification that does not "truly overshadow or change conventional sexist constructions of black female identity." As a result, although *Lemonade* seeks to "offer multidimensional images of black female life," it fails to move beyond the image of the black female victim.

When confronted with the bold images of female power in the visual album, it is hard to make sense of this claim. However, hooks means that the album (in particular, "Hold Up") offers a vacuous sense of agency because the solution to pain is violence. She writes:

> Among the many mixed messages embedded in *Lemonade* is this celebration of rage. Smug and smiling in her golden garb, Beyoncé is the embodiment of a fantastical female power, which is just that—pure fantasy. Images of female violence undercut a central message embedded in *Lemonade* that violence in all its forms, especially the violence of lies and betrayal, hurts. Contrary to misguided notions of gender equality, women do not and will not seize power and create self-love and self-esteem through violent acts.

As such, the album fails to provide us with "adequate ways to reconcile and heal trauma" (hooks 2016). While aesthetic appreciation of black female bodies is a necessary step to well-being, it is not enough for full emancipation. While "giving voice" to pain is a "vital and essential stage of freedom struggle," hooks writes, "it does not bring exploitation and domination to an end." I see hooks's critique as two-pronged. First, the solutions, or ways of moving through pain, offered in the visual album are facile—namely, beauty and violence. Second, there is no "real" address (i.e. protest) of institutional structures of oppression.[25]

However, engagement with the black spiritual traditions that move the narrative in *Lemonade* would provide a sense of agency that hooks misses. For instance, within *Envisioning Black Feminist Voodoo Aesthetics*, Kameelah Martin develops another framework than can be used to interpret *Lemonade*. She defines "voodoo aesthetics" as "the inscription of African ritual cosmologies on the black female body" through ceremony, adornment of the body, spirit possession or "mounting," etc. (Martin 2016, xvi–ii). Paying homage to Patricia Hill Collins's work, Martin provides a method of black feminist interpretation of "voodoo aesthetics" within film. For Collins, black feminist thought, as social critical theory, is developed within a *dialectic* of oppression and activism—or response to that oppression).[26] One example of this dynamic is the "controlling images" (stereotypes designed to dominate black women) and the cultivation of our own self-definition in response to those images. Martin contributes to this discussion by investigating in what ways the image of the "voodoo priestess" has been used, both by popular, mainstream culture and within our own cultural traditions.[27] In particular, Martin highlights how the use of the black female priestess figure can signal a "safe space" for other black women. That is, a space where "black women can actively resist being objectified" and that, as Collins writes, "nurture[s] the everyday and specialized thought of African-American women" (Collins 2009, 100).

Culling these insights into a method for film criticism, Martin writes that a film passes the "safe space" test if the black female priestess

> is depicted as an active subject rather than a passive object; if she is empowered by her black folk traditions and able-bodied to make decisions concerning her immediate circumstances; and if the image moves away from stereotypes and represents a healthy portrait of Africana women and spirit work. (2016, xviii)

Further, Martin suggests that this figure's "foundation in black folk traditions" could "denote a level of agency and resistance to objectification that is inaccessible" to the other controlling images (xviii). As a result, where hooks saw only images of victimization in *Lemonade*, Martin, through her attention to the figure of the black female priestess, saw radical empowerment. I argue that hooks mistakes the protagonist's power for "pure fantasy" because black spiritual traditions offer a *different* conception of power—one that cannot easily be read as protest or resistance. For, in the case of *Lemonade,* the protagonist's power to move through her pain is secured by traditions in which submission, such as in practices of spirit possession, is instrumental to developing a sense of agency.

"Formation" and Yemayá iconography

Applying Martin's framework to *Lemonade* orients us towards developing the rich context clues that spiritual traditions plant along the album. Tending to those clues enables us to reap a rich harvest of questions about conceptions of the self, agency, and the kinship between sexual love and freedom. Moreover, it makes sense of how hooks could mistake violence as the "central message" of the video. That is to say, it is tempting to read "Hold Up" as a central moment rather than part of a journey if one misses the context clues of that journey's passage. As others have noted in this reader, the blues woman tradition is infused with black spiritual traditions. Beyoncé continues in this tradition, as the visual album is replete with references to these traditions (such as hoodoo, Haitian Vodou, Santería, and Yoruba religious practices). Through a symbiosis of conjure and the blues, blues women were able to fashion an identity that was unavailable in mainstream, American society.[28] I am particularly interested in the spiritual aspect involved in fashioning these alternative identities. As Vanessa K. Valdés notes, "[i]nvolvement with these African diasporic religions … provides alternative models of womanhood" than that offered by "dominant Western patriarchal culture" (Valdés 2014, 2). For example, many of the feminine orishas in Yoruba religion defy dichotomies that restrict black women in mainstream society: they are "rich and complex" beings that are "beautiful, wealthy, fierce, sexual, and all warriors" (Valdés 2014, 11). Under this view, the sexualized violence and flirtatious rage that hooks notices in "Hold Up" is not a contradiction, but an expansive range of complexity that the orishas exemplify. As many scholars have noted, at the start of "Hold Up" the protagonist is mounted by the orisha Oshún known for the heat of both her love *and* vengeance.[29]

Reaching across the African Diaspora, *Lemonade*'s engagement with orisha worship is a meditation upon the creative act of black women's self-definition, for in ritual practices of spirit possession, a practitioner "can call upon ... identities as varying parts of the self," Solimar Otero argues, and "can shift between different registers of embodiment during ritual: male, female, black, white, ... *oricha*, healer, ancestor, relative" (Otero 2013, 96). Not only do Beyoncé and her cast appear as different black women across centuries in her album, relying upon this ritual as an organizing principle, but also I argue that we get a radically different read of *Lemonade* than hooks if we analyze its engagement with orisha worship.

While many analyses of orisha worship in *Lemonade* already focus on Oshún, I focus on the references to Yemayá in *Lemonade*'s concluding track, "Formation." With colors of blue and white to remind us of the deep waters from which all life came, Yemayá is considered the mother of all other orishas, the wellspring of intuition, and the fierce protector of women. She is also known as a patron of queer men and women.[30] Her symbols include: water, mirrors (or any reflective surface), pearls, cowrie shells, fish-tailed creatures, water fowl, the number 7, silver, and fans. Otero notes that Yemayá and Oshún are intimately connected, yet distinct (as mother and daughter, or as sisters) in a manner similar to the relationship between oceans (or lakes) and rivers.[31] Indeed, the floodwaters of Hurricane Katrina, referenced in "Formation," were formed by *both* the Mississippi River and Lake Pontchartrain over-spilling their bounds. And it is this space, where both waters meet, that sets the stage for "Formation."

I argue that if we read what hooks calls "messages of violence," such as the call to "slay," within the context of orisha worship, we gain access to an important tool for liberation. In queer orisha worshipping communities, as Elizabeth Pérez notes, Yemayá is "lauded as 'fierce'"—"intense, bold, and exceptional" (Pérez 2013, 28).

FIGURE 2.1 Video still from "Formation." *Lemonade*, Parkwood Entertainment, 2016

Madison Moore argues that the performance of fierceness can be subversive, especially "in its ability to crystallize a solid identity for people who might otherwise be overlooked" (Moore 2012, 84), for participation in fierceness "allows its users to fabricate a new sense of self that radiates a defiant sense ownership through aesthetics" (Moore 2012, 72). It is interesting to note as well that this sense of ownership is inextricably linked to a sort of "possession" in performance in Moore's analysis.[32] In the case of orisha worship practices, such as possession, Yemayá endows her children with "the license to be unapologetically fierce concerning their choices" (Pérez 2013, 29).

If we read Beyoncé's "Formation" under the lens of Yemayá's iconography—due to the floodwaters, the use of blue/denim when Beyoncé and the dancers align in formation, the backdrop of empty pools suggesting water—then the call to "slay" takes on richer meaning. Rather than mixed messages as hooks claims, understanding the protagonist as "mounted" by Yemayá *unites* various, seemingly contradictory aspects of personality:, such as her wealth ("earned all this money"), with her rural, slave-inflected, Southern roots ("but they'll never take the country out me");[33] her sexuality ("when he fucks me good") with her fierceness ("I slay");[34] and her individual fierceness with her collective warrior aspect ("ok ladies, now let's get in formation/cause I slay"), urging us, her children, to get into "formation." As Pérez notes, during spirit possession Yemayá "not only bears witness to the suffering of her children," but she also "offers practical strategies" in dealing with the effects of "economic exploitation, racial discrimination, and patriarchal oppression (Pérez 2013, 28).With these points in mind, the album's reference to making lemonade is not simply about "practic[ing] the art of money making" (hooks 2016). Rather, the act of making lemonade is bound up with a capacity that orisha worshipping communities often associate with Yemayá: "to make the most of what is at hand, with a mighty flourish" (Pérez 2013, 26).

Might this "formation" be a tool of imagining community, turning a personal problem into a mighty communal struggle? As Davis notes of Bessie Smith's "Backwater Blues," another song about a flood that brought devastation to black communities, songs like this have a very special role in the struggle for liberation. While they cannot be considered resistant in themselves, they "create the emotional conditions for protest" by "naming the problems the community wants to overcome" (Davis 1998, 113). As such, these songs can shape a people's capacity to forge a critical consciousness of their oppression (Davis 1998, 111). Similarly, Zandria Robinson argues that "formation" is "a metaphor, a black feminist, black queer, and black feminist queer theory of community organizing and resistance" that occurs *before* "overt action." It is not the protest movement itself, but "the alignment, the stillness, the readying, the quiet, before the twerk, the turn-up, the (social) *movement*" (Robinson 2016). The distinction Robinson and Davis are drawing here captures both the type of political agency I am pinpointing and its relationship to protest or resistance. Namely, they are pointing out the processes of self-definition that are needed for the development of the *capacity* to resist. In this essay, I have analyzed the role that black spiritual traditions play in forging this capacity in the kinship of sexual love and freedom—an insight that can be missed if we focus too narrowly on protest and resistance.

Notes

1 Wright writes: "In the main, her novel is not addressed to the Negro, but to a white audience whose chauvinistic tastes she knows how to satisfy. She exploits that phase of Negro life which is 'quaint,' the phase which evokes a piteous smile on the lips of the 'superior' race" (Wright 1937, 25). Comparatively, hooks writes: "Viewers who like to suggest *Lemonade* was created solely or primarily for black female audiences are missing the point. Commodities, irrespective of their subject matter, are made, produced, and marketed to entice any and all consumers. Beyoncé's audience is the world and that world of business and money-making has no color" (hooks 2016).
2 Wright states that Hurston's novel had "no basic idea or theme that lends itself to significant interpretation" (Wright 1937, 25); and hooks writes: "Images of female violence undercut a central message embedded in *Lemonade* that violence in all its forms, especially the violence of lies and betrayal, hurts" (hooks 2016).
3 Levine notes that some of the folk songs connect John Henry's hammer driving to his sexual prowess, due to a long penis. See *Black Culture and Black Consciousness,* page 421.
4 Hurston also reviewed Wright's *Uncle Tom's Children* in "Stories of Conflict." She noted that "[t]here is lavish killing here, perhaps enough to satisfy all male black readers,". for the black male hero "gets his man," or enacts revenge against the white man. However, the pretext for this revenge is sexual: securing justice for "his woman" (Hurston 1938, 32).
5 While his Marxism constrains him to jettison religion, many black folk traditions cannot be understood properly without the religious contexts that undergird them.
6 Jordan writes, "I believe we were misled into the notion that *only one kind* of writing—protest writing—and that *only one kind* of protest writing—deserves our support and study" (Jordan 2002, 286). She continues to draw out the gendered dimensions of this issue: "because Zora Neale Hurston was a woman, and because we have been misled into devaluing the functions of Black affirmation, her work has been derogated as romantic … and assessed as *sui generis*, or idiosyncratic accomplishment of no lasting reverberation, or usefulness" (Jordan 2002, 288).
7 See "High John de Conquer," page 922. Davis writes also takes up this theme of hope cultivated in "High John de Conquer" practices. See *Blues Legacies and Black Feminism,* pages 157–8.
8 See "High John de Conquer," pages 923–4. Hurston highlights the presence of John de Conquer during dark moments of slavery—the ship, the lashes, the dismal slave quarters.
9 Ibid, page 923.
10 Hurston writes, "[John de Conquer] had come from Africa … [The sea captains] knew about those black bodies huddled down there in the middle passage, being hauled across the waters to helplessness. John de Conquer was walking the very winds that filled the sails of the ships" (Hurston 1995b, 923).
11 That is, John de Conquer is not only a folk figure, but also a root used in hoodoo practices. See "High John de Conquer," pages 930–1.
12 Hurston writes, "High John could beat the unbeatable. He was top-superior to the whole mess of sorrow. He could beat it all, and what made it so cool, finish it off with a laugh" (Hurston 1995b, 923).
13 Davis writes: "Because the slaveocracy sought to extinguish the collective cultural memory of black people in order to confine them to an inferior social space, music, folktales, and hoodoo practices were always important ways black people could maintain connections—conscious or not—with the traditions of their ancestors" (Davis 1998, 155).
14 See "High John de Conquer," pages 925 and 931.
15 Ibid., pages 922–3 and 931.

16 For a detailed development of this point, see my "'I Ain't Thinkin' 'Bout You': Black Liberation Politics at the Intersection of Region, Gender, and Class" (Stewart 2017).

17 Indeed, one identifying characteristic of these "Race Champions," Hurston notes, is that "they call spirituals 'Our Sorrow Songs'" (Hurston 1999, 142). This is a pointed remark at W. EB. Du Bois, and Hurston later provides a different account of the origin of Negro spirituals that emphasizes joy through John de Conquer. See "High John de Conquer," pages 927–30.

18 The language used, such as an "ecstatic shiver" that sent the sacred tree's "root to tiniest branch creaming in every blossom and frothing delight," suggests the experience of female orgasm—especially the "thousand sister-calyxes" that "arch[ed] to meet the love embrace" (read: clitoris nerve endings) just before the "ecstatic shiver" (Hurston 2006, 11).

19 Hurston writes in "Conversions and Visions," "[t]here days is the traditional period for seeking the vision"; also, "[t]hree is the holy number (Hurston 1995a, 847).

20 In "Shouting," Hurston writes that during spirit possession, a spirit "chooses to drive out the individual consciousness temporarily and use the body for its expression" (Hurston 1995c, 851). This might be why the physical orgasm accompanies the vision of blooming.

21 Also similar to visions and conversions, where there is often an "unwillingness to believe" (Hurston 1995a, 847), hence the search for confirmation.

22 See *Their Eyes Were Watching God,* pages 10–11, 21, 32, 71–2, 76–8, 88–9, and 105–6. In these passages, Janie often "looks inside herself" to measure her life/affect against the love revelation before (signaled by references to foliage and blooming, such as petals, pollen dust, poignant smells, etc).

23 "To be truly free," hooks writes, "we must choose beyond simply surviving adversity, we must dare to create lives of sustained optimal well-being and joy."

24 hooks writes, "concluding this narrative of hurt and betrayal with caring images of family and home do not serve as adequate ways to reconcile and heal trauma."

25 Hooks writes, "Beyoncé's vision of feminism does not call for an end to patriarchal domination ... no call to challenge and change systems of domination, no emphasis on intersectionality."

26 See *Black Feminist Thought,* page 6.

27 Such as a way to demonize Haiti. For a development of this point, see *Envisioning Black Feminist Voodoo Aesthetics,* pages xvii–xxxv.

28 For example, see *Blues Legacies and Black Feminism,* pages 124–5 and 156–7 for a development of how blues women managed to become spiritual leaders in their communities.

29 Martin notes that the protagonist's "hem of a bright, yellow dress signaled the descent of Oshún. It mattered not that Beyoncé's face was not in the frame, in fact, the image is more powerful for doing so" (Martin 2016, 177).

30 See "Nobody's Mammy," page 29.

31 See "Yemayá y Ochún," pages 89, 92, and 97.

32 Focusing on Tina Turner, Moore writes, "[a]cross Tina's performance practice we witness fierceness as a spastic bodily possession—a seemingly uncontrollable, unrestrained energy" (Moore 2012, 83).

33 Pérez notes, for instance, that in some orisha worshipping communities Yemayá's "favorite foods—pork cracklins, sweet potatoes, black-eyed peas, salt-cured meat, grits—resemble Southern 'soul food' to a greater extent than that of other orishas and bring to mind slaves' accomplishment in building a cuisine from their paltry, monotonous provisions, larded with scraps from the master's table" Pérez 2013, 26).

34 Such as Yemayá's "spicyness," her "funky grace," her "sensuality and coolness" (Pérez 2013, 24).

Bibliography

Collins, Patricia Hill. 2009. *Black Feminist Thought: Knowledge, Consciousness, and the Politics of Empowerment.* New York: Routledge.

Davis, Angela Y. 1998. *Blues Legacies and Black Feminism.* New York: Vintage Books.

hooks, bell. 2016. "Moving Beyond Pain." May 9. Accessed Feb. 12, 2018. http://www.bellhooksinstitute.com/blog/2016/5/9/moving-beyond-pain.

Hurston, Zora Neale. 1999. "Art and Such." In *Go Gator and Muddy the Water: Writings by Zora Neale Hurston from the Federal Writer's Project,* by Zora Neale Hurston, edited by Pamela Bordelon, 139–145. New York: W.W. Norton & Company.

Hurston, Zora Neale. 1995a. "Conversions and Visions." In *Zora Neale Hurston: Folklore, Memoirs, and Other Writings,* by Zora Neale Hurston, edited by Cheryl A. Wall, 846–850. New York: The Library of America.

Hurston, Zora Neale. 1995b. "High John de Conquer." In *Zora Neale Hurston: Folklore, Memoirs, and Other Writings,* by Zora Neale Hurston, edited by Cheryl A. Wall, 922–931. New York: The Library of America.

Hurston, Zora Neale. 1995c. "Shouting." In *Zora Neale Hurston: Folklore, Memoirs, and Other Writings,* by Zora Neale Hurston, edited by Cheryl A. Wall, 851–853. New York: The Library of America.

Hurston, Zora Neale. 1938. "Stories of Conflict." *The Saturday Review of Literature,* April 2: 32–33.

Hurston, Zora Neale. 2006. *Their Eyes Were Watching God.* New York: Harper Perennial.

Hurston, Zora Neale. 2003. *Zora Neale Hurston: A Life in Letters.* Edited by Carla Kaplan. New York: Anchor Books.

Jacobs, Harriet. 2001. *Incidents in the Life of a Slave Girl.* Mineola: Dover Thrift Editions.

Jordan, June. 2002. *Some of Us Did Not Die: New and Selected Essays of June Jordan.* New York: Basic/Civitas Books.

Levine, Lawrence. 1977. *Black Culture and Black Consciousness.* New York: Oxford University Press.

Martin, Kameelah L. 2016. *Envisioning Black Feminist Voodoo Aesthetics: African Spirituality in American Cinema.* Lanham: Lexington Books.

Moore, Madison. 2012. "Tina Theory: Notes on Fierceness." *Journal of Popular Music Studies* 24, no. 1: 71–86.

Morrison, Toni. 2008. "Rediscovering Black History." In *What Moves at the Margin: Selected Nonfiction,* by Toni Morrison, edited by Carolyn C. Denard, 39–55. Jackson: University Press of Mississippi.

Otero, Solimar. 2013. "Yemayá y Ochún: Queering the Vernacular Logics of the Waters." In *Yemoja: Gender, Sexuality, and Creativity in the Latina/O and Afro-Atlantic Diasporas,* edited by Solimar Otero and Toyin Falola, 85–113. Albany: SUNY Press.

Pérez, Elizabeth. 2013. "Nobody's Mammy: Yemayá as Fierce Foremother in Afro-Cuban Religions." In *Yemoja: Gender, Sexuality, and Creativity in the Latina/o and Afro-Atlantic Diasporas,* edited by Solimar Otero and Toyin Falola, 9–42. Albany: SUNY Press.

Robinson, Zandria. 2016. "How Beyoncé's "Lemonade" Exposes the Inner Lives of Black Women." *Rolling Stone,* April 28. https://www.rollingstone.com/music/news/how-beyonces-lemonade-exposes-inner-lives-of-black-women-20160428.

Stewart, Lindsey. 2017. "'I Ain't Thinking 'Bout You': Black Liberation Politics at the Intersection of Region, Gender, and Class." Paper presented at the Society for Phenomenological and Existential Philosophy Conference "Philosophy In/Of the South." Panel. Memphis, TN, October 19–21.

Valdés, Vanessa K. 2014. *Oshun's Daughters: The Search for Womanhood in the Americas.* Albany: SUNY Press.

Wright, Richard. 1994. "Blueprint for Negro Writing." In *Within the Circle: An Anthology of African American Literary Criticism from the Harlem Renaissance to the Present,* edited by Angelyn Mitchell. Durham, NC: Duke University Press.

Wright, Richard. 1937. "Between Laughter and Tears." *New Masses,* October 5: 22–25.

3

GETTING TO THE ROOTS OF "BECKY WITH THE GOOD HAIR" IN BEYONCÉ'S *LEMONADE*

Janell Hobson

When pop star Beyoncé appeared on the 2014 cover of *Time*'s "100 Most Influential People" issue, the occasion prompted a visceral remark from renowned cultural critic bell hooks, who participated in an all-black women's panel on the subject "Are You Still a Slave?" at the New School in New York City in May of that year. Beyoncé's airbrushed black-and-white cover photo slimmed down her signature "bootylicious" curves as she posed in a bikini underneath a see-through over-shirt, while her long, bone-straight blonde hair had the effect of presenting her as a model-thin, near-white woman. For black feminists like hooks, such manipulative photoshopping indicated that the pop star had no control over her image, which in hooks's view made her a "slave" to the interests of a "white supremacist capitalist patriarchy." However, when fellow panelist and transgender activist-writer Janet Mock challenged this position by suggesting Beyoncé, as a successful entertainer and powerful entrepreneur of her own brand, is someone who has significant control over her self-image, hooks then accused the pop star of being a "terrorist"—one who can do significant harm to the self-esteem of young black girls who are exposed to images that seem to negate their blackness while also learning to adulate and glorify Beyoncé's light skin and wealth.

Hooks's comments stirred contentious debates among feminists and black feminists specifically, especially considering the pop star's embrace of a feminist politic that advocates for gender equality. For some, bell hooks's old-school critique—based in anti-capitalist and anti-racist analyses—brought some "clarity" to a radical discourse that had become murky during the millennial era when a new crop of black feminists proclaimed the virtues of sex positivity, conspicuous consumption as a site for political praxis, and "ratchet" feminism that pushed back against the dictates of respectability politics. For this younger generation, Beyoncé, and her claims to a feminist identity—one steeped in a hyperfeminine display of sexuality—felt authentic and in keeping with this new feminist ethos. For others, her claims seemed to be another marketing strategy, an attempt at rebranding, and even—as hooks would later argue in a keynote address at the National Women's Studies Association Conference in November 2014—a "hostile corporate takeover" of the feminist movement (hooks 2014).

What I find striking about hooks's remarks concerning Beyoncé is how personal they seem, far more rooted in emotionality than in intellectual rigor. After all, this is the same critic who once interviewed rapper Lil' Kim decades earlier, reveling in her raunchy and rebellious sexuality even though the black female rapper similarly sports blonde weaves and wears blue contact lenses (hooks 1997). And before these black sex symbols, hooks generously recognized how the white pop star Madonna, a natural brunette, embodied "blonde ambitions" as a way to "deconstruct the myth of 'natural' white girl beauty [that exposes] the extent to which it can be and is usually artificially constructed and maintained" (hooks 1992, 159). Whereas hooks is willing to recognize the artifice and performativity of the hypersexual personas of both Lil' Kim and Madonna, she does not afford Beyoncé the same performativity or subjectivity in crafting a potentially subversive public sexual persona that transcends the narrative of victimization or harm.

As Brittney Cooper observes,

> I think hooks read Beyoncé as flirting with whiteness and passing for white in ways that were fundamentally anti-Black and not affirming for women of color. I wish she had said that, rather than throwing around the very loaded language of 'terrorist' all willy-nilly. (Cooper 2018, 35)

However, hooks was intentional in her language, believing the pop star to be dangerous—if not in the political sense, then definitely in the cultural or psychological sense. Indeed, her remarks remind us that we are still somewhat invested in a racially essentialist definition of the black body, in which hair—as an extension of the body—seemingly captures our politics. Nonetheless, black cultural studies scholar Kobena Mercer challenges that we "de-psychologize" black hair styles as linked to racial politics by instead highlighting how black hair—straightened, extended, coiffed, dyed, afroed, or braided—represent "politically intelligible [and] creative responses to the experience of oppression and dispossession" (Mercer 1987, 34). It is this political intelligibility that I wish to explore in Beyoncé's critically acclaimed visual album *Lemonade* and the accompanying video for her single "Formation," both released in 2016.

For the purposes of this chapter, I trace this creative representation of black women's hair to the most memorable line from the visual album, Beyoncé's dismissive to her cheating partner: "You better call Becky with the good hair." Moving beyond famed video vixen Karrine Steffans's 2016 responsive think piece on being "Becky"—given her confessed one-night stand with Beyoncé's husband Jay-Z (né Shawn Carter)—or white Australian rapper Iggy Azalea's defensive misnomer of Becky as a "racial slur" against white women, I am interested in the phrase "Becky with the good hair" as signifying not only the "other woman" who poses a threat to black women's marriages and romantic partnerships, but also the "Other Woman" writ large: White Womanhood as a negation of black beauty and black femininity. Given hooks's repositioning of Beyoncé as the "Other Woman," in her critique of the pop star's appropriation of whiteness that negates a darker-skinned black sisterhood, Beyoncé strategically realigns her own body and self with other black women when calling out "Becky" as a racial and sexual threat.

As such, Beyoncé does not simply assimilate to whiteness with her blonde weaves, but disrupts the beauty codes of whiteness while also upending the white supremacist definitions of blondeness with one that encompasses creolization and the African Diaspora. She especially complicates this presentation—both in the video "Formation" and in *Lemonade*—through her use of braids and cornrows, signifiers of black womanhood, even with blonde coloration. This is a positionality that Beyoncé has managed throughout her career, as I explore in the subsequent pages, but which came to a head with this much-lauded feminist project.

Calling out Becky

On its most surface level, Beyoncé's *Lemonade* explores the emotional journey of a woman who reels from the discovery that her husband has cheated, each emotion serving as a subheading for the different segments of the visual album: *Intuition, Denial, Anger, Apathy, Emptiness, Accountability, Reformation, Forgiveness, Resurrection, Hope,* and *Redemption.* This is not the first time the pop singer has addressed infidelity in her relationship—songs such as "Resentment" and "Jealous" come to mind—and Jay-Z, with whom she has been coupled since the early millennium, confessed to his abusive behavior on his own album *4:44.* While Beyoncé's fans, the Beyhive, infamously went on an Internet hunt for the real "Becky with the good hair," and the lyrics to each song suggest the concerns of an intimate sexual relationship, the visual themes of the film gesture toward a wider historical and transnational context for the pop star's grief. Hair is a significant part of this engagement, which complicates Beyoncé's portraits of black womanhood—both of herself and others.

As previously stated, "Becky with the good hair" symbolizes the Other Woman, the White Woman as both historical and present-day nemesis for black women. "Becky" as a moniker for white women stems from rapper Sir Mix-a-Lot's infamous *Baby Got Back* music video (1992), in which two white women are shown at the start of the video (one who is called "Becky") making disparaging remarks about the size of a black woman's behind. Their fat-shaming comments betray their innate fear of a black female sexuality that might render their own sexuality as inauthentic and insufficient, given the racial expectations surrounding white women's supposed racial and sexual purity. However, "Becky's" dismissal of black women's beauty—represented by an ample butt size that Sir Mix-a-Lot celebrates—is further highlighted by her own expectations to top the racial hierarchy of beauty and femininity, often through the politics of "good hair," a vernacular term in black communities used to describe hair that is long and straight (or nearly straight). Beyoncé's star persona has merged these two racial aesthetic ideals of the black "bootylicious" body and blonde "good hair," even while the latter is depicted as artifice. Subsequently, she is successfully marketed as blurring the arbitrary racial color lines, despite not being biracial.

Beyoncé's light-skinned beauty is typically made fairer through blonde highlights, extensions, and weaves—often in contrast to darker-haired and darker-skinned members of her girl group Destiny's Child during her early career, or to her throng of background dancers and bandmembers with whom she regularly performs. The visual effect of her luxurious hair often presents Beyoncé as the "fairest" of the group, even when some of her background dancers are white. This is perhaps why, as Cooper argues, "Beyoncé … triggers a lot for us: about desire and beauty and skin color politics and access and being chosen and being the cool kid" (Cooper 2013). Indeed, an anonymous reader of the feminist magazine *Ms.* objected to its Spring 2013 cover of the pop star because "Beyoncé makes me feel bad about myself" (cited in Hobson 2016, 12).

Such triggers recall the character Maureen Peal from Toni Morrison's *The Bluest Eye*: the light-skinned pretty girl who ignites the envy of the narrator, Claudia MacTeer, and her sister, Frieda. As Claudia muses about her black peers' response to this beauty figure of childhood:

> Jealousy we understood and thought natural—a desire to have what somebody else had—but envy was a strange, new feeling for us. And all the time we knew that Maureen Peal was not the Enemy and not worthy of such intense hatred. The *Thing* to fear was the *Thing* that made *her* beautiful, and not us. (Morrison 1970, 74, emphasis in original)

The "thing" refers, of course, to a white supremacist heteropatriarchal worldview, which hooks pinpoints in her critique of Beyoncé. Nonetheless, her criticism was delivered without generosity and with explosive resentment, thereby suggesting that the lingering memory of the Maureen Peals of our own childhoods "triggers a lot for us," as Cooper warns. Indeed, Morrison admits in a conversation with the late fellow novelist, Gloria Naylor, that Maureen Peal was the only character in *The Bluest Eye* whose interiority she did not explore due to resentment from childhood memory; a powerful statement from someone whom many might describe as being light-skinned herself (cited in Montgomery 2004, 25).

In an intriguing way, Beyoncé's *Lemonade* entreats us to the interiority of the pretty light-skinned woman who seems to have it all, who tried to "be softer, prettier, less awake," only to have the "love of her life" dismiss her efforts with extramarital affairs with "Becky." Though she is never depicted in the visual album, the spectral figure of "Becky with the good hair" haunts the narrative, both in Beyoncé's embodiment and in the historical markers throughout the film. In a remarkable way, through hair politics, Beyoncé approximates "Becky with the good hair" as a way to divest her of the power of whiteness and to reposition her in the service of a collective black womanhood.

Hair journeys

Beyoncé Knowles's father, Mathew Knowles—who managed her girl group Destiny's Child, as well as her solo career until they parted ways in 2011—was quoted by social media as saying he married Beyoncé's mother, Célestine (Tina) Ann Beyincé, due to her proximity to whiteness. In an alleged interview with *Ebony Magazine*, Knowles describes this desire as "eroticized rage," a way to "get back" at white men for their racial oppression by sexually conquering white women and light-skinned black women by proxy (Gaynor 2018). In the same quote, he also admits that the light-skinned Louisiana Creole whom he married introduced him to a sense of black identity and pride.

Giving her daughter her unique maiden name as a continuation of her matrilineal Creole heritage, Tina Knowles, who became the stylist to her daughter's singing group and the fashion designer to her own House of Dereon—in homage to her own mother's maiden name and work as a seamstress—complicates this "eroticized rage" of approximating white womanhood. Mathew Knowles may have cynically demonstrated this rage in the aesthetic juxtaposition of his daughter, Beyoncé, as "almost white" through her highlighted blonde appearance that allowed her to visually stand out from her fellow Destiny's Child members Kelly Rowland, Michelle Williams, and (in the earlier iteration of the group) LaTavia Roberson, LeToya Luckett, and Farrah Franklin; however, Tina Knowles enabled the group to signify black womanhood through style and embodiment. It is these same hair politics that further allow Beyoncé to visualize a distinct black female subjectivity.

One of the earlier songs and videos of Destiny's Child, "Bills, Bills, Bills" (1999), takes place in a hair salon—based on Tina Knowles's own beauty salon in Houston, Texas. Here, Beyoncé is in black feminine space, where other black women are sitting under hair dryers, reading black beauty magazines, and the pop star herself is styling someone's hair. Against this backdrop, the song narrates the dilemma of dating a broke "trifling, good-for-nothing type of brother," with a chorus of women testifying to similar experiences. This will become a regular motif throughout Beyoncé's musical repertoire—the importance of women's financial independence and economic power since black men's own financial precarity is undependable, a subject she would address in 2014 when she penned the essay "Gender Equality is a Myth!" for the Maria Shriver Report to advocate for pay equity. The other motif—an unfaithful partner—pops up in the hit song "Say My Name" (1999), and in this video, Beyoncé rocks honey-blonde braids to convey a more aggressive attitude for a song based on a woman pointedly confronting her lover and demanding he say her name, which he actively avoids lest he inadvertently mentions the names of other women.

The honey-blonde hair color would become a signature look for Beyoncé, even as she maintains fluidity and chameleon-like transformations throughout her career. Although her musical and romantic partnership with hip-hop mogul Jay-Z oftentimes mirrors the same "eroticized rage" as her father—especially when the rapper is given to bragging about Beyoncé's "redbone" complexion and her status as "the baddest bitch in the game," based on her voluptuous figure heightened through provocative booty-enhanced dancing and her long, straight blonde hair—Beyoncé's stylized embodiment has been quite adept in balancing her status between hypersexual black woman and respectable All-American blonde girl-next-door, between a recognizable "sister" among fellow black woman (especially when forging narratives of friendships among her Destiny's Child bandmates) and the idealized "Becky with the good hair."

At times, Beyoncé signifies through her changing hairstyles different black women icons from the past, especially in movie roles. Think of her embodiment as a light-skinned, blonde-afroed, Pam Grier-like figure in *Austin Powers in Goldmember* (2002), or her allusions to Diana Ross and the Supremes with her darker-haired coif in *Dreamgirls* (2006), or the short blonde bob for her portrayal of blues singer Etta James in *Cadillac Records* (2008). Indeed, in 2009, she managed to embody different manifestations of black womanhood through her distinct hair expressions. She emerged as the tamed and sophisticated straight-haired blonde songstress serenading the first black president, Barack Obama, as he danced with Michelle Obama during their Inauguration Ball while Beyoncé crooned Etta James's signature ballad "At Last."

Aligned with the Obamas through this performance, Beyoncé's hair suggested both a political and cultural assimilation to the American national project—made manifest with the ascendance and acceptance of an African American president and First Lady. However, later that year, the pop star is seen with darker and curlier hair in *Obsessed,* her last live-action movie to date, in which she stars alongside black heartthrob Idris Elba in a thriller that has her defending her marriage and family from a crazed and dangerous white woman. Here, Beyoncé is made to perform and stand in for "every black woman" who rages against "Becky with the good hair" and her personal (and historical) damage to the black community— from the white women falsely accusing black men of rape to the present-day anxieties of such women waltzing into black communities and "stealing" available "good brothers," since more than a few black men seem to hold the same "eroticized rage" of racial and sexual one-upmanship waged against white men through white female bodies.

While Beyoncé has managed to affect an "angry black woman" persona through her movie role and through rage anthems like "Ring the Alarm" and "Irreplaceable," she has avoided the recreation of the loud-mouthed and unattractive Sapphire stereotype. However, she came close to becoming America's "mammy" at MTV's Video Music Awards Show in 2009 when she intervened on behalf of the emerging pop-country singer Taylor Swift, whose award-speech moment for Best Female Pop Music Video was scandalously interrupted by rapper Kanye West, who objected to her win over Beyoncé's immensely popular video for "All the Single Ladies." When Beyoncé won the more important Video of the Year award, she graciously brought Swift back on stage to finish her speech. In this moment, Beyoncé, who was adorned in a similar red dress to Swift's while sporting long, uncharacteristically black hair, got eclipsed by the "real" white woman represented by the slimmer and blonder Taylor Swift. Over the years, Swift's image would be mobilized as an Aryan ideal for the neo-Nazi "alt-right" movement, not just because of her perceived racial purity, but also because of the racial politics that framed this moment in 2009 when the white Barbie-like singer was accosted by a black male rapper who had the temerity to praise a black woman over her, especially one that some might view as a "fake white woman."

On a political level, Beyoncé's close relationship with the Obamas—from her partnership with the First Lady's "Let's Move" campaign on childhood obesity to her appearance at President Obama's second inauguration in the wake of his reelection—made her increasingly less palatable to a more conservative mainstream audience. Nonetheless, Beyoncé continued to both seriously and playfully adorn herself in various shades of blonde on diverse platforms: the Super Bowl halftime show in 2013, her majestic Eurocentric "Queen" imagery for her *Mrs. Carter* world tour commercial, and her platinum-blonde bombshell appearances that were mobilized for her game-changing *BEYONCÉ* visual album. Her trademark look became so convincing to audiences that, when she shared images of her daughter, Blue Ivy Carter, to whom she gave birth in early 2012, certain fans objected to what they viewed as Blue's unkempt and unruly hair.

Beyoncé's choice to keep her daughter's hair naturally kinky and in an afro was jarring against her own blonde tresses. She deliberately juxtaposed her blonde weave against the natural black naps of her daughter in an Instagram photo shared on February 5, 2014—in defiance of the public criticism of her daughter's natural hair, which she would defend in "Formation" with the lyrics: "I like my baby hair, with baby hair and Afros." Given that the fashion clothing line H&M once had to discontinue darker-haired images of the pop star when the public demonstrated a preference for her blonder image, Beyoncé's Instagram image seemed to suggest that, while she had to conform to mainstream beauty standards to attain her success—as her song and video "Pretty Hurts" from her self-titled album testifies—her daughter, who is often presented in tomboyish clothes and activities, will be free to be herself. This is a defiance that more reflects the hair politics of her younger sister, Solange Knowles, who cut her hair short and grew it into an afro that rocked the fashion world in wedding photos featured in *Vogue*'s online pages in 2014. Solange, subsequently, has provided black women with the ultimate hair anthem, "Don't Touch My Hair," from her critically acclaimed album *A Seat at the Table* (2016). These politics will set the stage for Beyoncé's more radical project illuminated in *Lemonade*.

Up(braiding) Becky

The video for "Formation," directed by Melina Matsoukas, features an intriguing scene of three black women of varying shades who don colorful wigs while posing in a beauty supply store. Expanding beyond the hair salon in "Bills, Bills, Bills," this setting highlights a raced, classed, and gendered experience pertaining to black women's beauty maintenance, as well as the global economy that has built an industry around this maintenance with "raw materials" of natural hair from India shipped to urban centers in the U.S., where vendors are typically Asian and consumers are mostly part of the African Diaspora. Such artifice in the maintenance of grown black women's hair rituals contrasts with Beyoncé's own affirming maintenance of the natural black-girl state of Blue. There is nonetheless a celebration of black women's creative hair and style expressions both globally and in the Gulf Coast region, akin to the "formations" of New Orleans-based women's groups, who don colorful outfits and elegant hairstyles while "getting in formation" to lead second-line jazz parades in the streets of the segregated black city. There are elements of local New Orleans flavor throughout the "Formation" video, from Mardi-Gras costumes to second-line parades and visual invocations of Vodou spirits, such as the loa (spirit) Maman Brigitte, guardian of the souls of the dead with a penchant for profanity, whom Beyoncé embodies with her obscene hand gestures, her eye-covering, wide-brimmed hat, and two long braided ponytails. Much like Beyoncé's manifestation of Maman Brigitte, local women's groups affirm the material side of this spiritual work: In their case, they are guarding the living community and its culture, and doing so while looking fabulous. As the pop star declares: "I slay!"

In "Formation," the long flowing braids of Beyoncé and Creole buns from a different era, combined with Blue Ivy's magnificent afro, suggest the pop star's engagement with *conjuring,* sometimes requiring the use of actual hair parts to create the power of "black girl magic." Here, Beyoncé conjures black culture and style in the service of a "black lives matter" politic, and black women's hair is at the heart of this assertion of blackness. This is made evident in the larger project of *Lemonade,.* which offers three images of Beyoncé's hair politics manifested at the beginning of the visual album. There is the opening close-up on her golden-colored cornrows, which suggest power and resistance given the more aggressive stance that Beyoncé takes when she adorns this style—especially when situated in contexts that find black women disciplined for donning this style in either a professional or military setting. Beyoncé next appears in a hoodie, which signifies the spirit of Trayvon Martin, whose death and acquittal of his murderer ignited the Black Lives Matter movement. The third image of Beyoncé in a tignon signifies her engagement with a more distant past as she dons a relic from Louisiana's history when laws required free, mixed-race women to cover their hair to downplay their beautification hair rituals and, especially, to racially distinguish them from white women. It is no coincidence that Beyoncé, who has been accused of appropriating whiteness, would signify on this particular history in which Creole women of color were regimented in their proximity to whiteness. That these women then transformed the obligatory tignon into its own aesthetic practice—which Beyoncé visualizes as a fashion statement—testifies to the legacy of black women's resistance, indeed turning "lemons" into "lemonade."

This history also recalls black women's perpetual placement as a racial rival to white women, the "sidechick" and "Becky with the good hair" whose absence-presence in this project causes significant pain and resentment. In her manifestation as the Yoruba orisha Oshún, adorned in her elaborate yellow gown and high platform shoes, Beyoncé's blonde tresses extend from darker braided roots, which reflect her duality: interweaving her smiling coquette persona with a bat-wielding and rage-filled fiery goddess as she performs the catchy song, "Hold Up." This orisha targets for destruction, aside from smashed cars and water hydrants, a store window advertising "free facials" and colorful wigs, symbols of commercial beauty. Such a fantastical scene precedes a documentary footage-based scene depicting black dancing girls in a high school marching band, the lightest-skinned one with long hair positioned at the front while the darker-skinned girls appear at the back. That they are all subject to wearing "nude" hosiery intended for white complexions invites an association between the cheating narrative and a critique of the wider racist and colorist society, especially when Beyoncé's spoken-word voiceover muses about the other woman: "If this is what you truly want, I can wear her skin over mine ... her hair over mine."

However, Beyoncé emerges at her angriest in her glorious golden cornrows and fur coat for the song "Don't Hurt Yourself," and at her most defiant for the song "Sorry," when she and a collective of black women with elaborate braids, afros, and weaves—including tennis champion Serena Williams—dance, prance, twerk, and let loose in the spaces once associated with racial and sexual oppression: the plantation house and a party bus, refashioned from their earlier respective histories of slavery and Jim Crow segregation. That "Sorry" closes on a dismissive to her husband—"you better call Becky with the good hair"—while Beyoncé sports intricate and stunningly gorgeous Nefertiti-style braids further upends the racial meanings of "good hair." Indeed, a transitional scene of women donning similar braids resembles a coven of witches, nude and walking in a trance into the wilderness, thus signaling their departure from the white patriarchal world.

FIGURE 3.1 Video still from "Sorry." *Lemonade*, Parkwood Entertainment, 2016

It must be noted, however, that by the time Beyoncé literally sings her "Freedom" song—performing on a stage within the grounds of a plantation for a community of black women, including the mothers of slain sons recognized in the Black Lives Matter movement—she appears at her blondest and most straight-haired. She also performs alongside Sierra Leone-born ballerina Michaela DePrince and the model with vitiligo, Winnie Harlow, who is shown grooming herself in a beauty ritual. The plantation site combined with these aesthetic choices seems to suggest that, as a collective black womanhood, we are not quite removed from the shadow of Becky with the good hair: the plantation mistress, the ballerina, or the fashion model gazing at herself in the mirror (the way Harlow does in one scene). Yet, the move toward coming together in the space of this history—with black women of various hair textures, styles, skin shades, and different ages, extending from a mossy tree or gathering on the porch of a slave cabin—suggests this is the path to redemption and even a healing circle that might include the "other woman" with whom we must reconcile. There is also the manifestation of Oshún, as these beauty rituals and gazing into mirrors—one of the orisha's symbols—indicate, which further invites black women to move beyond the gaze of Becky with a divine license to self-love, self-care, and self-definition.

Conclusion

In the aftermath of *Lemonade,* Beyoncé performed across the racial and sonic color lines: sporting her braids while splashing around in water with rapper Kendrick Lamar as the words of Martin Luther King, Jr. provided a prelude to the racial-struggle song "Freedom" at the BET Awards show, and donning her bone-straight long blonde hair as she sang the country song "Daddy Lessons" with the blond-haired trio Dixie Chicks at the Country Music Awards show. Whereas the BET performance captured the ethos of being "woke" and championing the racial jus-tice politics of Black Lives Matter, the CMA performance disrupted the mostly white affair by interjecting multiracial and joyous abandon rooted in the black origins of country music. It was subversive enough for certain country-music audiences to object to Beyoncé's presence, whose body-hugging attire conjoined both virginal lace and vixen-like see-through negligee. Her sexiness and Creole-based beauty, which reminds us of past Southern practices of interracial sexual violence and liaisons, upends the myth of white purity, and especially demonstrates how "Becky with the good hair" is both an approximation and a subversion. By the time she performed her digitized live performance while pregnant at the 2017 Grammy Awards show, Beyoncé made sure we all "bowed down" to the goddess who blessed her with twins: Oshún, the African Venus in trademark yellow made manifest as Botticelli's Venus, doubling as the Virgin Mary, and synergizing with the Hindu goddess Kali. This time, her luxurious and unruly blonde hair, like the women of *Lemonade* and the multiplying women on stage, "cannot be contained."

Beyoncé may have lost the Album of the Year award to the industry's preferred songstress Adele, who herself seemed embarrassed to have received the honor over her, but the pop star has transformed the way we listen to and even *see* music. Soul singer India.Arie may have also once crooned "I am not my hair," but in the instance of a pop diva who is often accused of wanting to be white or who is dismissed as just another "Becky with the good hair," she has proven that hair is integral to identity, agency, and a more complicated racial consciousness. This was again made manifest a year later when the pop star, in partnership with husband Jay-Z, filmed their video *Apeshit* at the famous Louvre Museum in Paris while they were touring in Europe. Not only did the two stars position their expensively attired bodies in front of the museum's most celebrated painting—Leonardo da Vinci's *Mona Lisa*—but they also subverted its aesthetics by placing another black couple in front of it as the woman picked the man's afro. In defiance of the dominant Eurocentric gaze, Beyoncé and Jay-Z accessed a cultural symbol of power and reclaimed it for black bodies and black aesthetics. In these ways, Beyoncé redefines raced and gendered aesthetics and subverts our cultural under- standings of "good hair." She does so in opposition to a dominant and normative construction of white womanhood, and in service to a versatile and racially fluid representation of black womanhood.

Bibliography

"Are You Still a Slave?" Panel at the New School, with bell hooks, Shola Lynch, Marci Blackmon, and Janet Mock. May 6, 2014. Available: https://livestream.com/TheNew School/Slave.

Cooper, Brittney. "The Beyoncé Wars: Should She Get to be a Feminist?" *Salon* (December 17, 2013). Available: https://www.salon.com/2013/12/17/a_deeply_personal_beyonce_ debate_should_she_get_to_be_a_feminist.

Cooper, Brittney. 2018. *Eloquent Rage: A Black Feminist Discovers Her Superpower*. New York: St. Martin's Press.

Gaynor, Gerren Keith. "Mathew Knowles Says Colorism Made Him Think Ex-Wife Tina Lawson Was a White Woman." *The Grio* (February 2, 2018). Available: https://thegrio. com/2018/02/02/mathew-knowles-tina-lawson-white-woman/.

Hobson, Janell. 2016. "Feminists Debate Beyoncé." In *The Beyoncé Effect: Essays on Sexu- ality, Race and Feminism*, 11–26, Adrienne Trier-Bieniek, ed. Jefferson: McFarland.

hooks, bell. 1992. *Black Looks: Race and Representation*. Boston: South End Press.

hooks, bell. "Hardcore Honey: bell hooks Goes on the Down Low with Lil Kim." *Paper* (May 1997). Available: http://www.papermag.com/hardcore-honey-bell-hooks-goes-on-the-down -low-with-lil-kim-1427357106.html.

hooks, bell. Keynote Address Delivered at the National Women's Studies Association Annual Meeting. November 14, 2014. San Juan, Puerto Rico.

Mercer, Kobena. 1987. "Black Hair/Style Politics." *New Formations* 3 (Winter): 33–54.

Montgomery, Maxine Lavon, ed. 2004. *Conversations with Gloria Naylor*. Jackson: University Press of Mississippi.

Morrison, Toni. 1970. *The Bluest Eye*. New York: Alfred A. Knopf.

Steffans-Short, Karrine. "I Am Becky with the Good Hair." *XOJane* (April 29, 2016). Available: https://www.xojane.com/sex/becky-with-good-hair-karrine-steffans-short-ja y-z-hookup.

4

PULL THE SORROW FROM BETWEEN MY LEGS

Lemonade as rumination on reproduction and loss

LaKisha M. Simmons

In Toni Morrison's novel *Beloved* (1987), a mother named Sethe is haunted by her murdered daughter who comes back to her in the flesh. In a review of the book shortly after publication, Marsha J. Darling emphasized the notion that "death is an integral part of living consciousness in African religious understanding." "Sethe's world," Darling explains, "was deeply inscribed with a concrete understanding of traditional African religion and its belief about mother's right, communality, and the continuum, that linked ancestors and unborn spirits with the incarnate; her consciousness reflects this deeply rooted cultural pattern."[1] Like the novel *Beloved,* Beyoncé Knowles-Carter's *Lemonade* centers a world-view where unborn spirts inhabit spaces, our ancestors' grief and wisdom are passed down, and a community of women work toward healing on the plantation landscape.

"Dismembered and displaced" bodies haunt the landscape of *Lemonade*'s past, present, and future.[2] These dismembered and displaced bodies provide a haunting—creating a "site of memory" and a place of mourning.[3] In this essay, through a reading of *Lemonade* and autobiographical life-narratives, I focus on just one of *Lemonade*'s sites of mourning: the maternal mourning for lost children. By mixing methods and genres, this essay considers black women's grief. But, as *Lemonade* and other seminal texts by black women writers teach us, "the dead are not dead."[4] According to theorist Sharon Holland, interdisciplinary inquiry is required for stories such as these because "speaking about death and the dead necessitates that critics move beyond familiar country and into liminal spaces."[5] *Lemonade* provides the opportunity to move into these liminal spaces—linking the historical with the present, the ancestors with the unborn.

Silence, dissemblance and black women's personal narratives

Colleen Burrell, mother to James Naim Burrell (May 19, 2018–May 19, 2018), began a blog called "Silent No More: A Journal about Infant Loss." Burrell bravely talks about her son, despite feeling a cultural taboo around sharing such stories: "I am going to talk about my son. I want to share my journey to have him, to lose him and to keep loving him even as he looks down on me from heaven." She notes how many women have suffered in silence:

> From aunts to grandparents to sister-in-laws to friends, so many people have lost a baby they so deeply loved and wanted. It is for all of them and all of those who are still holding on to the secret of losing a baby that I am "Breaking the Silence."[6]

Even in the face of a culture of dissemblance, where black women silence their innermost fears, black women have also engaged in "embodied testimony" to theorize the ways in which they experience their bodies, motherhood, and loss.[7]

Beyoncé Knowles-Carter has used autobiography to discuss her own experiences with motherhood and loss. Analyzing her autobiography helps situate *Lemonade* as a text that seeks to speak *to* black women about motherhood, fertility, loss, and rebirth. In a 2013 interview with Oprah Winfrey, Beyoncé discussed her first miscarriage as "one of the hardest things I've ever been through" and as a "big part of my story." Winfrey specifically asked the singer about secrecy and silence: "How did you keep that a secret?" Beyoncé's response is illuminating; rather than reveal the emotional labor of keeping the *miscarriage* a secret, Beyoncé moves to her next pregnancy, explaining that she never told people she was pregnant with Blue Ivy Carter in case that pregnancy ended in loss, too.[8] Presumably she would have remained silent if her longing for motherhood had remained unfulfilled. However, Blue Ivy's birth allowed Beyoncé to talk more specifically about miscarriage in her interview with Winfrey and in her HBO autobiographical documentary *Life Is But a Dream* (2013).[9]

Beyoncé is not the only black woman to have maintained silence and distance after miscarriage and/or infertility. Psychologists have studied this phenomenon among black women specifically—who have higher rates of adverse reproductive health outcomes than white women. In "Silent and Infertile" Rosario Ceballo, Erin Graham, and Jamie Hart find that African American women have few outlets for discussing journeys with infertility. They quote one informant as admitting that she doesn't talk "about that." "Yeah, I don't have kids," she says, "but girl, *I'm alright.*"[10] Here, the "alright" creates a needed emotional distance—maintaining the silence. Another informant said, "I never said anything to anyone else, because in our culture … it was not something that you shared."[11] Beyoncé's *Life Is But a Dream* documentary seems to do this same work—revealing loss and pain while also maintaining a curated distance. Beyoncé's critics often point to this distance to devalue her art, claiming she is too obsessed with fame and profit to reveal true vulnerability. For example, one critic panned the autobiographical documentary as a "contrived" "infomercial" that was "neither daring nor entirely truthful."[12] In this common interpretation of Beyoncé, she is an inauthentic, celebrity machine— doing whatever it takes to charm fans. But there is another word historians have used for this distance besides "inauthenticity"—dissemblance.

Historian Darlene Clark Hine has named the "girl, I'm alright" tendency among black women as a "culture of dissemblance." Hine describes dissemblance as an emotional culture that helps to hide black women's inner feelings from prying public eyes; dissemblance "involved creating the appearance of disclosure, or openness about themselves and their feelings, while actually remaining an enigma to whites."[13] Darlene Clark Hine draws a long genealogy for the "culture of dissemblance," noting that when looking for the "inner lives" of black women, we rarely see their thoughts and feelings articulated in the public archive. To explore this, she uses autobiographies as one example and the National Association of Colored Women (NACW) as another.[14]

Mary Church Terrell (1863–1954), elite clubwoman, activist, and president of the NACW, was perhaps the most polished of all dissemblers (despite Beyoncé's talents in this area). Historian Alison Parker argues that Terrell "inscrib[ed] her public body with wellness and decorum" while at the same time dealing with "private pain." Terrell nearly died the first time she gave birth. As Parker explains, "beginning with her first pregnancy in 1892, when she was in her late twenties, Terrell gave birth to three babies in five years, each of whom died within a few days of birth."[15] Yet her public articulations on this matter remained opaque. Terrell used her own autobiography, *A Colored Woman in a White World*, to carefully tell her own story as a mother who experienced loss. At the same time, she maintained an emotional distance. Recounting one of her losses, Terrell said,

> When my third baby died two days after birth, I literally sank down into the very depths of despair. For months I could not divert my thoughts from the tragedy, however hard I tried. Right after its birth the baby had been placed in an improvised incubator, and I was tormented by the thought that if the genuine article had been used, its little life might have been spared. I could not help feeling that some of the methods employed in caring for my baby had caused its untimely end.[16]

Yet Terrell never describes her personal emotions, her relationship with her husband, or what her "despair" looked like. Instead, she focuses most of the book on her long list of accomplishments as an activist. As she was working on a draft of her autobiography, Terrell received feedback from an editor saying, "the book is a little cold."[17] Yet there was a reason for the distance. Historian Deborah Gray White has argued that black clubwomen were

> cautious about putting their private lives and histories in the hands of a media that had for centuries stereotyped and slandered black women. Rather than

take such a risk, black women learned to practice ... the art of dissemblance. They let their public see only what they wanted them to see.[18]

Certainly, the current media landscape includes risk for black women in the public eye. Actress Gabrielle Union explores the public's insatiable desire for personal information and dirt on their favorite stars in her autobiography *We're Going to Need More Wine*. There, Union shares her experience with recurrent miscarriage: "Yes, Dwayne [Wade] and I would have such pretty babies. But I have had eight or nine miscarriages. In order to tell you the exact number, I would have to get out my medical records." In this chapter, Union never reveals her embodied experience with miscarriage or her private thoughts. Indeed, the chapter is framed through the "art of dissemblance"—revealing her losses while also making room for her private self. The chapter is titled "Everyone Get Out of My Pussy!" and ends with a gesture toward full transparency that is actually a request for privacy: "That's the real story. Gabrielle Union's Baby Hopes: 'Everyone Needs to Get Out of My Pussy!'"[19] Union says she shared her struggles in her autobiography because, "There is no reason to feel alone. There is no reason to suffer in silence."[20]

Like Union, Beyoncé says she shared her story of loss in *Life Is But a Dream* not only because "there are so many couples that go through that" but also to spread "hope."[21] In the documentary and Oprah interview, Beyoncé discusses her secret longing to be a mother. The public articulation of emotion around the miscarriage, I would argue, does not fully break the "silence" around black women, infertility, infant loss, and/or miscarriage—or even Beyoncé's own struggles around reproductive health and infant loss. As we know, these interviews also came in the wake of conspiracy theories that Beyoncé had not birthed a child (her daughter Blue Ivy) at all, and critiques that her security team barred other parents at the hospital from caring for/seeing their newborns the same day Beyoncé was in labor. As Beyoncé presented her life story in these moments, she was therefore still guarded, still dissembling. But a quotation from the "Silent and Infertile" study highlights the importance of Beyoncé's attempts at articulating her personal experience for her fans. One informant admitted,

I didn't think there were that many African American women out there that were having this problem. I mean, you know, because nobody talks about it and you know, there's nothing ever on the media about it. I mean, the media represents us as popping out babies left and right. You know, we're welfare mothers, we're this and that, you know, so I didn't think there was a problem with us.[22]

Blood, pain, and reproduction

Lemonade is (purposefully) a multilayered text. Each image, sound, and space holds multiple meanings. In my analysis of *Lemonade* here, I explore the meaning of blood as closely related to maternal mourning. Read alongside Beyoncé's discussion of miscarriage in *Life Is But a Dream,* it becomes clear that *Lemonade* honors black women's struggles as mothers in a world that cannot recognize their pain. By giving voice to this grief and linking death with rebirth, *Lemonade* works toward places of healing.

A woman dives from the top of a skyscraper—falling. She crashes not into the ground, but into water, sinking deeper into an underwater world. She swims above a bedroom, and looks longingly at the bed and her past self—imperfect and in pain. In "Denial," blood seeps through the water in the form of a scarlet cape. Beyoncé recites: "I threw myself into a volcano. I drank the blood, and I drank the wine." The bleeding in this section is closely related to religious iconography. The protagonist drinks the blood to attempt to fix the pain, the wrong of her body. Here, as throughout *Lemonade,* the narrator intertwines the pain of losing a lover, the pain of losing a child, and the pain of the African American past. This scene highlights the questions that frame the central narrative of *Lemonade*: How do you make yourself whole again after loss? How do you ease the longing? Here, the protagonist attempts to make herself clean and worthy by bathing: "I bathed in bleach and plugged my menses with pages in the Holy book." The image of blood, specified in menses, is significant for those attempting to get or stay pregnant. The return of the monthly flow can be evidence of (yet another) failed attempt to get pregnant; or, it can also be the evidence of the start of (yet another) miscarriage as fetal tissue is expelled from the body.

Yet it is the section "Apathy" that lays the foundation for my reading of *Lemonade* as a text that deals specifically with miscarriage and infant loss. In this section, a music box plays *Swan Lake* in the background, the soundtrack to images of a ghostly school bus; the scene is played out in black and white. The young women on the school bus sway back and forth in a trance; as if dead, Beyoncé sways right along with them.

FIGURE 4.1 Women seated and leaning, adorned with *Sacred Art of the Ori* by Laolu Senbanjo from "Sorry." *Lemonade*, Parkwood Entertainment, 2016

"Apathy" begins with "Here lies the mother of my children both living and dead," and ends with "Rest in Peace my True Love." The school bus is a portal, holding a dead mother and her dead and unborn children. All of the sounds and images conjure those children, infants, and unborn who have gone before us. Indeed, this section of *Lemonade* acts as if a wake, pointing the viewers to the bodies and spirits of the dead. Christina Sharpe notes that:

> Wakes are processes; through them we think about the dead and about our relation to them; they are rituals through which to enact grief and memory. Wakes allow those among the living to mourn the passing of the dead through ritual.[23]

The school bus highlights black women's grief. Beyoncé's deadened state on the bus represents the emotional deadness, weariness, and hopelessness that can accompany recurrent miscarriage and infant loss. But the repeated use of this imagery in *Lemonade* functions as more than just a wake that remembers the dead. Instead, it is a reminder that the dead are always with us. Throughout *Lemonade* this configuration of dancers and the school bus signifies the in-between world— the spirits always with us.

The transition into "6 Inch"—a section aptly titled "Emptiness"—explains, "she sleeps all day. Dreams of you in both worlds." Again, the metaphor of blood alerts the viewer to miscarriage: "Tills the blood in and out of uterus. Wakes up smelling like zinc." Beyoncé sits in the dark, within a circle of fire; a long red dress drapes down from her body. Next, the viewer enters a red (bloodied) hallway with a small bit of light at its endpoint—symbolizing both the uterus and the birth canal.

FIGURE 4.2 Video still from "6 Inch." *Lemonade*, Parkwood Entertainment, 2016

From within the hallway, sounds are distorted. Beyoncé begins chanting: "Loss. Dear Moon we blame you for floods. For the flush of blood." The haunting sound, of water mixing with some bass from "6 Inch," mimics the sound of a fetal heartbeat, or perhaps the sound of the placenta. The placenta is a revered organ that grows in the uterus during pregnancy. The placenta pulses with blood. It is the transfer point between the mother and fetus; all nutrients and oxygen flow through this organ.[24] Listening to the placenta on a Doppler machine sounds like the swishing of liquid at a beat—it is the low-pressure blood flow. During "Emptiness" the internal pulsing surrounds the viewer/listener as they move through the deep red hallway; the viewer is *inside* the woman's body. In some ways, this slow pulsing sound in the transition to "6 Inch" is a poignant sonic evocation of Prince's "Sex in the Summer." In that song, Prince sampled his own son's heartbeat. Prince's son died one week after birth, and the record, *Emancipation,* was released only days later.[25] Because the song "Sex in the Summer" was produced prior to the birth and death of his child, the heartbeat in the song is upbeat and joyful.

The pulsing at the start of "6 Inch" feels slower, more mournful. As the camera moves through the hallway and the viewer is "pushed" through the canal, the song "6 Inch" begins in full sound. But before the song continues there is an interruption, red filters and red lights, then a burst of bright light. A number of images flash quickly past the viewer just as "6 Inch" begins anew. The images flash so quickly they are barely seen. The pictures signify maternal mourning: again, an image of the hallway/birth canal; a bed with a woman fallen to the ground illuminated by red light; a black screen emblazoned with the word LOSS; a fiery red cross. The poetry, imagery, sounds, color and tones recreate the moment of miscarriage—the emptying of the uterus, the blood clots, the embryonic or fetal tissue.

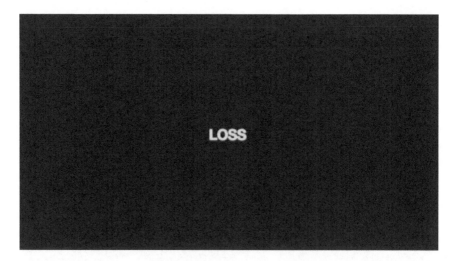

FIGURE 4.3 Video still of the title card for the chapter titled "Loss." *Lemonade*, Parkwood Entertainment, 2016

Genealogies of loss

Beyoncé purposefully places the black maternal struggle with loss within a historical context. In doing so, she creates a "present-past time-space"[26] that loops the experiences of the ancestors with the experiences of black women in the present. In *Lemonade,* this past-present time-space is produced through a "site of memory"[27] that acknowledges enslaved mothers' inability to protect and keep their own children. The video-album was filmed along Plantation Alley, located along the Mississippi River in Louisiana just outside of New Orleans—a site of sugar plantations. In one scene, Beyoncé recites: "One thousand girls raise their arms. Do you remember being born? Are you thankful for the hips that cracked the deep velvet of your mother and her mother and her mother? There is a curse that will be broken." At Laura Plantation, also along the river, in 1830 Nanette Prud'homme Duparc, the matriarch of her family, improved the family business by going to the city and purchasing thirty teenagers. Ten years later she had her first "crop of children." Her wealth and her business relied on breeding slaves and stealing children.[28] The past, present, and future loss of black children is highlighted, placing *Lemonade* at the site of these plantations. These themes and imagery in *Lemonade* were inspired by *Daughters of the Dust* (1991), an independent film by Julie Dash that explored the connections between ancestors and the unborn. *Daughters of the Dust* is narrated by an unborn child (who will be born in the future). In that film, Nana—the matriarch and elder—explains, "Those in this grave, like those who're across the sea, they're with us. They're all the same. The ancestors and the womb are one."[29] *Lemonade* takes this generative cosmology and asks, what happens when the Unborn Children of the womb stay forever in the spirit world? When our children cannot be our future?

Placed within the genealogy of loss in *Lemonade* are also the Mothers of the Movement—black mothers who have lost their children to police violence/white vigilantes and whose stories have incited the Black Lives Matter Movement. *Lemonade* features Lezley McSpadden (mother of Michael Brown), Gwen Carr (mother of Eric Garner), and Sybrina Fulton (mother of Trayvon Martin). Lezley McFadden sits, regally holding a graduation photograph of her son Michael Brown. (Brown was shot and killed the summer after his high school graduation.) The camera stays on her face as a tear slips down her eye. She then closes her eyes, her face infused with pain.

Healing comes by recognizing the connections between the living and the dead, the unborn, never born, and the ancestors. Just after the mothers lovingly hold photographs of young black men and boys killed by police and vigilantes, Queen Ya Ya (Kijafa Brown) of Washitaw Nation Mardi Gras Indians conjures the ancestors by walking a circle around a table, empty, yet full of spirits. There is no sound except for her tambourine until the whispered, "Magic." A picture flashes on the screen—it is a black and white image of Beyoncé with the unborn children on the school bus. This is a reminder that Queen Ya Ya is conjuring all of the dead and lost children. The camera then pans through the house to find an infant child in a bed. Here, "the ancestors and the womb are one." The unborn, never born, and children lost too soon are with the ancestors.

FIGURE 4.4 Video still of Lezley McSpadden. *Lemonade*, Parkwood Entertainment, 2016

Personal reflections on blood

In an interview with Toni Morrison, Marsha Darling asks, "[W]here's the healing? There's a healing in the memory and the (re)memory." Morrison takes up the question of healing by turning to silences. The story needs telling, but,

> no one speaks, no one tells the story about himself or herself unless forced. They don't want to talk, they don't want to remember, they don't want to say it, because they're afraid of it—which is human. But when they do say it, and hear it, and look at it, and share it, they are not only one, they're two, and three, and four, you know? The collective sharing of that information heals the individual—and the collective.[30]

The gestures toward infant loss, miscarriage, and infertility in *Lemonade* and in Jay-Z's title track "4:44"—"I seen the innocence leave your eyes/ I still mourn this death and/ I apologize for all the stillborns 'cause I wasn't present/ Your body wouldn't accept it"—open up public places for mourning. So, too, has Beyoncé's *Life Is But a Dream* autobiographical documentary.

On YouTube, for instance, women use the miscarriage clip from *Life Is But a Dream* to talk about their own experiences—or to simply mark them. One black woman commented:

> I know exactly how this feels. I heard baby's heartbeat at 8 weeks. Went back for a checkup two weeks later, no heartbeat. It was soul crushing. We had names, and our whole family knew. It was my first and only baby.

Another woman wrote of her experience with two late-term losses: "I lost my third baby boy @21 weeks and it almost killed me, it was one of the hardest things I ever experienced … #awareness of incompetent cervix." Yateesha[31] wrote:

> I lost my baby too. I wanted him so bad. I don't know what I did wrong. I know everything happens for a reason, it's just every time I go past baby clothes I wonder why did God take my baby from me.

And Khamina responded, "I promise it wasn't your fault." One woman simply wrote: "Kenny Jerome Bailey. 10-23-2016–10-23-2016. Mommy loves you and I see you when [I] get there."

To tell my own story of blood and loss I have to start with the first miscarriage. It was an ordinary miscarriage, as miscarriages go. I went to get an ultrasound, but there was no heartbeat. But then the news, discovered by the radiologist: I was told that I had a "uterine anomaly" or, a birth defect of the uterus. It turns out that my uterus was shaped like a heart, and that can make getting (or staying) pregnant difficult.

I sought out a specialist on birth defects of the uterus. Tests confirmed a heart shape; the doctor recommended surgery. The surgeon decided to schedule one last test, an MRI, before the surgery, now only a few weeks away. The result: I did not appear to have a uterine anomaly. Instead, massive fibroids had created a misshapen uterus. Instead of an uncommon birth defect, I was suffering from a condition that nearly every black woman has by her mid-thirties. The (white, male) doctor's advice thus shifted. He could not advocate for or against surgery—"many black women have fibroids; yet black women don't seem to have problems having children," he said.

Shortly after this, I became pregnant again. Things seemed fine until the blood started. The doctor recommended regular ultrasounds. Despite the blood there was a heartbeat and a growing fetus. But the blood did not stop. And then, there was no heartbeat. At this point we decided on surgery to remove the fibroids. And we'd try again.

Again, I got pregnant. The next time I bled, one of the specialists assured me it was not out of the ordinary. It seems that specialists think women have baseless anxieties. I bled the entire pregnancy. At some point, an excessive burst of blood sent me to the ER. I felt a growing sense of heaviness and dread as the pregnancy progressed. Eventually it became clear to the specialist that something was not right. For some reason, the placenta wasn't providing the necessary nutrition to the fetus, and the fetus was not growing very fast. This basically meant weekly appointments, ultrasounds, and tests to check to see if the fetus would continue growing at a slow rate or stop altogether, necessitating immediate delivery if possible.

One morning I "[woke] up to the smell of zinc." I was hemorrhaging. At home alone, I jumped in the car (did not clean the blood) and drove to a hospital a block away from my home. (My husband would later have to go home and clean all the blood.) When I was in the hospital and told him there was a mess, he said, "Don't worry about it. You don't have to see it. I already cleaned it." The diagnosis: a placental abruption (when the placenta detaches from the uterus). Luckily for me and the baby, the placenta did not tear completely off. After an emergency c-section, Layla Bell was born weighing only 3.5 pounds. Because of my ill health, I did not get to hold her right away.

These are a list of facts, not emotions. The facts say little about my inner world at the time. I cannot tell the story without dissembling. I cannot even perform the emotions of grief for an audience. What I can say is, "But *girl, I'm alright.*" What I can write is that I punished my body for the bleeding for a long time after. Running too soon and too hard was the only control I had of a body turned traitor to me and my unborn children. I can also write about the statistics: black women living in my zip code at the time were more likely to have a baby premature and underweight than not.

Conclusion: monstrous mothers and fertility

What happens when *Lemonade* "Pull(s) the sorrow from between my legs like silk; knot after knot after knot"? We have seen the genealogy of loss, enslaved women "could not, in fact claim her child."[32] And, too, *Lemonade* reminds us that "in the prevailing social climate" black motherhood is not seen as a "legitimate procedure of cultural inheritance"[33] by foregrounding the Mothers of the Movement. Placing them *on the plantation landscape, Lemonade* creates a conversation between their pain and the pain of our ancestors. I have attempted to put *Lemonade*'s discussion of loss in wider conversation with black women's experiences with infertility and miscarriage, highlighting how black women attempt to account for grief and pain in autobiographical acts.

After the release of *Lemonade,* Beyoncé became pregnant with twins—performing the Grammys five months pregnant.[34] Her set included her prominent belly and a glorious celebration of black female fertility. Yet I believe *Lemonade* leaves us not with Beyoncé mother goddess of the Grammys, but with an entirely different vision of motherhood that is more "monstrous."

In *Lemonade,* after the unborn and the ancestors are conjured by Queen Ya Ya, Beyoncé gives birth. She recites: "I awake as the second girl crawls head-first up my throat, a flower blossoming out of the hole in my face." This birth is a beautiful monstrosity, a creativity that forges a black feminist art future, where the young artists assemble on Destrehan Plantation—a plantation along the Mississippi River outside of New Orleans. There we find young black feminist artists such as sisters Lisa-Kaindé and Naomi Diaz of the duo Ibeyi, musicians Chloe and Halle Bailey, and actresses Amandla Stenberg and Zendaya. The birth of these artists comes not from Beyoncé's womb, but from her throat and her art. Hortense Spillers ends her essay "Mama's Baby, Papa's Maybe" with precisely this monstrous image of black motherhood. She suggests that because black women will never be properly gendered "female" in "the prevailing social climate," we should turn to our own definitions of black motherhood: to "make a different social subject."[35]

Thus, the mother with the radical potential at the end of *Lemonade* is not the mother to the twins Rumi and Sir Carter (born in June of 2017), but the mother who births hope from her throat in the form of the flower. She is the "other-mother"[36] who births another generation of black feminist artists, *without the help of any men.* The flush of blood made way for the hope of resurrection. This is a hopeful image because it tells a different story—black female fertility works in numerous ways. By the time of the Grammys, of course, this story had been rewritten. Because now, Beyoncé was pregnant with twins. And then, the end of the story became more about her as mother-goddess with Jay-Z as traditional father.

Notes

1 Marsha Jean Darling, "Ties That Bind," ed. Toni Morrison, *The Women's Review of Books* 5, no. 6 (1988): 5, https://doi.org/10.2307/4020268. Also see Sharon Patricia Holland, *Raising the Dead: Readings of Death and (Black) Subjectivity* (Durham, NC: Duke University Press, 2000), 52.

2 As Katherine McKittrick explains, "The various kinds of madness, the pathological geographies, the dismembered and displaced bodies, the impossible black places, the present-past time-space of cartographers, the topographies of 'something lost, or barely visible, or seeing not there'—these material and metaphoric places begin to take us" inside of black women's subjectivities. Katherine McKittrick, *Demonic Grounds: Black Women and the Cartographies of Struggle* (Minneapolis: University of Minnesota Press, 2006), 5.

3 Before I have talked about, for example, the 1811 slave revolt in plantations along the Mississippi River—and then the beheading of those enslaved found responsible. This happened at the very same plantation (Destrehan) where *Lemonade* was filmed. For site of memory see, Toni Morrison, "The Site of Memory," in *Out There: Marginalization and Contemporary Cultures*, ed. Russell Ferguson, Martha Gever, Trinh T. Minnh-ha, and Cornel West (Cambridge, MA: MIT Press, 1990), 299–306.

4 For more on "the dead are not dead," and for readings of black feminist texts that engage with this theme see Jean-Marc Ella, "Ancestors and Christian Faith: An African Problem", in *Liturgy and Cultural Religious Traditions*, ed. Herman Schmidt and David Power (New York: Seabury Press, 1977), 37; Bonnie J. Barthold, *Black Time: Fiction of Africa, the Caribbean, and the United States* (New Haven: Yale University Press, 1981); Julie Dash, Toni Cade Bambara, and bell hooks, *Daughters of the Dust: The Making of an African American Woman's Film* (New York: New Press, 1992); Venetria K. Patton, *The Grasp That Reaches Beyond the Grave: The Ancestral Call in Black Women's Texts* (Albany: State University of New York Press, 2013); Kinitra D. Brooks, *Searching for Sycorax: Black Women's Hauntings of Contemporary Horror* (New Brunswick, NJ: Rutgers University Press, 2017).

5 Holland, *Raising the Dead*, 149.

6 Colleen Burrell, "Breaking the Silence," *Silent No More: A Journal About Infant Loss* (blog), August 6, 2018, https://myjourneyafterinfantloss.blogspot.com/2018/08/breaking-silence.html.

7 Sarah Brophy, "On the Times and Places of Embodied Testimony: Remaking the World," *A/B: Auto/Biography Studies* 33, no. 2 (May 4, 2018): 437–440, https://doi.org/10.1080/08989575.2018.1445590.

8 "Oprah's Next Chapter with Beyoncé," T.V. (OWN, February 16, 2013), http://www.imdb.com/title/tt2714048/.

9 Beyoncé Knowles-Carter and Ed Burke, *Beyoncé: Life Is But a Dream*, Documentary, Music (HBO, 2013), http://www.imdb.com/title/tt2324998/.

10 Rosario Ceballo, Erin T. Graham, and Jamie Hart, "Silent and Infertile: An Intersectional Analysis of the Experiences of Socioeconomically Diverse African American

Women with Infertility," *Psychology of Women Quarterly* 39, no. 4 (December 1, 2015): 497–511, 505, https://doi.org/10.1177/0361684315581169.505 For more on these themes see also, Rosario Ceballo, "The Only Black Woman Walking the Face of the Earth Who Cannot Have a Baby: Two Women's Stories," in *Women's Untold Stories: Breaking Silence, Talking Back, Voicing Complexity*, ed. Mary Romero and Abigail J. Stewart (New York: Routledge, 1999), 3–19.

11 Ceballo, Graham, and Hart, "Silent and Infertile," 504.

12 Alessandra Stanley, "Another Cog in the Machinery of Divahood." TV Review. Beyoncé: Life Is But a Dream, *New York Times*, February 14, 2013, https://www.nytim es.com/2013/02/15/arts/television/beyonces-documentary-life-is-but-a-dream-on-hbo. html.

13 Darlene Clark Hine, "Rape and the Inner Lives of Black Women in the Middle West: Preliminary Thoughts on the Culture of Dissemblance," *Signs* 14, no. 4 (1989): 912–920, 912.

14 Hine, "Rape and the Inner Lives of Black Women," 914–917.

15 Alison M. Parker, "'The Picture of Health': The Public Life and Private Ailments of Mary Church Terrell," *Journal of Historical Biography* 13 (2003): 164–207, 170.

16 Mary Church Terrell, *A Colored Woman in a White World* (Salem, NH: Ayer Company, 1986), 107.

17 Deborah Gray White, *Too Heavy a Load: Black Women in Defense of Themselves, 1894–1994* (New York: W.W. Norton, 1999), 87.

18 Gray White, *Too Heavy a Load*, 87–88.

19 Gabrielle Union, *We're Going to Need More Wine: Stories That Are Funny, Complicated, and True* (New York: Dey Street Books, 2017).

20 "Food Can Fix It: Easy Ways to Alter Your Coffee Drinks for Boosted Energy and Longevity," *Doctor Oz* (ABC, November 3, 2017).

21 "Oprah's Next Chapter with Beyoncé."

22 Ceballo, Graham, and Hart, "Silent and Infertile," 506.

23 Christina Sharpe, *In the Wake: On Blackness and Being* (Durham, NC: Duke University Press, 2016), 21.

24 John S. Mbiti, *African Religions and Philosophy*, 2nd ed. (Oxford: Heinemann, 1990), 109–110.

25 Jason Draper, *Prince: Life and Times: Revised and Updated Edition* (New York: Chartwell, 2016), 134.

26 McKittrick, *Demonic Grounds*.

27 Morrison, "Site of Memory."

28 Laura Plantation, "Laura's Five Centuries of Habitation," accessed July 17, 2017, http://www.lauraplantation.com/general.php?id=51.

29 Dash, Bambara, and hooks, *Daughters of the Dust*, 94. See, Patton, *The Grasp That Reaches Beyond the Grave*, 160.

30 Marsha Jean Darling and Toni Morrison, "In the Realm of Responsibility: A Conversation with Toni Morrison," *The Women's Review of Books* 5, no. 6 (1988): 5, https://doi.org/10.2307/4020269.

31 All women's names are pseudonyms; lightly edited for spelling.

32 Hortense Spillers, "Mama's Baby, Papa's Maybe: An American Grammar Book," *Diacritics* 17, no. 2 (1987): 64–81, 80.

33 Spillers, "Mama's Baby, Papa's Maybe," 80.

34 Catherine Saint Louis, "Singing While Pregnant," *New York Times*, December 22, 2017, https://www.nytimes.com/2017/02/23/well/family/beyonce-singing-while-pregnant. html.

35 Spillers, "Mama's Baby, Papa's Maybe," 80.

36 Patricia Hill Collins, *Black Feminist Thought: Knowledge, Consciousness, and the Politics of Empowerment* (New York: Routledge, 2002), 180.

5

THE LANGUAGE OF *LEMONADE*

The sociolinguistic and rhetorical strategies of Beyoncé's *Lemonade*

Alexis McGee

The power of Queen Bey is an undeniable force with respect to what Gwendolyn Pough identifies as the Black public sphere. According to Pough, the Black public sphere is crucial to understanding the intersectional identities of Black women:

> Blacks historically navigated and negotiated the larger public sphere (and currently do so) by using what was available to them, namely, spectacle, representation, and the renegotiation of concepts such as the public/private split. In doing so, they helped to shape (and continue to shape) a Black public sphere that aims to evoke change in the larger public sphere. The change sought has taken a variety of forms throughout Black history in the United States. However, the consistent factors have always been collective struggles and the greater good for the Black community writ large. (Pough 2004, 33–34)

Questions of how Beyoncé navigates (Black) public spheres as a celebrity who explores her various personal and public identities arise when we ruminate on Pough's construction of the Black public sphere. This rise of Beyoncé as a mother, sister, daughter, and unapologetically Black woman from the South who is also a worldwide performer and entrepreneur has shown us various sides of this Black woman music artist from Houston. Therefore, the public presence of *Lemonade* makes space available for Black women to evoke change and validate collective struggle and identity.

However, these navigations are often discussed in conversations addressing her avant-garde metamorphosis, her personal aesthetics, and her non-heteronormative religious practices seen in *Lemonade*. They are broadly discussed as disaggregate identities of the same person, which limits the realities of her complex being. I posit that Beyoncé's navigation of the spectacle and representation of her intersectional identities in the public/private spheres is significantly and rhetorically demonstrated in her visual album, *Lemonade*. It is here that her rhetorical and socio-linguistic use of language and performance establish a complex Black woman identity cultivated in public/private spheres for personal and communal consumption. To do this, I first situate the conversation of *Lemonade* as a linguistic and rhetorical praxis. I define particular terminology to ground Beyoncé's practice of language as an important indicator of discursive communities. In this work, I primarily focus on the juxtaposition of two songs, "Hold Up" and "Daddy Lessons"; however, this analysis is not beholden only to these two songs. Then I frame the significance of language as a rhetorical method to better understand the navigation of intersectional identities, particularly for southern Black women. This analysis, more specifically, uses verbal and nonverbal gestures such as code-switching, indirection, silence, "g-dropping," and "r-lessness" to exemplify Beyoncé's navigation of identities between songs. Here, "nonverbal" is defined as part of human language but not recognized as a morpheme, or word. Rather nonverbal, as well as utterance (more precisely), is "a stretch of speech between two periods of silence or potential (perceived) silence" (Rowe and Levine 2015). Finally, I locate linguistic and rhetorical markers in *Lemonade* to provide real-world application and analysis of the manifestation recognized as intersectional identities. I argue that Beyoncé's use of African American Women's Language (AAWL) in *Lemonade* provides us with a rhetorical tool for re/addressing the intersectional workings of Black womanhood, and provides us with a roadmap for discussing the ways in which she navigates her fluid and evolving identity that is accessible and explicit by design (Brooks 2018, 72–76). As such, this chapter highlights Beyoncé's use of AAWL, which includes both verbal and nonverbal rhetoric and linguistic features connected to AAWL, reflecting her construction of a Black feminist identity.

With this in mind, this work bridges academic and community spaces to remind us of and to celebrate the power and possibilities resonating within Black women. This chapter analyzes rhetorical cues and speech sounds performed and heard in this album. I understand Beyoncé's use of language as a functional, rhetorical style which allows the flexibility of identities that signify the incorporation of multiple discourse identities—namely Black, Southern, woman—as part of her production, navigation, and excavation of the self within public/private spheres. She blurs the boundaries between one specific identity and another, effectively constructing a conglomeration of identities specific to her.[1] This marking of intersectional identities, by way of language, demonstrates an explicit connection with generational and communal practices creating, or rather *conjuring*, spaces for Black women's healing (Brooks, Martin, and Simmons 2018)—a method for enacting agency, activism, and self-care.

Defining foundational terms

To clarify the language used here, I ground my discussion more broadly in Geneva Smitherman's description of African American Language (AAL):

> Black Dialect is an Africanized form of English reflecting Black America's linguistic-cultural African heritage and the conditions of servitude, oppression and

life in America. Black Language is Euro-American speech with an Afro-American meaning, nuance, tone, and gesture. The Black idiom is used by 80 to 90 percent of American blacks, at least some of the time. (Smitherman 1977, 2)

Smitherman continues,

Think of black speech as having two dimensions: language and style ... Black English, then, is a language mixture, adapted to the conditions of slavery and discrimination, a combination of language and style interwoven with and inextricable from Afro-American culture. (Smitherman 1977, 3)

I incorporate Smitherman's definition here because it provides us with a working foundation for understanding the context of Beyoncé's rhetorical use of language, which expresses her navigation of intersectional identities in and between public/private spheres. The ways Beyoncé performs (i.e. "style") the various songs in *Lemonade* announces her reconciliation with the same sociopolitical and historic context of language Smitherman asserts. For example, Beyoncé's explicit inclusion of AAWL-like code-switching, in/directness, and nonverbal sonic rhetorics—specifically "hush harbors" and silence—varies between songs. This navigation is most visible when one listens to the difference of style, or delivery and performance, in "Hold Up" and "Daddy Lessons," two well-known, mainstream singles from the album. As rhetorical functions, these features show her explicit navigation of constructing agency through language.

Additionally, Sonja Lanehart notes that AAWL marks a more specific way of using language and rhetoric in a gendered construction as well as a sociocultural manifestation:

I have patterned my definition of AAWL to [Salikoko] Mufwene's (2001) definition of AAL: AAWL is the language spoken by African American women ... As with Mufwene's definition of AAL as the umbrella term for all varieties of speech by African Americans (including vernaculars, standard, and Gullah), AAWL includes the varieties of speech by African American women (vernaculars, standard, etc.). As such, to speak AAWL is to be an African American woman. (Lanehart 2009, 2)

With this in mind, Beyoncé's use of AAWL positions her in multiple Black public discourses (e.g. Black, woman, and Southern) from which she draws to substantiate her intersectional identity in *Lemonade*.

AAWL encapsulates the central networkings of intersectional, rhetorical, and cultural identities performed in sonic spheres. For example, we hear Beyoncé forego her Southern drawl and regional terminology like, "hot sauce in my bag" in her song "Sandcastles," for a performance that delivers a message through the use of Standard American English. This explicit code-switching positions Beyoncé in multiple spheres: attuned to Black Southern heritage (e.g. in "Formation") and assimilated to Standard American English practices and audiences in "Sandcastles." As a collective audience we see her deliver multiple styles between songs that resonate with the politics and cultural atmosphere of New Orleans at one point and the larger general population at another. This agency through language describes her maneuvering of multiple identities, politics, and locations for our consumption and reflection. Evelyn Brooks Higginbotham discusses a portion of these interrelated workings of identity reflected by language. She notes this "metalanguage of race," for instance, is integral to understanding AAWL. Higginbotham states,

> At the threshold of the twenty-first century, black women scholars continue to emphasize the inseparable unity of race and gender in their thought. They dismiss efforts to bifurcate the identity of black women (and indeed of all women) into discrete categories—as if culture, consciousness, and lived experience could at times constitute "woman" isolated from the contexts of race, class, and sexuality. (Higginbotham 1992, 273)

Therefore, AAWL not only includes the varieties of speech but also the ways in which Black women communicate culture, consciousness, lived experiences, processes of moment-creating, and/or conjuring feminist modes of being or healing (Brooks, Martin, and Simmons 2018).

Black women's rhetorical use of language, like Beyoncé's emphasis of instrumentation and silence in "Daddy Lessons," also reminds us of the intersectional complexities between verbal and nonverbal communication of Black women's language which is equally important for understanding AAWL as a method of rhetorical communication (Morgan 2002; Morgan 2004). In this line of thought, we begin to see the interrelatedness of language (in terms of sound and context) and the performance of meaning (in terms of interaction between non/verbal expression) as a method for Black women's delivery and navigation of multiple discourse communities—both public and private. Marcyliena Morgan asserts that the generational and historical role of creating identity through narratives, which include laughter and hollers for example, is a significant part of AAWL. This could easily be said of Beyoncé's *Lemonade* and her connection to the South for many of her listeners, including myself. Morgan's insistence of sociocultural context within language aligns cultural politics with language, body politics, place, sonic rhetoric, and translation. Like Morgan, Beyoncé theorizes the performances of everyday Black women in *Lemonade*. Morgan states:

> The daily lives of Chicago's Black women were wrapped in layers of contradictions, and they knew it. Yet they celebrated it. And they agonized over it too. Sometimes they buried their real fears and stories of discrimination in hilarious tales of adventure. At other times, the realities were revealed in retrospect—when one finally grasped in astonishment that what seemed out of place in a story was actually what was "really" going on. (Morgan 2004, 52)

This is what is happening in *Lemonade*. The celebration of Black womanhood in the midst of oppressive politics we see globally and in the South in "Formation" comes after the acknowledgment of loss and pain performed in "Freedom" and its preceding interlude. These stories and realizations of various ways of knowing developed in connection with the use and delivery of language—the speaking of their (generational Black women's) stories—and the recognition of the hidden performances and meanings of language within nonverbal communication.

Overview of intersectionalities in the language of *Lemonade*

This intersection of AAWL and public identities is reflected in Black women's music, making it useful as a generational method, one that Beyoncé utilizes. Like Morgan suggested with her ethnographic analysis of AAWL, Beyoncé's opening vocals of this album, a series of "huhs" and "voiced breaths," harken back to early blues women,[2] jazz singers, and Black women hip hop artists who also implement similar rhetorics, language practices, and stories with scatting and improvisation. "Voiced breath" here is recognized as an utterance—more specifically, breathing with sound. Bruce Rowe and Diane Levine describe voice, in terms of phonetic description, as "The air exhaled from the lungs does not in itself produce speech sounds. To create such sounds, the flow of air must be altered into sound waves of varying qualities and characteristics" (2015, 31). Furthermore, voiced sounds, in English, are often created in a sociocultural context. Beyoncé sings: "You can taste the dishonesty/It's all over your breath as you pass it/off so cavalier/But even that's a test/Constantly aware of it all/My lonely ear pressed against the walls of your world" ("Pray You Catch Me"). Her combination of nonverbal sounds and oral storytelling of relationships at the beginning of *Lemonade*, for example, works together to nuance what Morgan (2004, 51) suggested as "what is really going on." The expression of the spectacle and representation of selves are being conceived through AAWL. The pain, joy, and companionship, the expression of intimacy are delivered as multileveled interactions between herself and (presumably) her heterosexual husband; but this reality also speaks to numerous types of relationships one person—Beyoncé or any Black (Southern) woman—may find herself entwined with, such as familial relationships and internal or communal relationships. The nonverbal, audible epigraph of voiced breaths provides a multidimensional reflection of not only her exhaustion and expended energy lost in the relationship but also deepens her social condition and consciousness expressing recognition of her reality.

More so, the rhetorical use of AAWL signifies a connection to Black women's discursive communities. It insists that Bey is more than a public pop-culture icon; she is also part of the audience, part citizen who is disproportionately misrecognized as other by a solipsistic nation. This rhetorical listening to her identities and communities builds coalition and agency through sound and language. As Morgan points out,

This [recognition or validation of self within community] is because in the African American speech community, hearers and audience members construct meaning and intention along with the speaker. The cultural logic requires that individuals be aware of the consequences of their words. (Morgan 2004, 54)

Furthermore, "As an actor and observer, one's social stance and social face are defined as how others understand the speaker as part of a community of cultural and social actors" (Morgan 2004, 54). Therefore, one's selfhood is simultaneously constructed as a reflection of macro- and micro-community presences as well as an internalized reflection of the self as an individual with respect to multiple discourses. *Lemonade* acts as a discursive call and response formed with AAWL, and Beyoncé's linguistic and rhetorical use of language are manifestations of these intersectional identities.

Beyoncé asserts her reconciliation with fault, love, distance, fear, pain, pride, sexuality, and loneliness all at once: feelings many of us are familiar with. The "huhs" and hollers intimately connect the magnitude of her realities and her emotional and physical involvement of coming to consciousness repeatedly. These recognitions of emotions and communities cannot always be expressed in words alone but are accompanied by moans, groans, foot stomps, hand waves, sighs, and other nonverbal gestures. This is the sonic interlude representing her manifestation of dynamic, intersectional identities that are supported by the delivery and style of her lyrics.

Beyoncé's use of AAWL in *Lemonade* demonstrates her coalescing consciousness and provides examples of movement-creating, making her use of language a rhetorical tool. By movement-creating I am referring to what "A Black Feminist Statement" suggests as "the process of consciousness-raising, actually life-sharing, [hence,] we began to recognize the commonality of our experiences and, from that sharing and growing consciousness, to build a politics that will change our lives and inevitably end our oppression" (Combahee River Collective 2009, 4). In other words, upon analysis of Beyoncé's language in *Lemonade*, we see that her use of AAWL reflect and open dialogues in public spaces—such as politics, news media, and community organizing—and private spaces like home captures a range of emotions, selfhoods, places, and political coalitions that in/form Black women's. With this in mind, I see both Beyoncé and her album *Lemonade* as a performance; it is an aural/oral/visual work, a collective ensemble and testimony of shared life experience that explicitly incorporates AAWL marking methods of change and resistance to binary or linear transformations of the self. It is a tool for movement-making and consciousness-raising.

Contextualizing rhetorical functions of AAWL found in *Lemonade*

These spaces of sonic resonance, found in *Lemonade*, mark Black women's complexities through both indirect and direct practices. The smile portrayed in the video for "Hold Up," the scream heard in "Don't Hurt Yourself" tell of happiness and anger most explicitly. However, in other circles concerning Black women, for example, these acts also represent power, autonomy, and frustration or resolve indirectly. The recognition of these multiple meanings in both verbal and non-verbal gestures is central to recognizing the complexities conveyed through AAWL. In "Conversational Signifying," for example, Morgan suggests that cues marking indirectness—a method of conveying intention by means of hinting, circumlocution, insinuations, and the like—such as laughter and silence have particular linguistic resonance for AAWL. These features "characterize dialect ambiguity and opposition between African American English (AAE) and American English," and, as such, represent a way of communicating meaning, agency, support, and resistance to normative practices and/or policies that may be in opposition to the betterment of one's self. In addition, "prosodic features such as loud talking, marking, pitch and timing/rhythm" as well as "interactional features such as eye gaze, parallelism and rights to a topic," asserts Morgan, all suggest that verbal communication and nonverbal gestures instruct conversation, implying an engagement with one another to provide ways for Black women to subvert power structures and assert or validate experiences through developing and sustaining particular identities, individually and communally (Morgan 1996, 409). With this in mind, Beyoncé's explicit inclusion of AAWL markers like codes-witching, signifying, and nonverbal sonic rhetorics—"hush harbors" or silence—shows her navigation of constructing intersectional identities. This process-creating is a rhetorical network of movement thoroughly connected to Black women's communities and Black public/private spheres. The evolution of identity and consciousness within the public sphere, *Lemonade*, is particularly relevant in this movement of #BlackLivesMatter. Beyoncé gives us a tool to heal as Black women, individually and communally, as we continually face depreciation of our bodies. Simultaneously, she refuses to isolate the #BlackLivesMatter movement, making this conversation of healing and self-love a communal address—one that challenges systemic and intersectional oppressions.

Additionally, I look to Regina Bradley's presentation at the *Lemonade* Seminar. Bradley (2017) suggests that some of the starkest (and perhaps the most significantly audible) markers of meaning in Beyoncé's *Lemonade* are the silences. These aural/oral breaks highlight the tension and complementary workings of nonverbal and linguistic complexities that impact Southern, Black womanhood. I agree with Bradley that these silences are more than just pauses meant to draw listeners into the song. They signify a rhetorical maneuver of AAWL as a method of communicating multilayered meanings found within sonic resonances. This negotiation of silence and sound is explicit and rhetorical.

In a similar fashion, Vorris Nunley contextualizes this as an African American rhetorical tradition of what he identifies as "hush harbors." Nunley suggests that generations of Black authors, both men and women, have utilized silence in a rhetorical and metaphysical manner: "[Black rhetoricians] have demonstrated, diasporic Africans, women, and others have histories of developing raced and gendered distinctive interpretive communities to offset their exclusion from the public sphere" (Nunley 2004, 221–22). He continues to define the rhetorical use of "hush harbors" as "a rhetorical tradition constructed through Black public spheres with a distinctive relationship to spatiality (material and discursive), audience, African American *nomoi* (social conventions and beliefs that constitute a worldview or knowledge), and epistemology" (Nunley 2004, 222). Furthermore, Nunley states,

> Hush harbor rhetoric is composed of the rhetorics and the commonplaces emerging from those rhetorics, articulating distinctive social epistemologies and subjectivities of African Americans and directed toward predominately Black audiences in formal and informal Black publics or African American-centered cultural geographies. (Nunley 2004, 222)

He continues, "hush harbor places become Black spaces because African American *nomos* (social conventions and beliefs that constitute a worldview or knowledge), rhetoric, phronesis (practical wisdom and intelligence) tropes, and commonplaces are normative in the encounters that occur in these locations" (Nunley 2004, 222). For *Lemonade* then, Beyoncé's album not only re/creates individual and communal identities reflecting and connecting with Southern, Black womanhood, but the metaphysical spaces of her utterances also develop an intersectional Black feminist "hush harbor." Her hollers, laughter, and silences, as Bradley pointed out, all renegotiate Black public/private spheres to explicitly include AAWL as a central rhetorical method.

Silence, verbal gestures, and the hush harbor discourse, for example, are linguistic and rhetorical exercises especially important to Black women's speech. Denise Troutman acknowledges the use of silence in Black women's conversations as an extension of cooperative and collaborative speech. She refers to Gwendolyn Etter-Lewis's (1993) important work with oral narrative and Black women's autobiography when she asserts "non-verbal cues induced cooperation. When interviews used long pauses or made particular facial expressions, Etter-Lewis encouraged the women to express their pensiveness, in many instances allowing interviewees to uncover information that may have gone undisclosed" (Troutman 2001, 215). In this instance, silence is acting as a pathway to re/discovery and community building without the voiced or guided projections of a public discourse. The silence is a moment in which to challenge normative gazes and constructions of identity for Black women; it is a moment made for physical, ethical, and social shifting of identities and cognition, which, in turn, validate experiences. Beyoncé does not *announce* the coalition with #BlackLivesMatter or the entry of the mothers most notably impacted by police violence; she silently includes them in the conversation by way of visual expression. Understanding the pain, grief, strength, and hope accompanied by the presence of these Black mothers symbolizes the multiple dimensions and narratives re/covered with AAWL, that is, both verbal and nonverbal. The absence of utterances in "Daddy Lessons" or "6 Inch" gives us room to read Beyoncé's silence as part of her use of AAWL. This specific rhetorical and linguistic marker asks us to re/negotiate ideals of womanhood and counter the ways in which we implicitly or explicitly maneuver white, male, patriarchal constructs of womanhood as a binary.

Beyisms: a sociolinguistic approach to analysis

Beyoncé's unapologetically Black, Southern womanhood did not surface in the public sphere by chance. The sounds and silences in her music, poems, and images are rhetorical and linguistic markers of a specific identity, one that navigates Black (women's) discourses. The explicit, rhetorical exercise of using specific linguistic markers or the absence of certain linguistic markers has direct impact on the type of social contexts available to Black women. These audibles, if you will, are accompanied with "this ideology" (linguistic matter and sociocultural context as dependent of one another) that "is enmeshed in cultural beliefs of fairness and equality—about life and expectations in conversation," as Morgan explains. She continues: "Verbal skill is a force of both celebration and contestation as their identities and ethics of the past and present are negotiated through discourse" (Morgan 2004, 56, 58). Beyoncé uses this to her advantage in *Lemonade*. For example, some songs, like "Hold Up" and "Sorry," use AAL more frequently than other discursive features; however, the song "Daddy Lessons" rarely uses common linguistic markers often associated with AAL or AAWL. In contrast, "Hold up" uses five variations of AAL—such as "g-dropping" (the absence of the "g" sound) and "r-deletion" (the absence of the "r" sound)—in various words. However, in "Daddy Lessons" the potential for these same features are present, but Beyoncé explicitly emphasizes the hollering that accompanies the instrumentation as the most frequent trait. See Tables 5.1 and 5.2 for full descriptions of features and for juxtapositions of the two songs.

This rhetorical choice represents Beyoncé choosing various contextualized identities for her and her audience. As a result, we hear this rhetorical function (i.e. code-switching) in her use of language and delivery. These features are not only reserved for Black speech communities, however; some characteristics, like the absence of the "r," are more frequent in particular communities like Southern or working-class and Black communities, making Beyoncé's use of these features more compelling and pertinent to the validation of her intersectional identities which she proclaims in public/private spheres.

Moreover, the Black feminist tradition and use of AAWL translate linguistically into syntactical and phonetic occurrences. Beyoncé "g-drops" in her album *Lemonade* approximately 70 times, and incorporates nonverbal markers like laughter and hollers over 100 times. Although this data for nonverbal utterances is skewed by the overabundance and explicit use of hollering in one particular song, "Daddy Lessons," the recognition of these linguistic and rhetorical features as available tools is still relevant and important. These factors, like the phonetic constructions such as "r-lessness" (48 times), makes Beyoncé's linguistic and rhetorical navigation of Southern, Black womanhood interesting and valid. In fact, the incorporation of these linguistic markers suggest that Beyoncé's cultivation and demonstration of her Southern, Black woman identity *are firmly* constructed by the conditioning of her acceptance within various Black public/private spheres.

As such, we hear the rhetorical and linguistic features Beyoncé uses to code-switch, such as the use of Standard American English in "Daddy Lessons"

TABLE 5.1 Language Feature Frequency in *Lemonade* tracks, actual [potential]

Feature	Pray You Catch Me	Hold Up	Don't Hurt Yourself	Sorry	6 Inch	Daddy Lessons	Love Drought	Sandcastles	Forward	Freedom	All Night Long	Formation
G-dropping	11 [13]	5 [8]	8 [10]	17 [27]	2 [6]	4 [4]	8 [8]	0 [0]	0 [0]	8 [8]	1 [3]	3 [4]
r-deletion	0 [4]	9 [20]	10 [28]	6 [12]	6 [21]	0 [7]	0 [11]	0 [5]	0 [2]	5 [3]	11 [15]	4 [17]
nonverbal marker	54 [0]	4 [0]	20 [29]	3 [9]	4 [4]	125 [125]	0 [1]	3 [16]	0 [0]	2 [5]	1 [4]	1 [48]
copula absence	0 [8]	0 [44]	2 [39]	4 [46]	17 [22]	0 [9]	2 [16]	0 [9]	0 [0]	0 [26]	3 [9]	7 [19]
Absence of third person sing. "s"	1 [15]	0 [36]	0 [5]	0 [16]	8 [40]	0 [13]	0 [4]	0 [2]	0 [0]	0 [8]	0 [7]	3 [70]
Final consonant cluster deletion	0 [2]	10 [55]	4 [9]	5 [6]	3 [4]	0 [4]	3 [13]	0 [9]	0 [0]	2 [18]	19 [19]	7 [7]
Front consonant deletion	0 [0]	0 [0]	3 [4]	12 [10]	1 [1]	3 [3]	2 [2]	1 [1]	0 [0]	6 [6]	0 [0]	13 [16]
dis/dat/dem/dese (i.e. alveolar stops)	0 [0]	5 [51]	2 [7]	5 [10]	0 [23]	0 [1]	0 [13]	0 [10]	0 [0]	0 [7]	6 [6]	7 [9]

TABLE 5.2 Feature Frequency Comparison (%)

	G-dropping	r-deletion	Non-verbal marker	Copula absence	Absence of third person sing. "s"	Final consonant cluster deletion	Front consonant deletion	dis/dat/dem/dese) (alveolar stops)
Hold Up	0.625	0.45	0	0	0	0.18	0	0.10
Daddy Lessons	1.00	0	1.00	0	0	0	1.00	0

juxtaposed with AAL during her rap break in "Hold Up.". This flexibility of language ultimately opens various pathways for her to navigate and perform the complexities of womanhood through language in *Lemonade*. Although this feature has been marked as significant, her explicit use of r-lessness, for example, throughout her songs is most impressive and telling of her rhetorical weaving between various Black public and private spaces. Notice this example from "Hold Up": "Let's imagine fa a moment dat chu neva made a name fa yaself." We do not see these markers, the r-lessness, in "Daddy Lessons," which tells us that her use of AAWL is a rhetorical expression and extension of spectacle and representation of Black women's intersectional identities. Erik R. Thomas and Guy Bailey describe particular features in AAL. A common example of AAL represented throughout the album is r-lessness or the absence of "r." The importance of the r-lessness seen in AAL resonates:

> [H]istorically r-lessness occurred in White varieties in the Lower South, it is most often associated with AAE, and for good reason: r-lessness is characteristic not only of most traditional varieties of AAE in the South but also of many non-southern AAE varieties. (Thomas and Bailey 2015, 406)

Moreover, Thomas and Bailey include Walt Wolfram's studies to support this argument: "Wolfram ... showed that in Detroit r-lessness decreases as social class rises and speaking style becomes more formal" (Thomas and Bailey 2015, 407). Therefore, Beyoncé's explicit use of AAWL, specifically in terms of r-lessness, squarely and explicitly positions her in Southern, Black discourses.

As suggested by Thomas and Bailey, African American Language is more likely to utilize syntax with these characteristics, although Black speech does not hold exclusive privileges over these traits, as mentioned before. However, what this *does* suggest for Beyoncé, then, is that she is not only fluent in AAWL, but also that she has the autonomy and cultural cache to shift between various identities and discourses. *Lemonade* is exercising the complexities of her identity: Southern, Black woman. She develops and pushes the boundaries of intersectional identities including race, gender, class, and location.[3] The more frequent or more comfortable she becomes with this identity in public, the more often we hear these shifts that mark her as a part of the Black Southern (women's) community.

This explicit use of language between songs and within the same album shows her prowess in navigating Black public/private discourses, and shows us the rhetorical function of language enabling her to bridge musical genres while asserting Black women's and African American culture into predominately white, historically co-opted spaces. Beyoncé's public expression of the self manifests through language constructed by her communal discourses. She presents an unapologetically Black, Southern woman identity that challenges white, male patriarchy. It is in this cultural reading that I see Beyoncé's lyrics giving us insight into Black women's rhetoric, language, and discourse—like narrative strategies—as important methods of communication (Morgan 1996; Morgan 2002; Morgan 2004). To conclude, I argue that these characteristics, both linguistic and rhetorical phenomena, are examples of the navigation of identities seen within African American Women's Language. Beyoncé shows us ways to assert complex selfhoods and heal in public and private spaces. The combination of linguistic features, verbal and nonverbal, specifically demonstrates a structure for nuancing intersectional identities, thus providing an indicator for constructing a web of pathways validating Black women's experiences, healing, and acknowledging one's shifting identity in oral/aural platforms. Beyoncé's internal consciousness-raising through validating her cultural and communal identity is represented in linguistic and rhetorical fashion in *Lemonade*. Her language and sonic rhetoric make a political statement of being unapologetically Black, and this message, now, parallels her body as performing the concretization of her Southern (Black) identity.

Notes

1 See Tanisha Ford's chapter in this reader.
2 See Brooks and Martin's chapter in this reader.
3 See Tyina Steptoe's chapter in this reader.

Bibliography

Bradley, Regina. 2017. "Presentation: Beyoncé's Lemonade Lexicon: Black Feminism & Spirituality in Theory and Praxis." 12–15 October, Lane Hall, 204 State St., Ann Arbor, MI.

Brooks, Kinitra D. 2018. *Searching for Sycorax: Black Women's Hauntings of Contemporary Horror*. New Brunswick: Routledge.

Brooks, Kinitra D., Kameelah Martin and LaKisha Simmons. 2018. "Conjure Feminism: Toward a Genealogy of an Old Black Women's Intellectual Traditions." Presentation to Issues in Critical Inquiry Biennial Symposium. 4–6 September. Vanderbilt University, Knoxville, TN.

Combahee River Collective. 2009. "A Black Feminist Statement." In *Still Brave: The Evolution of Black Women's Studies*. Edited by Stanlie M. James, Frances Smith Foster, and Beverly Guy-Sheftall, 3–11. New York: The Feminist Press.

Etter-Lewis, Gwendolyn. 1993. *My Soul Is My Own: Oral Narratives of African American Women in the Professions*. New Brunswick: Routledge.

Higginbotham, Evelyn Brooks. "African-American Women's History and the Metalanguage of Race." *SIGNS* 17, no. 2(1992): 251–274.

Lanehart, Sonja. ed. 2009. *African American Women's Language: Discourse, Education, and Identity*. Newcastle: Cambridge Scholars Publishing.

Morgan, Marcyliena. 1996. "Conversational Signifying: Grammar and Indirectness among African American Women." In *Interaction and Grammar*. Edited by Elinor Ochs, Emanuel A. Schegloff, and Sandra A. Thompson, 405–434. Cambridge: Cambridge University Press.

Morgan, Marcyliena. 2002. *Language, Discourse and Power in African American Culture*. Cambridge: Cambridge University Press.

Morgan, Marcyliena. 2004. "Signifying, Laughter, and the Subtleties of Loud Talking: Memory and Meaning in African American Women's Discourse." In *Ethnolinguistic Chicago: Language and Literacy in the City's Neighborhood*. Edited by Marcia Farr, 51–76. Mahwah: Lawrence Erlbaum Associates.

Nunley, Vorris L. 2004. "From the Harbor to Da Academic Hood: Hush Harbors and an African American Rhetorical Tradition." In *African American Rhetoric(s): Interdisciplinary Perspectives*. Edited by Elaine B. Richardson and Ronald L. Jackson II, 221–241. Carbondale: Southern Illinois University Press.

Pough, Gwendolyn. 2004. *Check It While I Wreck It: Black Womanhood, Hip-Hop Culture, and the Public Sphere*. Boston: Northeastern University Press.

Rowe, Bruce M. and Diane P. Levine. 2015. *A Concise Introduction to Linguistics*. 4th ed. New York: Routledge.

Smitherman, Geneva. 1977. *Talkin and Testifyin: The Language of Black America*. Detroit: Wayne State University Press.

Thomas, Erik R. and Guy Bailey. 2015. "Segmental Phonology of African American English." In *The Oxford Handbook of African American Language*. Edited by Sonja Lanehart, 403–419. New York: Oxford University Press.

Troutman, Denise. 2001. "African American Women: Talkin That Talk." In *Sociocultural and Historical Contexts of African American English*. Edited by Sonja Lanehart, 211–237. Amsterdam: John Benjamins Publishing Company.

INTERLUDE C: HOW NOT TO LISTEN TO *LEMONADE*

Music criticism and epistemic violence

Robin James

With the 2016 premier of *Lemonade*, her second visual album, Beyoncé did not make the world stop so much as she made it revolve: around her, around her work, around black women. For all of the limitations of pop music as a medium (it's inherently capitalist, for one) and *Lemonade*'s various feminist strategies—"Formation," with its "Black Bill Gates" language, can be heard as a black parallel public to white corporate feminism[1]—the album nevertheless recentered mainstream media attention on black women's cultural and creative work.

As the conversation about *Lemonade* revolved around black women and black feminism, two white, male pop critics writing for major publications responded with "So what about the music?" articles. The description to Carl Wilson's *Slate* piece asks, "But how is it as strictly music?"; and Kevin Fallon's *Daily Beast* piece asks both "But is the music any good?" in the description and "But is the music worth listening to?" in the subtitle. Each time, the "but" sounds like the antecedent to its implied mansplainy consequent "actually … ." And just as "but actually" recenters men as authorities and experts, these three questions decenter features prioritized in black women's pop performance traditions, and in *Lemonade* itself. As posed in these two articles, the "so what about the music?" question frames "music" so narrowly that it both obscures or at best trivializes what the album does musically. Wilson's and Fallon's essays are good examples of how *not* to listen to *Lemonade*. [2]

I want to read Wilson and Fallon carefully so we can think about when this question makes for both technically correct and ethically/politically responsible theory and criticism, and when it makes for technically incorrect and ethically/politically irresponsible theory and criticism. My aim here isn't to argue that Wilson and Fallon are bad people. My focus is the definition or concept of "music" that's at the heart of the *method* they use in these two articles (and methods are bigger than individual writers). In more academic terms, I'm asking about research ethics. If, as Wilson's and Fallon's articles prove, the "so what about the music?" question can be a power move that establishes the critic's or theorist's epistemic authority over material they don't actually have adequate knowledge of, how can music scholars and critics ask about the music parts of pop music without making that power move? The answer to this question includes applying appropriate aesthetic and epistemic frameworks to our analyses of pop music, which is something neither Wilson's nor Fallon's pieces do.

For example, both articles evaluate the album according to inappropriate political and aesthetic metrics. Wilson invokes pre-Enlightenment European aesthetics to argue that the "reality show aspect" of the album is somehow aesthetically inconsistent with great pop music. Prior to the 17th century, it was commonly thought that the status of a work's form or medium ought to correspond to the status of its representational content: painting, the most highly regarded art form, should have subject matter of equal stature—gods and royalty. Wilson's claim that "the other distraction is the way that the album's central suite of music interacts with tabloid-style gossip (and a certain elevator video clip) about Beyoncé and her husband Jay Z" echoes that centuries-old sentiment, a sentiment which is about as alien to *Lemonade*'s aesthetic as, well, Boethius is. Fallon likewise assumes that relationship issues are inherently trivial. He begins his article with a genuflection to Prince (as does Wilson), scrunches its nose at the gossipy lyrical and narrative content, and then twice scoffs at the very idea of a visual album, "whatever that is," as though we in the West don't have precedents for this sort of *Gesamtkunstwerky* (the total artwork combining music, visuals, and lyrics) thing going back to Wagner and the Florentine Camerata (the collective attributed with inventing opera in the 17th century). He does talk more extensively about the sounds and music than Wilson does; but, given the rapid turnaround he also faced, there's not a lot of close listening to specific musical figures, performances, or compositional techniques, mostly just a survey of the different genres on the album. But for both Wilson and Fallon, the album's lyrical content detracts from its greatness or seriousness as an artwork. This analysis only works if intimate relationships—what we might otherwise call emotional labor—are less valuable or interesting than other topics. Wilson says that the cheating story detracts from the album's musical quality because it's an unoriginal narrative:

> a drama of jealousy, betrayal, and reconciliation, one of the most ancient and common of human experiences, and of songwriting fodder … that issue of thematic freshness may render some of the songs here less distinctive and invigorating than Beyoncé was.

I find this an odd criticism to level at a pop album, or even an artwork. Nobody would say that *West Side Story* or *Romeo and Juliet* were aesthetically diminished because they recycled that tired old theme of jealousy, betrayal, and (failed) reconciliation. Moreover, as Angela Davis argued in *Blues Legacies and Black Feminism*, these themes of jealousy, betrayal, and reconciliation are the foundation of black feminist pop music aesthetics in a personal-is-political kind of way. As Davis explains,

> Sovereignty in sexual matters marked an important divide between life during slavery and life after emancipation … The former slaves' economic status had not undergone a radical transformation … It was the status of their personal relationships that was revolutionized. For the first time in the history of the African presence in North America, masses of black women and men were in a position to make autonomous decisions regarding the sexual partnerships into which they entered. (4)[3]

While full political and economic freedom was—and still is—denied black people, they did win autonomy with respect to their sexuality. So, for black women especially, sexuality and intimate relationships are more politically salient than what white Western philosophy defines as "politics." And, as Davis emphasizes, it's this understanding of politics that informs the aesthetics and performance practices of classic blues singers like Ma Rainey and Bessie Smith. This is the frame of reference one should use to interpret *Lemonade*'s politics. Both Wilson's and Fallon's articles force a contextually incorrect definition of "politics" onto the album, one which sees the most intimate details of relationships, sex, and kinship as merely personal and apolitical. Fallon, for example, says, "there's no doubt that the music on the album is far more personal than it is political." Both critics fail to consider it in terms established in black women's pop performance traditions.

They also rely on implicitly gendered and racialized double standards to evaluate the artistry on the album. Even in Wilson's attempt to focus strictly on the music, he spends most of the time talking about visuals and lyrics. He hears a wide range of sonic references in *Lemonade*, from Dolly Parton to Donna Summer to the Lomax recordings to calypso. But he thinks this makes it sound derivative: "as an *aural* album, *Lemonade* is a little less fascinatingly singular and eccentric than *Beyoncé*." Fallon makes an almost identical remark in his article: "*Lemonade* doesn't hurl itself toward any genre in a statement of artistry. Instead it masters … um, all of them, but in turn doesn't make the same powerful statement of Beyoncé's artistic mission, like her last album did." Contrast this with the way Jonathan Shecter talks about Diplo's post-genre eclecticism as "fresh and cutting-edge," part of an "ongoing artistic evolution."[4] As philosopher Christine Battersby has argued, the habit of thinking that flexibility is a sign of innovation when attributed to white men, but a sign of regression when attributed to anyone else, is a habit that goes back to the 19th century.[5] It's not surprising that Beyoncé gets dinged for the same thing that garners Diplo praise: in her case, what Fallon calls "the most daringly genre-hopping music she's ever produced" is evidence of unoriginality, whereas in Diplo's case post-genre eclecticism is evidence of his ability to distinctively transcend provincialism. Even when Wilson's article does manage to talk about sounds and music, it trivializes Beyoncé's other artistic achievements on the album.

Both articles rely on some gendered and racialized interpretive habits to address the song's aesthetic value, lyrical content, and Beyoncé's artistry. But what about their discussion of the music? These same racialized, gendered habits tune Wilson's and Fallon's listening and mask the sonic dimensions of *Lemonade* that don't fit their narrow concept of music. Both critics make a conceptual move that separates musical practice from black feminist practice. Fallon uses parentheses and a "but...?" question to put rhetorical and grammatical space between *Lemonade*'s black femininity and its musical and sonic features: "(By the way, it's powerful, and feminist, and unapologetically black, and transfixing, and gorgeous, and assured, and weird, and confusing, and dumb, and groundbreaking.) But hey: Is the music any good?" This framing defines "the music" as something distinct and independent of the album's black femininity, as though black women's and black feminist musical traditions didn't infuse the album's music ... or, to the extent they do, they don't count as "music." Wilson makes an identical move. Following the white liberal feminist aesthetics that influence lots of contemporary post-feminist pop, Wilson's piece locates the black feminist message primarily in the video:

> In video form ... it's more evident that [*Lemonade*] is equally the cyclical story of generations of black women dealing with men and balancing their struggle for R-E-S-P-E-C-T (as well as S-E-X) against the violations and injustices of race and gender.

He sees the politics in the visuals, but doesn't consider the sounds as having anything to say or do about that story and that struggle.

This approach isn't limited to well-meaning but ignorant white men pop critics: even bell hooks's now (in)famous essay on *Lemonade* looks at but doesn't listen for its politics. She argues that it is a "visual extravaganza" whose "radical repositioning of black female images does not truly overshadow or change conventional sexist constructions of black female identity."[6] Locating the politics entirely in *Lemonade*'s visuals, hooks's essay treats black feminism as something contested solely in terms of images (and divorcing the images from the sounds fails to consider the fact that the sounds impact how viewers interpret what they see). This is the wrong method to use for thinking about *Lemonade* and Beyoncé's work as a whole (and pop music in general). Sounds on this album don't operate independently of black femininity, black women's performance traditions, or individual artists' black feminist politics.

On the one hand, thinking with Daphne Brooks and Regina Bradley, it's more accurate to say that Beyoncé's sound game has generally led the way and been more politically cutting-edge than her visual game.[7] As Bradley explains,

> Beyoncé uses instrumentation and sound production to fragment her persona limited by investments in her visual image. It blurs clean-cut negotiations of black women's identity and respectability as literal discourse by introducing the concept of sound as an alternative form of black (feminist?) expression and its analysis.[8]

FIGURE C.1 Video still of Beyoncé singing while composing on the piano from "Sand-castles." *Lemonade*, Parkwood Entertainment, 2016

Beyoncé has a track record of using sounds whose class, sexual, and regional associations (with working-class southern black people) work against her more "respectable" visual self-presentation to depict a more radical set of political commitments than one can see. On the other hand, sound can also be what does the heavy lifting for patriarchy and other systems of domination. As I have argued elsewhere, in Meghan Trainor's and Charlie Puth's duet "Marvin Gaye," "sound recodes white women's transgressions of traditional femininity as racially and sexually normal."[9] The song pairs lyrics that allude to sex with music from before the sexual revolution that today sounds especially white; the racial and temporal associations of this music reassure listeners that even though Trainor's performance of sexually forward femininity may shake up traditional gender norms for women, the underlying white patriarchal order isn't budging. Separating the music itself out from the political content misrepresents what music is and how it works. And it is a particularly gendered misrepresentation: critics are not so eager to separate Kendrick Lamar's sounds from his politics. In both white and black philosophical traditions, dominant concepts of politics and the political are normatively masculine (just think about the gendered public/private distinction, for example), so from these perspectives feminine and feminized sounds don't feel or seem "political."

But in these two cases the divorce between music and politics is also what lets white men pop critics have authority over black feminist music. If they can distill *Lemonade* down to its "solely musical" aspects, then they can plausibly present themselves as experts on generic, depoliticized sound, sounds disconnected from knowledges and values tied to particular lived experiences and performance traditions. Problem is, in the same way that there is no generic "person" without a race or a gender, there is no generic, depoliticized sound. As Jennifer Stoever-Ackerman has argued, even though Western modernity's occularcentric epistemology obscures the sonic dimensions of white supremacist patriarchy and the subaltern knowledges developed under it, sounds nevertheless work politically.[10] Digging deep into the music on *Lemonade* or any other pop song does not involve abstracting the music away from every other aspect of the work and its conditions of production. Digging deep into the music part of pop music means digging deeper into these factors, too. When Regina Bradley and Dream Hampton, Laur M. Jackson, Zandria Robinson, and Joan Morgan talk about how *Lemonade* makes them feel, what affects and knowledges and emotions it communicates, *they are talking about the music*—they just work in a tradition that understands music as something other than "the music itself" (that is, they don't think music is abstracted away from visual and cultural elements, from structures of feeling common to black women with shared histories and phenomenological life-worlds).[11] As I have tried to show in my own work, the sounds and musical performance are central to Beyoncé's and Rihanna's work because they engage traditions of black women's and black feminist knowledges. Aesthetic practices develop and emerge as types of implicit (i.e., non-propositional or non-verbal) knowledge, knowledge created in response to lived experiences in a particular social location. Aesthetic practices can communicate and perform knowledges that reinforce systems of domination, and they can also communicate and perform subordinate knowledges that map out strategies for survival amid domination. Dominant institutions (like the music industry) and people from dominant groups (like Iggy Azalea or Eric Clapton) separate the aesthetic practice from the implicit knowledges that make it meaningful, and thus neutralize those knowledges and make the aesthetic practice fungible and co-optable. Talking about "the music itself" or "solely music" does the same thing: it is a form of what philosophers call epistemic violence.

In a year-end reflection, Wilson called his *Lemonade* review "the biggest mistake I made as Slate's music critic this year." Citing the original version of this article, he admits that separating the music from the rest of the work was the wrong way to approach the album. However, he attributes his mistake to a poor attempt to account for his social position and "to aging: My aesthetic reflexes weren't fast enough to kick it with *Lemonade*'s immediate multimedia paradigm shift. I've been fretting about it ever since." And while I sincerely appreciate his humility and openness here, these were not the problems I claimed his review exemplified. Remember, I argued that the review applies an incorrect interpretive method, one which fails to situate not the critic, but the *artwork*, in the right interpretive traditions. The point is less "check your privilege" and more "you need to fully understand the terms and traditions you are using to evaluate the work in question." He and Fallon used the terms and traditions someone in their social position would likely be most fluent in (i.e., have implicit knowledge of), but these were not the ones the work primarily appeals to. Like them, I am white, but I have developed some fluency in black feminism and black feminist aesthetics through decades of academic study. That kind of study is necessary for critics to be able to accurately interpret and evaluate works grounded in aesthetic and philosophical traditions that we aren't granted fluency in by virtue of our social position. And that study isn't itself sufficient. Mariana Ortega identifies a type of epistemic violence she calls "loving, knowing ignorance," wherein white feminists use their knowledge of women-of-color feminist theory to reproduce white supremacy, often by theorizing away the implicit knowledges WOC feminist theorists appeal to in their work.[12]

So, asking "but what about the music?" is a way to dig into those implicit knowledges to show where much of this epistemic work is happening. As Jennifer Nash notes, "poetry" and other "non-objective and often non-linear theoretical formations" (7) have been the most successful tools black feminists have used to think through and discuss intersectionality, i.e., black women's experiences of multiple marginalization.[13] Such methods work because they make use of both explicit and implicit knowledges. So perhaps one way music critics can include implicit knowledges in their analyses is to work at the level of poetics (in the sense of poesis, meaning creativity not just literary poetry) and with full fluency in the poetic traditions musicians appeal to in their works. It demonstrates what Stoever-Ackerman calls "an ethical responsibility to hear African American cultural production with … assumptions about value, agency and meaning" (31) that are appropriate to them. But you can also ask "but what about the music?" in a way that abstracts away from these implicit knowledges. That's what Wilson's and Fallon's pieces do, and that's why they're both epistemically violent and objectively poor methods of musical interpretation. But we can and do better when we write about and theorize the music part of pop music. And, to riff on Ortega, doing better means listening to and with black women, black women's music, and black feminist aesthetics. You can't divorce music or listening from politics; listening better can and will follow from practicing more than just politics.

Notes

1 "Black parallel public" is political scientist Lester Spence's term for black subcultures that adopt logics and formations present in mainstream white culture. His study focuses on how black politics reproduces neoliberalism within black communities. See Spence, Lester. *Stare in the Darkness*. Minneapolis: University of Minnesota Press, 2011.

2 Wilson, Carl, "*Lemonade*, the Aural Album." *Slate*, April 25, 2016. https://slate.com/culture/2016/04/beyonces-lemonade-is-incredible-as-a-visual-album-but-how-is-it-a s-just-music.html; Fallon, Kevin, "Beyoncé's 'Lemonade' Is Breathtaking. But Is the Music Any Good?" *Daily Beast*, April 24, 2016. https://www.thedailybeast.com/beyon ces-lemonade-is-breathtaking-but-is-the-music-any-good.

3 Davis, Angela. *Blues Legacies and Black Feminism: Gertrude "Ma" Rainey, Bessie Smith, and Billie Holiday*. New York: Vintage 1999.

4 Shecter, Jonathan. "Diplo & Skrillex are Jack Ü: The Cuepoint Interview." March 19, 2015. https://medium.com/cuepoint/how-diplo-and-skrillex-became-the-coolest-guy s-in-music-230c8fa7475e.

5 Battersby, Christine. *Gender and Genius: Towards a Feminist Aesthetics*. Bloomington: Indiana University Press, 1990.

6 hooks, bell. "Moving Beyond Pain." *Bell Hooks Institute*. May 9, 2016. http://bell hooksinstitute.com/blog/2016/5/9/moving-beyon-pain.

7 Brooks, Daphne A. "'All That You Can't Leave Behind': Black Female Soul Singing and the Politics of Surrogation in the Age of Catastrophe." *Meridians* 8, no. 1 (2008): 180–204. http://www.jstor.org/stable/40338916.

8 Bradley, Regina N. "I Been On (Ratchet): Conceptualizing a Sonic Ratchet Aesthetic in Beyoncé's 'Bow Down'." RedClayScholar blog. March 19, 2013. http://redcla yscholar.blogspot.com/2013/03/i-been-on-ratchet-conceptualizing-sonic.html.

9   James, Robin. *Resilience and Melancholy: Pop Music, Feminism, Neoliberalism*. Alresford, UK: Zero Books, 2015.
10 Stoever-Ackerman, Jennifer. "The Word and the Sound: Listening to the Sonic Colour-Line in Frederick Douglass's 1845 Narrative." *SoundEffects* 1 no. 1 (2011): 20–36.
11 See Bradley, Regina and Dream Hampton, "Close to Home: A Conversation about Beyoncé's Lemonade." The Record: Music News from NPR. April 26, 2016, https://www.npr.org/sections/therecord/2016/04/26/475629479/close-to-home-a-conversation-about-beyonc-s-lemonade; Jackson, Lauren M, "I Can Tell You All About Lemonade." April 26, 2016, https://www.complex.com/music/2016/04/beyonce-lemonade-essay; Robinson, Zandria, "We Slay, Part I," February 2016, http://newsouthnegress.com/southernslayings; Morgan, Joan, "Beyoncé, Black Feminist Art, and This Oshun Bidness," April 30, 2016, https://genius.com/a/beyonce-black-feminist-art-and-this-oshun-bidness.
12 Ortega, Mariana. "Being Lovingly, Knowingly Ignorant: White Feminism and Women of Color." *Hypatia* 21, no. 3 (2006): 56–74.
13 Nash, Jennifer C. "Re-thinking Intersectionality." *Feminist Review* 89 (2008): 1–15.

INTERLUDE D: WOMEN LIKE HER CANNOT BE CONTAINED

Warsan Shire and poetic potential in *Lemonade*

Shauna M. Morgan

"Accountability," the sixth chapter of *Lemonade*, opens with a voice-over of Beyoncé reciting lines from the third stanza of Warsan Shire's poem "How to Wear Your Mother's Lipstick." The black and white scene begins on a long muddy path bracketed by Spanish-moss-covered trees, and travels to a house where elaborate wood architectural features are softened by the presence of young children. It begins: "You find the black tube inside her beauty case, where she keeps / your fathers old prison letters, / you desperately want to look like her," and then continues by pulling lines from different stanzas of the poem before flowing into the song "Daddy Lessons." Much of director Kahlil Joseph's conception of *Lemonade* continues in this vein with the song lyrics buttressed by Shire's poetry and Joseph's stunning visuals. While in her essay "'Where Do You Go When You Go Quiet?': The Ethics of Interiority in the Fiction of Zora Neale Hurston, Alice Walker, and Beyoncé" Sequoia Maner asserts that "Beyoncé embraces an ethical engagement with interiority as a strategy for moving toward liberatory social action," I contend that it is, rather, the juxtaposition of Joseph's concept and filmic representations of Black womanhood with Shire's womanist poetry which exudes a kind of freedom—or at least the quest for one (Maner 2018, 185). What Beyoncé embraces is the artistic vision of Kahlil Joseph which included the poetry of Warsan Shire. Focusing on a myriad of women's pain and grief coupled with the enduring and restorative power of women's communal spaces and legacy, Joseph and Shire offer a work of art, rich with imagery, metaphor, personification, and symbolism, which declares both the depth of vulnerability and the enduring strength of Black womanhood.

This would not be their first collaboration, however, as Joseph recorded the initial reading of Shire's celebrated poem "For Women Who Are Difficult to Love" on his personal laptop years ago.[1] When developing this project, about which Joseph asserts "The whole thing was my idea ... I helped [Beyoncé] think through how to present it as a visual project and the people to cast, such as Tray-von Martin's mom and Serena Williams" in an interview with Amelia Abraham for *The Guardian* (2017), he naturally reached out to his friend, Warsan Shire, one of the most profound young poets of our time. Shire has expressed the significant impact Joseph's chosen artistic medium has on her poetry. In a 2013 interview with Katie Reid for *Africa in Words*, she stated: "My writing is always inspired by film. If I don't watch a film, I won't write. I watch about ten films a week".[2] According to Carolina Miranda (2015), "For Joseph, the film is an opportunity to render African American life in a creative, nuanced way." She also notes that:

> In music circles, [Joseph] is best known for producing pieces that violate just about every rule of the music video: There are no choreographed dance sequences, no jiggling backup dancers, no literal interpretation of the lyrics. Instead, there is simply a mood—and worlds where strange things happen. (Miranda 2015, par 3)

This is a stark contrast to the tropes which typically drive Beyoncé's performances. What Shire accomplishes with her poetry, Joseph does with film, and their aesthetic connection is clear: they both move to deliver distinct representations of Black life which depart from commonplace stylistic offerings.

With *Lemonade*, Joseph has answered the call made by James Baldwin, who argued that: "It is very strange to be a black artist in this country—strange and dangerous. He must attempt to reach something of the truth, and to tell it—to use his instrument as truthfully as he knows how" (2011, 108). In his 1969 essay "The Price May be Too High," Baldwin considers the role and responsibility of the Black artist. He dedicates much of the short essay to considering filmic representations of Blackness, and the "exasperated" Black artist who navigates that world. Baldwin asserts that in Hollywood, for example "what is being attempted is a way of involving, or incorporating, the black face into the national fantasy in such a way that the fantasy will be left unchanged and the social structure left

FIGURE D.1 Video still of women seated and leaning, adorned with *Sacred Art of the Ori* by Laolu Senbanjo from "Sorry." *Lemonade*, Parkwood Entertainment, 2016

untouched" (2011, 108). Even now in the 21st century, there are examples of Black film which tangle with caricatures and stereotypes of Blackness in ways that merely enhance the insidiousness of those vile images. However, we have a legacy of film which moves against those images rooted in a white imaginary—films which answer Baldwin's call to "reject a doctrine" of white supremacy (2011, 108). Kahlil Joseph accomplishes that very thing with *Lemonade*, and his film's inclusion of Warsan Shire's poetry explicitly situates Black women at the center of that freedom. The director's cut of *Lemonade* features Shire reading her own work—something which was altered once Beyoncé saw Joseph's final version.[3] Even with the alterations this adaptation, for which Shire was credited, renders a womanhood that cannot be contained. Each of the chapters are lyrically framed by lines from several of Shire's poems as noted by the numerous articles that emerged shortly after the film's release. This brief examination will attempt to unpack some aesthetic qualities of the work which helped to make *Lemonade* such a striking success for Beyoncé.

"Intuition," chapter one of the film, begins with lines adapted from Shire's "For Women Who Are Difficult to Love"—arguably her most well-known poem, and one that was, ironically, brought to its mass of followers through a short film.[4] Beyoncé opens with "I tried to make a home outta you," adapted from "you can't make homes out of human beings" (line 29), and the result of that change is a focus on the individual making the declaration versus the instructive and communal lines of the original. Revised lines from this poem also appear in chapters two and nine, "Denial" and "Resurrection" respectively. In chapter nine the original lines that close the poem— "you are terrifying/and strange and beautiful/something not everyone knows how to love (34–36)—are voiced by Beyoncé without the closing line. This poem is repurposed to eliminate the possibility of "something not everyone knows how to love," and unfortunately loses the degree of vulnerability faced by the female subject. When the medium is reshaped, as with any work of art, it forms something entirely new and often something which carries its own new beauty. What is lost, however, in the adaptation and unfamiliar voicing of Shire's poetry is the artful and meticulous crafting of poetic devices which offer us rich metaphor, imagery, personification, and symbolism, among other things. "For Women Who Are Difficult to Love" opens: "You are a horse running alone/and he tries to tame you/compares you to an impossible highway/to a burning house/says you are blinding him/that he could never leave you/ forget you/want anything but you/you dizzy him, you are unbearable" (1–9). The poem at once indicts the accusing subject for his inability to accept the beauty and power and wonder of the "women" whom the speaker presumably addresses. The metaphor of the horse conveys her perceived unbridled spirit racing much like the blaze she is accused of being—her name also incendiary—both in the literal and figurative sense dousing the women "before or after" (12). The adaptation for *Lemonade* eliminates this fire and any suggestion of her supposed difficult characteristics.

While the revisions of Shire's poems draw the audience closer to Beyoncé's personal narrative, it effaces the opportunity for this Black art to render a world of emotive possibilities for Black women. These poems, which appear on Shire's album *warsan vs. melancholy: the seven stages of being lonely*, are dismembered and distributed throughout several chapters of the film. Appearing in chapters three "Anger," four "Apathy," and five "Emptiness," "the unbearable weight of staying (the end of the relationship)" resonates through the sections which expose the most severe emotional affliction in the visual album. In fact, the echo of Malcolm X's voice declaring "the most disrespected woman in America is the Black woman" further illuminates these wrongs, and Joseph's visuals—the image of women entangled and lithe in white fabric, hands interconnected, a community struggling yet beautiful with a necessary harmony—mirror the poem's interior conflict. This chapter's further inclusion of lines from "dear moon (the distraction)" and "Grief Has Its Blue Hands in Her Hair" emphasizes the complex on-screen dynamics related to sensuality and desire, sexual and otherwise, captured in "Emptiness." The segment marks one of two sections in *Lemonade* which present Shire's poems in near entirety. Beyoncé recites five of the six stanzas in "Grief Has Its Blue Hands in Her Hair," and it is certainly worth citing here as well: "She sleeps all day/dreams of you in both worlds/tills the blood in and out of uterus/wakes up smelling like zinc./Grief sedated by orgasm/orgasm heightened by grief" (1–6). Here grief is personified—empowered and sexualized. The uterus becomes a metaphor—a field seeking a harvest, while the orgasm is a symbol of both satisfaction and longing. Standing as a symbol of another kind of nourishment, the nipple extends that longing: "Sometimes when he had her/ nipple in his mouth she'd whisper/*Allah*/ this too is a form of worship"—at once feeding and yet representing the pining for a child that does not come and is revealed as the loss in the last stanza "whenever he pulls out" (14–17; 25–26).

Her body is the mortar and pestle whose efforts are unrewarded. Freedom does come, however, in chapter ten ("Hope") and presents itself on screen as a child lying on a bed, and then as the longed-for children in the poem "Nail Technician as Palm Reader"—the only unrevised full poem in the film:

> That night, in a dream, the first girl emerges from a slit in my stomach. The scar heals into a smile. The man I love pulls the stitches out with his fingernails. We leave black sutures curling on the side of the bath. I wake as the second girl crawls head first up my throat—a flower, blossoming out of the hole in my face. (6–14)

Here the birth of twin daughters and the subsequent scar that heals serve as larger symbols for *Lemonade*'s broader narrative. The love interest participates in the journey to healing. The different birth passages taken by each girl represent the diverse emotional landscape across which our speaker travels. Her awakening comes at the moment of new growth—"a flower, blossoming" so unlike the unfulfilled longing in the previous poem where merely the smell of a flower lingered. The presence of the palm reader in this poem adds a spiritual element—the speaker's body, specifically her hand, serves as a divining tool—and the presence of twins makes "a visual statement on the wonders of black women who dare to trifle with the divine," as noted by Kameelah L. Martin, in her book *Envisioning Black Feminist Voodoo Aesthetics* (2016, 177). This section leads us into the closing assertion of the film with the final chapter's affirmation of love and resilience.

Lemonade presents a woman and her emotional journey—entities which, like the words of poet Warsan Shire, cannot be contained. Kwame Dawes, on the cover of *Our Men Do Not Belong to Us*, says:

> [Shire's poems] are direct, but they are works of such delicate construction and layered insight that one quickly realizes what seems "direct" is necessarily wholly indirect, questioning, uncertain, and vulnerable. Her poems are about how women deal with the violence of all kinds of exploitation, but they are never didactic or simplistic. (Shire 2014)

Indeed, Shire's rich and complex poetry serves as a major artery through the body of the film, but the difficulties the corpus of her work deals with is enacted upon her poetry in *Lemonade*. The sacred wholeness and potential offered by each of her poems experiences a rupture and injury in the pulling apart of stanzas and lines. Still, despite the revisions and abbreviations—a seeming constraint—the literature used to support the film's visuals offers a poetic potential for freedom rich with imagery, metaphor, symbol, and the personification of wrenching emotions.

Notes

1 Personal interview with Kahlil Joseph in Lapwai, Idaho, 27 May 2016.
2 Interview between Warsan Shire and Katie Reid. https://africainwords.com/2013/06/21/qa-poet-writer-and-educator-warsan-shire/.
3 Hilton Als, "The Black Excellence of Kahlil Joseph," *The New Yorker*, 6 November 2017.
4 https://everydayfeminism.com/2016/05/for-women-difficult-to-love/.

Bibliography

Abraham, Amelia. "How Artist Kahlil Joseph Restored Faith in the Music Video." *The Guardian*. 19 October 2017.
Baldwin, James. 2011. *The Cross of Redemption: Uncollected Writings*. Edited by Randall Kenan. New York: Vintage Books.
Beyoncé. 2016. *Lemonade*. New York: Parkwood Entertainment.
Joseph, Kahlil. Personal Interview. 27 May 2016.
Maner, Sequoia. 2018. "'Where Do You Go When You Go Quiet?': The Ethics of Interiority in the Fiction of Zora Neale Hurston, Alice Walker, and Beyoncé." *Meridians: Feminism, Race, Transnationalism*. 17. 1: 184–204.
Martin, Kameelah L. 2016. *Envisioning Black Feminist Voodoo Aesthetics*. Lanham, MD: Lexington Books.
Miranda, Carolina. "Kendrick Lamar's Video Director Kahlil Joseph Takes His hypnotic Art to MOCA." *Los Angeles Times*. 25 March 2015.
Shire, Warsan. 2017. *Penguin Modern Poets 3: Your Family, Your Body*. London: Penguin.
Shire, Warsan. 2014. *Our Men Do Not Belong to Us*. Sleepy Hollow, NY: Slapering Hol Press.
Shire, Warsan. 2012. *warsan versus melancholy (the seven stages of being lonely)*. Bandcamp.com. 14 February.

PART II

Of her spiritual strivings

6

LOOKING FOR BEYONCÉ'S SPIRITUAL LONGING

The power of visual/sonic meaning-making

Valerie Bridgeman

In 2014, Rudy Rasmus, co-pastor of St. John's Downtown, a United Methodist church, defended Beyoncé against her Christian critics. She is a "consummate entertainer," he said of her, noting that no one asks Arnold Schwarzenegger whether his movie persona and his real life are the same. Of Beyoncé, Rasmus said: "I think she is tremendously gifted and I think she expresses that gift in some amazing ways. I think the world would be void an extreme talent if we silenced her or censored her."[1]

Three years later, I am sitting on the front row of a dimly lit church, waiting to preach. The ambience is more concert than congregation, but the praise and worshipful atmosphere is unmistakable. And suddenly, musical bars of Beyoncé's "Freedom" come from the band, and the congregation clearly recognizes the beat to one of its favorite daughter's songs. The church is St. John's. Beyoncé grew up in this congregation, and congregants love her and her family, who remain a part of the congregation at this writing. She is the quintessential church-girl-made-good to them, like Aretha Franklin or the Pointer Sisters before her. Her gifts and her stage presence were nurtured in the shadow of this congregation and by the "go` on, baby" of church mothers. This congregation is one of the nurturers of her spiritual longing.

Hebrew Bible scholar Yolanda Norton has capitalized on Beyoncé's longing, to which I will return, and her journey to adulthood in order to teach a course at San Francisco Theological Seminary titled "Beyoncé and the Hebrew Bible." On the surface, a correlation might not be evident. But, as Norton explains after noting she will likely never be as well-known as Beyoncé, the artist provides a window into black women's lives. Norton explains:

> as a Black woman I know what it means to have my body and clothing policed; people judging my hair, makeup, and style choices, and making judgments about my appropriateness. As a Black woman I know what it

means to be consistently underestimated. I know what it means to have to do more and better than my peers, and still not be taken seriously in my craft. I know what it means for my value to be attached to the men in my life. Beyoncé's unique status in the world gives me the unique opportunity to narrate the realities of Black women in the church and in the world.[2]

Norton's words are specifically mundane or non-religious. But she locates the mystery of God/s in the everydayness and struggle of black women, the starting point for Womanist biblical interpretation and Black Feminism. What Norton points to is the constant policing of black women's bodies; but what we learned with *Lemonade*, as with other of Beyoncé's work, is that black women's spirituality also often is policed. Enter into any website search engine the words "Beyoncé and spirituality" or "Beyoncé and religion" and you will find comments as diverse as disparaging ones among people entrapped in a certain form of Christianity, to comments that praise her esoteric embrace of Africanisms. Beyoncé, we can see, is fascinated by the Mystery, especially as Mystery has manifested itself among African and African-descendant people.

Even so, we cannot say that Beyoncé has embraced a hybrid religious sensibility, since we have no direct statement from her declaring her religious allegiances. But we do have her nod in the direction of honoring what are the practices of black ancestors. A "Texas bama" is the result of a history of people who knew how to both conjure behind closed doors and shout in black churches. In this way, Beyoncé participates in an artistic tradition in which writers, dancers, and singers remember the African traditions that sustained oppressed black people throughout the African Diaspora.[3] Her lyrics are both holy and profane, and cannot be separated because life is not sectioned off in such categories. Cheddar Bay biscuits at Red Lobster after unbridled and unashamed sex is holy. But these lyrics also are the ones that make people uncomfortable with women's desire—black women's desire—squirm.

Lemonade, her visual album, is a visual and sonic exhibit of Beyoncé's "extreme talent." It also is a recognition that she grew up in the stew of black church tradition, American black Southern conjuring traditions, black esotericism, and longing. The collection in its visual form may also be an expression of her own spirituality at most, or her homage to a diverse Africana spirituality at least. The album must be viewed as much as heard in order to see what I am saying. She is, as Melanie Jones notes, an embodiment of Divine Mother, seen in the visuals in a variety of ways, from community mother on the porch to angry lover on a rampage with a baseball bat. Jones argues that "Beyoncé recovers the warrior power of Hindu goddess Kali, whose name means 'she who is black' in Sanskrit, *slaying* her white opponents and seeking liberation for her children at whatever cost." Following Jones, we also see Beyoncé as the Black Madonna, as a matriarch who may also be the god-head figure of a feminine/Black Feminist Triune Divine, which Jones sees in the image of Beyoncé dressed in a regal way during her 2017 Grammy performance, and flanked by her mother and daughter, who themselves reflect an age-diverse trinity, and "offers a model of healing and liberation that is transgenerational."[4]

But if we are to understand fully what Beyoncé has conjured for us, we must turn quickly to Africa and to the African-derived traditions, like Santería, Vodún, and Candomblé, whose practitioners managed to preserve for enslaved people a memory of home and healing. Beyoncé embodies the orisha Osun, who personifies beauty and sexuality.[5] In *Lemonade*, she dresses in the gold of Osun; she surrounds herself in the waters as does this orisha; and she is violent and unpredictable when protecting what is hers. Like Osun, she sees her image mirrored to her, and it emboldens her to continue. She is destructive in the way storms are destructive, reflecting the power of the orisha. But we are reminded that destruction is the substance of creations. What Beyoncé does is conjure a new beginning, then asks us to get in line/in formation. If conjurers also have the ability to read the future,[6] Beyoncé has read us well. If this hybrid way of knowing the divine leads us to freedom, she dances us to liberty. These visions are consonant with stories we've heard from fierce Southern religious women, as well as significations of ancient African traditions in Yoruba/Ifa.

What Beyoncé has done for us is given us an artist's way to freedom through spiritual r/evolution and longing. She does not tell us as much as she shows us the way to pursue our longings, whether they are for power, resources, or sexual ecstasy. She has embraced her ancestors' lemonade *and* Southern (U.S.) sweet tea. In this way the "extreme talent" that her pastor points us to is a gift of longing, of searching; and if we would find and experience Mystery, Beyoncé invites us through this visual/sonic conjuring to get in formation.

Notes

1 Chris Witherspoon, "Beyoncé's Pastor, Rudy Rasmus, Defends Her Image from Christian Critics." June 2, 2014. https://thegrio.com/2014/06/02/beyonces-pastor-rudy-rasmus-defends-her-image-from-christian-critics/.
2 Yolanda Norton, "Giving Voice: Beyoncé and the Hebrew Bible," https://btpbase.org/giving-voice-beyonce-and-the-hebrew-bible-beyoncemass/.
3 See especially Yvonne P. Chireau, *Black Magic: Religion and the African American Conjuring Tradition* (Los Angeles: University of California Press, 2003), p. 137 *passim*.
4 Melanie C. Jones, "Clothed in Glory: Beyoncé Fashioning the Black Feminine Divine and Spinning Gold," https://btpbase.org/clothed-in-glory-beyonce/. I would also invite you to read Teresa N. Washington's work, *Our Mothers, Our Powers, Our Texts: Manifestations of Àjé in Africana Literature* (Oya's Tornado, 2015).
5 Philip John Neimark, *The Way of the Orisa: Empowering Your Life Through the Ancient African Religion of Ifa* (New York: HarperOne, 1993).
6 Chireau, *Black Magic*, 50.

7

BEYONCÉ'S *LEMONADE* FOLKLORE

Feminine reverberations of *odú* and Afro-Cuban *orisha* iconography

Nicholas R. Jones

Social media outlets worldwide—BuzzFeed, Facebook, the *Huffington Post*, Instagram, Quartz, and Twitter, to only name a few—went into a frenzy celebrating and deconstructing Beyoncé's depiction of African diasporic religions and spirituality. Even superstar JLo—an initiate of Oshún—cheered enthusiastically after Bey's 2017 Grammy performance. It was all the rage; all the (lemon) tea to sip! In academic circles, numerous scholars from a variety of disciplines and across all stages of their careers remarked that Beyoncé's *Lemonade* offers a musical and visual journey through the African diaspora. In doing so, *Lemonade* captures conceptually, spiritually, and visually Yoruba diasporic religious iconography and practices in the Atlantic world—most notably in Cuba and Louisiana. Even further, *Lemonade* is an undeniable African diasporic poetic treatise and visual text that brings life and meaning to a broader Yoruba diaspora located within the Americas more broadly—and Cuba more specifically—that is rooted in the experiences of the slave trade, but also highlights the ongoing processes of making and establishing connections with an ancestral homeland that exists long after the abolition of slavery.[1] In a black feminist context, *Lemonade* reflects the power and strength of black women via the variety of African diasporic cultural traditions and spiritualities that connect women of the diaspora together. At its very beginning, the film transports its audience to the origin of the diaspora, where images of stonewall tunnels allude to any of numerous dungeons and fortresses littered across the Gold Coast or the Bight of Biafra, or even early-colonial port cities throughout the Atlantic World. To that effect, Beyoncé's black feminist aesthetic and intellectual labor in *Lemonade* privileges the Gulf region of the U.S.-American South—an important site of the African diaspora that is all too often marginalized; a locale where Afro-Cuban religion practices were also alive. For instance, the visual economy in "Love Drought" captures beautifully the majesty and grace of primordial female water *orishas* such as Naná Burukú, Yembó, and Yewá.

This chapter explores and situates the fecundity and profundity of Afro-Cuban Lukumí religious iconography and symbolism of female *orisha* in Beyoncé's *Lemonade*. [2] To be clear, while this essay only focuses on Afro-Cuban divinatory practices and religious contexts, it does *not*, by any means, position the Yoruba *orisha* tradition of Cuba as superior to other black Atlantic religions. Throughout the *Lemonade* film, waterways and other kinds of aquatic imagery abound in its celebration of the female *orishas* Oshún (sweet water), Yemayá (salt water), and Naná Burukú (fresh water lagoons and mountain springs). [3] Amongst friends and colleagues, anecdotally speaking, I've been known to parallel snippets of Beyoncé's life and glimpses of her personal narratives shown in *Lemonade* as a revelation of the *orisha* Obba Nani. In my view, Obba Nani captures a fuller, yet more nuanced, picture of the long trajectory of Beyoncé's life and romance with Jay-Z. To arrive at a deeper and more nuanced understanding of how *Lemonade* thematically treats and visually frames Afro-Cuban *orisha* images and metaphors, I turn to an examination of *odú* and its variety of proverbial meanings in the corpus of Afro-Cuban Lukumí divinatory knowledge and practices. To achieve this analysis, I will thus concentrate on *Lemonade*'s visual culture, its spoken-word poetic corpus (recited by Beyoncé), and its lyrics (sung by her). To that effect, this study uncovers the various ways in which the presence of *odú* helps us to theorize a new way of interpreting how *Lemonade* articulates Beyoncé's African diasporic aesthetics and black feminist framework.

Orisha iconography and the Afro-Cuban *orisha* tradition

Lukumí religion is based on the cosmology and religion of the peoples of the ancient Yoruba city-states, a conglomeration of numerous and diverse tribal groups united by a common language and a belief system linked to those of the neighboring kingdoms of Benin and Dahomey (today the Republic of Benin), who shared with the Yoruba the claim of descent from Oduduwa, the founder of the sacred city of Ilé Ife, the cradle of their civilization. [4] At the apex of the hierarchical organization of Yoruba worship was the universe's creator, Olodumare a remote being and supreme deity who is the ultimate embodiment of *ashé*—a spiritual-mystical energy, grace, or power found in varying degrees and in many forms throughout the universe. Olodumare is considered an inaccessible and omnipotent god who abdicates its powers to divine intermediaries. Beneath Olodumare operate the pantheon of deities known as the *orishas*, forces or spiritualities of nature created either prior to the creation of human beings *or* others who were once human and then evolved into deities due to some remarkable quality. *Orishas* intercede in the daily lives of humans and, if appeased, can help mankind. Neither gods nor deities in the Western sense, *orishas* are personified natural forces that interact with human beings, whereas in West Africa each *orisha* had his or her own cohort of priests, fraternities and sororities, and sanctuaries. But in Cuba the dispersion caused by slavery precluded this specialization. Orishas are identified with specific numbers, foods, and plants used in their worship, and explicit chants, drum rhythms, dance movements, and sacred narratives of their lives and relationships. As a result, each *orisha* possesses its own vital force: *ashé* permeates all aspects of life; the propagation of *ashé* in rituals and ceremonies is believed to bring balance, well-being, and harmony.

The persistence and predominance of Yoruba worship in the Afro-Cuban Lukumí religious tradition, arguably the best-preserved practice and the most influential, is observable in the worship of the *orishas*, styles of divination practices, ritual relationships, sacrifice and possession, as well as conservation of the ritual language. Its success is due to the creation of a complex Yoruba religious structure prior to their arrival in the New World, and to it having been the most recent and most massive of all African groups, which allowed them to replenish and strengthen African transplanted culture.[5] They were also aided by the fact that many of the Yoruba prisoners of war who had been taken as slaves were from the priestly class, and thus possessed a realm of knowledge of their religious beliefs and practices. Among these practices is the noteworthy Odu Ifá divination practice, the Yoruba corpus of wisdom in the form of parables and proverbs that codified the wisdom of an entire culture and kept it alive so far from its source. Ifá divination is the cornerstone of Lukumí divination.[6] Everything that exists is catalogued within the constellation of *odu*: containers of meaning and experience through experience and oral recitation.[7] According to Eugenio Matibag in "Ifá and Interpretation":

> Ifá itself is a vast information-retrieval system that preserves, accesses, and processes the texts of mythological, naturalist, medicinal, and spiritual knowledge. At the heart of the Ifá system lie the thousands of narratives that the *babalawo* [high priest] has memorized as part of his training and that he recites to clients in consultations.[8]

In Cuba these Yoruba narratives, or *ese Ifá*, have become the *patakí* myths recited in divination. And in *Lemonade*, I see these *patakí* operating symbolically as foils to the spoken-word narratives recited by Beyoncé in the film. Born out of the sixteen *meyi* corpus of the Ifá divination system, *dilogún* divination, for example, has been made more complex.[9] Two hands of shells are thrown, making a new *odu* from the combination of the two composite signs: 16 × 16 or 256 *odu*. Again, each *odu* has a specific name accompanied by its own list proverbs/refrains and *patakís*.

For the intents and purposes of this chapter, I would like to highlight the myths surrounding the *orishas*—their family ties, adventures, affairs, problems, arguments, loves—referred to as *patakís*; the explanatory stories of Afro-Cuban Lukumí thought. The divination practices of *dilogún* and Ifá utilize the *patakís* in their diagnosis and prediction of a client's situation. These stories have been likened to fables or parables in their moral message or etiological explanations of nature. Esteban Montejo, the former slave interviewed by Miguel Barnet in his famous work, *Biography of a Runaway Slave*, describes the process he witnessed in the nineteenth-century slave barracks of Cuba as follows:

Lucumí are more allied to the Saints and to God. They like to get up early with the strength of the morning and look at the sky and pray and sprinkle water on the ground. When you least expect it, the Lucumí is doing his work. I have seen old blacks kneeling on the ground for more than three hours speaking in their tongue and telling the future. The difference between the Congo and the Lucumí is that the Congo does things, and the Lucumí tells the future. He knows everything through the diloggunes, which are snails from Africa. With mystery inside.[10]

Patakís have been compared to the creation myths of the Bible and to the mythological tales of many cultures that explore the problems of life and the mysteries of the cosmos. The diviner will decide which narratives best apply to the life and problems of the client as well as the *ebó*—the sacrifice or offering that must accompany every request—prescribed by the *odu*. The song "Sandcastles," wherein Beyoncé speaks of the breaking of curses, highlights the importance of performing ebó—giving offering and making sacrifices in order to restore balance and strength to one's life. Like the spoken-word narratives chanted in *Lemonade*, the odu-derived *patakís*, I contend, negotiate and reconcile a variety of problems specific to black diasporic women such as domestic violence, infanticide and miscarriage, and reproductive health. And on many levels, these prefatory statements narrated by Beyoncé in the film further operate as if they carried a symbolic meaning that represents instances of explanatory myth and clarification, as well as the required *ebó* needed for black women to grow, heal, and resist. A clear example of this occurs in the spiritually haunting, yet emotionally raw, "Resurrection" scene that introduces the interlude song "Forward." A track that dedicates space, reflection, and time to the mothers of the memory and souls of their unjustly murdered sons is showcased. Representative of the feminine Odu Oyekun Meyi, we are exposed to the darkness of the night as well as funerary rites such as ancestor worship (e.g. the *Mardi Gras* Indian sounding a tambourine to call and resurrect spirits at an empty, candle-lit dinner table). Fashion model Winnie Harlow's presence in the scene is also astounding, for her image mirrors a syncretized visualization of the *orisha* Obatalá Obá Moro and his crown of thorns. Moreover, her vitiligo also alludes to the story where Obatalá created deformed human bodies, where Oduduwa then had to step in and take over the manufacturing of the (ideal) human form. Then, at the scene's closure, Beyoncé exclaims "Magic!" thereby teleporting us to an Afro-futuristic moment where black women across all generations are centered.

Locating female *orisha* and *odu* in *Lemonade*

Odu represent the energies and embody a collection of prophets—referred to as *omolodu* or *omodu*—that walked the universe. Another way to look at it: *odu* contains worldly and religious experience, past, present, and future.[11] What is particularly apropos and fascinating about *odu*, in relation to the broader themes addressed in the *Lemonade Reader*, is the fact that *odu*'s metaphysical embodiment and personification are *feminine*. Either indirectly or, perhaps, in an inverted way, *Lemonade*'s black feminist aesthetics and conjuring feminism analytic frame, define, and underscore the gendered constitution of *odu*, or what I term as its "feminine reverberations." Hence, when I reiterate the idea of *odu* embodying the sacred feminine and reproductive femininity, I am referring specifically to *Igba iwa-odu*. Igba iwa-odu is joined with the deity of divination and wisdom, Ifá, whose meaning is derived out of the symbolic translations: the calabash of existence, or container of the universe/planet. A female entity, Igba iwa-odu encompasses knowledge and wisdom disseminated through divination and imparted to humankind.

At this juncture of the chapter, I identify and link the presences of female *orishas* and the wealth of corresponding *odu* that not only describe them, but also illuminate, more broadly, the fascinating discourses and matrices of ancestor worship, material culture, and black feminist thought, among other issues related to black women. To be clear, what I signal in this imagery is not conclusive or finite. Just as I see Beyoncé via her *Lemonade* visual album inaugurating—arguably for the first time in popular culture—a powerful, racially gendered dialogue with Afro-Cuban religious and spiritual thought, this does not suggest that it is *the* only way in which to access and analyze the work. *Lemonade* shows and reflects upon many kinds of African diasporic spiritualities and religions that require further scholarly attention.

In my uncovering of the presences and representation of Afro-Cuban thought in *Lemonade*, I proceed by examining several tracks' accompanying spoken-word narratives (or poetry)—which I treat symbolically twinned with the *pataki* of *odu*—in order to illustrate the important role Afro-Cuban Lukumí religious thought plays in *Lemonade*.

"Intuition" (Track 1, "Pray You Catch Me")

This opening chapter haunts and reports inherited curses from the past. While seated in a wooden bathtub reminiscent of another era, Beyoncé's tignon-inspired head covering speaks to the legacy, lives, and material culture of African-descended women who wore these garments. The sub-title "Intuition" is wrought with messages from *Egun*, spirits of the dead who are related to us by blood or by religious ties. Egun communicate to us in dreams and potentially at any other point in time. Their messages to people can manifest in the form of a vision or a "second" sight. Symbolic of Egun communicating with their kin, the narrative of the opening scene that Beyoncé recites in the "Intuition" chapter cautions and mourns against "the curses of men" and women's forefathers. When Beyoncé says in the film, "you remind me of my father; a magician, able to exist in two places at once," some of the misgiving of the Odu Osa Rete and the figure of the magician come to mind. The divinatory corpus of the Odu Oshe, in particular the Odu Oshe tonti Ofun (5–10), illuminates the various inherited curses that are passed down genealogically—*to* women *from* men, in the context of *Lemonade*—to which

Beyoncé alludes. For example, the vast *odu* Oshe Meyi acknowledges heightened spiritual senses and reminds us proverbially that the blood (ancestral, biological, and genealogical) runs through the veins. The misfortunes (*osogbo*) of the Odu Oshe reign in "Intuition," as Beyoncé asks "where do you go when you go quiet?" and then reveals: "in the tradition of men in my blood, you come home at 3 a.m. and lie to me. What are you hiding? The past and the future merge to meet us here. What luck! What a fucking curse!" A masculine *odu* that always sees Death—corporeally, literally, metaphysically, spiritually—Oshe Meyi fornicated with his mother and signals matters related to the blood, sadness, tears, and work. It is in this *odu* where the *orisha* Oshún had to return to the work of transactional sex in order to live. In "Intuition," the poetic and visual narratives therein articulate the emotional energy captured in the Odu Oshe tonti Unle (5–8). In this *odu*, people are taken for granted, thus reminding us of the good that has been lost or marginalized.

"Denial" (Track 2, "Hold Up")

Arguably, this has to be the most iconic track in the *Lemonade* film because it set in motion popular reactions, both positive and negative, amongst the masses that launched a redemptive statement about the agency, joy, and resistance of black women via female *orisha* in Yoruba diasporic religions in the Americas. The opening narrative that introduces the subject matter of the "Denial" chapter resonates with so many fans and spectators because it uplifts them. The prefatory verses spoken in this scene and the display of its watery dominion symbolize rebirth and the activation of self-protection and preservation. For instance, the reference to African diasporic initiations is important. For our interests, Beyoncé speaks directly of the year-in-white initiation of diasporic Yoruba religious practices: the *iyaworaje*. "I wore white; abstained from sex and mirrors," the songstress says. For Lukumí priests and priestesses, known as *olorishas* (owners of *orisha*), the act of not cutting one's hair and sleeping on mats clearly references some of the new life changes and expectations of a newly ordained initiate—known as an *iyawo*, or the "bride" of their tutelary *orisha*.

This iconic scene when Beyoncé, personified as Oshún, exits the pair of doors with water gushing lets the entire world know that Oshún is present and ready to clean house. In the film, Beyoncé channels this female *orisha* figuratively and literally. In all her glory and power, the plethora of Oshún references in "Hold Up"—ranging from a joyous Beyoncé donning a free-flowing, ruffled gold dress adorned with a gold anklet to the omnipresence of water at various stages of the video—position this song in *Lemonade* as an ode to Oshún, more specifically, and the veneration of the *orishas*, more broadly (Even the young boy who gives Beyoncé a bat and then proceeds to follow her throughout the video can be likened to the omnipresent messenger *orisha* Eshu-Elegba.)

The Odu Ifá Oshe Tura best captures the *ashé* of Oshún's gleeful, yet wrathful presence in the *Lemonade* film. Oshe Tura restores the harmony between Oshún and the sixteen major *odu* that exist in the universe. And it is in this *odu* that Oshún thus saves the planet from eternal chaos. Like Beyoncé's black feminist embodiment of Oshún in *Lemonade*, the *orisha*'s role in Oshe Tura functions as the ultimate representation of feminine power, womanhood, and women's salvation of humanity. In Ifá ceremonies and rituals, *ebó cannot* begin or end without reciting this *odu*.

"Anger" (Track 3 "Don't Hurt Yourself")

African women's *ashé* does not end with the Oshún imagery Beyoncé extols in "Hold Up." As the visual narrative transitions into the third track, titled "Don't Hurt Yourself," we encounter women whose faces are painted in white chalk or kaolin (*efún*, in Yoruba). Throughout *Lemonade* this imagery recurs, and its repetition must not be overlooked. I read the repetition of African-descended women painted in white as a clear nod to and recognition of a broader ideation of the secret sorority of Íyàámi, or the guild of feminine *ashé*, and the Geledé masqueraders that honor women and the innate power of their life-giving forces. Although not readily visible in "Hold Up" and, perhaps, throughout *Lemonade*, the popular attention given to Oshún must be balanced by Yemayá's presence as owner of all waters. As Martin Tsang explains:

> Being owner of all waters, Yemayá doled out specific aquatic domains to her children and other related deities: Oshún, Oyá, Obba, Yewá, and Erinle received freshwater streams and deep-water tributaries in which to repose. Olokun resides in the depths of the vast oceans. Naná Burukú dwells in freshwater lagoons and mountain springs. Orisha Abatán received the ponds and marshlands, and Olosa the saltwater lagoons. Water chemistry and physics are similarly meted out by Yemayá. Boromu oversees underwater currents. The waves of the sea and the treasure they bring to the surface are governed by Olokun and Yemayá in her aspect as Ibú Mojelewu. Despite the co-optioning of domains, Yemayá is the true sovereign of all waters and all activity that takes place therein.[12]

Through Oshún's image, *Lemonade* captures and introduces this diverse representation of water-related *orishas*.

"Apathy" (Track 4 "Sorry")

"Sorry" is a celebratory anthem for black women and black girls. With respect to female *orisha* imagery in the video, Beyoncé focuses on queens and queenship—specifically that of Queen Nefertiti. To an extent, we can venture to say that this imagery mimics the path of Oshún called Ibú Adesá. The owner of the peacock, this aspect of Oshún lived in Egypt and the greater Nile River basin and valley. She owns all precious minerals and fine stones; a goddess in every sense of the word. But what is particularly striking in the "Sorry" video, at least to me, is its ending where we see an assortment of women with triangular-shaped hairdos, walking a in a grass field with their backsides facing us viewers. This scene alludes to Oshún Ibú Itimú, a warrior amazon, who goes to war while riding ostriches. An inhabitant of lagoons and a lover of crocodiles, Ibú Itimú also works closely with Egún, the formidable *orisha* Babalú-Ayé and the regal Erinle. Collectively, such imagery then transitions into the next narrative sequence, or spoken word verses, "Emptiness," which prefaces "6 Inch."

"Emptiness" (Track 5 "6 Inch")

The narrative that foregrounds "Emptiness" is powerful. A text that relies heavily on sounds—murmurs, pulses, and vibrations—the sonic register that adorns this entire track signals a woman's reproductive organs. The Odu Odi, for example, is where the vagina and holes (orifices) are born. In the opening statement to "6 Inch," Beyoncé narrates: "Dear moon: we blame you for floods." In Yoruba cosmology, the moon is known as *oshupa*. Born in the *odu* Ogbe Sa, this astral entity cannot be disassociated from its connection to sacred femininity and womanhood. The *odu* Oyekun Meyi—a feminine *odu* that speaks of Ikú (Death), darkness, and funerary rites—reverberates in the song "6 Inch" by way of the various metaphors stated in the prefatory spoken word verses of "Emptiness." When Beyoncé discusses acts of worshipping women's body, such as "suckling on the nipple and breast" and "hips grinding cinnamon, like mortar and pestle," she is describing the avatar of Oshún Ibú Kolé. Like the wardrobe and head gear worn by Beyoncé and the women in the "6 Inch" video, this manifestation of Oshún is a powerful sorceress and owns five mortars and pestles and a hanging gourd loaded and charged with medicinal plants and other secret ingredients. In the natural world, Oshún Ibú Kolé is the vulture, a representation of her disfigurement because she sacrificed her beauty for humankind.

Conclusion

In closing, this chapter has set out to expose its readers to Afro-Cuban Lukumí religious iconography and symbolism of female *orishas* in Beyoncé's *Lemonade*. Throughout this study's discussion of Lukumí divination and the presence of *orishas* in the *Lemonade* film, readers of this collection can see how black women take folklore and syncretic religious practices in their creative fiction and use it as a place of power and subversion against other forms of classic readings of black women in populate culture. Like *Lemonade*'s last track, "Formation," Beyoncé's ground-breaking masterwork has beckoned numerous African-descended women across the globe to reclaim their ancestral and spiritual pasts. And it is through the *Lemonade* film that the Afro-Cuban Lukumí religious thought will continue to thrive and touch the lives of many.

Notes

1 Falola, Toyin and Matt D. Childs, eds. *The Yoruba Diaspora in the Atlantic World* (Bloomington: Indiana University Press, 2004), 10.
2 When discussing the *orisha* religious traditions of Cuba, I opt to refer to them as Lukumí or La Regla de Osha. Alternative names for Lukumí are Santería and, in Spanish, *la religión*.
3 Clarification, Yemayá owns all water.
4 Fernández Olmos, Margarite and Lizabeth Paravisini-Gebert, eds. *Creole Religions of the Caribbean: An Introduction from Vodou and Santería to Obeah and Espiritismo* (New York: New York University Press, 2001).
5 See Brown, David, *Santería Enthroned: Art, Ritual, and Innovation in an Afro-Cuban Religion.* (Chicago: University of Chicago Press, 2003).
6 Tsang, Martin, "A Different Kind of Sweetness: Yemayá in Afro-Cuban Religion." In *Yemoja: Gender, Sexuality, and Creativity in the Latina/o and Afro-Atlantic Diasporas.* Eds. Solimar Otero and Toyin Falola (Albany: State University of New York Press, 2013), 113–130, 123.
7 Ibid., 123.
8 Matibag, Eugenio, "Ifá and Interpretation: An Afro-Caribbean Literary Practice." In *Sacred Possessions: Vodou, Santería, Obeah, and the Caribbean.* Eds. Margaret Fernández Olmos and Lizabeth Paravisini-Gebert (New Brunswick, NJ: Rutgers University Press), 151–170, 153.
9 Writing on *odu* in Lukumí divination, Tsang succinctly explains that "the *odu* cast for an individual will indicate the current and future situations of importance to the querent faces. The diviner ascertains if the *odu* is accompanied by *iré*, which can be translated as blessings or positivity balance. *Osogbo*, also known as *ibi* [sic] indicates something that may be troubling a person's life." For clarity of the names of the major *odu*, or *omolodu* of Ifá, I list them as follows: Ogbe, Oyekun, Iwori, Odi, Irosun, Owani, Obara, Okana, Ogunda, Osa, Ika, Otrupon, Otura, Irete, Oshe, and Ofun. When cast, the *odu* of *dilogún* are determined by the number of the cowry shells' mouths facing up. Listed in sequential order, these are the *odu* of *dilogún*: (1) Okana, (2) Ejioko, (3) Ogunda, (4) Irosun, (5) Oshe, (6) Obara, (7) Odi, (8) Unle, (9) Osa, (10) Ofun, (11) Owani, (12) Eyilá, (13) Metanla, (14) Merinla, (15) Marfunla, and (16) Merindilogun. When none of the cowries land face up, this is called *opira*. For additional context information, see Tsang, "A Different Kind of Sweetness," 128.
10 Qtd from Fernández Olmos and Paravisini-Gebert, *Creole Religions*, 70–76.
11 Tsang, "A Different Kind of Sweetness," 124.
12 Ibid., 115–116.

References

Barnet, Miguel. 1994. *Biography of a Runaway Slave.* Trans. W. Nick Hill. Chicago: Northwestern University Press.
Brown, David. 2003. *Santería Enthroned: Art, Ritual, and Innovation in an Afro-Cuban Religion.* Chicago: University of Chicago Press.
Falola, Toyin, and Matt D. Childs, eds. 2004. *The Yoruba Diaspora in the Atlantic World.* Bloomington: Indiana University Press.
Fernández Olmos, Margaret, and Lizabeth Paravisini-Gebert, eds. 2000. *Sacred Possessions: Vodou, Santería, Obeah, and the Caribbean.* New Brunswick, NJ: Rutgers University Press.
Fernández Olmos, Margaret, and Lizabeth Paravisini-Gebert. 2001. *Creole Religions of the Caribbean: An Introduction from Vodou and Santería to Obeah and Espiritismo.* New York: New York University Press.

Matibag, Eugenio. 2000. "Ifá and Interpretation: An Afro-Caribbean Literary Practice." In *Sacred Possessions: Vodou, Santería, Obeah, and the Caribbean*. Eds. Margaret Fernández Olmos and Lizabeth Paravisini-Gebert. New Brunswick, NJ: Rutgers University Press, 151–170.

Tsang, Martin. 2013. "A Different Kind of Sweetness: Yemayá in Afro-Cuban Religion." In *Yemoja: Gender, Sexuality, and Creativity in the Latina/o and Afro-Atlantic Diasporas*. Eds. Solimar Otero and Toyin Falola. Albany: State University of New York Press, 113–130.

8

THE *SLAY* FACTOR

Beyoncé unleashing the Black Feminine Divine in a blaze of glory

Melanie C. Jones

Ntozake Shange's opening poem, "Dark Phrases of Womanhood," in *For Colored Girls Who Have Considered Suicide When the Rainbow is Enuf,* calls for the melodies, rhythms, struggles, dramas of a Black girl's song to be born.[1] Beyoncé's sixth studio and second visual album, *Lemonade* (2016), "sings a righteous gospel"[2] and answers this revolutionary call as a lyrical and cinematic biomythography of Black women's multi-dimensional and generational experiences of love and loss.[3] *Lemonade* time travels through dimensions of Black southern culture and African Diasporic sacred wisdom to craft a creation story of sacrifice, redemption, and healing. Something magical happened during Beyoncé's live 2017 performance of *Lemonade* at the 59th Annual Grammy awards.[4] Beyoncé emerges as an "uncontainable" global icon who controls the penetrating gaze by crafting and creating Black counter-looks that reposition Black women beyond pejorative imaging and stereotyping in media and music. Beyoncé's pregnant body, adorned in the golden splendor of a thousand ages, conjures the radical radiance and oceanic depth of the Black Feminine Divine across African Diasporic religious traditions. Beyoncé crafts a glorious vision of a Black Mothering Goddess channeling the creolized cosmologies and composite energies of multiple deities, namely the Yoruba orisha Oshun, the iconic Black Madonna, and the ancient Near Eastern Goddess Kali.[5]

Taking seriously the convergence of the prophetic and the popular in Black women's moral formation, this essay locates Beyoncé's *Lemonade* as a sacred multi-layered source for Black women and girls discovering and reclaiming the Black Feminine Divine in themselves, their mothers, daughters, and sisters. This essay interrogates Beyoncé's embodiment of the lyrics "I Slay/ We Gon' Slay" as belonging to the dark, ancient, radical, warrior Goddess tradition that celebrates erotic power and affect (i.e., anger, rage, fury, etc.) as moral virtues for self-awareness and communal wellness. The slay factor that Beyoncé unleashes bears power that is recognizable to cis-queer-trans Black women alike, and is akin to the mystery of the sacred—its witness cannot be wholly explained, but Black women know *what it is and what it ain't*. Slay takes on a double-edged meaning as an outer display of sartorial grace and an inner courage for Black women who leverage their power (i.e. resources, talents, gifts, wealth, etc.) to command the moment. Slay as a spiritual force emanating from the Black Feminine Divine, drawing on the poetry of Lucille Clifton in the line of the Goddess Kali, is no stranger to Black women, but spawns from within Black women's body dramas, transnational realities, and blood lineages.

This essay makes the following moves. First, I argue that Beyoncé's 2017 Grammy performance represents the culmination of the *Lemonade* album and fully realizes Black Goddess traditions on centerstage. Second, I analyze historic and contemporary Goddess debates in feminist theology and popular culture that inform the significance of Beyoncé's Goddess imaging. Third, I claim that the gift of Beyoncé's Goddess-ing in *Lemonade* is the slay factor, which offers radical ways of being for Black women in particular and, by extension, all women universally.

Bow down, bitches: Beyoncé as the Holy Grail

Beyoncé Knowles (Carter) debuted as a Grammy performer at the top of the new millennium in 2000 under the banner of the accomplished girl group, Destiny's Child. By 2004, Beyoncé was a showstopper, winning five awards in one night and returning to the Grammy mainstage as a solo artist to perform her classic ballad "Dangerously in Love 2" and a sensational duo with Prince. Rising up the musical charts as one of America's Dreamgirls, Beyoncé took the 2007 Grammy stage to tell the world to "Listen." Beyoncé performed "Proud Mary" in 2008, paying homage to the musical legend Tina Turner; and, in 2010, she had the world rethinking gender norms with her hit single "If I Were a Boy." The year 2014 featured a sizzling performance of "Drunk in Love." Her 2015 act then caused quite a controversy when she sang the Thomas Dorsey classic "Take My Hand, Precious Lord" as critics questioned why pop-songstress Beyoncé would perform this selection when jazz vocalist Ledisi, who had never performed on the Grammy soundstage, was set to sing a Mahalia Jackson-inspired soulful rendition in the movie *Selma* later that year. According to *Entertainment Tonight*, songwriter John Legend confirmed that Beyoncé approached the Glory duo (Legend and rapper Common) to sing the Gospel hymn as their introduction. Legend told *ET*'s Kevin Frazier, "You don't really say no to Beyoncé if she asks to perform with you."[6] From a first-time performer in 2000 to the Queen of the Grammys in 2015, Beyoncé emerges as a diva who controls her spotlight and commands the moment. From the Grammys to the MTV Video Music Awards (VMAs) to the Super Bowl to the Presidential Inauguration, when Beyoncé performs live there is a message she aims to convey and an aspect of her superpower she seeks to reveal. *Lemonade* is no exception.

On Sunday, February 12, 2017, Beyoncé re-awakened the world to the Black Feminine Divine in her culminating live performance of the *Lemonade* album. From the heartfelt introduction of her mother, Tina Lawson, to the opening hologram of generations of women coming together in search of their mothers' gardens, Beyoncé's 2017 Grammy performance is a sight to behold. The performance unlocks a magical portal luring her viewers into the cosmic world of the Goddess as a pregnant Beyoncé adorned in a golden headdress and gilded, crystal-encrusted bikini and gown rises to centerstage while women dancers bow at their knees.[7] Though she has sought to convey representations of royalty in past works, Beyoncé's 2017 Grammy performance creatively employs her pregnant body through dramatic stylization as a countermove to re-inscribe Black female bodily presence into America's focus as capable of embodying divinity, beauty, and glory. From her gilded embroidered look to her expecting body to her picturesque poses to her sultry music to her sacred power, American viewers—whether in the Los Angeles Staples Center or from home televisions—were fixated on Beyoncé's grandeur as she commands the Grammy soundstage for ten full minutes. The struggles of a broken relationship that Beyoncé sings of in the two songs sampled for the Grammy performance, "Love Drought" and "Sandcastles," do not drown her in despair, but emerge as living waters birthing a glimpse of a beatific vision of healing and redemption on Earth.

Similar to the diverse African spiritualities introduced in *Lemonade*, Beyoncé's Goddess representation pays homage to multiple female deities of African religious traditions, and enables Black women across religious traditions to see themselves in the likeness of the Black Feminine Divine. Following the release of the *Lemonade* visual album in 2016, womanist theologian Yolanda Pierce described feeling as if she had "been to Church" as she reflected on Black women encounters with the sacred from the Black Church traditions of water baptism, testimony service, Sunday morning worship, healing practices, and preaching depicted in the album. Pierce further affirms that the album moves beyond the Christian imagination and "evokes other gods and other faiths, particularly the traditional religions of the Yoruba in Africa and the Caribbean."[8] *Lemonade*'s second single, "Hold Up," channels the Yoruba Goddess and orisha Oshun as a sensual Beyoncé bursts out of the waters adorned in a Roberto Cavalli yellow dress, smashing windows and breaking cameras with a bat in tow while serving notice to her betrayer of her fiery willfulness and fierce resilience with a sinister smile. Themes of African spirituality persist in *Lemonade*'s "Sorry" with body art and faces painted in the Yoruba tradition Ori, Voodoo-inspired ring shout in "Don't Hurt Yourself," the water ritual in "Sandcastles," Nefertiti-styled braids, and consistent interaction with the ancestral world through photographs, chants, and sounds. Beyoncé's 2017 Grammy performance follows suit and opens pathways for the revelation of multiple Goddess figures across African Diasporic spiritualities and religious traditions, including but not limited to Oshun and the Black Madonna.

"Everybody is watching Beyoncé," according to Harvard University Professor of African Religious Traditions Jacob Olupona.[9] Beyoncé's Grammy performance enlivens the Yoruba orisha Oshun, the mother of orisha twin deities Ibeji, who heals with her sweet waters and honey, governs money affairs, represents fidelity and youth, and receives honor through the colors of yellow and gold. Some myths of the Yoruba tradition point to Oshun as an integral creator and savior of the Yoruba world. Oshun's story is replete with experiences of suffering facing neglect and deep betrayal; likewise, she celebrates sensuality and pleasure as virtues that make life worth living. The remarkable chair tilt in Beyoncé's Grammy performance illustrates Oshun's power to turn the world right side up as she walks on water and flaunts her star power. Olupona contends, "She is speaking to the world, she is speaking to America … Beyoncé is educating the masses on Oshun. She is seeing how indigenous spirituality can be a powerful tool for changing the world." Beyoncé representing Oshun at the Grammys makes visible the universal value of the particularity of Yoruba spirituality for America and the global world with Black women at the center.

"Do you remember being born? Are you thankful for the hips that cracked?"[10] The opening lines of the Grammy performance give clues that Beyoncé's Goddess origins begin with her mother both watching and emulating her pain and her love. Displayed mostly in Europe and in the Americas, the Black Madonna represents statues, paintings, sculptures, and shrines depicting Mary, the mother of Jesus, and an infant Jesus with black skin. The Black Madonna is often adorned with a halo to symbolize that she is a divine mother. The headdress Beyoncé wears also resembles a crown of light signaling her Queen Mother status. Beyoncé restores the righteousness of the Black Madonna beyond mother to son, but to fully embody a female-headed family pattern that also values the matriarchal and maternal lineage as divine. The dynamic pose at the opening of the performance of her mother Tina Knowles Lawson on the left, pregnant Beyoncé in the middle, and daughter Blue Ivy Carter on the right—with all three clad in the regal line of Nefertiti showcased during the 2017 Grammy performance—offers a model of healing and liberation that is transgenerational. Like *Lemonade*, the performance is a liturgy encompassing a mixture of word, drawing from the poetry of Kenyan-born Somali-British poet Warsan Shire, and song. In her 2017 Grammy Award speech for Best Urban Contemporary Album, Beyoncé acknowledges,

> It's important to me to show images to my children that reflect their beauty so they can grow up in a world where they look in the mirror—first through their own families, as well as the news, the Super Bowl, the Olympics, the White House and the Grammys—and see themselves. And have no doubt that they're beautiful, intelligent and capable.

Through *Lemonade*, Beyoncé reveals the Goddess as a mother who casts a vision for her children near and far, but also reaches back to transform old magic through lessons learned from the past. Beyoncé re-aligns maternal inspiration and mother wit at the center of the universe: "Your mother is a woman and women like her cannot be contained!"[11] The Goddess that self-avowed feminist Beyoncé awakens in *Lemonade* and unleashes at the Grammys to a global audience is Black, divine, feminine, and cannot be tamed; but what does this mean for feminism?

I met God, she's Black? Goddess debates in feminist theology and popular culture

Since the early work of radical feminist theologian Mary Daly,[12] white feminist theologians have discussed at length the significance of the female imaging of the divine. Daly's classic maxim, "If God is male, then the male is God," presented in her second book *Beyond God the Father: Toward a Philosophy of Women's Liberation* (1973), illustrates the need for a new language of the divine to dismantle and transcend patriarchal theological methods that establish and perpetuate a sexist society. Daly writes,

> The biblical and popular image of God as a great patriarch in heaven, rewarding and punishing according to his mysterious and seemingly arbitrary will, has dominated the imagination of millions over thousands of years. The symbol of the Father God, spawned in the human imagination and sustained as plausible by patriarchy, has in turn rendered service to this type of society by making its mechanisms for the oppression of women appear right and fitting. If God in "his" heaven is a father ruling "his" people, then it is in the "nature" of things and according to divine plan and the order of the universe that society be male-dominated.[13]

Daly moves beyond simply calling God a new name, but calls for the death of a patriarchal God through a re-ordering, re-framing, and re-positioning of systematic theological categories of soteriology, Christology, ecclesiology, anthropology, and eschatology to enact women's liberation. In Daly's third book *Gyn/Ecology: The Metaethics of Radical Feminism* (1978), she articulates an otherworldly dis/course that creates newspeak and new space for women to both come into being and become. Daly's method is gynocentric in that:

> [It] requires not only the murder of misogynistic methods (intellectual and affective exorcism) but also ecstasy, which [she] calls *ludic cerebration*. This is the "free play of intuition in [women's] spaces, giving rise to thinking that is vigorous, informed, multi-dimensional, independent, creative, tough." It arises from the lived experience of being.[14]

Gyn/Ecology participates in the radical feminist process of spinning into a women's centered otherworld outside of the bounds of patriarchy that fosters an exorcism of the Godfather, and by way of three passages an entry into the gates of the Goddess. Daly asserts,

> The metaethics of radical feminism means simply that Zeus, Yahweh, and all the other divine male "Mothers" are trying to retrieve their dolls from the ashcan of patriarchal creation, women on our own Journey are discovering Metis and the third-born Athena: our own new be-ing. That is, we are be-ing the Triple Goddess, who is, and is not yet.[15]

Here, Daly constructs Goddess theology as a reclaiming of past sources of female wisdom throughout ancient Greek literature and connecting women's be-ingness as made in the image of Goddess while eclipsing the empowering ancient divine feminine traditions of nonwhite women.

Black feminist poet and theorist Audre Lorde raises this critique of Daly's willful ignorance in *Gyn/Ecology* in her "Letter to Mary Daly," first sent to Daly on May 6, 1979 and four months later published as an open letter after allegedly receiving no response. Lorde recalled approaching Daly's work with excitement and expectation about Daly's perspective on ways the Goddess has been hidden historically and the suppression of female power in the West. After reading Daly's *Gyn/Ecology*, Lorde later becomes suspicious of Daly's pale articulation of the Goddess. Lorde queries,

> So, I wondered, why doesn't Mary deal with Afrekete as an example? Why are her goddess images only white, western european, judeo-Christian? Where was Afrekete, Yemanje, Oyo, and Mawulisa? Where were the warrior goddesses of the Vodun, the Dahomean Amazons, and the warrior women of Dan? Well, I thought, Mary has made a conscious decision to narrow her scope and to deal only with the ecology of western european women.[16]

Lorde argues that Daly eclipses the experiences of nonwhite women and fails to address the cosmic female power that is ancient, dark, and deep. Lorde writes, "What you excluded from *Gyn/Ecology* dismissed my heritage and the heritage of all noneuropean women and dismissed the real connections that exists between all of us."[17] Lorde critiques Daly's use of nonwhite sources and experiences as the barriers to the flourishing of gyn/ecology, particularly Indian sutee, Chinese footbinding, and African female genital mutilation. In addition to European witchburning, Daly identifies the aforementioned ancient traditions as sado-rituals that perpetuate the reenactment of Goddess murder. Lorde criticizes Daly's missing engagement with the empowering ancient traditions of nonwhite female Goddesses that can be found in religious orders older than Europe. Such a dismissal of noneuropean goddesses by Daly reinforces a historic white feminist erasure of nonwhite women's sacred female energies and virtues. Lorde retorts,

> Mary, I ask that you be aware of how this serves the destructive forces of racism and separation between women—the assumption that the herstory and myth of white women is the legitimate and sole herstory and myth of all women to call upon for power and background, and that nonwhite women and our herstories are noteworthy only as decorations, or examples of female victimization … When patriarchy dismisses us, it encourages our murderers. When radical lesbian feminist theory dismisses us, it encourages its own demise.[18]

Lorde does not wait for Daly to demonstrate inclusion, but instead she writes several poems capturing ancient Black Goddess traditions and a full-length biomythography,

Zami: A New Spelling of My Name, which tells Lorde's coming of age story and illustrates her lesbian encounters with old magic found in the African trickster Goddess Afrekete. Almost four decades after Mary Daly's *Gyn/Ecology* and Audre Lorde's "Letter to Mary Daly," Goddess feminist theology largely remains a white feminist project making self-avowed feminist Beyoncé's representation of the Goddess oppositional in *Lemonade* and at the Grammys, thus pushing back against the paleness of radical feminism.

Articulations of the Black Feminine Divine are not new to Black popular culture and Black theological traditions. Most notably, Ntozake Shange's last line—"I found God in myself and I loved her. I loved her fiercely"—in *For Colored Girls,* [19] first published in 1975 prior to the work of Daly, articulates both a recovery of the Black Feminine Divine and radical affirmation of a theological anthropology of Black women's bodies as bearers of divinity and glory even in a hostile world that denies Black substance and virtue. Spawned from the radical Black prophetic tradition including voices like Bishop Henry McNeal Turner, who first declared "God is a Negro" in the late nineteenth century, early Black theologians in the mid-twentieth century—particularly Albert B. Cleage, Jr., J. Deotis Roberts, and James Cone—championed perspectives that "God is Black" and expanded theological discourse of a Black Christ who bears witness to/for/with the suffering and oppression of Black people in America.[20] While Black theology linked blackness with divinity to confront racist white theologies, first-generation Black theologians on the whole failed to fully integrate the voices and experiences of Black women and children in these early theological constructions.[21]

Drawing from novelist Alice Walker's four-part framing of "womanist" as a Black feminist or feminist of color in her classic collection of essays *In Search of Our Mothers' Gardens: Womanist Prose,* [22] Black women theologians—namely Katie Cannon, Jacquelyn Grant, and Delores Williams—birthed womanist theology formed in the 1980s as a prophetic theology of liberation affirming the full humanity of Black women as made in the *imago dei* (image of God) while also confronting both the missing analysis of gender in Black theology's struggle for Black liberation and race in white feminist theology's rally against patriarchy. Alice Walker's protagonist Celie in *The Color Purple* reveals the image of an old, white, gray-haired male God offering no redemption for Black women. Celie laments, "If he ever listened to poor colored women the world would be a different place I can tell you.[23] Systematic theologian Delores Williams, the first to use the term "womanist theology" in her seminal 1987 essay "Womanist Theology: Black Women's Voices," links Walker's quadripartite definition of "womanist" with four intentions of a Christian womanist theological method with Black women's voices and experiences at the center. For Williams,

> Christian womanist theological methodology needs to be informed by at least four elements: (1) a multidialogical intent, (2) a liturgical intent, (3) a didactic intent, and (4) a commitment both to reason and to the validity of female imagery and metaphorical language in the construction of theological statements.[24]

Williams uses the fourth intention to encourage womanist theologians to rethink the question, "Who do you say God is?" Where Black and feminist theologies ignored and overlooked perspectives of the Black Feminine Divine, womanist theologians like Delores Williams, Kelly Brown Douglas, and Monica Coleman have articulated the importance of female images and imagery of the divine as necessary for Black women doing and engaging theology. And there is still more work to be done here. Black women must see themselves in the face of the divine. Quite frankly, even if Black, feminist, and womanist theologies fail to take seriously the Black Feminine Divine, Beyoncé gives new vision by recovering and representing a Goddess that bears witness to Black women across numerous geographical locations, experiences, and religious traditions.

Though not the originator of the slogan, self-avowed Jewish atheist Dylan Chenfield claims to have popularized the phrase "I Met God, She's Black" by placing it on a $30 T-shirt. When asked about his motivation, Chenfield told *HuffPost*, "I like poking fun at sacred cows … I'm taking the idea that God is a white male and doing the opposite of that, which is a black woman."[25] Chenfield's statement exposes the conception of Black women associated with divinity depicted in the broader culture as strange, ridiculous, and often exploited. Beyoncé's *Lemonade* and iconic performances of her music like the Grammy 2017 performance signal the re-emergence of continuing representation of the Black Feminine Divine in popular culture. Queen Bey has opened the altar doors. So, now what? What does Beyoncé's Goddess symbol grant to her devotees?

The slay factor: the future is Black and feminist

First delivered at the University of Santa Cruz "Great Goddess Re-emerging" Conference in the spring of 1978 and published in *Heresies: The Great Goddess Issue* (1978), pioneering Goddess feminist theologian Carol P. Christ's classic speech, "Why Women Need the Goddess," discusses the contribution of the Goddess symbol to the feminist movement. At the heart of the essay, Christ probes the question: "Does the emergence of the symbol of Goddess among women have significant political and psychological ramifications for the feminist movement?"[26] Unlike Daly, Christ affirms at the outset the "ancient Mediterranean, pre-Christian European, Native American, Meso-American, Hindu, African, and other traditions" and modern women's interpretations as "rich sources for Goddess symbolism."[27] Christ stresses that deep psychological effects of religious symbols extend beyond one's belief in God or practice of patriarchal religions leaving even the secularized beholden to male dominance by divine sanction and distrust of female power. Engaging the works of thinkers Clifford Geertz, Mary Daly, and Simone de Beauvoir, Christ argues four primary reasons the Goddess is a necessary religious symbol for the feminist movement and worth modern women fully interpreting its meaning.

First, the Goddess symbol promotes the affirmation of female power and defeats patriarchal psychologies that maintain "women's power as inferior and dangerous."[28] Second, the Goddess symbol "aids the process of naming and reclaiming the female body and its cycles and processes" while connecting women's bodies with creativity, life-giving potential and old wisdom in nature.[29] Third, the Goddess symbol through ritual of music and movement values the woman's will. Christ asserts, "A woman is encouraged to know her will, to believe that her will is valid, and to believe that her will can be achieved in the world, three powers traditionally denied to her in patriarchy."[30] Fourth, the Goddess symbol promotes the coming together of women through a "revaluation of women's bonds and heritage."[31] Beyoncé's representation of the Goddess symbol in her 2017 Grammy performance of *Lemonade* bears witness to each of Christ's core elements while further embodying a fifth sense, a particular characteristic of the Black Feminine Divine which I call the "slay factor."

Beyoncé's Goddess representation is not new. As Lorde suggests, "The woman's place of power within each of us is neither white nor surface; it is dark, it is ancient, and it is deep."[32] Beyoncé as Goddess raises a poignant query: "What do divine figures do?" Or better stated: "What about Beyoncé's divine figuring gives new representation to Black women's moral wisdom?"

From the hit single "Formation," the catchphrase of the *Lemonade* album is the phrase "slay." Popularized on every product imaginable and enveloped into everyday speak, there is a shared understanding whenever it is evoked among Black women of all ages, backgrounds, nationalities, and social locations. Slay as a way of being in the world that encourages Black women to command the moment and claim their power by self-possession. In a *Good Morning America* (2006) interview with Diane Sawyer about her *B'Day* album mirroring the artistry of Josephine Baker, Beyoncé claimed a desire to follow Baker's example and make room for a sense of woman possession (or self-possession) and freedom in her artistry. Undoubtedly, ten years later, *Lemonade* reveals a mastery of possession of her body, story, and multiple spiritual belonging. In "Policing Beyoncé's Body: Whose Body is this Anyway?" writer Noel Siqi Duan speaks to Beyoncé's ability to control the gaze: "In her performance both on-and off-stage, Beyoncé reverses the panoptic vision of the male gaze—you, the viewer, are self-conscious in her presence, and she is commanding your attention."[33]

> I will give you the looks of me I want you to have
> I will tell the parts of my story I want you to know
> I will create what I want you to enjoy
> This is power, this is slaydom!

Beyoncé's embodiment of the lyrics "I Slay/ We Gon' Slay" belongs to the dark, ancient, radical, warrior Goddess tradition that celebrates erotic power and affect (i. e., anger, rage, fury, etc.) as moral virtues for self-awareness and communal wellness, while also demonstrating significant linkage to Kali, the Hindu Goddess of war and liberation. Even in the 2017 Grammy performance, the opening silhouettes of dramatically moving arms resemble the many arms of the fierce Kali. In the use of the affirmation "slay," Beyoncé' recovers the warrior power of Kali, whose name means "she who is black" in Sanskrit, representing, on one end, the mother of creativity and fertility (shakhti), and, on the other, an unrelenting slaying of her white opponents and seeking liberation for her children at whatever cost. Much like Lucille Clifton, who retrieves Kali in her poetry, Beyoncé spins the expressions of anger, fury, and rage as powerful weaponry to self-protect and eradicate all manners of oppression.

Though her self-titled, fifth studio and first visual Beyoncé album may be named her debut album as a feminist, *Lemonade* is the album that Beyoncé first takes up a feminist analysis as a framework for executing her artistry. The music matches the historical moment for Black women belonging to her generation. Though any comparison falls short, Beyoncé's *Lemonade* is the millennial generation's *The Miseducation of Lauryn Hill*, both bearing the significance of tracing the saga between love, loss, and liberation for Black women.[34] *Lemonade* represents deeply personal, but also the most explicitly political songs in Beyoncé's catalogue. Moreover, the inclusion of the Mothers of the Movement in the visual album makes it possible for you to not only hear the stories of the painstaking loss due to devastating state-sanctioned violence, police brutality, and gun violence, but also to see the pain and resilience that lingers in their faces. *Lemonade* offers a new layer of Beyoncé's iconic platform that unleashes the Black Feminine Divine in a blaze of glory.

Notes

1 Ntozake Shange, *For Colored Girls Who Have Considered Suicide/ When the Rainbow Was Enuf: A Choreopoem* (New York: Scribner, 1997), 17–18.
2 Shange, *For Colored Girls*, 18.
3 Biomythography is a term coined by Audre Lorde to define the weaving of myth, autobiography, history and fantasy to form a narrative that demonstrates unbridled courage and blends the ordinary and extraordinary experiences of women. Beyoncé's *Lemonade* represents a lyrical and visual biomythography capturing the terrible, timeless and triumphant experiences of Black women journeying love and loss. Audre Lorde. *Zami, A New Spelling of My Name* (Berkeley: Crossing Press, 1982).
4 *59th Annual Grammy Awards Live Performance*, by Beyoncé Knowles-Carter, California, Los Angeles, February 12, 2017.
5 I am building upon an argument that I express briefly in a previous online article about Beyoncé's 2017 Grammy performance. See Melanie C. Jones, "Clothed in Glory: Beyoncé Fashioning the Black Feminine Divine and Spinning Gold," base: Black Theology Project, June 16, 2017, accessed November 13, 2018, https://btpbase.org/clothed-in-glory-beyonce/.
6 Philiana Ng, "GRAMMYs 2015: Ledisi, John Legend Respond to Beyonce 'Selma' Controversy," *Entertainment Tonight*, February 9, 2015, accessed November 16, 2018, https://www.etonline.com/awards/grammys/159381_ledisi_john_legend_respond_to_beyonce_selma_controversy.
7 Beyoncé's dress was made by Peter Dundas, first look in the eponymous collection (under his name) since the designer left Roberto Cavalli. The dress was inspired by African Goddess Oshun, and includes Beyoncé's face in the embroidery and two cherubs on her hips. See Nicole Phelps, "Exclusive: Peter Dundas Dresses Beyoncé at the Grammys, Launches Solo Label," *Vogue*, May 26, 2017, accessed November 16, 2018, https://www.vogue.com/article/beyonce-grammys-peter-dundas-dress.

8 Yolanda Pierce, "Black Women and the Sacred: With 'Lemonade,' Beyoncé Takes Us to Church," *Religion Dispatches*, June 07, 2018, accessed November 13, 2018, http://religiondispatches.org/black-women-and-the-sacred-Beyoncé-takes-us-to-church/.

9 See Matthew Wright, "Beyoncé's Grammy Award Inspiration Could Be Oshun," *Daily Mail Online*, February 14, 2017, accessed July 25, 2018, http://www.dailymail.co.uk/news/article-4221100/Was-Oshun-Beyoncé-s-Grammy-Award-inspiration.html.

10 59th Annual Grammy's Live Performance, by Beyoncé Knowles-Carter, California, Los Angeles, February 12, 2017. These lines are sampled in the "Forgiveness" chapter of *Lemonade* on the visual album and during the 2017 Grammy performance.

11 Drawing from the poetry of Warsan Shire, this is a phrase from Beyoncé's 2017 Grammy performance as holograms and images of her statuesque poses are displayed.

12 Mary Daly (1928–2010), a brilliant theologian and philosopher earning two PhDs in sacred theology and philosophy from the University of Fribourg, Switzerland, is one of the most controversial figures in feminist theology and philosophy. Daly's work is still widely used in white feminist circles and also heavily critiqued for her radical lesbian feminist exclusivity toward nonwhite women, men, and the trans-community. It is debated whether Daly was forced out of tenure or chose to retire from her faculty position at Boston College in 1998 because of her unyielding decision to teach women only in her classes.

13 Mary Daly, *Beyond God the Father: Toward a Philosophy of Women's Liberation* (Boston: Beacon Press, 1973), 13.

14 Mary Daly, *Gyn/Ecology: The Metaethics of Radical Feminism* (Boston: Beacon Press, 1978), 23.

15 Daly, *Gyn/Ecology*, 14.

16 Audre Lorde, *Sister Outsider: Essays and Speeches* (Berkeley, CA: Crossing Press, 2007), 67.

17 Lorde, *Sister Outsider*, 68.

18 Lorde, *Sister Outsider*, 69.

19 Shange, *For Colored Girls*, 87.

20 For an expansive academic treatment of Bishop Henry McNeal Turner and Black theological perspectives of Black God and Black Christ, see Albert B. Cleage, Jr., *The Black Messiah: (The Religious Roots of Black Power, a Strong and Uncompromising Presentation by Americas Most Influential and Controversial Black Religious Leader)* (New York: Sheed and Ward, 1969); James Hal Cone, *God of the Oppressed* (Maryknoll, NY: Orbis, 1997); J. Deotis Roberts, *Liberation and Reconciliation: A Black Theology* (Louisville, KY: Westminster John Knox Press, 2005); Kelly Brown Douglas, *The Black Christ* (Maryknoll, NY: Orbis, 1994); Andre E. Johnson, *Forgotten Prophet: Bishop Henry McNeal Turner and the African American Prophetic Tradition* (Lanham, MD: Lexington, 2014)..

21 Some Black religious scholars may argue that Albert B. Cleage, Jr. is an exception to early Black theologians imagining the Black Divine Feminine because of his unveiling of the mural of the Black Madonna and Child on Easter Sunday, March 12, 1967 and the founding of the Pan African Orthodox Christian Church (PAOCC), more commonly known as the Shrine of the Black Madonna, in Detroit, Michigan. Though the Black Madonna and Child remained a central religious symbol for Cleage's Black Christian nationalism, there is still a question of whether such a liberating symbol translated into full affirmation of Black women in PAOCC practices and clergy leadership. See Jawanza Eric Clark, ed., *Albert Cleage Jr. and the Black Madonna and Child* (New York: Palgrave Macmillan, 2016).

22 Alice Walker, *In Search of Our Mothers' Gardens: Womanist Prose* (New York: Harcourt Brace Jovanovich, 1983), 4.

23 Alice Walker, *The Color Purple* (New York: Harcourt Brace Jovanovich, 1982), 193.

24 Delores Williams, "Womanist Theology: Black Women's Voices," in *Voices of the Religious Left: A Contemporary Sourcebook*, ed. Rebecca T. Alpert (Philadelphia: Temple University Press, 2000), 30.

25 Carol Kuruvilla, "Jewish Atheist's Controversial T-Shirt: I Met God, She's Black'," *Huffington Post*, December 7, 2017, accessed November 12, 2018, https://www.huffing tonpost.com/2015/01/03/i-met-god-shes-black_n_6406928.html.

26 Carol P. Christ, "Why Women Need the Goddess," in *Womanspirit Rising: A Feminist Reader on Religion*, ed. Carol P. Christ and Judith Plaskow (San Francisco: Harper & Row, 1992), 273.

27 Christ, "Why Women Need the Goddess," 275.

28 Christ, "Why Women Need the Goddess," 276.

29 Christ, "Why Women Need the Goddess," 279.

30 Christ, "Why Women Need the Goddess," 281.

31 Christ, "Why Women Need the Goddess," 282.

32 Lorde, *Sister Outsider*, 37.

33 Noel Siqi Duan, "Policing Beyonce's Body: 'Whose Body Is This Anyway?'" in *The Beyoncé Effect: Essays on Sexuality, Race and Feminism*, ed. Adrienne Trier-Bieniek (Jefferson, NC: McFarland & Co, 2016), 55–74.

34 *The Miseducation of Lauryn Hill* represents the height of hip hop music, as the most decorated album of 1999. Lauryn Hill maintains high recognition because of her work taking hip hop to its highest achievements, winning Grammy Album of the Year, and her identity as a Black woman. *Lemonade*, though belonging to the genre of pop rather than hip hop, did not earn Album of the Year; however, the album did evoke similar attention to Black women's struggles from the personal to the political to the popular.

Bibliography

Christ, Carol P. 1992. "Why Women Need the Goddess." In *Womanspirit Rising: A Feminist Reader on Religion*, edited by Carol P. Christ and Judith Plaskow, 273–287. San Francisco: Harper & Row.

Cleage, Albert B.Jr. 1969. *The Black Messiah: (The Religious Roots of Black Power, a Strong and Uncompromising Presentation by Americas Most Influential and Controversial Black Religious Leader)*. New York: Sheed and Ward.

Cone, James Hal. 1997. *God of the Oppressed*. Maryknoll, NY: Orbis.

Daly, Mary. 1973. *Beyond God the Father: Toward a Philosophy of Women's Liberation*. Boston: Beacon Press.

Daly, Mary. 1978. *Gyn/Ecology; The Metaethics of Radical Feminism*. Boston: Beacon Press.

Douglas, Kelly Brown. 1994. *The Black Christ*. Maryknoll, NY: Orbis.

Duan, Noel Siqi. 2016. " Policing Beyoncé's Body: 'Whose Body Is This Anyway?'" in *The Beyoncé Effect: Essays on Sexuality, Race and Feminism*, edited by Adrienne Trier-Bieniek, 55–74. Jefferson, NC: McFarland & Co.

Johnson, Andre E. 2014. *Forgotten Prophet: Bishop Henry McNeal Turner and the African American Prophetic Tradition*. Lanham, MD: Lexington.

Jones, Melanie C. "Clothed in Glory: Beyoncé Fashioning the Black Feminine Divine and Spinning Gold." .base: Black Theology Project. June 16, 2017. Accessed November 13, 2018. https://btpbase.org/clothed-in-glory-Beyoncé/.

Knowles-Carter, Beyoncé, performer. *Lemonade*. Recorded April 23, 2016. Parkwood Entertainment.

Kuruvilla, Carol. "Jewish Atheist's Controversial T-Shirt: "I Met God, She's Black"." *Huffington Post*. December 07, 2017. Accessed November 13, 2018. https://www.huffing tonpost.com/2015/01/03/i-met-god-shes-black_n_6406928.html.

Lorde, Audre. 2007. *Sister Outsider: Essays and Speeches*. Berkeley, CA: Crossing Press.

Ng, Philiana. "GRAMMYs 2015: Ledisi, John Legend Respond to Beyonce 'Selma' Controversy." *Entertainment Tonight*. February 09, 2015. Accessed November 16, 2018. https://

www.etonline.com/awards/grammys/159381_ledisi_john_legend_respond_to_beyonce_
selma_controversy.

Pierce, Yolanda. "Black Women and the Sacred: With Lemonade, Beyoncé Takes Us to
Church." *Religion Dispatches*. June 07, 2018. Accessed November 13, 2018. http://reli
giondispatches.org/black-women-and-the-sacred-Beyoncé-takes-us-to-church/.

Roberts, J. Deotis. 2005. *Liberation and Reconciliation: A Black Theology*. Louisville, KY:
Westminster John Knox Press.

Shange, Ntozake. 1997. *For Colored Girls Who Have Considered Suicide When the Rainbow Was
Enuf: A Choreopoem*. New York: Scribner.

Townes, Emilie Maureen. 1995. *In a Blaze of Glory: Womanist Spirituality as Social Witness*.
Nashville, TN: Abingdon Press.

Walker, Alice. 1982. *The Color Purple*. New York: Harcourt Brace Jovanovich.

Walker, Alice. 1983. *In Search of Our Mothers' Gardens: Womanist Prose*. New York: Harcourt
Brace Jovanovich.

Williams, Delores. "Womanist Theology: Black Women's Voices." In *Voices of the Religious
Left*, edited by Rebecca Alpert, 26–33. Philadelphia: Temple University Press.

Wright, Matthew. "Beyoncé's Grammy Award Inspiration Could Be Oshun." *Daily Mail
Online*. February 14, 2017. Accessed July 25, 2018. http://www.dailymail.co.uk/news/a
rticle-4221100/Was-Oshun-Beyoncé-s-Grammy-Award-inspiration.html.

Williams, Delores. 2000. "Womanist Theology: Black Women's Voices," In *Voices of the
Religious Left*, edited by Rebecca Alpert, 26–33. Philadelphia: Temple University Press.

9

BEYONCÉ'S DIASPORA HERITAGE AND ANCESTRY IN *LEMONADE*

Patricia Coloma Peñate

Beyoncé's latest album, *Lemonade* (2016), has received a lot of attention due to its exploration of the singer's conflict with her husband, Jay-Z, and because in it she provides a complex picture of her identity. *Lemonade*'s visual content centers not only on Beyoncé herself, but also points to New Orleans's history and people as specific markers of her identity and consciousness. The specificity of this site connects Beyoncé's identity to Louisiana and its Creole culture; as the singer explains in "Formation," the first released single from *Lemonade*: "My daddy Alabama, Momma Louisiana. You mix that negro with that Creole make a Texas bama."

Lemonade takes us on a journey with different stages that address and celebrate Beyoncé's ancestry and heritage. Through the album's development, the singer elaborates on how her private life—the allusion to her husband's infidelity and her immediate family's dynamics—shapes or influences her public life, and vice versa. The juxtaposition of these two spheres generates a conflict that marks *Lemonade*'s progression while affirming and celebrating the singer's identity and ancestry. Such simultaneous consideration of private and public life issues illustrates Toni Morrison's analysis about both spheres in her essay "Rootedness: The Ancestor as a Foundation," in which the writer states:

> There is a conflict between public and private life, and it is a conflict that I think ought to remain a conflict. Not a problem, just a conflict. Because they are two modes of life that exist to exclude and annihilate each other. It's a conflict that should be maintained now more than ever because the social machinery of this country at this time doesn't permit harmony in a life that has both aspects. (Morrison 1984, 339)

In *Lemonade,* Beyoncé continuously intersects these two realms in order to illustrate the complexity generated by their collision, and employs the ancestor figure as a key presence in both of them. As Farah Jasmine Griffin points out, the forebear constitutes an identity paradigm rooted in the South that serves as an individual's "recursive touchstone" and "posture of remembrance" (Griffin 1995, 3–12); moreover, in *Lemonade* the ancestor figure works as a marker of Beyoncé's celebration of Creole tradition and heritage and of African-descent women in particular. Additionally, this presence provides the solution to the conflict stated at the album's beginning. *Lemonade* generates a space in which the singer articulates her Southern Creole identity together with its diasporic elements, specifically its spirituality, folklore, and ways of knowing. This space has the ancestor figure at its center acting as a bridge between the past, present, and future.

Private vs. public: the space

The overall theme of Beyoncé's album deals with the singer's realization about her husband's cheating; and through its eleven phases—Intuition, Denial, Anger, Apathy, Emptiness, Accountability, Reformation, Forgiveness, Resurrection, Hope, and Redemption—it signals a possible resolution. *Lemonade*'s journey from Intuition to Redemption interchanges images of the couple's private life, the singer's subjectivity, and her public persona. Characteristic of Beyoncé's depiction of her public personality is the sense of community; *Lemonade*'s cameos of prominent black women such as Serena Williams, Winnie Harlow, Amandla Stenberg, and the French-Cuban duo Ibeyi, among others, achieves this communal space. These outstanding characters participate in *Lemonade*'s narration working as a chorus to echo and illustrate the singer's attempt to solve the ongoing conflict. Beyoncé's struggle as a public figure and as a person becomes evident in the album's juxtaposition of these two spheres and in the juxtaposition of simultaneous scenes that take place in different timelines, but appear to be happening at once. This dualism also signals the *double-consciousness* characteristic of diasporic identities, and of Beyoncé's Creoleness. Within this duality *Lemonade* highlights and celebrates femaleness embodied in the singer's family and the prominent African-descent celebrities of its chorus and the wisdom of her female ancestors. It is not until the end of the visual album—at its last stage, Redemption—that the singer explicitly evokes the ancestor by talking about a grandmother's healing powers, as well as by showing images of the celebration of Jay-Z's grandmother, Hattie's, 90th birthday. When talking about her grandmother Beyoncé states:

> Take one pint of water, add a half pound of sugar, the juice of eight lemons, the zest of half lemon. Pour the water into one, then to another several times. Strain through a clean napkin. Grandmother. The alchemist. You spun gold out of this hard life. Conjured beauty from the things left behind. Found healing where it did not live. Discovered the antidote in your own kitchen. Broke the curse with your own two hands. You past these instructions down to your daughter, who then passed them down to her daughter.

Beyoncé addresses how a grandmother incorporates healing, and the ancestral wisdom it carries, in a lemonade recipe, transforming it into a life lesson. Similarly, when talking about Jay-Z's grandmother the singer reveals that it is Hattie who, in some way, names the album. When we hear Hattie speak during her 90th-birthday celebration, she states how she has dealt with difficulties in her life, but that this colloquial expression helped her to transform her sufferings into victories: "I had my ups and downs, but I always find the inner strength to pull myself up. I was served lemons, but I made lemonade." Beyoncé's description of the grandmother figure coincides with Toni Morrison's illustration of the ancestor figure as that of an elder, or "timeless people whose relationships to the characters are benevolent, instructive, and they provide a certain kind of wisdom" (Morrison 1984, 343). It is in this connection to the ancestor's recipe that Beyoncé finds the resolution of *Lemonade*'s conflict; in hearing the voice of the ancestor's teaching, she finds the mechanisms to pull herself up and face her challenges with the assumption that "nothing real can be threatened." Given the communal nature of *Lemonade*'s narrative, is the album only celebrating Hattie's coping mechanisms, or is it celebrating/acknowledging something bigger?

Redemption resolves some of the questions that the first scene, Intuition, asks. In this first chapter the singer is lying in a bathtub in what seems to be a Southern building. This image of Beyoncé submerging herself in water is intrinsically linked to intuition, which Charles Laughlin defines as:

> a type of experience in which the answer to a question, the solution to a problem, guidance in following some goal, a creative impulse resulting in the emergence of some image, idea, or pattern springs into consciousness whole cloth - as if it were seemingly out of nowhere. (Laughlin 1997, 20)

Intuition emanates from an unspecific source, and in this way it sets the tone for the album's timing, which at the same time is reaffirmed through Warsan Shire's opening verse: "The past and present merge to meet us here. What luck. What a fucking curse." This merging of past and present not only conveys *Lemonade* as a circular chronicle, but also signals the convergence of different simultaneous scenes that take place in each chapter. Intuition is also connected to imagination since both are creative, spontaneous forces; and, as *Lemonade* shows, both are connected to memory. As Morrison clarifies:

> Because, no matter how "fictional" the account of these writers, or how much it was a product of invention, the act of imagination is bound up with memory. You know, they straightened out the Mississippi River in places, to make room for houses and livable acreage. Occasionally the river floods these places. "Floods" is the word they use, but in fact it is not flooding; it is remembering. Remembering where it used to be. All water has a perfect memory and is forever trying to get back to where it was. Writers are like that: remembering where we were, what valley we ran through, what the

banks were like, the light that was there and the route back to our original place. It is emotional memory—what the nerves and the skin remember as well as how it appeared. And a rush of imagination is our "flooding." (Morrison 1995, 98–99)

In a similar narrative strategy *Lemonade*'s Intuition initiates this relationship with the singer's past. The past points to Beyoncé's individual history, as well as to that of people of African descent on the North American continent. This liminality of time is consistent with ancestry's time frame. When speaking about the ancestor, Matthew Ikechukwu Nwafor specifies: "In Igbo ontology, often called Ndiichie or Ndibunze are those men and women who led good and exemplary lives when they were in the physical world, and are believed to continue their existence in the spiritual world" (Nwafor 2017, 37). That is, the ancestor's influence extends its time from the living sphere to the spiritual one. This figure influences cultural tradition and personal identity. Furthermore Amy Yeboah points out that *Lemonade* has a diasporic scope since:

[It] invokes so much of the Yoruba tradition, which is grounded in African tradition … but it spreads across the diaspora. So you see it in Cuba, you see it in Louisiana. It's a cultural tradition that connects women of the diaspora together. (Roberts and Downs 2016)

This cultural sharing across the diaspora is evident in how important a role the communal plays within the album's narrative and visual discourse. Morrison also identifies this collective character as something particular about black art, and links it to its oral quality:

To make the story appear oral, meandering, effortless, spoken—to have the reader *feel* the narrator, without identifying that narrator … To use even formally, a chorus. The real presence of a chorus. Meaning the community or the reader at large, commenting on the action as it goes ahead. (Morrison 1984, 341)

Lemonade's inclusion of prominent African-descended women who participate in the visual album seems to incorporate this choral ensemble. A group activity that calls for a shared tradition whose preservation has been possible given the presence of the ancestor as well because it is this relationship with the forebear that determines individual success or failure (Morrison 1984, 343).

The way in which *Lemonade* includes the chorus and Beyoncé's female heritage enhances both the oral and visual aspects that Morrison talks about. It also signals how Beyoncé's addresses her healing to the connection with the ancestor. In bringing a chorus to her album the singer exposes her victory to them, thus celebrating their shared diasporic tradition. As Zandria F. Robinson points out:

The video album writes black women back into national, regional and dia-sporic histories by making them the progenitors and rightful inheritors of the Southern gothic tradition. Beyond "strong" and "magic," *Lemonade* asserts that black women are alchemists and metaphysicians who are at once of the past, present and future, changing and healing the physical, chemical and spiritual world around them. (Robinson 2016)

Robinson's statement echoes Beyoncé's description of her grandmother as an alchemist and coincides with Morrison's depiction of the ancestor. This antecedent is the root of identity and community for people of African descent.

Another important connection between the first and last stages of *Lemonade* is the inclusion of a stage in each of these episodes. *Lemonade* starts with Beyoncé seated on a theater stage with no audience, and in the last scene she appears on the stage singing to all the participants in the video and says, "The audience applauds but we cannot hear them." Such a statement connects the journey to a private and public performance, to the two life spheres that Morrison talks about. It is also a personal reaffirmation about not needing anyone's approval, and a proclamation of how her ancestry has been the driving conductor of such progression.

New Orleans: the city of the ancestor

In a similar way to the metaphor created by the platform in Intuition and Redemption, in which the stage symbolizes Beyoncé's public persona, New Orleans is the setting that frames *Lemonade*'s journey from Intuition to Redemption. The city's landscape works as a narrative and mnemonic device. In Joseph Roach's words: "to walk is also to gain experience of the cityscape that is con-ducive to mapping the emphases and contradictions of its special memories." New Orleans is a city, according to Roach, where life is "like living on the edge of the world, between cultures, between languages, and between races" (Roach 1996, 13, 180). This life in between, a life on the frontier, is representative of the diasporic experience, as well as of its spirituality. It generates a space where past and present converge, where history is made present. The synchronicity of past and present is consistent with Shire's statement about their encounter in Intuition and the employment of New Orleans's landscape as the album's setting becomes its meta-phor. As LaKisha Michelle Simmons explains:

But the landscapes are unambiguously part of the geography of Louisiana; the visual album is haunting because of its specificity to place. Barely visible, in the discussion thus far, is the history of slavery—and its remnants—all over the landscape of the album. Beyoncé's representation of madness, jealousy, anger, and hurt are intertwined with the madness and pain inherited from our ante-bellum past. (Simmons, 2016)

Moreover, the specificity of landscape generates an incursion of past history in Beyoncé's present signaling how scenery also enacts the ancestor's presence, and how it activates the singer's *rememory*. This exercise is explained as follows by Sethe's character in *Beloved*:

> I used to think to it was my rememory. You know. Some things you forget. Other things you never do. But it's not. Places, places are still there. If a house burns down, it's gone, but the place—the picture of it—stays, and not just in my rememory, but out there, in the world. What I remember is a picture floating around out there outside my head. I mean, even if I don't think it, even if I die, the picture of what I did, or knew, or saw is still out there. Right in the place where it happened. (Morrison 1997, 36–37)

This pointing out of a particular site as the embodiment of trauma calls for memories that are orally and genetically transmitted. Places that played an important role during a historical time are capable of narrating stories even if they are not occupied because in remembering the history of a community, of its forebears, some of their memories become one's own—as Sethe continues to explain when Denver questions whether or not other people can see that picture:

> Oh yes, yes, yes, yes. Someday you be walking down the road and you hear something or see something going on. So clear, And you think it's you thinking it up. A thought picture. But no. It's when you bump into a rememory that belongs to somebody else. Where I was before I came here, that place is real. It's never going away … So, Denver, you can't never go there. Never. Because even though it's all over- over and done with- it's going to always be there waiting for you. (Morrison 1997, 37)

Intuition, *Lemonade*'s first stage, opens up the space for rememory by recalling how slavery marks the history of the African diaspora in the Americas; and in the second episode, Denial, the album evokes its origins in the African continent. It opens up with Beyoncé falling from a window into a body of water and immersing herself in it. The singer seems to become a mermaid. The mermaid is a powerful symbol in African spirituality since it represents Oshun, the orisha that rules sweet or fresh waters and embodies sensuality, love, sexual attraction, and flirtation. Despite her sweetness, Oshun has also a malevolent and tempestuous temper. After her immersion, Beyoncé, dressed in yellow (Oshun's color), opens a door resembling what Amy Yeboah perceives as "images of stonewall tunnels allude to the dungeons of Elmina in Ghana … the last place many African people were brought to before being brought to the Americas" (Roberts and Downs 2016). It seems that Denial acts as a bridge, thematically as the singer's first reaction after her intuition and spatially because it appears to connect Beyoncé's present moment to the diaspora's spatial origins, the dungeons in Africa and to the female spirit that travelled with the ancestors to the Americas. The presence of water in this scene reinforces this connection, since the liquid element represents a literal or symbolic return to the Atlantic Ocean waters which are part of the ancestral past and collective memory (Wardi 2011, 6–8). The presence of water from Intuition's bathtub to Denial's ocean frames this mnemonic continuum and points out both to the Atlantic journey from Africa to the Americas, as well as from Beyoncé's unconscious which *Lemonade* visualizes.

In the following chapter, Anger, Malcolm X's voice becomes that of the ancestor, as he proclaims at the beginning of this chapter: "The most disrespected woman in America is the black woman. The most unprotected person in America is the black woman. The most neglected person in America is the black woman" (Malcolm X 1962). His statement contextualizes anger within the specificity of a history of abuse that reverberates in present day. It also enacts the oral quality of ancestry and diasporic art that Morrison identifies as essential. Consequently, Malcolm X's voice participates in *Lemonade*'s choral ensemble. Folkloric figures also permeate this episode's symbolism contributing to its message.

Concretely when Beyoncé appears disguised metaphorically as what Kinitra D. Brooks identifies as a Boo Hang or Soucouyant. Both are folkloric characters from the Gullah and Caribbean culture, respectively, who are known for shedding their own skin (*soucouyant*) or wearing the skin of another (Boo Hag) (Jackson 2016). Both characters are female and considered evil. Zora Neale Hurston describes this character as follows:

> There was a witch woman wid a saddle-cat who could git out her skin and go ride people she didn't like. She had a great big looking-glass. When she git ready to go oout she'd git befo dat glass naked. … Then she shake herself and she'd say: "Gee whiz! Slip 'em and slip 'em agin!" And de old skin would slip off and she'd git out on her and she'd look back and say "umph! I forgot sumthin." And she'd go back to her keyhole and she blow and say "Open door, lemme come in again." And she'd go back and spread de old skin out at the fire place and tell de skin, "So remember who you are." (Hurston 1990, 63)

FIGURE 9.1 Video still "Don't Hurt Yourself." *Lemonade*, Parkwood Entertainment, 2016

The way in which this folk creature tells the old skin to remember its identity replicates the title of the song that frames Anger, "Don't Hurt Yourself," and represents the importance that history and tradition have for the development of personal identity. Furthermore, in not hurting herself the singer accepts and reconciles the sides in her identity—the skin that the *socouyant* sheds—that were in conflict, and integrates them through her cultural tradition inherent in the ancestor's wisdom.

Beyoncé's knowledge in this regard is the overall theme of *Lemonade*'s next chapter, Apathy, which combines images of a modern bus trip and a plantation. Beyoncé participates in both scenes as if she was wearing two different skins, which she merges. In the bus trip Beyoncé and some of her dancers dance together wearing Ori face painting, which Yeboah identifies as a Yoruba tradition: "This idea of inscribing who you are on your face and your body is seen throughout the diaspora" (Roberts and Downs 2016). Ori visualizes personal history by marking ethnographic origins. The central settings of the second plane are Destrehan Plantation, which provides the exterior images, and Madewood Plantation, where the interior pictures were shot. Both locations in Louisiana constitute important memory frameworks, as Simmons explains:

> At Destrehan, an army of plantation owners and white elites confronted the black rebel army. The plantation elites won the battle and captured the men responsible for the uprising. As punishment, and as a reminder to the enslaved to fear white power, they executed those responsible and cut off their heads. The plantation owners placed the severed heads of the revolutionaries on poles and lined them up for 40 miles along the river to New Orleans. (Simmons 2016)

The overlapping of the ethnographically marked bus journey with the plantation's historical role contextualizes in a modern time frame the trip from the African homeland to the Americas. Such timing is also expressed through Beyoncé's performance of a historically impossible role for her within the plantation. It is in this scene where Beyoncé and Serena Williams dance and twerk, thus appropriating a space historically denied to them and charged with the pain and abuse of the enslaved African-descent population. They perform a modern type of dance that originated in New Orleans, and which, linked to the African diaspora, appropriates and modernizes, culturally, such a setting. Additionally, Beyoncé and Serena's performance challenges the geographical implications of this site because, as Katherine McKittrick clarifies, "black women, unprotected—it is in the material landscape, at work, in the home, and within the community, where the body is rightfully retranslated as inferior, captive and accessible to violence" (McKittrick 2015, 82).

Beyoncé and Serena's inscription of their bodies through dance within this confined space proves that black women's bodies no longer occupy a marginal space. They centralize the history of abuses to talk about their experiences and defy traditional notions of place: providing a new use for it, rather than seeing it as a place of pain, Beyoncé and Serena reclaim it as a performative site. As Simmons signals:

For Beyoncé's *Lemonade*, the dance in this space is an act of defiance, of claiming self and freedom. Beyoncé's throne is an impossible black place. Beyoncé Knowles-Carter's and Serena Williams's bodily freedom does not belong here, yet they have claimed it for themselves. (Simmons 2016)

The singer's self-reclamation acknowledges Nwafor's interpretation of Senghor and Rohio's definition of culturally returning to one's origins, as the writer states, "Then the word 'return' which is far from a mere homecoming to a perceptual space means 'a deconstructive term which symbolizes many aspects of the struggle of the peoples of African origin to control their own identity'" (Nwafor 2017, 36). This idea of controlling one's identity is evident in Apathy and the singer's reclamation of an impossible space, one that rejects external assumptions, stereotypes, and judgment to close the circle by proclaiming the authenticity of her own self—not only by remembering who she is (like the Soucouyant tells the old skin), but by reaffirming such knowledge. The space that Beyoncé creates in Apathy and through *Lemonade* is not only a space for rememory, but also one of reaffirmation. It is the space where the public and the private spheres converge according to her own terms.

Emptiness, which follows Apathy, is a chapter in which the theme of body performance is also central. In it Beyoncé sings about a woman described thus: "Six-inch heels, she walked in the club like nobody's business, Goddamn, she murdered everybody and I was her witness" as well as "She works for the money." Beyoncé praises women's effort to be independent economically. From Emptiness, *Lemonade* takes us to Accountability, where she talks about her father and family history, thus reintroducing family heritage into the conversation:

Mother dearest let me inherit the Earth. Teach me how to make him beg. Let me make up for the years he made you wait. Did he bend your reflection? Did he make you forget your own name? Did he convince you he was a god? Did you get on your knees daily? Do his eyes close like doors? Are you a slave to the back of his hand? Am I talking about your husband or your father?

Beyoncé addresses her family history and questions her mother about her relationship with her husband, Beyoncé's father. The singer ponders how her close family history influences her own. In this way she continues to establish a dialogue between past and present to identify the root causes of her current marital problem.

In Reformation's "Love Drought" the signer addresses self-love and resolving her doubts. This episode's main setting, a football field, overlaps with that of Beyoncé's unity with other women in the water, an image also used in Anger, but here with color. The intersection between both sites plays again with the idea of public (a football stadium) and private (the water, symbol of memory) spaces. Forgiveness follows Reformation and extends the conversation of female unity as a spiritual and essential relationship because it addresses healing and how healing is a rebirth. Warsan Shire's poem in this episode deals with ancestry:

Baptize me … now that reconciliation is possible. If we're gonna heal, let it be glorious. 1,000 girls raise their arms. Do you remember being born? Are you thankful for the hips that cracked? The deep velvet of your mother and her mother and her mother? There is a curse that will be broken.

Healing implies breaking a curse, one that can only be broken through a connection with womanhood as transmitted from mother to daughter, through ancestry. Once that cycle is untangled, a new start follows.

Resurrection starts with a voice that is not that of Beyoncé, but questions "how do we lead our kids to the future?" Different images emerge in this segment: at the beginning, women are walking around the slave cabins dressed in brilliant colors, contrasting the black and white images of the beginning. The images move from the slave cabins to a plantation mansion where the mothers of recently murdered African American young men hold their pictures. As Janell Hobson points out, such unity is representative of *Lemonade*'s communal dialogue and a celebration of ancestry:

The basis for the album is the story of a woman reeling from an unfaithful partner and traveling through the different emotions: denial, anger, apathy, emptiness, forgiveness, hope. But when this most personal narrative is situated in the larger context of other black women, including the mothers of slain sons Trayvon Martin, Michael Brown and Eric Garner, who also make an appearance, as well as our more distant ancestors whose memories we hold dear, *Lemonade* is the feminist proclamation that "the personal is political" and that "black lives matter." (Hobson 2017)

This inclusion of the political is repeated in *Lemonade*'s last episode, its first released single, Formation. In this segment, the singer includes her daughter Blue Ivy in the song and video narrative—signaling how having future descendants implies that one day Beyoncé will embody the ancestor role sharing ancestral wisdom.

Formation: performing the ancestor

Joseph Roach points out in *Cities of the Dead* (1996, 3) that "a performance offers a substitute for something else that preexists it" and that such replacement indicates that performance replays and actualizes history and memory. Beyoncé has performed two times at the Super Bowl, and both of them in New Orleans. Such coincidence has not been random because both occasions have coincided with the singer's praise of what lies at the base of her artistic endeavors. During her first performance in 2013, Beyoncé described herself as a feminist, and in the most recent one, February 2016, she performed "Formation" for the first time and gave a statement about self-love, the love for her identity as a black woman. Beyoncé's performance at this last spectacle was also charged with political implications. Her dancers were dressed as members of the Black Panther Party, during the 50th anniversary of the organization, and Beyoncé herself paid homage to Michael Jackson when she appeared dressed in "Jacksonish" attire. The dancers also formed, while dancing, an X, in reference to Malcolm X. Through this public performance Beyoncé paid tribute to the artistic tradition that inspired her, and exemplifies what Roach defines as "counter memory" in the genealogies of performance; that is, through her visual album and Super Bowl performance Beyoncé made visible "the disparities between history as it is discursively transmitted and memories as it is publicly enacted by the bodies that bear its consequences" (Roach 1996, 26).

Similarly, her employment of a public space, the football stadium, replicates the stage setting that appears in Intuition. This setting opens up Beyoncé's public and private narrative and signals the political as its artistic manifestation. As Morrison states: "It seems to me that the best art is political and you ought to be able to make it unquestionably political and irrevocably beautiful at the same time" (Morrison 1984, 345). The political is Morrison's answer to the conflict, the crack, between the public and private life. This individual and communal struggle can only be culturally and artistically sustained with the presence of the ancestor. This timeless figure roots one's identity while providing freedom to transform spaces of oppression into creative realms, as *Lemonade* has proven. Such transformation generates a space where the past orally transmits to the present its wisdom while the future impatiently awaits.

If you cut your chains you free yourself. If you cut your roots, you die.

(African proverb)

Bibliography

Beyoncé. 2016. *Lemonade*, Parkwood Entertainment.

Griffin, Farah J. 1995. *"Who Set You Flowin'?": The African-American Migration Narrative*. New York: Oxford University Press.

Hobson, Janell. "Lemonade: Beyoncé's Redemption Song." *Ms. Magazine Blog*. August 02, 2017. Accessed February 07, 2018.

Hurston, Zora Neale. 1990. *Mules and Men*. New York: Harper & Row.

Jackson, Panama. "An Interview with Dr. Kinitra Brooks, Who Teaches a Class on Beyoncé." *Very Smart Brothas*. October 14, 2016. Accessed February 19, 2018. https://verysmartbrothas.theroot.com/an-interview-with-dr-kinitra-brooks-who-teaches-a-cla-1822521935.

Laughlin, Charles. 1997. "The Nature of Intuition: A Neuropsychological Approach." In *In Intuition: The Inside Story: Interdisciplinary Perspectives*. Ed. Robbie E. Davis-Floyd and P. Sven Arvidson, 19–39. New York: Routledge.

Malcolm X. 1962. "Who Taught to Hate Yourself?" Accessed August 7, 2018: https://www.youtube.com/watch?v=xaXPhR7aWvo.

McKittrick, Katherine. 2006. *Demonic Grounds: Black Women and the Cartographies of Struggle*. Minneapolis: University of Minnesota Press.

Morrison, Toni. 1984. "Rootedness: The Ancestor as Foundation." In *Black Women Writers (1950–1980): A Critical Evaluation*. Ed. Mary Evans, 339–354. New York: Doubleday.

Morrison, Toni. 1997. *Beloved*. London: Random House.

Morrison, Toni. 1995. "The Site of Memory." In *Inventing the Truth*. Ed. William Zinsser, 84–102. New York:Houghton Mifflin.

Nwafor, Matthew Ikechukwu. "The Living-Dead (Ancestors) among the Igbo-African People: An Interpretation of Catholic Sainthood." *International Journal of Sociology and Anthropology* 9, no. 4(2017): 35–42. doi:10.5897/ijsa2017.0719.

Roach, Joseph. 1996. *Cities of the Dead: Circum-Atlantic Performance*. New York: Columbia University Press.

Roberts, Kamaria, and Kenya Downs. "What Beyoncé Teaches Us about the African Diaspora in 'Lemonade'." PBS. April 29, 2016. Accessed October 08, 2018. https://www.pbs.org/newshour/arts/what-beyonce-teaches-us-about-the-african-diaspora-in-lemonade.

Robinson, Zandria F. "How Beyoncé's 'Lemonade' Exposes Inner Lives of Black Women." *Rolling Stone*. April 28, 2016. Accessed February 07, 2018. https://www.rollingstone.com/music/news/how-beyonces-lemonade-exposes-inner-lives-of-black-women-20160428.

Simmons, LaKisha Michelle. 2015. *Crescent City Girls: The Lives of Young Black Women in Segregated New Orleans*. Chapel Hill: University of North Carolina Press.

Simmons, LaKisha Michelle. "Landscapes and History in Beyoncé's Lemonade." *UNC Press Blog*. May 25, 2016. Accessed February 07, 2018. https://uncpressblog.com/2016/04/28/lakisha-simmons-beyonces-lemonade/.

Wardi, Anissa Janine. 2011. *Water and African American Memory: An Ecocritical Perspective*. Gainesville: University Press of Florida.

10

SIGNIFYING WATERS

The magnetic and poetic magic of Oshún as reflected in Beyoncé's *Lemonade*

Martin A. Tsang

I experienced Beyoncé's *Lemonade* with awe, and within it I connected the powerful spoken and visual poetry of the album as resonating deeply with the Yorùbá-diasporic deity, or orisha, Oshún, and her characteristics as a strong, black female symbol of survival and regeneration. In this piece, I connect characteristics of Oshún (Figure 10.1)—in particular the multiplicity of her eponymous river and refractive, moving waters—with the many knowable characteristics of this Yorùbá goddess, and use these facets to draw attention to the parallels and synchronicity of the imagery and symbolism crafted in the visual album. Further, I seek to read *Lemonade* in terms of the orisha religious devices used across the Atlantic: *itán* and *oríkì*. Engaging and performing *itán*, special and vital orisha tales, gives these stories efficacy through vocalization. The tradition of orature, or praise poetry called *oríkì*, strives, through deeply poetic words, to flatter and eulogize the essence of a person as practiced in orisha worship across the globe. In *Lemonade*, we witness the weaving of a sort of visual *itán* or tale(s) composed with the orated *oríkì*, together creating a spiritually laden journey of survival and victory—two repeating characteristics in the *itán* and *oríkì* of the orisha Oshún.[1] Here, I explore Oshún and her waters and how they are possibly reflected in Beyoncé's masterpiece, demonstrating how an Afro-Atlantic religion, its goddess, praises, and tales are central tenets, with its deities making appearances in the mainstream through the inspired work of artists, in new and imaginative ways.

Oshún, goddess of the living, moving waters

Resplendent mother of rivers and humanity, whose sweetness and elegance belies her strength and tenacity. Oshún's *itán* (legends) speak of the hardships, sacrifices, and tribulations she has had to endure in order to survive. Oshún instills and insists in us courage, understanding, and strength; she is the light and success that comes

FIGURE 10.1 Painting of Oshún incorporating many of her symbols and flowing water. Titled *Iyalode Oxum* (2018), by André Hora. With permission of the artist

through perseverance. Shining with true beauty and majesty, she reminds us that we have a duty to be filled with honor and good character in order to be worthy of the crown, and not think that a crown bestows these virtues. Oshún is a multifaceted goddess; her complexity and sagacity are too often ignored for popular yet erroneous representations that arise out of repeating superficial and erroneous characteristics, mostly by non-practitioners. Oshún, like the experiences of many women, has been charged with being coquettish, flirty, and playful, which serve to give a thin description of the serious and sacred manifestations of the orisha. In turn, Oshún's worshippers are characterized as valorizing shallow traits which could not be further from her ritual and liturgical vernaculars.

This chapter takes a deeper look at Oshún, the transatlantic goddess of survival and elegance, and how Beyoncé and *Lemonade* can be read in terms of nuanced ideas of Oshún's sumptuous symbolism, her adroit bravery, and reflections on the need to connect these seemingly inchoate dots. In recent years, Yorùbá-derived culture has become ever more pronounced, globally. These tributes, affiliations, and artistic expressions have come to us from a myriad of sources that were created by a mesmerizing history of interconnectedness, communication, and empowerment.

When we feel pain, be it of emotional, physical, or spiritual origin, we might clutch our chest while choking tears or feeling the prickly, flushing sensations of the skin and exclaim, "Oh god, my heart!"; but we should really be exclaiming, "Oh goddess, my heart!" for it is Iyalode Oshún that powers the beat. According to Diedre Badejo, Oshún is "the giver of children, wealth, and power to women; she is the leader of the Aje (powerful beings), a ruler, and protectress of Òsogbo township" (Badejo 1996, 73). Badejo cites Filomena Steady in casting Oshún as the original feminist, and I would add strong role model and protector for women. Many of the characteristics of Oshún found in Nigeria follow the same theme of Oshún worship in Cuba and Brazil, where she is considered an expert diviner, and the first *iyalorisha,* or initiatory priestess, the deity in charge of ratifying the initiation process for orisha priests. In remembrance of this, all initiates—no matter into which orisha priesthood they will individually be initiated—must first visit the river and pay their respects and their debt to Oshún as architect of the religion.

Oshún is the orisha of fresh, or sweet, running water, delineating her from Yemayá, who is deemed the original owner of all forms and sources of water and often shorthanded as owner of vast expanses such as the sea. This tells part of the story of Oshún as she is indeed the owner of sweet waters, but also all that it entails. Rivers are the lifeblood of civilization, allowing for sustenance in terms of potable water, food, and the development of agriculture. Cities around the world have prospered on the banks of famous rivers, waterways that allow for commerce and communication, people, things, and ideas in constant movement. Indeed, Oshún owns the veins and arteries of the body, that is our life support system. The *odu* Oshe meji, one of the paramount *odu* associated with Oshún, speaks specifically about the "blood that runs through our veins," and thus we see that Oshún is essential not only to living together, but also to each of our lives. She can warn when something is not right through *odu,* when blood-borne illnesses and conditions may be present, and she is the one who can create healing possibilities and perform miracles. Beyoncé's *Lemonade* thus creates in a visually arresting manner the importance of flowing water, particularly the need to cleanse and flush out all that is blocking our paths, the ferocity by which flowing water can change a life, or even take it.

Although Yemayá is considered the owner of all waters, and each female orisha has her particular river, Oshún is considered *the* river goddess, par excellence. She is praised as Iyalode, the mother of the outdoors, senior market titleholder; and cries of *Ore Yeye O* ("Oh, Gracious Mother") accompany her worship. Afolabi Kayode tells us that Oshogbo, the name of the river, is another praise epithet or *oríkì* for Oshún, which is connector of Yorùbá Oyo and Ijesha kingdoms. Kayode notes that the River Ọ̀ṣun in Nigeria is the physical manifestation of Oshún, which moves from the area known as Igede Ekiti and flows through Ilesha or Oshún territory, and in doing so, "meanders through the thick forest and encircles the present-day Oshogbo" (Kayode 2006, 143). The river flows to the Atlantic Ocean, where it mingles with the waters of other orisha. Thus, the Oshogbo River is a constantly dynamic, replenishing expression of the power and multiplicity of Oshún, making moving water a testament to the many obstacles, twists, and turns that life and destiny bring to worshipers. Susanne Wenger, the Austrian-Jewish artist and initiate of Obatalá responsible for saving Oshún's sacred grove in Nigeria, sums up Oshún's importance and universality as:

> the goddess of the living waters is, as it seems, indispensable, not only to all Yorùbá cults but also to most religions of the world, including Christianity and Islam. The holy water in the church font, Islamic ablutions, the Hindu ritual bath are only some examples. According to Yorùbá tradition, the authority of the gods in Heaven broke down but was restored when they admitted Oshún into the council. (Wenger and Chesi 1983, 115)

Water and fire: music and motion

The tale of Oshún overcoming Ina, who in this tale is fire personified, affords us a view of Oshún and the ways that *itán* or tales are more than fables, but are truly revelations of the spirit and spiritual revelations that resonate in contemporary sonic and visual work, like *Lemonade*. An important Afro-Cuban tale tells us that one day, like most days, Oshún was sitting by the river in a rocking chair embroidering and humming to herself, peacefully creating knowing that her domain was in good order and without incidence. She had been warned, though, by Orunmila and Eleguá that the *odu* Ejila Shebora, which is one of the chapters of the orisha divination system, spoke of an immense fire that was on its way to her realm. This intentional fire was ignited and fueled by the negativity of the world. Every time a person was hurt, wronged, shunned, or embarrassed the force of those events big and small left like smoke from where they happened and coalesced, like tumbleweed, and grew in momentum, becoming its own entity with a fury and will to destroy everything in its path. This ferocious, disconsolate, destructive fire went from town to town consuming everything in its way and growing stronger with every soul it took and incandescent with indignant rage until he had reached Oshún's empire.

Spotting Oshún, from the other bank of the river, fire rose and extended to his full height, roaring at Oshún to rouse her attention and with the purpose to intimidate and take her life. Oshún paused, her hand holding the gold crochet hook gently rested on her lap, and without looking up, smiled and said in a level voice, "Ah, hello, *Ina* [Fire], I guess you have come to finish me off?" The stoic serenity of Oshún's response brought out every ounce of vehemence in Ina, which was like adding pure oxygen to a flame, the crescendo of heat, smoke, and violence in the form of an immense blazing wall. "Yesss," he hissed, "I will be taking your life and your kingdom, you will be no more," spitting sparks with rage. "I see, well if it is to be, and now is my time, I won't resist. I can't run, you are too fast and clever for me, I can't reason with you because this is what you are here to do. So, please, come forward." With that, Fire in his flagrant zeal to destroy such sweetness and resolve, rushed to Oshún from the bank and into the river. Ina didn't know that the antidote to his wrath and destruction was pure, sweet water and within a matter of moments, he was extinguished and gone for good. Oshún went back to humming her tune and continued with her embroidery. Indeed, we see fire interspersed throughout *Lemonade*, in explosions and in one scene, surrounding Beyoncé on three sides as well as burning down the mansion in the background. Beyoncé as present and counterfoil to the destructive energy communicates that which no longer serves is gone, leaving space for regenerative renewal, standing in power and transformation.

When Oshún employs her waters, it is without mercy or forgiveness. Beyoncé's *Lemonade,* especially in "Intuition/Hold Up," uses the imagery of water flowing, covering, drenching as a symbol of dousing the fire as enemy, and the feelings of hurt, pain, and suffering. As orisha priests who actively worship Oshún and many other deities or orisha, we are intimately aware of the nuances in her symbolism. How deep is the water? It is deeper than you can ever quantify or vocalize; it has a spiritual profundity that we are reminded of by every libation paid in honor of God, the ancestors, and the divine. Water is indispensable in the worship and veneration of the orishas, and Oshún's gift to humanity is the ability to enlist water in removing our enemies, be they human, deleterious feelings, or self-doubt. She is the nurturing mother who survived life's hardships; and for this, Beyoncé's work resonates with this strong female energy, created consciously or not with reference to Oshún.

As an orisha worshipper and someone who has the deepest love and respect for Oshún, it saddens me profoundly that people focus on the superficiality of Oshún, that she is popularly defined as coquettish and flirtatious. These descriptors are things too often seen as the domain of *la mulata*—the mixed-race, light-skinned black woman in Cuban popular culture who is depicted in art as devastatingly beautiful and a temptress to men, even though she is the very figment of male desire and the two-dimensional conjuration of sexuality. It is easy to see how Oshún was glossed as the tragic, mixed-race temptress given that she governs love, sensuality, music, beauty, and elegance; however, she is much more. Oshún is a warrior orisha who is a ferociously protective mother to all of her adherents; but she is also one of the most difficult orishas to please as she expects nothing but the very best for and from her devotees. The skin-deep and casual connections to female beauty that Oshún has become known for, especially by non-practitioners, are not peculiar to any one geography. Light-skinned connotations of Oshún are popular in Cuba and Brazil, two countries where her worship is well known even outside of religious circles, and there are traces of it in Nigeria. Ulli Beier, on writing about the restoration of the Oshún grove in Oshogbo, Nigeria, notes that Oshún is an old orisha, as she was present long before the official founding of the relatively young town that she had protected from invasion. Beier states that although she has been around for a very long time, "ambivalently, Oshún is both seen as a young woman, the velvet-skinned concubine and as the ancient woman, steeped in magic. She is the concubine. Desirable and seductive - because her life-giving force must be accessible to all" (Beier 1975, 36). Both Oshún's character and Beyoncé's work can be read in multiple ways, some being surface deep and in other ways that bring to the fore conundrums and ambivalence.

Itán and oríkì Oshún: stories and orature

There are many distinct *ibú*, streams or riverways, whose distinctive characteristics are related through important fables or *itán*. While each is Oshún, collectively these variations in Oshún's energy are further prismatic aspects of the divine, refracted *ashé* or life-giving and sustaining divine energy that can be encountered and experienced in culturally specific terms. In the Afro-Cuban worship of the orishas called Lukumí, as in many other global expressions of Oshún worship, the *ibú* or tributaries are the ways of knowing Oshún. Below are some of the most well-known Lukumí *ibú* with brief descriptions of their important traits.

Ibú kole	The vulture and sorceress who saved mankind by reaching Olodumare, the distant omnipotent God to tell of a time of severe drought.
Ibú Ololodí	The wife of Orunmila, deity of wisdom and divination.
Ibú Akuaro	The Oshún who transforms herself with quail feathers and hunts with the orisha Oshosí.
Ibú Yumú	An ancient Oshún, who is the original owner of brass and governs the Aje, collective ancestral female power.
Ibú Anyá	The queen of the sacred Anya drums and the dance, consort of Shangó.
Ibú Doko	The wife of the orisha of fertilization and agriculture, Orisha Oko. It is through Ibú Doko's messenger, the bee, that pollination can occur and we are given the gift of honey.
Ibú Ipondá	A warrior Oshún who, with Erinle (hunter deity of the river as father), gave birth to Lógun Ede, the princely orisha of wealth.

For the Yorùbá in West Africa, Pierre Verger tells us that *ibú* are particular parts of the Ọ̀ṣun River that flows through Oshún's sacred grove in Oshogbo. These distinct locations are deep water eddies that are each home to an aspect of Oshún. We find some names here—such as *Ọ̀ṣun Ijùmú*, the queen of all the Oshúns, and *Ọ̀ṣun Àpara*, the youngest of the all the manifestations—that are shared with Oshún in both Cuba and Brazil (Verger 1982, 172–3). Beier notes that the flowing Ọ̀ṣun River in Oshogbo is the perfect symbol for Oshún's countenance:

usually very smooth and calm, it flows so gently that the movement of the waters is almost imperceptible in certain places. Then, only half a mile downstream, it gets noisily entangled in numerous outcrops of rock and shows the orisha's wild dominating face. (Beier 1975, 36)

Consequently, in times when life is good and sweet, the water moves smoothly and serenely; when there are obstacles in the way, water meets them with vim and energy to dominate and continue with forward momentum. In *Lemonade,* perhaps the most arresting visual element of the piece is the opening of the doors and flooding of the water. Here, Beyoncé is transformed into the power of *ibú*, overcoming impediments in the water's path as its untrammeled energy is released. Beier goes on to give us further understanding of *ibú* and the connectivity to the land:

There used to be some forty sacred sites of worship, where the water spins in dangerous and deceptive whirlpools. In these places (*ibú*) the water delves down into the soil, is in touch with potent and ancient rocks and minerals, and such close union with the earth gives it special magical force. (Beier 1975, 36)

Oshún is all of these aspects, these energies, and these experiences; and where flowing and whirling water is found, so too is Oshún present.

Thus, Oshún "represents the sacred dimension of water" (of which we almost exclusively consist) and her kinetic essence and power are akin to "the mandala of water's eternal movement, which proceeds and never returns" (Wenger and Chesi 1983, 115). We turn to *oríkì* to grasp some of Oshún's character, and her *itán* help narrate the important lessons in survival, strength, and pride. Similarly, the *oríkì* that are composed and intoned in *Lemonade* are accompanied by contemporary renderings of *itán* in visual form. *Oríkì* is a thoroughly Yorùbá concept that inflects many performances and practices across the Atlantic and the Americas. It can be roughly defined as poetry intoned for the purpose of defining and flattering, traditionally the orisha which helps delineate the prowess and power of a deity by devotees at important occasions and in crucial moments of ceremony and worship. Individuals, including and especially their names, form personal *oríkì* that delve into lineage, significant events, and feats and achievements. It is praise poetry that can be recited and, like a biography, grows with time to express greater understanding of the deity or person and highlight their prestige. The function of *oríkì* is to express the essence or inner nature of the person or deity being eulogized; the phrases and words go deep and bring out to the audience all that makes him or her incomparably unique. *Oríkì* are cumulative and communal. As Karin Barber explains, "[*oríkì*] are composed by different people, on different occasions, and with reference to different experiences. Any subject's corpus of *oríkì* are therefore composed of a number of autonomous items" (Barber 1990, 315). Thus, epithets for any entity can be overlapping and are not to be deemed a singular holistic narrative. Crucially, Barber notes from her experience conducting fieldwork in Nigeria that the *oríkì* tradition is under the aegis of women—both in their performance and composition. *Oríkì* also have a direct relationship with *itán* wherein *oríkì* (praises) are the main form of oration for the orisha, and that they are bolstered by *itán*, the accompanying narratives or fables, rather than the other way around. In applying these terms and relationship to *Lemonade* we can understand that it is a composition of orature—*oríkì* elements that praise and define—and visual and deeply symbolic narratives that support the essence-making project. By framing *Lemonade* in such a way, the sometimes continuous, sometimes different parts of the visual album are congruous with the nature of composing *oríkì*, which is an expert art in the purview of women. Judith Gleason delves poetically into Oshún's pools and banks along her river in Oshogbo:

> A walk along her varied edges ... describes some of the richness of her personality. For example, the meditative visitor may come upon a quiet pool overhung with branches whose varied twig and leaf patters, intricate as crinkled lines on the palm of a deeply experienced person, make the whole seem like the reflection of an adiré [prized, patterned indigo] cloth in the pool below. Such pools enclose the gaze so that again and again the eye is compelled to look down into the dark water, immobile save for here and there at the brim of the cup a slender ripple around a stalk of tilted grass. (Gleason 1971, 93)

Of the above list of Oshún aspects, Oshún Ibú Anyá is perhaps the closest corollary to what we witness in Beyoncé in *Lemonade*: Oshún whose path is governess of the Anya drum is the Oshún that brings the joy, knowledge, and power of music and dance to humanity and lifting our collective souls. Percussion, as well as call and response singing, is essential for communication between the realms of living, the orishas, ancestors, and God. Oshún is the pulse of life; our hearts pound out the rhythm of our lived reality, and she fires passion and energy with every step. Who hasn't felt the hammering of the heart in times of love or excitement? Or the soothing beat of the heart that begins in the womb and ends with the last breath that we will each eventually take? In all of our moments in life, we are accompanied and guided by the heart, and its rhythm measures the pace of time and echoes the meaning we give to our place in the world. Oshún's signifying waters, her tributaries and meanderings, are what Diedre L. Badejo terms these and more "pathways" that form "ways of knowing Ọ̀ṣun through the metonymic system of her orature, rituals, iconography, and fine and performing arts" (Badejo 2008, 191) which are precisely expressed in *Lemonade*.

Marysol Quevedo's work on the ability of touring Cuban symphonic music to cross borders and effect change in politics from the Cold War period to the present day notes the powerful and layered effect of Beyoncé's visit to Cuba and *Lemonade*'s religious iconography. In 2012, Quevedo notes, the Cuban Symphonic Orchestra toured the US with relatively little fanfare and media attention.

However, in comparison, Beyoncé and Jay-Z's visit to the island in April 2013 was highly publicized, and covered by major press outlets in both the US and Cuba. The mass dissemination of *Lemonade* and the global visibility of its creator allow for it to act as a more powerful and effective tool to promote cultural understanding and cooperation than any attempts (by government organizations or cultural institutions) to foster mutual understanding through classical music (Quevedo 2018, 8).

Rachel Elizabeth Harding's reflection on the presence and meaning of Oshún in the lives of six African American women brings together many of the elements discussed here in terms of the goddess's wondrous form and countenance as expressed through water, art, and narratives, and Beyoncé's iconic visual and musical performance and direction that continue the legacy of Afro-Atlantic ways of knowing and being. For Harding and the women she interviewed, Oshún has particular relevance to North American and female spiritual power that simultaneously reinforces Oshún's reign from Nigeria and the Americas and creates new ideas and avenues for her expression in these new spaces in relevant ways, as an evolution and continuation of Oshún's power and gifts. Harding reports that Oshún may manifest in different ways and through different cultural means in North America, making it more inclusive, as Oshún devotee Osunguunwa spoke:

> In the city, going to the river, to the Hudson to talk to Her is a little different. I was initiated upstate, in the ricer ... It was so special. So beautiful. I associate Her with nature, nature in the upstate-cold of New York ... I see Her on the city's streets as the consummate businesswoman, or artist. I see so many Òsuns who don't even know they are. (Harding 2001, 185)

Beyoncé, using the visual and verbal cues and clues located and made present in the black Atlantic, provokes us to think deeply about the aesthetics being presented and performed. How we interpret the use of water, how it is coalesced with color, music, movement and dialogue evokes and invokes Oshún and all of the other deities to be present. We journey like flowing water, aided in removing our pain and obstacles by tracking with Oshún and taking umbrage in her strength, to find, experience, and celebrate the divine in ourselves and each other.

Note

1 The spelling of Yorùbá-derived words varies from region and dialect as well as in the American diasporas, where worship of the orishas was established and maintained by the legacy of the enslaved Africans over the centuries. For example, in this chapter I use Oshún; however in Nigeria her name would be written as Òṣun, in Brazil as Oxum, and in Cuba Oshún or Ochún. For readability and to reduce confusion, I do not deviate from the "sh" convention in this and other Yorùbá words. For quotes, I have retained the published orthography. The reader is advised that spelling and pronunciation do vary.

References

Afolabi, Kayode. 2006. *Osun in Colours: Pictorial History of the River Goddess, Osun.* Charleston, N.C.: BookSurge.

Badejo, Diedre. 1996. *Osun Seegesi: The Elegant Deity of Wealth, Power, and Femininity.* Trenton, N.J.: Africa World Press.

Badejo, Diedre. 2008. "The Pathways of Ọ̀ṣun as Cultural Synergy." In Jacob Obafẹmi Kẹhinde Olupọna and Terry Rey (eds), *Òrìṣà Devotion as World Religion: The Globalization of Yorùbá Religious Culture.* Madison: University of Wisconsin Press, 191–201.

Barber, Karin. "'Oríkì', Women and the Proliferation and Merging of 'Òrìṣà'." *Africa: Journal of the International African Institute* 4 no. 2 (1990): 313–337.

Beier, Ulli. 1975. *The Return of the Gods: The Sacred Art of Susanne Wenger.* Cambridge: Cambridge University Press.

Gleason, Judith, art by Aduni Olorisa. 1971. *Orisha: The Gods of Yorubaland.* New York: Atheneum.

Harding, Rachel, 2001. "'What Part of the River You're In': African American Women in Devotion to Òsun." In Joseph M. Murphy and Mei-Mei Sanford (eds), *Ọ̀ṣun Across the Waters: A Yorùbá Goddess in Africa and the Americas.* Bloomington: Indiana University Press, 164–188.

Quevedo, Marysol. "Wither 'the Cold War' in Music Studies Today?" Paper presented at the American Musicological Society, Rochester, New York. 10 November 2017.

Verger, Pierre Fatumbi. 1982. *Orisha: Les Dieux Yorouba en Afrique et au Nouveau Monde.* Paris: Editions A.M. Metailie.

Wenger, Susanne, and Gert Chesi. 1983. *A Life with the Gods in their Yoruba Homeland.* Wörgl, Austria: Perlinger.

11

BEYONCÉ REBORN

Lemonade as spiritual enlightenment

Lauren V. Highsmith

On April 23, 2016, at 9 pm Eastern Standard Time, over 787,000 viewers tuned into HBO for, unbeknownst to them, spiritual revival. Like secular Eucharist, this impressive audience virtually congregated to consume the dramatic breaking, unmaking, and transformation of Beyoncé's spirit. In doing so, the congregation received the call and power to also spiritually transform, or—as Beyoncé put it—"get in formation." Creole and proud, Beyoncé is known to unashamedly put on for (yet simultaneously commodify) her Louisiana roots in her art, and did so again when using Vodún as the aesthetic and ideological thread for her 2016 visual album *Lemonade*. Engaging and deploying motifs of Yoruba Orisha, BaKongo cosmology, and Mende ritual, Beyoncé created a contemporary narrative for Black femme spiritual liberation. In this text, Beyoncé embodies the roles of initiate and practitioner, priestess, and goddess. Through spiritual rebirth, Beyoncé finds the inner strength to free herself from patriarchal oppression. This strength not only empowers her singularly from within but also through the restoration of power via the practice of forgiveness. Her journeying allows her to achieve a level of power and enlightenment which then positions her to teach, lead, and empower others. Beyoncé's process of becoming was literally and thematically incited by marital discord; but it has higher stakes than to solely save a celebrity marriage. Whether for commodity or to use celebrity for public service, Beyoncé's platform permitted her to evangelize to thousands of people by (literally) recording, publishing, and distributing her spiritual account: *Lemonade*, Beyoncé's gospel of Black femme liberation via Pan African syncretism.

From bottom bitch to candid convert

Beyoncé's *Lemonade* mimetically and diegetically teaches self-love. The album echoes the sentiments of woman-empowerment composed in Beyoncé's previous self-titled visual album (2013). In the eponymous album, Beyoncé performs what has been colloquially named a kind of "bottom bitch feminism," explained in the viral article "The Problem with Beyhive Bottom Bitch Feminism" by Christa Bell and Mako Fitts Ward as "an image of feminism wrapped in the gold chains of hip hop machismo."[1] As Bell and Ward describe, Beyoncé's self-titled visual album exhibits a complicated autonomy primarily via sexual and spiritual eroticism and a juxtaposition of strong bravado of a personal feminine imperialism with intentional submission to her husband. The release features the singles "Drunk in Love" and "Flawless." The former, the hip hop ballad featuring Jay-Z in which the couple gushes over their bacchanalia, shows Beyoncé shedding her constructed R&B-crossover princess persona for that of a woman who does not ascribe to the trope of lady, dismantling European patriarchal standards of *wifey material*. In the video for "Drunk in Love," instead of playing coy and hitting all of her marks perfectly, she performs mostly improvised choreography, trades her iconic long tresses for a wet bob, and displays rawer vocals with rasp and less-than-perfect pitch as she nuances her married sex life. The latter is Beyoncé's attempt at a feminist anthem that credits materiality and making through the external as the foundations of her self-confidence. "Flawless" defines energy of the raw aesthetic as agency and subjective perfection, although superficial. The song first presents Beyoncé as an authority commanding respect because of her legitimate and referent powers; it later shifts and becomes a call for other women to recognize their power as well, sampling (and misappropriating) Chimamanda Ngozi Adichie's *We Should All Be Feminists*. [2] Overall, the self-titled album marked the convoluted beginnings of Beyoncé's passage into a liberated selfhood.

While *Beyoncé* evoked the sensual fruition of the Black woman's liberation, *Lemonade* takes on the Black woman's spiritual journey. When one cannot rely on the strength of her marriage to be her own strength, how does she then define herself? *Lemonade* rethinks arguing in the case for bottom bitch feminism, and seeks to find an internal source of power that can then be shared and combined to create a greater communal power. What appears superficially as a story that unveils the struggles and beauty of Beyoncé's familial relations, primarily focusing on her marriage, is actually an artistic depiction of grieving, healing, and progression of the Black femme self individually and collectively. Joining a phenomenon of the seeming resurgence and reformation of the Black Arts mission, Beyoncé evokes the aesthetics of various West African and Black diasporic religious traditions in the presentation of her spiritual journey from brokenness to fulfillment in this album.

On the surface, *Lemonade* tells the story of a woman coping with her husband's infidelity. It is organized into eleven chapters that poetically and theatrically stage how she works through the ordeal: Intuition, Denial, Anger, Apathy, Emptiness, Accountability, Reformation, Forgiveness, Resurrection, Hope, and Redemption. The titles allude to the reconciliation between husband and wife. Less obvious is the soul-searching that takes place within the wife to reach this happy conclusion. Before the wife can reconcile with her husband, she must first reconcile herself. What is outwardly recognized as a broken heart is actually a shattering of the self, a kind of spiritual death. When Beyoncé speaks the line "So what are you gonna say at my funeral now that you've killed me?" she is acknowledging that the woman's identity is bound to her marriage; hence, when the marriage breaks, so does she. Who is she if not a wife? Ironically, the wife must die in order for the woman to (re)claim her individual identity. To find herself, the woman must go on a spiritual journey. She must tap into the supernatural and experience death, seeking, and rebirth in order to (re)discover her true self. Velma E. Love, a scholar of cultures and religions with West African origins, records this seeking of self as the Yoruba Orisha process called the "hero's journey"; the three stages of this process are "departure, fulfillment, and return."[3] This death or departure is the move from the physical realm to the spiritual realm. One who is seeking must navigate through the spiritual realm and overcome personalized challenges before successfully returning to the physical realm as a new, enlightened being. *Lemonade* adds many more stages as it marks the impetus for traveling, divvies fulfillment into some of the challenges faced before success, and includes the prelude to life after resurrection as well as the testimony. The chapters Denial, Apathy, Reformation, and Hope feature the most compelling allusions to Beyoncé's liberating syncretism.

Denial

The second chapter, Denial, begins with Beyoncé jumping off of a ledge stories above an empty street. This suicide is the death of the wife. Rather than splatting on the street, Beyoncé instead plunges into water. Water is the most significant symbol in *Lemonade* as it is the means by which she crosses over from the physical to the spiritual. This visual transition is represented in the *tendwa kia nza-n'kongo*, also called the *dikenga* or the Kongo cosmogram. As Robert Farris Thompson explicates in *The Four Moments of the Sun*, the Kongo cosmogram signifies the circle of life.[4] The horizontal line dividing the cosmogram represents water. To exist above the water is to exist in the land of the living; and to exist below is to exist in the spirit world. The surface of the water acts as the line of separation between the two realms; this line is referred to as the Kalunga line.[5] When Beyoncé jumps off the ledge into the water, she is transitioning to begin her spiritual journey. The narration reveals that her god before this journey had been her husband. The "you" addressed in the chapter for whom she flagellated herself and from whom she asked for dominion is the same "you" of whom she asked "Are you cheating on me?" The conclusion of Denial is acceptance that her husband cannot be her god. She cannot continue to deny his unfaithfulness and worship his mere humanity. With this revelation, Beyoncé progresses in her travels and is introduced to the Orisha Oshún.

Beyoncé *meets* Oshún by embodying her. The music video for "Hold Up" is a representation of spirit possession and the beginning of conversion. The lyrics present Beyoncé's case for conversion: why serve an immature god? Beyoncé realizes also that her husband is only a god because she built him up to be one, saying that without his celebrity he would be powerful to no one but her because she has chosen to submit to him. Hence, they (the public) don't love (worship) him (her former god/husband) like she does. After giving up her former god, Beyoncé becomes an open vessel for the Orisha to enter and introduce her to true internal power.

The embodiment is represented in costume and performance. Beyoncé wears a floor-length yellow dress that reveals her cleavage and flaunts her curves; the cut of the dress evokes sentiments of regality and femininity. She also wears gold jewelry, plays in water, and performs a joy that cannot be inhibited by her anger. Velma Love's *Divining the Self: A Study in Yoruba Myth and Consciousness*, a synthesis of information about the Orisha compiled from practitioners and scholars, affirms that these choices in dress and performance all allude to the goddess: "[Oshún's] colors are yellow and gold."[6] She is the goddess "who heals with cool water"; she is associated with the sun because "her presence is felt to bring lightness and effervescence to illness, want, and gloom"; "She is healer, artist, mother, bringer of joy and laughter … the feminine principle of sensuality, of luxuriant sexual arousal"[7]

In addition to the dress, the jewelry, and the joy, Beyoncé's embodiment of Oshún non-traditionally involves the wielding of a baseball bat. With the bat, Beyoncé busts the windows out of a car, forces a fire hydrant to spew the water in which she and the community children jubilantly play, breaks a security camera, and even seems to commit battery against the viewer, breaking the fourth wall. While one could simply chalk this aggression up to rage towards her husband, Beyoncé-as-Oshún is performing something different. This performance of anger juxtaposed with seemingly eternal joy is a kind of cleansing, a spiritual release, as signified by the yellow fire hydrant (the yellow connects the body of the fire hydrant to the body of the being possessed by Oshún). The possession allows Beyoncé's spirit to communicate with the Orisha in order to be read and cleansed on a personal level. Love explicates the significance of Oshún's divinity further, noting that Oshún's "symbolic representation of fertility, creation, birth, and source of new life" characterizes the goddess as "an aje power with a redemptive quality for an enslaved and oppressed people."[8] With this cleansing, Beyoncé-as-Oshún destroys the oppression of the (male) gaze represented by windows, cameras, and screens.

In addition to removing the worry of being spectacle, Beyoncé begins to rid herself of the concern for her husband's approval (an issue which she returns to in the following chapter, "Anger"). The meeting of Oshún also acts as an introduction to Beyoncé's spiritual awakening: An interpretation of Oshún against the Wimbush/Ford paradigm—how they understand "the hero's journey"—suggests that she be placed in phase one of the triparte schema. Phase one, flight or deformation in the Wimbush paradigm and departure in the Ford paradigm, is consistent with Oshún as deity of birth/beginnings.[9] Chapter two of *Lemonade* marks the official start of Beyoncé's conversion from bottom bitch feminist to self-divining womanist. Her deformation or shattering/her departure from worship of her husband permits new space to be formed into a new being. Here, her possession foreshadows her transformation into a full practitioner of her syncretism.

Apathy

Chapter four of *Lemonade* is a more positively powerful depiction of emptiness than the following chapter that is *actually* titled "Emptiness." While chapter five reminds listeners of Drake's "Hotline Bling" girl who goes out and explores more of life to fill the void of her indifferent lover, chapter four provides a look at her genuine independence, one not motivated by a need to prove that one has moved on. She also builds a new community, surrounding herself with other strong, independent women. As Beyoncé sings about her lack of concern for her husband and her new focus on building herself, she dances with the troupe of women, she laughs, and she does not censor herself as she once did. With the gaze destroyed, Beyoncé can focus on her traveling without distraction. Beyoncé, posed with nonchalance, and tennis legend Serena Williams, twerking unreservedly, both wear all black and look directly at the viewer as if to satirically mourn the gaze that once constricted them. The community of other women commune with Beyoncé on a bus. Because they all wear chalk, perform in-sync choreography, and travel together on the bus, it can be assumed that these women who accompany Beyoncé are also in an initiation process. Sylvia Ardyn Boone's *Radiance from the Waters: Ideals of Feminine Beauty in Mende Art* supports this theory: "White is Sande's color [Sande is a West African secret society that initiates girls into adulthood via ritual practices; girls are initiated in groups] … and white clay [*hojo*—kaolin, porcelain clay] is used to paint the initiates-in-training."[10] While the women do not endure all of the same tribulations in their spiritual journeys, as they have all been painted with white clay but with different markings, they still come together to support one another and find the sameness in their stories to be in tune with one another's movements. In this part of Beyoncé's journey, she begins to see the spirit leading her towards a purpose greater than her own individual overcoming; in her personal travels she sees the strength of the potential collective.

Reformation

When considering the Wimbush/Ford paradigm, chapter two of *Lemonade* is stage one of self-divining, chapters three through six are stage two, and chapter seven is stage three. Of course, chapter seven is fittingly titled "Reformation," but that alone does not justify it being the end of Beyoncé's training to be initiated as a practitioner of her syncretic faith. It is the ritual and the noticeable change in narrative that signify Beyoncé's spiritual maturation.

In the beginning of the video for "Love Drought," Beyoncé is wearing a white baby-doll dress while lying in a fetal position on the 50-yard line of the Mercedes-Benz Superdome in New Orleans. Her costume and position signify that she is a fetus about to be born. A Black woman dressed in eighteenth-century European attire observes her from stadium seats far away. In this scene, the spirit of an elder of the religious community awaits the (re)birth of the newest member. Just as the other initiates met each other during their travels, so elders and spirits have means of observing the spiritual journey of the initiate-in-training as well. The presence of the older woman is another allusion to Sande society; the presence of a female elder instead of a male one stresses a focus on the Black female community and an unconcern for the male gaze. Rather than performing for the gaze, Beyoncé's full focus is on completing her spiritual formation in order to be reformed in the physical realm. The 50-yard line of the Superdome represents the Kalunga line that holds Beyoncé between the land of the living and of the dead.

Being in this in-between gives Beyoncé spiritual vision in the physical realm and helps her to see beyond the pain her husband has caused and into his heart. When they are intimate, she can look him in the eyes and discern what is troubling him. She says, "Why do you deny yourself heaven? Why do you consider yourself undeserving? Why are you afraid of love? You think it's not possible for someone like you. But you are the love of my life." With this spiritual vision, Beyoncé can see her husband in his truth: he is seen not as a weak god but as a broken man who also needs to be taught love. Teaching her husband love is her first assignment as a new initiate. Despite her devotion, however, to give him *all* of her energy would be backwards. Instead, she continues to be guided by the spirit and rely on the power of her spiritual community. To love herself is a means of teaching her husband self-love by example; to receive love and support from her spiritual community is to show her husband how she should be loved. To "stop this love drought," as Beyoncé sings, and successfully take up this assignment, she must once again call upon Oshún. The goddess who heals with cool water then bestows upon Beyoncé her powers of restoring and maintaining balance, peace, and harmony.[11]

Beyoncé addresses both her husband and Oshún when singing "Love Drought." While not adhering precisely to an AB song form (meaning the song only consists of two distinct sections), Beyoncé's song does use two different timbres when she switches her address from husband to Oshún. In the first section, Beyoncé sings with a fuller, more forwardly placed mix of head and chest voice; her phrases are slightly truncated and sound more compressed. The production of her vocals is a single, centered lead vocal track. This first section is Beyoncé's directness in confronting her husband in order to move forward in their relationship. She tells him honestly how he has made her feel, and asserts that her love for him is greater than their pain. In the second section, Beyoncé uses an airy head voice that sounds relaxed. Her phrases are more legato and her riffs, while exceptionally clean, do not sound artificial or strained; they too have a sense of ease and even a hint of playfulness. Beyoncé layers the tracks in the second section and spreads them out as if in a chorus effect in order to represent the collective of new initiates who join her in the video. This section represents her/their prayer to Oshún. The prayer begins, "You and me could move a mountain," repeating the word "you" like a chant. Love notes that Oshún "owns the odu Oche," the power of feminine energy; with this power, "even the greatest mountain can be felled."[12] The change from section A to section B represents Beyoncé's ideological maturation from worshipping a false god (her husband) to realizing the power in herself and in her femme collective.

When Beyoncé matures enough to forgive and love her husband through their pain, she comes to the end of her spiritual journey and is reborn. This rebirth is then represented via the ceremonial crossing of the river. Beyoncé and her fellow initiates walk single-file into the body of water. They all wear white dresses with black crosses on the chest. The white dress symbolizes connection to the spirits, enlightenment, and initiation;[13] and the black crosses evoke the BaKongo cosmogram. In "BaKongo Identity and Symbolic Expression in the Americas" by Christopher C. Fennell, the BaKongo cosmogram is explored in more depth:

> The crossed lines provide a more focused and selective invocation of the spirit world and the land of the living for immediate social action. The crossed lines could also be drawn or etched onto objects in combination with vocalized prayers to create protective objects and amulets. Thus, an abbreviated version of the emblematic form of the dikenga usually served more private and instrumental purposes.[14]

These simple crosses were used primarily during ceremonies/rituals in which persons were being sworn in or seeking spiritual guidance.[15] As the white dresses indicate, the viewer is witnessing the private ritual of initiation. When the initiates take their places in the water and raise their held hands, they signal to the viewer the completion of their initiation.

Beyoncé is at the front of the line, leading the initiates into the water. Her position at the front represents her acceptance of her role as a spiritual leader. During formation/seeking, initiates-in-training learn their spiritual gifts and roles in the community. Beyoncé's role can be classified as a future *nganga*. Ras Michael Brown defines banganga (nganga, singular) in *African-Atlantic Cultures and the South Carolina Lowcountry* as spiritual experts; they are the practicing healers who access, communicate with, and control the power of minkisi, what Brown defines as consecrated objects (objects holding spirits) or nature spirits (ground spirits within pools of water or running water, individual rocks and mountains, and forests).[16] In chapter seven alone, Beyoncé is connected to a river, a clearing in the forest, and even a football stadium; these act as her minkisi (with a contemporary addition).

Beyoncé's leadership is confirmed when the video suddenly cuts to her and the initiates in the clearing of a forest. The scene begins with a close-up on Beyoncé's face, the camera panning slowly in a full circle. Beyoncé's face is once again painted with white chalk. Her gaze shifts from the camera to the sky. Then the frame suddenly zooms out and shows that she is not alone. The other initiated girls surround Beyoncé with their hands outstretched towards her. The rotating frame represents BaKongo cosmology and the circle that signifies the completion of the hero's journey. Beyoncé's shifting gaze shows her spiritual transition from fixation on the external to a focus on the spiritual and the internal. The girls extending their hands anoint Beyoncé's divinity, represented by the white chalk around her eyes. Wyatt MacGaffey's *Kongo Political Culture: The Conceptual Challenge of the Particular* explains that white chalk around the eyes signals an ability to see the invisible, or to see with the eyes of the spirits who are more aware and more sensitive to their environments and the interplay of past, present, and future.[17] In this moment, the initiates, her spiritual sisters, anoint Beyoncé as a divine leader.

This chapter is so significant because it is in this part of the visual album that the multiple narratives of working on a marriage, (re)discovering self, and directly preaching to the community neatly converge. The setting of the Superdome is what finally brings these three stories together more explicitly. In the aftermath of Hurricane Katrina, many of the refugees who could be rescued found themselves in the Louisiana Superdome. For five days, the stadium was used as a shelter. However, the structure that was once thought to be able to withstand any natural disaster began to fail. The space was overcrowded and disorganized. Some survivors made it to the Superdome only to die there for lack of proper medical attention and resources. Some families were separated. The Superdome held/holds the memories of these traumatic moments after Hurricane Katrina hit New Orleans. But the Superdome was rebuilt and renamed. For the ten-year anniversary of Hurricane Katrina, Les Carpenter wrote "The New Orleans Superdome: A Great Comeback Story." Carpenter asserts that the Superdome's *death* was necessary for its rebirth:

> But of all the New Orleans revival stories, none might be more important than the rebuilding of the stadium that was a shelter of last resort for 30,000 people. In the days during and after Katrina, the Superdome became the symbol of a city falling apart; the lights went out, the roof ripped open and the flooded streets outside made it an island of panic. Repairing and re-opening it a year after Katrina sent a message to everybody that they can rebuild, too.[18]

Thus, when Beyoncé uses the rebuilt stadium, renamed the Mercedes-Benz Superdome, as her nkisi, she juxtaposes her broken relationship and hero's journey with the deconstruction and reformation of the Superdome and the victims who once resided there. Just like Beyoncé and the Superdome, New Orleans can make a comeback. While the people have suffered, some have not sacrificially died or have not opened themselves to work through their traumas and release their pains to move on. *Lemonade* is their signal to complete the journey.

Hope

In this chapter, Beyoncé's maturation in her syncretic faith is signified by her assimilation into her religious community and the performance of her spiritual leadership. The first scene of this chapter shows Beyoncé on a bus with more initiates-in-training. The women wear faces painted with white chalk, but Beyoncé's face is bare. This time, Beyoncé is the elder guiding the initiates-in-training in their spiritual travels. The scene then cuts to a baby lying on a bed. This baby symbolizes the rebirth of others post-Beyoncé rebirth. Here, Beyoncé signifies that others must find themselves via spiritual liberation—and they will.

The chapter continues with Beyoncé narrating the extraordinary mundaneness of her life as a full-fledged nganga. She goes to the nail salon, receives a spiritual reading from her technician, and then receives visions for her next spiritual assignment in a dream. This narration is set to the visuals of women cooking food in the kitchen and gathering for what appears to be a recital. In her assimilation to the lifestyle of her syncretic faith, communicating with the spirits in these ways is as common as familial congregation.

The motif of the extraordinary ordinary returns with the chapter's sociopolitical all–Black, mostly female, all–star cast. Notable ensemble members include the mothers of Trayvon Martin, Mike Brown, and Eric Garner and Quvenzhané Wallis, the youngest Oscar nominee for Best Actress. These women belong to Beyoncé's community of enlightened practitioners.

The mothers of the three young Black men unjustifiably murdered by police are recognized as mothers of the #BlackLivesMatter Movement. In the previous chapter, they are given special attention in *Lemonade* as each mother has a solo in which she looks directly at the audience while holding a picture of her deceased son. Through their grief, they are able to use their inner-strength to confront the gaze that framed their sons as unworthy of life and reframe their narratives for their new missions for social justice. Chapter ten unifies the mothers. They are always grouped together to show their own sisterly connection and common purpose and vision.

Wallis successfully transformed a role originally written for a white boy when she was only six years old; while the recognition for her work was not acknowledged until she was nine; and although she did not win the Oscar for Best Actress, she still made history with her nomination (for *Beasts of the Southern Wild*).[19] Wallis is depicted both with and without white body makeup in the visual album, representing her private and public activity in the syncretic faith as one to continue Beyoncé's legacy of liberation. She also holds the hand of Beyoncé's daughter, Blue Ivy, representing the continuation of a legacy to the next generation through mentorship and sisterhood.

Blue Ivy is the first daughter recognized in the nail technician's spiritual reading. She is the product of a rekindled love between Beyoncé and her husband. Therefore, she symbolizes their healing. The second daughter is Beyoncé's testimony: "I wake as the second girl crawls headfirst up my throat. A flower blossoming out of the hole in my face." This testimony is presented at the recital. Beyoncé wears a white dress and sings the song "Freedom." This song echoes the sentiments of the second section of "Love Drought" much more aggressively and pointedly. Her declaration of raining on thunder and wading through waters while wearing her spiritual white return Beyoncé to the moment of calling upon Oshún in the in-between. As the goddess of hope and redemption from oppression, Oshun speaks through Beyoncé to minister to the community a call to action and to remember their power: "I break chains all by myself/Won't let my freedom rot in hell/Hey! I'ma keep running/Cause a winner don't quit on themselves."

Conclusion

Beyoncé publishes this message of hope to inspire the next wave of self-realization and spiritual rebirth in the greater Black femme community. She also presents herself as a bard of New Orleanian culture and activism for the Black/New Orleans community. However, one should question if her project truly allows for the representation and healing of the people of the city. From the album's debut to the present, Beyoncé has fought lawsuits (copyright infringement, lack of payment for creative work) from creatives connected to New Orleans. While the text itself reads as Beyoncé's attempt at relatability, awareness, and activism via magical realist performance, the extra-textual politic of Beyoncé's project and performance do not fully support a social justice activism agenda. Despite this complication, *Lemonade* still effectively serves as a vessel to share the message of finding, freeing, and fostering the development of the Black femme self and collective. The compelling allusions to Yoruba, BaKongo, and Mende cultural traditions recall a history of ritual to self-identification and empowerment. In selling/reminding the audience of this cultural lineage through the evocative visual album, Beyoncé proposes the next step in Black femme progression: getting in formation by seeking the spirits for self-liberation.

Notes

1   Christa Bell and Mako Fitts Ward. "The Problem with Beyhive Bottom Bitch Feminism." *Real Colored Girls* (blog), 15 Dec. 2013, https://realcoloredgirls.wordpress.com/2013/12/15/the-problem-with-beyhive-bottom-bitch-feminism/.
2   Chimamanda Ngozi Adichie, *We Should All Be Feminists* (New York: Anchor, 2015).
3   Velma E. Love, *Divining the Self a Study in Yoruba Myth and Human Consciousness* (University Park: Pennsylvania State University Press, 2012), 58.
4   Robert Farris Thompson and Joseph Cornet. *The Four Moments of the Sun: Kongo Art in Two Worlds*, exh. cat. (Washington: National Gallery of Art, 1981), 27–28 and 43–52.
5   Ibid., 44.
6   Love, 88.
7   Ibid., 95.
8   Ibid.
9   Ibid.
10 Sylvia Ardyn Boone, *Radiance from the Waters: Ideals of Feminine Beauty in Mende Art* (New Haven: Yale University Press, 1986), 18.
11 Love, 89.
12 Ibid., 49.
13 Boone, 196.
14 Christopher C. Fennell, "BaKongo Identity and Symbolic Expression in the Americas" in *Archaeology of Atlantic Africa and the African Diaspora*, eds. Toyin Falola and Akin Ogundiran (Bloomington: Indiana University Press, 2007) 204–205.
15 Ibid., 205.
16 Ras Michael Brown, *African-Atlantic Cultures and the South Carolina Lowcountry* (New York: Cambridge University Press, 2012) 20.
17 Wyatt MacGaffey, *Kongo Political Culture: The Conceptual Challenge of the Particular* (Bloomington: Indiana University Press, 2000), 207.
18 Les Carpenter, "The New Orleans Superdome: A Great American Comeback Story," *The Guardian*, last modified 21 Aug. 2015, https://www.theguardian.com/sport/2015/aug/21/new-orleans-superdome-stadium-hurricane-katrina.
19 David Denby, "Beasts of the Southern Wild," *The New Yorker*, last modified 29 Jun. 2012, https://www.newyorker.com/culture/culture-desk/beasts-of-the-southern-wild. *Beasts of the Southern Wild* is an adaptation of Lucy Alibar's play *Juicy and Delicious*. Hushpuppy is the name of the young protagonist in both versions of the story. However, Hushpuppy is a "sweet little Southern" white boy in the play; and in the film adaptation, Hushpuppy is a six-year-old Southern Black girl. The decision to make the

cast interracial, and to tell this story of a father and child from the perspective of a little Black girl, decenters the traditional white and male narrative. *Beasts of the Southern Wild* instead grounds itself in conversations about impoverished communities (of people of color), constructing strong Black women, father–daughter dynamics, and much more that give voice to the diversity of American society.

Bibliography

Beyoncé. *Beyoncé*, recorded 2013, Parkwood Entertainment/Columbia, Visual Album.

Beyoncé. *Lemonade*, recorded 2016, Parkwood Entertainment/Columbia, Visual Album.

Boone, Sylvia Ardyn, and John Thomas Biggers. *Radiance from the Waters: Ideals of Feminine Beauty in Mende Art*. New Haven: Yale University Press, 1986.

Brown, Ras Michael. *African-Atlantic Cultures and the South Carolina Lowcountry*. New York: Cambridge University Press, 2012.

Carpenter, Les. "The New Orleans Superdome: a great American comeback story." *The Guardian*, last modified 21 Aug. 2015, https://www.theguardian.com/sport/2015/aug/21/new-orleans-superdome-stadium -hurricane-katrina.

Fennell, Christopher C. "BaKongo Identity and Symbolic Expression in the Americas." *The Archaeology of Atlantic Africa and the African Diaspora*, eds. Toyin Falola and Akin Ogundiran. Bloomington: Indiana University Press, 2007.

Denby, David. "Beasts of the Southern Wild." *The New Yorker*, last modified 29 Jun. 2012, https://www.newyorker.com/culture/culture-desk/beasts-of-the-southern-wild.

Love, Velma E. *Divining the Self a Study in Yoruba Myth and Human Consciousness*. University Park: Pennsylvania State University Press, 2012.

MacGaffey, Wyatt. *Kongo Political Culture: The Conceptual Challenge of the Particular*. Bloomington: Indiana University Press, 2000.

Thompson, Robert Farris and Joseph Cornet. *The Four Moments of the Sun: Kongo Art in Two Worlds, exh. cat.* Washington: National Gallery of Art, 1981.

INTERLUDE E: FROM DESTINY'S CHILD TO COACHELLA

On embracing then resisting others' respectability politics

L. Michael Gipson

> There will always be one more thing.
>
> *Toni Morrison*

When Nobel Prize-winning author Toni Morrison uttered this now infamous paragraph closing line in 1975 to a Portland, Oregon audience she was speaking as part of a panel discussion organized by the Portland State University Black Studies Center. What she was referencing was racism and how those who are invested in its function use racism to constantly move the line for an oppressed people to be considered a whole human being worthy of dignity and respect. Below is a fuller excerpt of Morrison's explanation.

> The function, the very serious function of racism is distraction. It keeps you from doing your work. It keeps you explaining, over and over again, your reason for being. Somebody says you have no language and you spend twenty years proving that you do. Somebody says your head isn't shaped properly so you have scientists working on the fact that it is. Somebody says you have no art, so you dredge that up. Somebody says you have no kingdoms, so you dredge that up. None of this is necessary. There will always be one more thing.

This steely-eyed observation is hard won. Learned from decades, even centuries, of Black people pouring forth the sweat of overachievement and justification for a perpetually remote reward. Observed by the literary matriarch from bearing witness to countless talents and intellects exhausting themselves to prove their value, worth, integrity, and the right to just "be" unequivocally accepted as an equal by the majority. Morrison reminds us that such efforts are an exercise in futility. That for those the game works for, for whom the game is rigged, there is little incentive in *not* moving the goal post again and again and gaslighting those who dare question why the line is never in the same place long enough to recompense oppressed people once they've finally hit the illusory mark.

While the named game is a multi-headed hydra for everything from capitalism to white supremacy as its purpose and end game, at the root of the effort for Black people is an indefatigable belief that a certain level of blood offering to the God of Respectability will one day open the door to the promised land of equality, if not equity, for them and their children. That if one can educate themselves enough, garb themselves humbly enough, speak precisely enough, exhibit manners and etiquette at the levels of royal households enough, rear children meek and obedient (and compliant) enough, order the steps of their lives with enough discipline and restraint at levels their oppressors have seldom mastered or demonstrated en masse themselves, propaganda aside, then maybe, *maybe* they and their offspring get to be accepted as a whole and valuable human being. Of course, that day never arrives, as most devastatingly demonstrated by the collective response to President Barack and Michelle Obama, the pinnacle of Black achievement and its resulting white backlash in the election of #45.

A similar argument can be made for women, particularly Black women. Only, those holding the keys to the gate are just as likely to be Black men and patriarchal-supporting women of every hue as they are to be the pale, cold hands of the white capitalist patriarch. "Black women are the mules of the Earth," author and anthropologist Zora Neale Hurston wrote in 1937; and despite the stunning advances made by Black women in the decades following the golden era of the ongoing Civil Rights Movement, there seems to be a concerted effort to make Hurston's now popularly clichéd statement a permanent mantra for Black women in the U.S. A moving of the line, if you will, despite the successful conditioning of many Black women to adhere to the God of Respectability and seek the fruits that deity will supposedly bear.

According to the National Center for Education Statistics, in 2014 Black women became the most educated group in the U.S, by both race and gender, eclipsing even Asian women. The Centers for Disease Control recently highlighted that between 2006 and 2016, Black girls' teen birth rates were cut nearly in half, itself a decline that followed a steady drop in Black teen pregnancies going back to 1995. The Nielsen Company trumpeted how Black women represent the fastest growing group of female entrepreneurs in the U.S., growing 67 percent between 2007 and 2012 to a whopping 1.5 million Black woman majority-owned businesses as of 2015. In homeownership trends since the 1970s, female-headed households have been outpacing male-headed households, including, of course, among Black women. It's Black women that are driving and controlling total Black spending power to 1.5 trillion dollars by 2021. In 2014, the Pew Research Center reported Blacks to be the most religious group in America, led in those stats by Black women. In 2012, a *Washington Post* and Kaiser Family Foundation survey of 800 Black women found that "living a religious life" was very important to them, higher than any other racial group interviewed. Even among Black millennials, the least religious generation, nearly two-thirds identified themselves as highly religious. By markers and measures economic to spiritual to "personal discipline," Black women collectively have stepped up to the line drawn in the sand of "respect-ability," but to little reward in either public perception or actual financial gains.

Despite doing so much the "right way," Black women still comprise only 8 percent of private sector jobs and 1.5 percent of leadership roles. Their overrepresentation in the public sector, teaching, and helping professions is under constant attack and budget cuts by the Right, with the exception of the military, where they are, too, over-represented (at least until they become a vet and deign to need a service). Fewer than 4 percent of women of color are executive officials and managers at S&P 500 compa-nies, and that's for all women of color together, not just Black women. Sisters earn 61 cents for every dollar paid to white men, meaning it takes nineteen months for a Black woman to take home what a white man takes home in twelve. Even when better educated, Black women with a college degree can expect to make less lifetime earn-ings than a white man with just a high school diploma. Despite the fact that single women are more reliable in paying their mortgages, they were more likely to be denied mortgage loans at higher rates than single men; this statistic is likely to be compounded by, you name it, race. Despite significant reductions in teen pregnancy and child birth, drug use, and white endurance as the majority of those accessing public assistance of every kind, Black women still are more likely to be labeled as "promiscuous," "crack whores," or "welfare queens" than any other women in the public narratives about Black women, and deemed the "least desirable" by men searching for intimate partners through dating apps. It seems despite Black women's loyalty to the God of Respectability, "there will always be one more thing" to keep them from the promised land of their well-earned respect and value as viable, con-tributing citizens to our "fair" land.

The arc of Black women's progress and the intractability of prevailing narratives that would deny them their "Atta boys" (or girls, as it were) follows the rise of one of the most universal symbols of #BlackGirlMagic around the world, Beyoncé Giselle Knowles-Carter. This rocket ship of Black women's collective achievement mirrors the beginning of this star's rise on November 11, 1997 with Columbia Records' release of R&B girl group Destiny's Child's first single, "No, No, No." Arguably, the pinnacle of that achievement came in the success of Beyoncé's sixth solo album and second visual album release, *Lemonade*, on April 23, 2016, almost twenty years later. The Peabody and Grammy Award-winning album would be the artist's sixth #1 album in a row and go on to become the bestselling album of 2016, shipping 2.5 million copies globally that year alone. It would be the second most critically acclaimed album of that year and listed by National Public Radio as the sixth greatest album of all time made by a woman.

Lemonade would also represent the moment when Beyoncé, once and for all, publicly shed an image that had been carefully and calculatedly informed by a father that had managed the first half of her career and had catered to the God of Respectability in many respects, with little upside in the consistent and often irra-tional barrage of charges made against her as both a woman and artist. The moment also appeared to define Beyoncé's own line in the sand of no longer serving that trickster God and following her own muse, with everything since *Lemonade*'s first single—from the Super Bowl to the Coachella performance— representing a new devotion to an unapologetic Blackness; an embrace of Southern roots, both country and urban; a spirituality more complicated than traditional Judeo-Christian praxis; and, a womanhood that dares and succeeds in eclipsing a husband as wealthy and globally popular as she is. By walking a different, self-directed path, explaining very little as she moves and letting the moves speak for themselves, Beyoncé has quietly signaled a way forward for other Black women being driven crazy and maligned by a rigged game they were never slated to win. And, in doing so, she's winning in ways few other Black women in entertainment ever have on their own terms.

The lead-up to the image liberation of Beyoncé was one that happened as it has for many Black women, as one of subtle degrees of loosening the chains. In early interviews and in award show appearances, the lead singer of Destiny's Child seldom spoke for the group and, when she did, it was brief and appeared highly scripted. Indeed, much of the Destiny's Child initial "girls next door" persona was scrupulously cultivated from their presentational image by Beyoncé's mother, Célestine "Tina" Knowles, and in their business and art by Beyoncé's father and longtime manager, Matthew Knowles.

The Houston, Texas daughter of a former IBM executive and a creative entrepreneur, Beyoncé was reared in a public model of Black, post-Civil Rights, middle-class respectability that often goes unexamined by those who besmirch her. Her Omega Psi Phi father holds three college degrees, including two BAs from lauded Historically Black College and University (HBCU) Fisk University, and an MBA from the Cornerstone Christian Bible College. Her multi-medium artist mother had deep professional experience in dance, make-up arts, and cosmetology when she opened her successful salon, Headliners, in Houston, before going on to be a fashion designer and author. A well-to-do two-parent household with deep spiritual and cultural roots in Louisiana Creole and Black Alabama lore, the home of Matthew and Tina Knowles could've served as the foundation for its own Southwestern version of *The Cosby Show* in the '80s and '90s and informed Beyoncé's early and perhaps even present-day values.

It is instructive that Beyoncé grew up in an era where integration and Black success was defined in purely capitalistic terms and proximity to mirrored white middle-class living as presented by *The Cosby Show*, that the girl-child was raised by two shining examples of Black respectability, one corporate and one entrepreneurial. A schizophrenic era that both episodically espoused Black pride within the Black community, but would then turn around and consistently measure its own achievement and respectability in terms and models defined by whiteness and its Western capitalist patriarchal hegemonic traditions. Both Knowles daughters, even in their current, "radical" iterations, also represent both an embrace and a rejection of those values and traditions—though Solange, a high-couture style icon, often escapes such critiques solely on the foundation that she seldom boasts of her economic prowess and might in the way that her elder sister so often does throughout her catalog and branding.

The home and quality of life Beyoncé experienced prior to her rise also belie a dogged public desire to paint the singer as inarticulate and uneducated, despite being raised by parents whose mastery examples were one of devotion to both formal and informal education. Denial of Beyoncé's public voice early in the group's career to avoid unflattering comparisons to Diana Ross and The Supremes, with Matthew Knowles portrayed in the Svengali role of Berry Gordy, perhaps aided in shaping the presumption that Beyoncé's little-observed voice meant one purposely being hidden because of its distasteful class presentation. It likely didn't help the performer's cause that her cadence is one unabashedly Southern, with a noticeable drawl that Americans have long characterized as uneducated despite Southern regional dominance in both degree holders and esteemed higher learning institutions, particularly among Black Americans. So, the singer was painted as a dumb blonde early on even without any of the social privileges traditionally afforded blonde white women. And, being quiet, humble, and meek in the background of her own group for the first two albums at least granted Beyoncé little social cache in much the way it rarely grants other Black women who arm themselves with these accoutrements to avoid charges of being considered loud, angry, or ghetto.

The backlash against Matthew Knowles' portraiture, whether real or curated, of his daughter grew as the rise of the supergroup elevated. By the release of the group's third and most successful album, *Survivor* (2001), Black media charges of colorism, nepotism, and promoting hyper-sexualized images of Black girlhood were nipping at the stilettos of its members, most especially of Beyoncé and her father. This despite performing respectability, pro-patriarchal heavy lyrics in hit songs like "Nasty Girl" that celebrated fashion modesty in the "independent" woman and Beyoncé's mother dressing the young ladies in attire that barely showed more than the midriff or the middle of a thigh in most videos and concert performances. These curious charges didn't hurt the sales of *Survivor*, with the album going on to sell 12 million copies internationally; but it would set the template for the public discourse on Beyoncé by the time of her solo debut for *Dangerously in Love* just two years later. She was now the pimped-out young woman seeking to poison your daughters with her lasciviousness, ties to the Illuminati, and an unearned commercial position that was only achieved through her suitably light skin and blonde weave, and her father's business acumen. This, despite writing on every album following Destiny's Child's 1998 debut album, boasting a behaviorally unmarred brand image for decades, and tripling the economic value of her own brand and financial worth since leaving her father's management and self-directing her career with a salaried management team of her own choosing. Black women not given credit for their sexual discipline, behavioral restraint, or their laborious contributions to their own success are familiar with such ad hominem attacks.

In the run-up to Beyoncé's solo career, it is important to note that none of the group members found themselves linked to any relationship or sexual controversies or scandals, with the group assiduously maintaining a cookie-cutter image and espousing patriarchal-propping virtues like "catering" to their man in the ways of a

'50s-era Stepford wife all the way to the group's disbandment following their fourth and final album, *Destiny Fulfilled*. Throughout, these precocious young women achieved a now near unimaginable decade-long run of thanking "their Lord and Savior Jesus Christ" at every awards show and interview, sought the zenith achievement of matrimony to a "good man," always appeared fashion-model coiffed, and promoted independently making their own money so as not to be too dependent or burdensome on his coin, all in what was then generously called "Girl Power" by the media—in other words, representing the flawlessly respectable "wife material" for the millennial male and the perfect bestie for their sisters. Together, Destiny's Child represented the respectability aspiration for their generation, the girl next door who was well paid and the ride or die survivor for— and of—her friends, but submissive and beautiful to the man they'd eventually land to be socially complete. It was an image goal they'd maintain even into their solo careers, one few stars today under the social media glare could match or would even be expected to maintain.

Perhaps the best of these "good girls" of Girl Power propaganda was Beyoncé herself. Throughout it all, as the lead singer throughout her teen and early adult years, Beyoncé had little to no press related to her dating life until her linkage to now-husband, rapper and businessman Shawn "Jay-Z" Carter. No secret pregnancies. No homewrecking. Not even serial monogamy. Nothing. This is instructive because so much of what is never said about Beyoncé is that she has facilitated a wholesome or "good girl" image for her entire girl group life and even most of her adult career, toothless writhing in wet bathing suits and hair choreography aside, a near misstep-free run of two-plus decades. As a woman, in the public's eye, she jumped right from Daddy's girl to the girlfriend and then wife of Jay-Z. Something a devout American Taliban member would cheer, and did, briefly, for singer/actress Jessica Simpson. So devoted was Beyoncé to her wholesome image for much of her life that in 2008 she felt compelled to introduce an alter ego, Sasha Fierce, to the public to justify having any sexuality or creative liberation at all; an act of dissonance and distancing that was a part of her first loosening of the chains to the respectability deity, even if she had to borrow from the DSM to do it. By 2011, she'd further loosen those chains by dropping her father as her manager and further stepping into the creation of something … else.

Since then, Beyoncé has become the mother of three children, all had within the bounds of wedlock. Her debut documentary, *Life Is But A Dream* (2103), intimately details in soft focus her modern experience as the sometimes exhausted young woman juggling career and marriage, her tragic miscarriage, and the completely ordinary process and concerns of becoming a new mother in contemporary times. Yet, she's often labeled an out-of-touch Jezebel and a whore by those who disparage her despite having never been linked to sexual scandal, of her own making anyway, at any point in her life and career, and ordering her marriage and motherhood steps in ways that many conservative Christians and some of her greatest opponents fail to do in their own glasshouse lives. This speaks to the fragility of respectability for any "good girl," but particularly for the Black Madonna, who doesn't break the rules and yet is still deemed unworthy of respect for adherence to conventional propriety and "responsible" behavior.

Indeed, the once private marriage would seem to be used against her rather than work for her. The first visual album by the star, often labeled her intimacy project, *Beyoncé* (2103), is an all-out celebration of marriage and sexuality within the bounds of marriage. Critically acclaimed as her magnum opus at the time, the project that valiantly tried to bring sex back to the ailing marriage industry that nearly half of the country has abandoned is also among the most cited when discussing the hyper-sexualization of Beyoncé in the public realm; and yet it is the most pro-marriage centered album ever developed by a secular woman artist in the American music canon. The tour that preceded the December release of the *Beyoncé* album by a few months beginning in April of 2013, *The Mrs. Carter Show World Tour*, both paid homage to her husband and her marital status in the tour's name and later in its incorporation of the songs from *Beyoncé* for the rest of its run into 2014. Even as she promoted a version of what some on the Left dismissively called Black "feminism-lite" through songs like "Flawless" (featuring author and feminist Chimamanda Ngozi Adichie), the multimedia star was still publicly positioning her most valuable achievements as those of wife and mother. Rather than media celebrated as scores of hip millennial-motivating pastors were during that same period for talking openly about keeping "marriage sexy" for young parishioners, Beyoncé was said to be crossing the line with a bold new sexuality that was unbecoming of a wife and mother.

Prior to *Lemonade*, it is because she had for so long served the God of Respectability and bowed to the altar of patriarchy in so many ways, even as she championed professional women to follow their ambitions and their bliss, that Beyoncé has been attacked as often by feminists on the Left as she has by conservatives on the Right. Perhaps none more famously than esteemed academic bell hooks have taken the artist to task for performing womanhood in ways that most caters to the "white male gaze." While Beyoncé has not been known exactly for rocking prairie skirts, her attire would barely bat an eye on a cheerleading squad, an ice rink, or a gymnastics floor, all public spaces of sports entertainment where such attire is normative and usually unremarkable. In fact, during a time when Black women in entertainment were pressured to wear thongs and bikinis onstage, Beyoncé seldom appeared in anything more revealing than a woman's ice skater's uniform, tights and all. Vegas showgirls are more revealing. And, as Janet Mock tried to point out to hooks during a now infamous 2014 panel discussion at the New School entitled "Are You Still A Slave? Liberating the Black Female Body," rather than something feminist-lite, perhaps Beyoncé represents a lipstick feminism that is dressing up for its own gaze, its own pleasure, regardless of who else participates in its enjoyment.

Somewhere between the management release of Matthew Knowles in 2011 at the advent of *4* and *Lemonade*, multiple shifts happened. One of those shifts, following a rather public berating by elder actor/singer/activist Harry Belafonte of her and her husband, was a jump in Beyoncé's public philanthropy on everything from anti-gun violence to campaigns on women's empowerment and the Flint water crisis to First Lady Obama's childhood obesity program. Permanent service and educational programs for the needy bear her name in both Houston and New York. By December 2016, Do Something would name Beyoncé the Most Charitable Celebrity of that Year. In charitable giving, Beyoncé reflected the millions of Black women who are the backbone of service, educational, and community organizations throughout the nation and the leaders of charitable giving within the Black community, regardless of income.

Another one of those shifts was the death of superstar Whitney Houston in 2012. An artist with a somewhat rougher, if musically storied background than Beyoncé, Houston had too been pigeon-holed into a "good girl" persona, one that promoted her to white audiences and alienated her to Black audiences. Only in Houston's case, the persona couldn't have been further from the girl reared in Newark and East Orange, New Jersey and exposed to drugs and the music industry life at an early age. Questions and rumors about the nature of Houston's relationship with longtime friend, confidant, and one-time manager Robin Crawford further fuels speculation as to whether Houston's public identity sacrificed an early love and stabilizing relationship in her life and was yet another layer to the lack of authenticity Houston was allowed to exhibit for the first few albums of her career. As outlined in numerous biographies, memoirs, and documentaries, the dissonance between the public and private and the cost of portraying a woman she was not was said to have been a driving factor in Houston's struggle with substance abuse and mental health, and ultimately led to her untimely demise.

In so many ways, a student of the Black female stars who paved the way for Beyoncé surely paid attention to what Houston lost by playing the respectability game and then not playing it—not in a controlled and calculated way, but as a drug and mentally challenged spiral down the drain. Just as Beyoncé never allowed her husband, an artist who managed other careers on his Roc-A-Fella roster, to manage her career the way Aretha Franklin had under Ted White's reportedly abusive hand and Nina Simone had to the equally abusive Andrew Stroud's heavy hands to disastrous effects, Beyoncé learned how to sidestep the female star trap of letting others, especially controlling and powerful men, determine her image and manage her resources. Once from under her father's thumb, her next three solo albums and recent duet album would each find her stepping further and further away from the image carefully crafted for her by her parents and record labels to one that better represented her own vision of herself, her journey, and her brand in ways that Svengali-curated icons like Donna Summer and Diana Ross would not gain for themselves until late in life. Even Beyoncé's portrayals of sexuality were fairly tame and restrained following the lessons of how far a Black woman with a powerful sexuality could be publicly accepted when the dominatrix-era Janet Jackson's titty was said to stop the world and, for more than a decade, her career. There were lessons in the stories of these and so many other Black women in the industry—in so many of the Black mothers, grandmothers, sisters, aunts, and cousins—on how trying to toe lines they did not create too often was met with terrible costs and consequences. Like many women of her generation, Beyoncé watched and learned, even as she fell into the pattern of reliving her mother's experience of marrying a powerful provider and professional partner, but an unfaithful spouse.

What did it mean to Beyoncé to finally and publicly confront her experience with her husband's infidelity, indiscretions that reportedly happened on a number of occasions episodically over multiple years? What did it mean to take a different path from her more private mother in addressing her father Matthew's reported infidelity to Tina Knowles, potentially breaking the pattern or chain of what Beyoncé's own daughters would witness and tolerate from partners in their futures? One can infer from the lyrics, visuals, and selected poetry and prose of British-Somali poet Warsan Shire that *Lemonade* represented a final breaking of many yokes in the artist's life and ended Beyoncé's service to the God of Respectability once and for all.

Suddenly other Gods of Yoruba faith traditions like Oshun and, later, Oya appeared in her visual iconography. *Lemonade*'s eleven chapters—titled "Intuition", "Denial", "Anger", "Apathy", "Emptiness", "Accountability", "Reformation", "Forgiveness", "Resurrection", "Hope", and "Redemption"—could as much be interpreted as the process of healing from years of devoted service to respectability and a reclaiming of self that is unconcerned with anyone else's gaze, expectations, and projections as it was a healing from her partner's faithlessness. In its unabashed embrace of its Black and Creole cultural and religious traditions far beyond the boundaries of Anglo, Judeo-Christian, middle-class respectability and its celebration of Southern 'hood and country ethos, values, and aesthetics, Beyoncé healthily shed all the care of what anyone says or thinks of her in a way that might have saved Whitney Houston's life had she known of another path to break her chains. In making the globally observed Super Bowl performance of "Formation" a political commentary on police brutality and an affirmation of both the Black Panther Party of old and Black Lives Matter today, Beyoncé staked her claim as a member of the "Unapologetically Black" side of the intracultural fence rather than the assimilationist/accommodationist side whose sentiments dominated Black life in Beyoncé's formative early years and marked an out-of-step deference to "coonery" and white supremacy today. *Lemonade* would go on to be rightly seen as an album explicitly speaking to Black women by a Black woman who understood the layered, conflicted, political, and personal experience of living as a Black woman who had been betrayed by husband, country, and too often even community. An album that represented the experience of Black women making lemonade, #BlackGirlMagic, and impossible advances less than sixty years out of Jim Crow out of the lemons of this American life.

As if to make it plain that *Lemonade* was not a one-time marketing gimmick or a creative fluke, but instead the watershed moment for the rest of Beyoncé's life as a resistance fighter to any other drum beat but her own, Beyoncé followed *The Formation Tour* promoting *Lemonade* with a performance for Coachella as its first Black woman headliner in its near twenty-year history (and only the third woman to ever headline the festival). In 2017, Beyoncé's first performance was to follow the 256 million-dollar, bestselling, forty-nine date tour experienced by 2.24 million attendees around the world. However, Coachella was one put on hold for a year while Beyoncé gave birth to twins, and during which she appeared to extend her interest in the African deities referenced in *Lemonade* by appearing as the Yoruba goddess Oya at the 59th Annual Grammy Awards in 2017, ignoring concerns that she was no longer a good Christian woman and that some of her fans had started practicing "Beyism" with the star as their deity.

With her two and a half-hour "Beychella" performance on April 14, 2018, Beyoncé delivered more of her resistance songs, bringing along 100 performers, sister Solange, Destiny's Child, and her freshly redeemed husband, whose own album *4:44* co-signed the accusations made on his wife's album and offered its own introspections and public apologias. Critics noted the twenty-six-song set included samples of Malcolm X and Nina Simone and served as a celebration of the Black diaspora with Southern Black band traditions, Caribbean dancehall, urban hip hop, Texas chopped and screwed, West African Afrobeat, and traditional rhythm and blues all finding space on a stage witnessed by 41 million total viewers and counting. The prevailing attitude on that stage was not anything remotely interested in being "ladylike" (despite modestly appearing in tight-clad Daisy Dukes and a made-up HBCU sweatshirt), but was instead bold, powerful, unafraid of drifting into coarse and provocative language, and was rich in political statements, Southern and street euphemisms, and feminine strength every bit as brass and braggadocio as any man.

Even while quietly exalting HBCU traditions and performing the Black National Anthem, the Coachella performance illustrated a Black woman uninterested in white gazes or respectability or any traps or games she couldn't ultimately win, and one that may have cost her her life, if not just her soul, to play. It was one that didn't listen to the feminists on the hard Left as she openly celebrated the joys of being a wife and mother but also clearly operated as an equal partner with a legendary husband whose star she'd already measurably eclipsed as they began announcements for their *On the Run II Tour* and would later release their trap and trap soul album, *Everything Is Love*, for the streets. *Everything Is Love*, like *Lemonade* and *4:44*, continued the artists' conversation with their Black audience that others were simply allowed to eavesdrop on. Arguably, the Coachella performance was an extension of that intracultural dialogue. It was also a performance that turned a deaf ear to the critics on the far Right who never respected or honored Beyoncé's efforts at toeing the line at any point in her career anyway. It was a performance clear on the lessons learned and the blood spilt by far too many Black women and artists.

It was, alas, a Beyoncé who had arrived to herself as if with an understanding of Morrison's resonating words: "There will always be one more thing." So, better to get on with the work of your life on your own terms, with your own values, principles, politics, and spirituality that needn't make sense to anyone else but you and, possibly, home. To let none of the distractions steer you away from the North Star of the self. To be a student of Morrison's evergreen words, embody their resistance melody, and apply them to your life regardless of one's social identity struggle. If oppressed by this system of ours, the words will usually apply. Learn as Beyoncé Giselle Knowles-Carter has learned, avoid the mistakes of the fallen, and determine your own course for winning and just "being" in the end. Be graceful with yourself in the journey, we aren't all able to so carefully avoid keeping up the masks and hiding the missteps in the ways of a global superstar just finding her way.

INTERLUDE F: "FORMATION" AND THE BLACK-ASS TRUTH ABOUT BEYONCÉ AND CAPITALISM

Tamara Winfrey Harris

On February 6, 2016, Beyoncé dropped the first single from *Lemonade*, her aural and visual masterpiece about marital and social strife. "Formation" is a pro-dirty South, pro-Cheddar Bay biscuit, pro-Black everything anthem. In it, Bey celebrates that Black that makes white America uncomfortable: Nappy Black, 'Bama Black, queer Black, sexual Black, militant Black. In a country that likes its Blackness smiling, agreeable, passive, straight, and as close to white as possible, this is a radical act. That is why the last line of "Formation" is dissonant: "Always stay gracious. Best revenge is your paper."

The quest for private wealth, American capitalism, is the engine for oppression—the devaluing and destruction of black bodies, distrust of queerness, and disempowering of womanhood. Getting rich is not radical. But Beyoncé—the woman who is proudly backed by an all-woman band; who features gay couples loving each other in the video for "All Night"; who launched the Homecoming Scholars Awards program to benefit historically black colleges and universities—is also about "stacking money, money everywhere she goes," as she purrs on *Lemonade*'s "6 Inch." Or, as she will eventually sing in Apeshit," her most recent (as of this writing) collaboration with her husband Jay-Z:

> Gimme my check, put some respeck on my check/ Or pay me in equity … Or watch me reverse out the debt (skrrt)/He got a bad bitch … We livin' lavish … /I got expensive fabrics I got expensive habits.

Forbes lists Beyoncé's net worth as somewhere around $355 million. Critics would say the capitalist cheerleading often dropped in the middle of Beyoncé's pro-Blackness and Black feminism is a tell. What appears to be the revolutionary elevation of Blackness and Black womanhood is really just the typical commodification of it in service to one woman's wealth-building. In a review of the work for the bell hooks

FIGURE F.1 Video still of Beyoncé referencing "paper" from "Formation." *Lemonade*, Parkwood Entertainment, 2016

Institute at Berea College, the feminist scholar, bell hooks, dismissed *Lemonade* as "the business of capitalist money making at its best." hooks says Bey's "radical" imagery only serves to distract from the same old, same old marketing of commodified Black bodies, sexualized violence, and "conventional sexist constructions of black female identity." In a post-*Lemonade* world after we've put our middle fingers up to men who cheat and pumped our fists to Kendrick Lamar's bars in "Freedom," Black folks will be no better off, but Beyoncé will be richer. (Indeed, it may even cost the Black female scholars editing this book to include an analysis of Beyoncé's capitalism. As I write this, it remains to be seen whether quoting Bey's lyrics about wealth qualifies as fair use or whether there is a heavy price tag attached to repeating "Gimme my check!")

The Queen Bey is not leading a socialist revolution, true. But critics who diminish the importance of *Lemonade*'s transgressive presentation because its creator is a successful player in the game of capitalism are misguided. They ignore the importance of representation and the power of popular culture; make the perfect the enemy of the good; and, as is too common, blame Black women for not saving others from "their fool selves." Black people collectively own less than 3 percent of America's wealth. Descendants of enslaved Africans who, post-abolition, were Black-coded, Jim Crowed, and red-lined out of economic stability have historically had little material wealth to share with future generations. And it will be very hard for modern Black families to catch up to white ones, with the heads of most Black households—women—making 63 cents for every dollar paid white men, and the wage gap between Black and white men widening to Black men's disadvantage, too. It is no wonder that 33 percent of Black children live in poverty.

In an economic context where African Americans commonly lose, it is powerful to see Beyoncé—a Black woman—winning. She has become arguably the most successful performer in the world in an industry that has used and discarded many a Black artist. She had the power to release *Lemonade* exclusively for streaming on Tidal, a service her husband owns and in which she holds equity. She had the ability to keep her previous release, 2013's *Beyoncé*, a secret until she stopped the world by dropping it in the middle of the night. The fact that she is able to commodify and control her own image and work is extraordinary in a society where Black women have so little control. She won. And some of us refuse to hate the player, rather than the game. Bey's "paper" is our figurative revenge, too. It means someone like us has found a formula for making it in this broken-ass, biased-ass, rigged system that isn't going to change anytime soon. Representation matters.

Beyoncé is not an anarchist; she is a pop diva. There is value in that alone. Movements need agitators and artists. Music has a powerful ability to shape social values and beliefs, and Black artists have always provided the support and soundtrack for civil rights. Billie sang "Strange Fruit"; Nina sang "Mississippi, Goddam"; Sam sang "A Change is Gonna Come"; Aretha asked for "Respect." And the day after "Formation" was released, Beyoncé performed the song during the Super Bowl 50 halftime show, flanked by an army of dancers styled like Black Panthers—all big, glorious afros, black leather, and berets.

By the time Beyoncé took the stage at halftime in Levi's Stadium, California, "Formation" was already being viewed as a challenge to police brutality against Black people and a show of support for Black Lives Matter. That message coupled with Black Power imagery made the upholders of white supremacy wail. Former New York City Mayor Rudy Giuliani wrung his hands on Fox News and pronounced the performance "Outrageous!" At the most American and capitalist of sporting events (2016 Super Bowl ads hit $5 million a pop), in front of more than 111 million people, a Black woman called out police violence and reclaimed the image of two Black activist groups that misguided mainstream, white America sadly associate more with terror than liberation. That is the power of popular culture.

And it is the power of capitalism. It is unfair, but she who amasses money amasses power to do what others cannot. Critics call for Beyoncé to toss off her extensions, makeup, and booty-baring sequined onesies, to eschew all talk of Lambos and yachts, to quit stacking money, money, and just talk revolution, when they know good and damn well that broke Bey without all the artifice wouldn't have a platform or power to speak on feminism or Blackness to the masses. Political purists don't become pop stars. The very thing that makes *Lemonade*'s social justice bent possible is the thing that makes people doubt the sincerity of the message and messenger. Most every American, except for the most disadvantaged few, benefits from and is complicit in the destruction caused by capitalism. It is the system under which we all have to find a way to move. Few of us have chosen to be purists, to drop out, to defy the system. We stack our paper—even if the stacks are short. This is the kind of bald hypocrisy that so often undergirds analysis of Black women's actions. We are uniquely and consistently called on to be better, purer, perfect—even when we do good. Beyoncé has leveraged her financial success to highlight the oppression of her people. That is something—a big something. Getting rich may not be radical, but richness can be leveraged for radical things.

PART III

The lady sings her legacy

12

THE LADY SINGS HER LEGACY

Introduction

Daphne A. Brooks

Now more than ever, *Lemonade* seems like an encapsulation of past as well as very present epochs. Though it dropped some seven months before Agent Orange would fully ascend to power, it is a catalogue of histories of collective subjugation and urgent, of-the-moment, personal as well as communal cata-strophe. Into this maelstrom comes a work that offers a vision of the black feminist elsewhere that is Othered temporality and spatiality. It is both histori-cally and speculatively dense at the level of the visual as well as the sonic. By way of its scale and length, ravishing imagery and black feminist verse delivered as voice-over narration, it demands that viewers reorient themselves in relation to our contemporary pop landscape by reckoning with a black woman's inter-ior lifeworld writ large.

This vision of black feminist alterity, *Lemonade* suggests, is one that is contingent upon the extent to which black women might take what was available to them and what they resourcefully and defiantly make out of that to which they have access and ultimately transform their lives. This exquisite work hits its emotional denouement with a recipe for how to turn a sour fruit into sweet drink with one's own hands. It is a recipe passed on to Beyoncé by her husband's family matriarch, Miss Hattie, and it sums up the terms of her own improvisational survival and will to thrive. "The past and the future merge to meet us here," declares Ms. Knowles in the opening minutes of her long-form video, reciting the quietly combustible verse of British-Somalian poet Warsan Shire that flows like an imposing body of water through and around each of the songs on the visual album. And it's this "here" that Beyoncé conjures for us, envisions for us, sings to us as she invites us to dwell and journey forth with "Black being in the wake," as cultural critic Christina Sharpe has famously put it in her prodigious meditation on this subject. This is a kind of "mourning" that "might be interminable." It finds Beyoncé "memorial [izing] ... an event that is ongoing."[1]

Our pop phenom walks the fields in the tragically iconic garb of the slain, as my colleague Claudia Rankine remarked to me when we first discussed Beyoncé's work with one another. She surrogates the precarity of modern black life in this opening sequence while singing a minor key testimonial (co-penned with Brit melanchol-iac crooner James Blake) about betrayal and distrust: "Pray you catch me whispering/I pray you catch me listening/I pray you catch me." The stealth work of a woman seeking answers is also the supplication of the abandoned, the forgotten, the dispossessed. Find me. Don't forget me. Break my fall. Hovering throughout are those there to bear witness: sisters dressed in nineteenth-century finery and haunting the scene, some in black and white and others in color; silently resolved women and girls meeting the camera's eye. All hold forth in stillness as they occupy the grounds that constitute the afterlives of slavery: New Orleans' Madewood Plantation, New Orleans' Destrehan Plantation, New Orleans' Fort Macomb, the site where Confederate troops holed up at the start of the war until the Union army got a hold of it in 1862.

"I tried to make a home out of you" declares our gravelly voiced heroine before concluding that "a stairway leads to nothing." The polyvalent "you"—a philandering lover, America the nation state—are all possible targets of admonishment here, the person and/or thing that is a source of emptiness and sorrow that must be confronted before the real work can be done. This is sonic pop performance art that insists on staying close to "those whom the state positions to die ungrievable deaths and live lives meant to be unlivable," as Sharpe puts it.[2] This is work that draws the throughline between personal and historical injury: "unknown women wander the hallways at night." The chasm of infidelity in a romance gone wrong turns, through visual citation, into an ode to the departed whom we loved as well as the ones whose names we do not know but who stand with us in the "*long durée*" of "a blackened consciousness" that might "rupture the structural silences produced and facilitated by, and that produce and facilitate, Black social and physical death."[3]

As many have noted, *Lemonade* is, to be sure, doing a kind of "wake work" with, for instance, its inclusion of the mothers of the Black Lives Matter movement who appear late in the video alongside Queen Ya Ya Kijafa Brown of the Washitaw Nation, the female Mardi Gras masquerader who stands near while the maternal sovereign hold up portraits of the dearly departed. The video insists on staging these rituals of acknowledging the perpetuity of black grief and disaster, of that which can never be repaired or reconstructed. These resonances with Sharpe's brilliant work are specific and poignant, but *Lemonade*, it should be noted, is no Afro-pessimist joint. While Afro-pessimism, that impactful field of current academic debate, cogently interrogates the putative certainty of black social death in the long arm of slavery and at the hands of racial capitalism, while it boldly exposes the ruse of a kind of "political hope" that, as Calvin Warren argues, remains invested in "temporal linearity, perfection, betterment, struggle, work, and utopian futurity" (key tenets of Beyoncéology, it should be noted), *Lemonade* conversely extols the potential for the "redemption" of forms of black intimacy that do not deny historical ruin but coexist with and in spite of it.[4]

It manages and addresses individual and collective turmoil by way of the narrative of solitary journey, sonic duets, and compositional ensemble work, the *mise en scène* of the communitarian, and the overarching trope of reconciliation with a life partner; and it suggests the necessity of ending a "love drought" before ultimately turning again, ready to "slay all day," outward and toward the Great War that continues to rage and rain down on black folks. Hers is a kind of cultural work that refuses the terms and strategies of black resistance in any single register (Afro-pess or otherwise), stretching itself across multiple expressive forms and aesthetic dimensions in ways that produce new sonic cartographies of black feminism in this perilous moment in time—one of the reasons that it remains such a monumental, impactful, critically adored, and history-making text of this millennium—Grammy Awards be damned.

As I have noted elsewhere about Beyoncé as well as her baby sis Solange, we might recognize the ways that these two sisters are united in addressing the problem of black subjugation in ways rarely seen in contemporary popular music culture, and certainly in ways that are all too rarely performed in black popular music culture in particular.[5] The Knowles sisters' spectacular statements of resolve, resistance as well as black grief recall the postbellum "Woman's Era" cultural activist politics of Ida B. Wells, who sounded the alarm on lynch law and public sphere black death; Anna Julia Cooper, who called out the inextricable links between patriarchy and black oppression; and Pauline Hopkins, who realized the exceptional responsibility that black women artists were tasked with in forging a path toward communal futurity. Still more, their work builds on the second black women's renaissance in thought and liberation politics summed up famously by the Combahee River Collective, which declares that "[o]ur politics initially sprang from the shared belief that Black women are inherently valuable, that our liberation is a necessity not as an adjunct to somebody else's"—surely a sentiment crossfaded across the epic reach of these artists' two pathbreaking albums from 2016, *Lemonade* and *A Seat at the Table.* [6]

Beyoncé and her sister Solange have used the pop pulpit to speak truth to power about the politics of liberation from the specificity of their intersecting experiences as black women from the South whose histories of racial, gender, and class struggle course through their work. Each made records that insist on the importance and value and beauty of black life under duress. The new millennium resistance movement in pop is in full bloom now—thanks much to the unapologetically agit-prop work of two *boss* siblings. It's their hour now standing at the hot center of pop music's most urgent and robust era of sociopolitical activism in nearly half a century. And *Lemonade* is the masterwork in this movement that broke open the floodgates, enabling a new and historically unprecedented level of critical engagement with intersectional politics in popular music culture. So let the Lady sing her legacy.

★★★★★★★

This final section of the *Lemonade* reader showcases a range of critical essays that convey the vast scope and breadth of Beyoncé's masterpiece as an immersive counter-historical text that tenaciously asserts: radical black feminist self-representation; the potency of regional blackness; the twinned agency of sacred and profane aesthetics as black women's restorative stratagems; the manifestation of pluralist genius in the form of "transmedial storytelling"; and the "spiritual praxis of black female performativity" reverberating from one queen's archive to the next. The very fact of *Lemonade*'s rich complexities in terms of form as well as content offers "boy-bye" rejoinders to the critical racial and gender biases that Beyoncé the artist has faced in the patriarchal world of music criticism that this volume's closing chapters address.

Tanisha Ford's essay, "'Beysthetics': 'Formation' and the Politics of Style," insists that we recognize how crucial the visual and sartorial economy of Beyoncé's repertoire is to her socio-historical and political vision. From the iconic yellow *Lemonade* dress that propels her into the diasporic realm to the charged choreography that invokes the confrontational aesthetics of avant-garde performance art, Ford's work traces the evolutionary lexicon of "Bey-arts" as insurgent expressive culture. Tyina Steptoe takes us to the "sonic borderlands of the Western South" in her chapter entitled "Beyoncé's Western South Serenade" in which she examines the specificity and the heterogeneity of the Knowles family's roots as well as the cultural influences of the Western South in Yoncé's musical formations. As her work reveals, we are out on the frontier in *Lemonade*, navigating cartographies steeped in the histories of West Africa, Spain, France, and Mexico that live on in her elsewhere. Kinitra D. Brooks and Kameelah L. Martin's "'I Used to Be Your Sweet Mama': Beyoncé at the Crossroads of Blues and Conjure in *Lemonade*" show us the tools by which the artist who has been called by critics "a one-woman storm system" reigns as both a sonic sorceress and a blues empress, as well as a formidable musician who draws on a dazzling array of vernacular black women's practices— voodoo, blues aesthetics, conjure rituals, and spiritual cosmologies—as methods of radical healing. Their study theorizes a kind of black feminist opaque physics in Beyoncé's work that rejects systemic structures of oppression and reorders the universe according to black women's desires.

Kyra Gaunt pursues the question of impossibility in her essay "Beyoncé and the 'Black Swan Effect' of *Lemonade*." As a remarkable "outlier" work of art, Beyoncé's visual album bucked industry presumptions about what sonic culture made by a black female artist can look and sound like, as well as who it is for and what kind of stories it is capable of telling. This is a tale of both the sweep of *Lemonade*'s accomplishments as a multimedia epic that attacks the long arm of patriarchy both head on and as a meta-narrative about the industry itself. Gaunt's chapter threads the needle between Beyoncé's shrewd battle and that of her forebear, Ethel Waters. Michele Prettyman Beverly explores *Lemonade* through the luminosity and the prodigious aesthetic power of Aretha Franklin. Beverly considers the ways in which we might invoke Queen Re Re's spiritual virtuosity as a hermeneutic, as a critical lens through which we might interrogate what she poignantly refers to as the "ecological spirituality" of Queen Bey's magnum opus. One black feminist archive of sound meets another in Beverly's stirring essay, which centers the importance of "natural woman" as "metaphysical force" that offers us more life "in the wake" of past and present disaster. Birgitta J. Johnson closes out the *Lemonade* reader with "middle fingers in the air." Her pointed chapter, "She Gave You #Lemonade, Stop Trying to Say Its Tang: Calling Out How Race-Gender Bias Obscures Black Women's Achievements in Pop Music," dissects the crisis in cultural criticism ill-equipped to manage and analyze the rigor and complexities of black feminist sonic cultures through a sophisticated lens. Rooted in racist and sexist presumptions about taste, rigor, and culture-making itself, the egregious critical blindspots that Johnson dissects here sink like a police cruiser under her critical eye.

Notes

1 Christina Sharpe, *In the Wake: On Blackness and Being* (Durham, NC: Duke University Press, 2016), 20.
2 Sharpe, 22.
3 Sharpe, 22.
4 Calvin L. Warren, "Black Nihilism and the Politics of Hope," *CR: The New Centennial Review* 15:1 (Spring 2015): 215–248, 243.
5 Daphne A. Brooks, "The Knowles Sisters Political Hour," unpublished essay manuscript.
6 The Combahee River Collective Statement (1978). http://circuitous.org/scraps/comba hee.html.

13

TO FEEL LIKE A "NATURAL WOMAN"

Aretha Franklin, Beyoncé and the ecological spirituality of *Lemonade*

Michele Prettyman Beverly

> You make me feel ... you make me feel ... you make me feel like a natural woman.
> *Lyrics from "(You Make Me Feel Like) A Natural Woman"*
> *written by Carole King and Gerry Goffin*

Like every text, the song lyrics quoted above, written by then married couple King and Coffin and sung with aching poignancy by Aretha Franklin, leave room for a range of interpretations. But this song has a particular currency that continues to resonate in the public sphere as a seminal articulation of a woman's power to express how her lover makes her "feel" and how this feeling allows her to touch the essence of her own being. Having long been a staple of Franklin's vast repertoire, "A Natural Woman" vibrates with a depth of longing that has characterized her music for over sixty years. Franklin's phrasing, her elocution, and the way in which she redefines genre and structures of feeling are no superficial exercise, as Barack Obama muses in a piece written by David Remnick: "Nobody embodies more fully the connection between the African-American spiritual, the blues, R. & B., rock and roll—the way that hardship and sorrow were transformed into something full of beauty and vitality and hope."[1] Like others whose vocal and performative power had origins in black church and religious experience, Franklin voiced the sacred and the secular as twin-voices, twin-souls, shared occupations.[2] Franklin's vocal and musical prowess, her song-writing ability, and her propensity for acting in the best interests of vulnerable black people birthed new relationships between politics, activism, entertainment, and performance, embodying what Arthur Jafa refers to as the "the power, beauty and alienation of black music."[3]

Jafa whose films, art, and philosophical perspective explore the metaphysics of black creative life, understands well the power of vocality and intonation as they relate to the visual sphere as he explains in an interview with Tina Campt how:

the black voice was at the core (technically, formally, and spiritually) of why black music was powerful. People typically talked about cinema in terms of stories, narratives, thematics—but it quickly became clear that we needed (additionally) different concepts. For example, the idea of black visual intonation was conceived as the cinematic equivalent of the black voice.[4]

To further explicate this connection between the power of vocal intonation and the cinematic, consider footage of Aretha Franklin recorded live in 1973 at the New Temple Missionary Baptist Church in Watts, a suburb of Los Angeles, California. There she performed arguably the most powerful rendition of the classic "Amazing Grace" alongside gospel legend Rev. James Cleveland. Rembert Browne describes the performance as "more than in your bones; it's cellular."[5] He recounts his own almost metaphysical reaction: "She makes you cry, she makes you smile, she makes you want to jump up and holler at her as she hollers at God."[6] Franklin's performance was filmed by the late director Sydney Pollack for a concert documentary whose release was held up for decades.[7] What is notable is the intensity with which Pollack (and other influencers like Robert De Niro, dispatched to apply pressure on Franklin) pursued her to obtain permission rights in the hopes of making available (and profiting from) the full metaphysical power of her "black visual intonation."[8] And the sheer force of Franklin's intonation reproduces more than a narrative or a feeling, but catapults us through multiple realms of experience.[9]

A final piece of introductory context about Franklin as a "natural woman" comes from Cinque Henderson, who eloquently writes:

> There's nothing expressly religious about "Natural Woman." But it is of course inevitably haunted by the verse from Paul's letter to the Corinthians about a natural man, who "receiveth not the things of the Spirit of God … neither can he know them." It may be that a natural man cannot know the things of God, but it was the radical gospel of Aretha that first made known that a particular type of women could. That a natural woman can know God and erotic longing, ravenous spiritual and sexual need all at once, and that they can live uproariously in on buoyant, life-giving body.[10]

Henderson's exegesis frames the "natural man"—who is carnal, *un*godly, and incapable of knowing God *and* more "worldly" preoccupations, like sexual desire—in opposition to a "natural woman" whose embodied performance liberates her from scriptural constraints. Building upon Henderson's reading, I imagine a "natural woman" as a contravening rupturous/rapturous force that breeches the hermeneutic split between the sensual and the sacred. "Natural women" are willing to affect and be affected, to touch and be touched, activating powers that are both sensory and ethereal in ways beyond the theoretical constructs of the "affective" and the "tactile." I am reminded of the power of "natural women" when I hear Fred Moten articulate Franklin's impact in a recent interview with Mark Anthony Neal saying, "She put her hands on us."[11] Evoking the spiritual (biblical) tradition going back many generations of "laying of hands" where black folks used rituals of touch meant to heal, make whole, or free of maladies, channeling energetic power to a sick child or a wayward soul. "Natural women" touch us in this way.

In this essay, I think through the archive of a "natural woman" looking for traces in both Franklin's and Beyoncé's creative footprint and likeness where performance and form conjoin the sensual and the sacred along with other spiritual pursuits of self-discovery, self-making, knowing, and desire. While Aretha was the pre-eminent voice of the twentieth century and Beyoncé is a seminal figure of the twenty-first, they were, in many ways, worlds apart.[12] But both were reared in the church, strongly influenced by their fathers; and each woman strove not simply to be relegated to the domains of stage, church, or screen, but to explore other kinds of performative/spiritual awareness.[13] My work fosters a connection between them where Aretha Franklin's performative power might be seen as the portal or conduit through which we gain entry into an interpretative framework for *Lemonade*, not simply as Beyoncé's magnum opus but as a polyvocal, intertextual field of creative performance. Aretha, like the countless blues, gospel, and soul women before her, helped us understand how black women in performance could tap into feeling as a transformative ontology; and *Lemonade*, too, interrogates and relishes in these same powers. To account for the work that these figures, images, and texts perform I use the term "ecological spirituality," a term which draws from, in part, Merriam-Webster's definition of ecological: as "of or relating to the environments of living things or to the relationships between living things and their environments."[14] "Natural women" are able to cultivate meaningful inquiries and connections to themselves and to the spiritual—the ecosystem of human, material, natural, and supernatural "environments" around them. Thus, I view *Lemonade* as a performance of ecological spirituality that explores how the *self* finds it*self* in relationship to its environment.

Moved by Franklin's extraordinary life, performative power, and the ways in which mourners have contemplated her work since her recent death, I write to proclaim, in part, what Christina Sharpe has powerfully pronounced as "wake work," that space which "does the important work of sitting (together) in the pain and sorrow of death as a way of marking, remembering, and celebrating a life. Wake: grief, celebration, memory and those among the living who through ritual, mourn their passing and celebrate their life."[15] This essay imagines how language/ scholarship might perform a "wake"—not simply in the form of a eulogy or an obituary, but as way of catalyzing the energy of person; as a mode of grieving that attends to their artistry and being; as a reckoning with the very life-force of a person that simultaneously moves on and is left behind in us. Thus, the next phase of this essay asks, "how do ... performance and visual culture observe and mediate this un/survival?"[16] Specifically, how might we interpret the performative poetics of *Lemonade,* and other emergent forms of visual culture, as remnants of this un/ survival or as an ecological, spiritual praxis of black female performativity?

The archive of the natural woman

In her keynote at the Association for the Study of the Arts of the Present (ASAP)—delivered fittingly, in light of my discussion of *Lemonade*, in New Orleans in October of 2018—Daphne Brooks reminds us that black women are rarely in control of their own archive, a claim impacting how we might read the work and legacies of Franklin and Beyoncé.[17] Central to this question of archival agency are ways in which they evolve through the various modes of archival indexicality: the photographic, the digital, the performative; and through the very praxes of being performers, artists and human, mothers, lovers, activists—what Brooks might describe as "sensuous forms of archiving."[18] Much of the essay will focus on Beyoncé's visual album *Lemonade* and how it reflects back to us the power of many "natural women" through the varied filmic, visual, artistic, literary, and spiritual influences and references it contains, which reach into the natural and the super-natural to get to us. Through *Lemonade* we are compelled to contemplate the influences of an ever-expanding archive of "natural women": performers like Nina Simone; filmmakers like Julie Dash and Kasi Lemmons; artists like Beverly Buchanan, Betye Saar, Carrie Mae Weems, Xavieria Simmons, and Allison Janae Hamilton (who I discuss later); writers like Alice Walker, Mari Evans, Toni Cade Bambara, Toni Morrison, Gwendolyn Brooks, and Lucille Clifton; and the work of contemporary figures whose work is deeply invested in the liberatory possibilities of ecologies and geographies like Katherine McKittrick and Dionne Brand, and contemporary poets with an explicit focus on eco-criticism/nature.[19] These figures mobilize material culture and memory, magical realism, natural and super-natural mysticism, black gothic mythology, tradition and ritual, grief and desire into tableaus where the performative becomes probative, the sensual is one with the sacred, and where hurt becomes hallowed. This archive of black life (and arguably the performative power of Beyoncé), once rooted in the hardness of the earth, is often uprooted by writerly, filmic, and performative energies, making the earth tender and malleable again. *Lemonade* channels a "woman done wrong" bio-graphical narrative into an hour-long spasmodic elegy where Beyoncé's feeling, flailing, drowning, aching, raging, body moves in and through the afterlives of slavery, racial violence, and natural disaster, reconstituting itself in the presence of other "natural women" as spectral and spiritual guides. I trace some of the aesthetic conditions that might help us see (and feel) the precise moments where these "natural women" emerge illuminating black female performance and artistry as spiritual and metaphysical force—literally forces of nature.

Evidence of the "natural woman" can be found in Franklin's archive of album covers, photographs, and footage where she is marked as a "spiritual" body and an equally sensual one. Countless images of Franklin center on her face in the throes of ecclesiastical ecstasy: head thrown back, eyes closed, voice reverberating through every muscle in her face and body. I want to briefly address two particularly telling images of Franklin which are also evocative of the many "faces" of Beyoncé in *Lemonade*. In the first image, a photograph from 1971, she stands between her father, Rev. C.L. Franklin, and her sister Carolyn, recalling the powerful influence both fathers wielded on the careers and lives of their daughters.[20] (A segment of *Lemonade* captures Beyoncé's paternal influence in the song "Daddy Lessons.") In this image, a full-figured Franklin wears an African-inspired dress, more pronounced cleavage, and a perfectly round afro, while Rev. Franklin dons "Jim Jones" styled sunglasses and Carolyn is carefully coiffed and neatly dressed. Aretha wears no smile here, just the wry curl of her lips; her afro reminding us of the emergence of "natural" hair in the lives of black women of the time. She seems well aware of the irony of the photo and of her position in the family as both icon and breadwinner, and as a woman coming into her own as an attractive, now more secular performer still flanked by her father's imposing religious influence. The photo reminds us of her propensity to use and transform her bodily presentation as an archival record of cultural and self-awareness, and also perhaps a reminder that she was still her father's daughter, still wrestling for independence and the capacity to make herself in her own image. This interpretation resonates given that both Franklin and Beyoncé came into a sense of themselves as performers under the watchful eyes of fathers and the collective eyes of audiences trained to police and evaluate their public presentations.

In a second image, the cover for her 1975 album entitled *You*, Franklin poses outdoors lying on the ground. She reclines in front of a resplendent, idyllic botanical garden of flowers and trees. This naturalistic setting is punctuated by Franklin's presence as she dons a bright yellow halter top tied at the bustline revealing cleavage and her slenderer figure. She reclines on the grass, yellow sandals beside her bare feet, propped up on her elbows, the yellow providing an interesting parallel to the golden Roberto Cavalli dress worn by Beyoncé in the section of *Lemonade* labeled "Denial." Her hair, an ever-changing feature, is now auburn, slightly pressed worn in a bouffant, and she wears a sexy grin. Aretha's body here is sleek, modern, and confident and at ease in a more pastoral setting. In both images, her image is malleable, able to move through different meanings and connotations, yet shifting between her inner and outer environments. While Franklin often fought for control over her image, as she reveals in her push back against the release of the *Amazing Grace* documentary, these images to me are nonetheless instructive. They emphasize ways in which "natural women" navigate self-awareness and self-making and create space for themselves to trouble, even subtly, the expectations and demands that others placed on them.

Making *Lemonade*: collaboration as spiritual praxis

Beyoncé's *Lemonade*, which premiered on HBO in April of 2016, is a traditional album of songs and a visual album/film segmented into eleven chapters: Intuition, Denial, Anger, Apathy, Emptiness, Accountability, Reformation, Forgiveness, Resurrection, Hope, and Redemption. While Beyoncé is listed as a director, *Lemonade* draws from an experimental style heavily influenced by groundbreaking director and visual artist Kahlil Joseph. Joseph's metaphysical aesthetic—seen in his short film collaboration with Flying Lotus, *Until the Quiet Comes* (2012), and more recently in *Fly Paper* (2018)—collapse movement and stunning photography into fragments of memory and forgetting.[21] *Lemonade* is also shaped by five other directors, seven cinematographers, and a host of set and costume designers and visual artists.[22] In addition to the behind-the-scenes collaborators it features a number of on-screen personas, including: tennis great Serena Williams; young actresses Zendaya, Amandla Stenberg, and Quvenzhané Wallis; Beyoncé's protégés Chloe and Halle; model Winnie Harlow; dancer Michaela DePrince; and the mothers of Michael Brown Jr. (Lesley McSpadden), Trayvon Martin (Sybrina Fulton), and Eric Garner (Gwen Carr). *Lemonade* dissects and reconstitutes Beyoncé's experiences, emotional anxieties, and self-doubt alongside broader narratives of the afterlife of slavery and natural disaster. *Lemonade* embeds Beyoncé's performative presence within black women's past and present histories' resilience and survival as interrogates of the politics of intimacy, equity, beauty, fidelity, and sexuality. The film's onscreen co-creators, some listed above, shape the film's figural index of blackness as: fairer/darker skinned, braided/flowing hair, famous/unknown, cis and queer, and those from the multiple regions of the African diaspora. This community of collaborators, onscreen and off, is a central trope of how I see the visual album as performing a kind of spiritual work.

Much of my thinking about spirituality is influenced by Judylyn Ryan's analysis of film and literature, *Spirituality as Ideology in Black Women's Film and Literature*. In it Ryan argues that both *Daughters of the Dust* (Dash, 1991) and *Eve's Bayou* (Lemmons, 1997) excavate black ancestral pasts, memory, and empowerment by tapping into female artistry and creative vision. After seeing *Daughters of the Dust*, Ryan explained:

> I realized that spirituality was not simply being depicted as an aspect of characters' lives. Rather, spirituality had a more integral function in the work, a function connected to the artist's vision and to the objectives she set out to accomplish through the film or literary text.[23]

Ryan's conception of spirituality "focuses on the ways in which spirituality anchored or encapsulated a set of ideas related to the Black woman artist's view of human relationships and human possibilities" and how "spirituality sustains the mechanisms of transformation that Black women's narratives generate for characters, actors, readers, and viewers, as well as for other writers and filmmakers, critics, and scholars"—a premise central to my reading of *Lemonade* as a text that relies on various modes of collaborative creativity, an investment in black women's past lives and texts as archival memory.[24]

Lemonade vibrates with the frequencies of African diasporic ancestral references and with spectral memories of a black southern past. In an ancestral context, it foregrounds fabric, art, movement, and elements from the natural world highlighting the powers of female bodies as art objects and elements of the natural world. Yoruba spirituality figures prominently through the art of Nigerian artist Laolu Senbanjo, whose body art is featured during the segment between "Anger" and "Apathy." Filmed in black and white, Senbanjo's designs—drawn with white body paint—create stark contrasts that adorn the black bodies complementing the ornate braided hair designs. At times in other color segments Beyoncé's face is similarly painted and she dons Masai-inspired neck ornaments. Called "The Sacred Art of the Ori," Senbanjo describes his work as creating a powerful "connection between the artist and the music."[25]

The film forges connective tissue between collaborators, not just as skilled artists but as individual energies shaping a broader vision. This kind of co-creative collaborative energy is certainly not new, but has gained powerful currency in visual culture: Kehinde Wiley's work on *Empire*; Mickalene Thomas's recent photographed portraits of Cardi B; Wiley and Amy Sherald's portraits of the Obamas; Arthur Jafa's multi-vocal collaborative poetics in *Dreams Are Colder Than Death* (which features the voices/presence of Hortense Spillers, Fred Moten, Saidiya Hartman et al.); Bradford Young's direction of a short film for Common's album *Black America Again*; Kahlil Joseph's work with Flying Lotus, Sampha, and Shabazz Palaces; and the work of dancers, artists, poets, filmmakers, and musical innovators across commercial and artistic spaces, platforms, and worldviews. The collaborative energy in *Lemonade* is one that is intertextual, multi-vocal, polyphonic quality; as Carol Vernallis puts it, "*Lemonade* encourages the listenerviewer to make sense of a complex whole" and the film's formal attachments to music video and experimental style are necessary to "contain the past, present and future." In a section of her essay on *Lemonade* she titles "Summoning Community," she writes, "All of *Lemonade*'s parameters—from sound effects to cinematography—work to incorporate an everwidening community."[26]

While the film's creation values the necessity of community and the power of collaboration, one might quarrel with Beyoncé's centrality in the film (she is often literally centered in the frame, her gaze fixed on the viewer); and she appears as the voice, the object, the subject, the temptress, the teacher, the student, the performer, the auteur, and is prominently featured in segments which depict the resilience of people surviving the wake of natural disaster in New Orleans. I would argue that this too is an invariable part of the unevenness of the nature of creative and spiritual praxes. While artists and performers typically want control over these processes and must learn to navigate egos, resources, creative differences, etc., what is critical here, what is at stake, are, to reiterate Ryan, ways in which "spirituality *sustains* the mechanisms of transformation that Black women's narratives generate for characters, actors, readers, and viewers, as well as for other writers and filmmakers, critics, and scholars." Thus, the generative collective energy, the merging of past, present and a speculative future, is where the power of this work will maintain a sense of meaning, not just for the creatives, but for the community spectral, ancestral, and imagined communities that are "summoned" in *Lemonade*.

I also recognize how *Lemonade* might also embody Moten's notion of "black sociality," particularly in light of Kahlil Joseph's aesthetic influence. Describing Joseph's practice and aesthetic in *Fly Paper*, Alessandra Raengo draws from Moten's notion of the "ensemble" as "a form of black sociality that eschews individuation and takes place in a constant productive dynamic between the 'solo' and the 'group': artists congregating and socializing."[27] Part of the spiritual praxis of

Lemonade then is the ebb and flow of a collective, creative dance that grapples, interrogates, and pursues answers to questions around love, self-awareness, and self-acceptance in a complex universe of other people and forces.

The politics of the natural woman

Another central element in *Lemonade*'s construction is the adapted poetry of British-Somali poet Warsan Shire heard in Beyoncé's voiceover narration. While at times there is some slippage between the song lyrics and Shire's poetic voice, Shire's piercing use of language and metaphor provides an incisive and complex reading at the intersections of intergenerational grief, loss, violence, and longing beyond that which Beyoncé's lyrics can do alone. Shire describes her work as "documentation, genealogy, preserving the names of the women [who] came before me. To connect, honor, to confront"; and much of this energy helps fuel Beyoncé's visual intonation, via Jafa.[28] That is, the poetic and political potency of the film relies on Shire's words more than the song lyrics. Similarly, in Beyoncé's 2013 song "Flawless" she excerpts a section of Chimamanda Ngozi Adichie's now-famous speech, "We Should All Be Feminists":

> We teach girls to shrink themselves
> To make themselves smaller
> We say to girls
> "You can have ambition
> But not too much
> You should aim to be successful
> But not too successful
> Otherwise you will threaten the man"
> Because I am female
> I am expected to aspire to marriage
> I am expected to make my life choices
> Always keeping in mind that
> Marriage is the most important
> Now marriage can be a source of
> Joy and love and mutual support
> But why do we teach girls to aspire to marriage
> And we don't teach boys the same?
> We raise girls to each other as competitors
> Not for jobs or for accomplishments
> Which I think can be a good thing
> But for the attention of men
> We teach girls that they cannot be sexual beings
> In the way that boys are
> Feminist: the person who believes in the social
> Political, and economic equality of the sexes.[29]

While I will not recount the lyrics to Beyoncé's song, Adichie rightly distinguishes her feminism from Beyoncé's, saying:

> Still, her type of feminism is not mine … I think men are lovely, but I don't think that women should relate everything they do to men: Did he hurt me, do I forgive him, did he put a ring on my finger? We women are so conditioned to relate everything to men. Put a group of women together and the conversation will eventually be about men. Put a group of men together and they will not talk about women at all, they will just talk about their own stuff.[30]

Given the legitimate differences between Adichie's and Beyoncé's articulations of feminism, and the discontinuity between the lyrical voice of Beyoncé and Shire, I want to briefly revisit some of Beyoncé's earlier music video work to note some important ways in which her own archive is evolving.

Consider the video for "Déjà Vu" from the 2006 *B-Day* album.[31] This video, directed by Sophie Muller, features some of the same visual cues, similar locations, and some of the shared aesthetic and formal concerns that shape the Beyoncé performative universe: frenetic, hypersexualized choreography and movements, erotic costuming, flailing limbs, blowing hair, etc. Daphne Brooks generously describes the album, saying:

> Beyoncé's latest recording imagines her growth as an artist by stretching (until it's taut) the emotional register of her lyrical and musical content. Although she returns time and again to conflicts between love and money, the material on *B-Day* examines an ever-sophisticated range of emotions tied to black women's personal and spiritual discontent, satiation, self-worth, and agency.[32]

While Brooks claims that the album crafts a "voice of black female discontent in black female popular culture," I find that the video is a precursor to many of the themes in *Lemonade*. It was filmed at the Oak Alley Plantation[33] and the Maple Leaf Bar, both in Louisiana. In "Déjà Vu," Beyoncé's body is not her own and she is driven to a frenzy by Jay-Z's high-angle gaze as she hovers around his crotch. In various scenes she is the girlfriend, the virgin, the whore, the primitive; quivering, gyrating at break-neck speed, as her lyrics proclaim, "boy I try to catch myself but I'm out of control, your sexiness is so appealing I can't let it go." Ironically, this video repeats visual cues from *Lemonade*, with scenes of her walking through the tall grasses, the plantation house, the bayou. Brooks describes it as "a tricked-out plantation setting with Knowles alternately draped across ornate Victorian furniture and dashing haltingly through ever-glades and (cotton?) fields looking like a deer in headlights, or perhaps more accurately, like a fugitive (house) slave on the run." While Brooks also points to the vocal and physical labor Beyoncé performs here, I also argue that her lover has brought her to a point of "feeling"—not perhaps like the natural woman I have described, but like a natural woman navigating an evolving personal journey.

Natural and supernatural aesthetics

As many in the popular press have noted, *Lemonade* resonates with influences from Julie Dash's pioneering *Daughters of the Dust*. [34] Dash and cinematographer Arthur Jafa collaborated to mine the beauty of the Gullah women juxtaposed with the naturalistic splendor of the Sea Islands. The film juxtaposes sequences where the camera lingers along water, land, and sky-scapes to frames of women as whirling figures in lacey cotton dresses, and at other times in still-life portraiture emphasizing how the sun hits the skin, teeth, bone structure, and the lilting layers of antique white fabric falling against a female frame. Central to how beauty is constructed here is the notion that beauty is endemic to human life and the natural world, and that it need not be wielded as a commodity or exploitative fantasy. *Lemonade* unapologetically references *Daughters'* visual template in the synched "formations" and movements of figures who sit still in trees, or bend in the wind, or just remain still. In *Lemonade*, "natural" might refer simply to nature; but it is also evoked in the wearing of "natural" hair or how hair might also resemble flowers, like tiny soft knots or hanging loosely like strands of Spanish moss that hover softly in the frame. In other scenes, women are surrounded by thousands of flowers and there is no distinction between flora and fauna. Black women in the after-life of ecological disasters like Hurricanes Katrina and Rita take an active form: dancing, like the elegant ballet dancer Michaela DePrince featured in several pivotal scenes. Her movements are elegant, long, and precise, similar to the choreographies of architectural bodily "formations"—lines, circles, and undulating waves. At other times, movement uproots and disrupts the unrepentant ecosystem. Musculature, in the thighs of Serena Williams, exorcizes demons (perhaps recalling what Hortense Spillers calls "flesh memory") using the force of physical form to drive away what haunts us in the plantation space. Some scenes in *Lemonade* embrace a kind of naturalistic, pastoral stateliness, while others disavow a noble presentation, instead unleashing a spectral ratchet-ness that smashes, quakes, gyrates, twerks, and grinds, crushing the memory of infidelity and sexual and racial violence into the foundation of the plantation house and into the dust.

The earth here is an essential trope, organic to the cultivation of the relationship between the body and a kind of rootedness. [35] Earth is a source of grounded-ness, a space where we grow where we are planted, but also a space where uprooted-ness might also take place. In the wake of the hurricanes, the earth, beaten into submission and grieving, is remade as new seedlings in the form of young actresses and performers, and new life appears. [36] In more contemporary visual culture, I notice a paradoxical emphasis on both rootedness—which aesthetically operates as a stabilizing force of continuity, knowing, ritual—and uprootedness as an unruly, unwieldy property more aptly where the interior and exterior states of being collide, sometimes in the form of agitation, rage, fugitivity, and protest.

A formative example of an image of southern uprooted-ness is seen in an act that reinforced the continuing relationship between violence and anti-black racism. Activist and artist Bree Newsome hoisted herself up the South Carolina state house flag pole in the wake of the massacre of nine members of the Emmanuel A.M.E. church. I read this act as an appeal to use our bodies, work, art, and sensibilities in ways that ground us in our commitment to black life and humanity while also offering a metaphysical critique of space, landscape, and power uprooting Newsome, and black life symbolically, from the firmaments of white authority. It embodies ways in which acts of public protest and political agency are rooted and uprooted. Black life and creativity in southern spaces, particularly the wave of music, film, and TV production, have a similar capacity to destabilize and reimagine the plantation regimes of power. *Lemonade* finds its ancestral and aesthetic "roots" in *Daughters*, Kasi Lemmons's *Eve's Bayou*, and, more recently, in films/TV including the series *Queen Sugar*, envisaged and adapted by Ava DuVernay, in Dee Rees's feature *Mudbound*, and in Bree Newsome's short film *Wake*, whose opening sequence depicts a figure laboring in red clay to dig a ditch for a grave.[37] This would also include art and visual culture that relishes in the material and the ethereal in work of the aforementioned Beverly Buchanan and more recently Xaveria Simmons and Allison Janae Hamilton (which I discuss later). These works collapse the spaces between earth, soil, and the natural work with human form and performativity creativity.

Wanderlust, or the spiritual practice of wandering outdoors

In this final section I want to contemplate the sensibility of being outdoors as a spiritual practice, noting that the outdoors figures prominently in recent work across many disciplines and creative practices. In many of the works I have already mentioned—but especially in contemporary acclaimed film/TV shows like *Queen Sugar, Atlanta, Mudbound* et al.—blackness and outdoor space have been reimagined; and innovative scholarship, creative writing, and poetry have done important work in reinvigorating discourses around nature, geographies, and architectures of space. Contemplating the lives and work of black women in particular, I am reminded of Katherine McKittrick's claim that "the relationship between black women and geography opens up a conceptual arena through which more humanly workable geographies can be and are imagined."[38] This conceptual opening, a clearing of space, is central to the practice of seeing and being out of doors. In this final section, I trace the movement of a particular figuration of Beyoncé in *Lemonade*, watching how that presence moves in the earlier and later parts of the film. And I find that this presence has some resonance with another "figure" in the work of artist Allison Janae Hamilton, who was recently the artist-in-residence at the Studio Museum of Harlem.

In Sarah Jane Cervenak's *Wandering: Philosophical Performances of Racial and Sexual Freedom*, she introduces us to a way of reading Gayl Jones's book *Corregidora* (1975), which she describes as "a story about the haunted life of a Southern blues singer."

Cervenak is precisely interested in a bus ride that the character, Ursa, takes during which she "wanders to recover a lost privacy and, with it, a grip on a landscape that cannot be encroached: a locale where she might roam without surveillance, out of harm's way."[39] Using language like "private pain and public trespass" Cervenak navigates the spaces in which Ursa must live, the hospital in which she attempts to heal, which are part of her daily comings and goings. Notable are the influence and impact of Ursa's lovers, part of the "traffic" of her life whose needs feel "impatient." Cervenak reads Jones's poignant narrative as a way to think about how we might feel the ways in which this character is encroached upon, but also how we might be attentive to ways she finds to carve out a semblance of an unencroachable space, where she can retreat to her own inhabitable space, as she chooses. Returning to the bus ride, Cervenak writes:

> It's on the bus that Ursa finally achieves some privacy, a rare occasion to wander and dream without interruption. To imagine the possibilities for her "own life," beyond the push and pull of other people's memories, or other people's desires.[40]

Cervenak theorizes that this practice of "wandering—daydreaming, mental and rhetorical ramblings—offers new pathways for the enactment of black female philosophical desire."[41] I conclude here by thinking with Cervenak to imagine the practice of *wandering* as a seminal feature of aesthetic and spiritual practice in *Lemonade*, and its liberatory possibilities in Southern spaces.[42]

In the film's opening of sorts we are introduced very quickly to several important images: Beyoncé in blonde cornrows; exterior shots drained of all color; shots of dry, tall grasses growing outside of a ruinous fortress (an almost 200-year-old Civil War relic in Louisiana). Cuts happen slowly in some moments, but then a quicker intercutting of Beyoncé first on a dramatic stage with a red backdrop; and then she appears outdoors, wandering among these very tall reeds.

Wearing a black hoodie—likely an homage to Trayvon Martin, but also a symbol of the melancholic loss of her self—she wanders. There is some sound here, women's voices softly chanting monosyllabic phrases, but no lyrics, no voiceover, not yet. Beyoncé here is not so much a character, but as I describe earlier, a figuration, a presence. Wearing minimal makeup, the body moving slowly and deliberately but without a sense of narrative motivation. It is difficult to find these moments in the film of some stillness, some quiet, without an emphasis on costuming, blocking, choreography, presentation. Quiet, as Kevin Quashie reminds us, is a powerful tool of both resistance and self-possession, but in *Lemonade* it is rarely deployed.[43] Later in the segment called "Redemption" a slightly different version of this figure reappears, this time wearing an African-inspired gown and with hair tightly bound. In this later series of images, she wanders again around a specific historical site, Fort

FIGURE 13.1 Video still from "Pray You Catch Me." *Lemonade*, Parkwood Entertainment, 2016

Macomb, a Civil War fortress built in 1822. Here Beyoncé sings, but the singing feels a bit intrusive as it interrupts what is an important contemplative moment. Unlike in other parts of the film where Beyoncé is an active force, exorcizing demons, here she takes just a few moments to indulge the unmotivated movement, the unscriptedness of being without narrative or artistic imposition. While the frenetic energy of *Lemonade* also has powerful resonance, it is here in these spaces where some stillness and even partial quiet provides a much-needed respite, emptying the moment of all dramatic, sometimes indulgent sensibilities.

In this vein, consider the Southern-influenced ecological tableaus of artist Allison Janae Hamilton. Hamilton's work is a majestic fusion of the ecological, biological, and material culture of the south as she collects animal carcasses, skins, found objects, and aspects of material culture, assembling them into dramatic southern sensoriums. Her work is often playful, ironic, and whimsical but undergirded by an abiding awareness of southern spatiality as a sphere that expands how we might see and inhabit outdoor space. In an essay by Siddhartha Mitter, Hamilton explains: "Even in trauma, after all, the land is beautiful. So I want you to feel that. The lightness and beauty, but wait a minute—there's something amiss, something that's not quite right."[44]

Consider here an image from Hamilton's series *Sweet Milk in the Badlands*, a series which, according to her website:

> looks toward ritual, storytelling, and trance in search of the connections between landscape and selfhood, place and disturbance. It invites an uncanny

cast of haints to lead the viewer through the beginnings of an epic tale that animates the land as a guide and witness.

Hamilton's piece, entitled "Dollbaby Standing in the Orchard at Midday" (2015, a year prior to *Lemonade*), provides a particular reading of outdoors-ness where the figure seems to have a particular kind of self-possession simply through its unmotivated presence in outdoor space.

A black female figure stands in a small grove or clearing. Trees seems to bend towards her pulled by the force of her presence—perhaps bent by her curiosity; she senses that she knows what she is and what she is doing there. A human Rorschach test, this figure is an unknown—is it a person facing the forest or a person facing the camera? Given the body's anatomical bearings and the long braid, I interpret the image with the figure's arms behind her, as she looks inquisitively at the natural world around her. Both woman and child, the figure is aware of the slight exposure of her buttocks/vaginal region, but feels untethered from an exploitative gaze. This sexual and figural ambiguity allows her a kind of freedom to amble, to discover herself here, in the present moment, as both of nature and one with it.

Part of *Lemonade*'s power, then, is its capacity to leverage the creative powers of black women and of a broad community of ideas, aesthetics, and lived-experiences. But perhaps its greatest contribution is to push through the aesthetics, the ancestral memory, and thematic density to create space to just be.

Notes

1 See David Remnick's "Soul Survivor: The Revival and Hidden Treasure of Aretha Franklin." https://www.newyorker.com/magazine/2016/04/04/aretha-franklins-american-soul. (Accessed November 18, 2018).
2 Aretha Franklin's song "Spirit in the Dark" is an important song in this key.
3 See Tina Campt's interview with Arthur Jafa, "Love is the Message, The Plan is Death." *e-Flux* 81 (2017) https://www.e-flux.com/journal/81/126451/love-is-the-message-the-plan-is-death/.
4 Ibid.
5 See Rembert Browne's piece, "A Friend in Aretha: The Spiritual Power of the Queen of Soul's 'Amazing Grace.'" https://www.theringer.com/music/2018/8/16/17705602/aretha-franklin-amazing-grace-life-career. (Accessed November 17, 2018).
6 Ibid.
7 See Chris Willman's "How Robert De Niro Helped Thaw Aretha Franklin Documentary Negotiations." https://www.billboard.com/articles/news/6898440/aretha-franklin-documentary-robert-deniro-tribeca-amazing-grace. (Accessed November 17, 2018).
8 Ibid.
9 Within Jafa's framework, we might imagine *Lemonade* as another iteration of what black visual intonation would look like.
10 See Cinque Henderson's "Aretha Franklin on Heaven and Earth." https://www.nytimes.com/2018/08/16/opinion/aretha-franklin-gospel-music.html (Accessed November 17, 2018).

11 Fred Moten is interviewed by Mark Anthony Neal on "Left of Black." November 5, 2018.
12 For discussion of a tense moment between Franklin and Beyoncé see Sean Michaels's piece, "Queen Aretha Not Amused By Beyoncé." https://www.theguardian.com/music/news/story/0,,2256370,00.html. November 5, 2018.
13 Aretha Franklin was reared in her father Rev. Clarence LaVaughn Franklin's church in Detroit; Beyoncé grew up in and maintains a connection to St. Luke's United Methodist Church in Houston, TX.
14 https://www.merriam-webster.com/dictionary/ecological.
15 See Christina Sharpe's *In the Wake: On Blackness and Being*, page 11.
16 Ibid, 14.
17 See Daphne Brooks's keynote address at the Association for the Study of the Arts of the Present, Oct 20, 2018.
18 Ibid.
19 See editor Camille Dungy's anthology of black poetry, *Black Nature: Four Centuries of African American Nature Poetry*. Athens: University of Georgia, 2009.
20 This photograph was published in Cinque Henderson's previously cited essay "Aretha Franklin on Heaven and Earth" and was taken by Anthony Barboza.
21 *Fly Paper* debuted in Europe in April of 2018.
22 Other directors include: Melina Matsoukas, Dikayl Rimmasch, Todd Tourso, Jonas Akerlund, and Mark Romanek.
23 See Judylyn Ryan's *Spirituality as Ideology in Black Wonen's Film and Literature*. Charlottesville and London: University of Virginia, 2005, 1.
24 Ibid.
25 See Alyssa Klein's essay at http://www.okayafrica.com/beyonce-lemonade-laolu-senbanjo-sacred-art-of-the-ori/.
26 See Carol Vernallis's piece, Beyoncé's Lemonade, AvantGarde Aesthetics, and Music Video: "The Past and the Future Merge to Meet Us Here."
27 See Alessandra Raengo's piece on *Fly Paper* at http://liquidblackness.com/lb-art-reviews-kahlil-josephs-fly-paper-by-alessandra-raengo/
28 See Alexis Okeowo's take at https://www.newyorker.com/culture/cultural-comment/the-writing-life-of-a-young-prolific-poet-warsan-shire.
29 Chimamanda Ngozi Adichie. 2015. "We Should All Be Feminists."
30 See Adichie's take in Lisa Blake's essay, https://www.billboard.com/articles/news/7534428/chimamanda-ngozi-adichie-beyonce-flawless-interview.
31 In "All That You Can't Leave Behind" Daphne Brooks provides a compelling reading of the music video for the song "Ring the Alarm."
32 Brooks, "All That You Can't Leave Behind."
33 Location details here: https://oakalleyplantation.org/filmed-here.
34 See some of the press's interest in this subject at these links: https://www.nytimes.com/2016/04/28/movies/daughters-of-the-dust-restoration-beyonce-lemonade.html; https://www.theguardian.com/film/2017/may/31/daughters-of-the-dust-review; https://www.vanityfair.com/hollywood/2016/08/daughters-of-the-dust-exclusive; https://www.bfi.org.uk/news-opinion/news-bfi/features/beyonce-lemonade-julie-dash-daughters-dust.
35 Here I think of Edouard Glissant's "poetics of landscape" and Katherine McKittrick's work in *Demonic Grounds*.
36 See in particular Toni Morrison's essay "Rootedness: The Ancestor as Foundation."
37 We might think of much of Erykah Badu early music videos as a product of this tradition of rootedness and uprootedness. Also for an excellent description of the ecological importance of the bayou in *Eve's Bayou* see Anissa Janine Wardi's book, *Water and African American Memory: An Ecocritical Perspective*.
38 See McKittrick's *Demonic Grounds*, xii.
39 Cervenak, *Wandering*, 1.
40 Ibid., 2.
41 Ibid.

42 See also the influential essay by Sarah Jane Cervenak and J. Kameron Carter, "Untitled and Outdoors: Thinking with Saidiya Hartman."

43 Here I am thinking of the importance of Kevin Quashie's work on quiet in *The Sovereignty of Quiet: Beyond Resistance in Black Culture*.

44 See Siddhartha Mitter's piece "Allison Janae Hamilton's Spirit Sources," https://www. nytimes.com/2018/10/26/arts/design/allison-janae-hamilton-mass-moca.html. (Accessed November 19, 2018.)

Bibliography

Blake, Lisa. "Chimamanda Ngozi Adichie Speaks Out on Being Featured on Beyoncé's Flawless." https://www.billboard.com/articles/news/7534428/chimamanda-ngozi-. (Accessed November 19, 2018).

Brooks, Daphne. "The SuperDome Basement Tapes: Black Feminist Sonic Revolutions in the Archive." Keynote Address, Association for the Study of the Arts of the Present, Annual Conference. New Orleans, October 20, 2018.

Brooks, Daphne. "All That You Can't Leave Behind": Black Female Soul Singing and the Politics of Surrogation in the Age of Catastrophe." *Meridians: Feminism, Race, Transnationalism*, vol. 8, no. 1 (2008), pp. 180–204.

Browne, Rembert. "A Friend in Aretha: The Spiritual Power of the Queen of Soul's 'Amazing Grace.'" https://www.theringer.com/music/2018/8/16/17705602/aretha-franklin-amazing-grace-life-career . (Accessed November 17. 2018).

Campt, Tina and Arthur Jafa. "Love is the Message: The Plan is Death." *e-Flux* 81 (2017) https://www.e-flux.com/journal/81/126451/love-is-the-message-the-plan-is-death/.

Cervenak, Sarah Jane. *Wandering: Philosophical Performances of Racial and Sexual Freedom*. Durham, NC: Duke University Press, 2014.

Dungy, Camille. Ed. *Black Nature: Four Centuries of African American Nature Poetry*. Athens: University of Georgia Press, 2009.

Henderson, Cinque. "Aretha Franklin on Heaven and Earth." https://www.nytimes. com/2018/08/16/opinion/aretha-franklin-gospel-music.html. (Accessed November 17, 2018).

Klein, Alyssa. "How Nigerian Visual Artist Laolu Senbanjo Brought His Sacred Art of the Ori to Beyoncé's 'Lemonade'." http://www.okayafrica.com/beyonce-lemonade-laolu-senbanjo-sacred-art-of-the-ori/. (Accessed November 17, 2018).

McKittrick, Katherine. *Demonic Grounds: Black Women and the Cartographies of Struggle*. Minneapolis: University of Minnesota Press, 2006.

Michaels, Sean. "Queen Aretha Not Amused By Beyoncé." https://www.theguardian. com/music/news/story/0,,2256370,00.html. November 5, 2018.

Mitter, Siddhartha. "Allison Janae Hamilton's Spirit Sources." https://www.nytimes.com/2018/10/26/arts/design/allison-janae-hamilton-mass-moca.html. (Accessed November 19, 2018).

Morrison, Toni. "Rootedness: The Ancestor as Foundation." In *Black Women Writers (1950–1980): A Critical Evaluation*. Ed. Mari Evans. Garden City, NY: Anchor/Doubleday, 1984.

Moten, Fred. Interview with Mark Anthony Neal. "Left of Black." webcast. November 5, 2018.

Remnick, David. "Soul Survivor: The Revival and Hidden Treasure of Aretha Franklin." *The New Yorker*. https://www.newyorker.com/magazine/2016/04/04/aretha-franklin-s-american-soul. (Accessed November 18, 2018).

Sharpe, Christina. *In the Wake: On Blackness and Being*. Durham, NC: Duke University Press, 2016.

Vernallis, Carol. "Beyoncé's Lemonade, AvantGarde Aesthetics, and Music Video: 'The Past and the Future Merge to Meet Us Here'." *Film Criticism*, vol. 40, no. 3, 2016.

Willman, Chris. "How Robert De Niro Helped Thaw Aretha Franklin Documentary Nego-tiations." https://www.billboard.com/articles/news/6898440/aretha-franklin- documenta ry-robert-deniro-tribeca-amazing-grace. (Accessed November 17, 2018).

14

BEYONCÉ'S WESTERN SOUTH SERENADE

Tyina Steptoe

The road from Houston to New Orleans passes through a landscape filled with gator farms and oil refineries, casinos and Catholic churches, bayous and bridges. This is a part of the South where old-timers might speak French or Spanish as their first language, where people love boudin balls and zydeco. As one of the most iconic performers from that region in the early twenty-first century, Beyoncé provides a sonic and visual roadmap of the place she calls home. As sociologist Zandria Robinson writes, "Beyoncé rides a southern genealogy that traverses the Deep South from Alabama to Louisiana to Texas, back and through, with stops in between."[1] Indeed, *Lemonade* takes us on a journey through the sights and sounds of the South. The Jim Crow South speaks in "Freedom," which samples field recordings of southern black preachers and inmates at Mississippi's Parchman prison farm, reminding us of the South's personal relationship with heaven and hell. We hear it in the prominent horn riffs of OutKast's "SpottieOttieDopaliscious" incorporated into "All Night." We see it in the plantations and city streets featured in the accompanying visual album.

Yet the southern genealogy of *Lemonade* is most deeply rooted in the *western* South, that stretch of the Dirty that lies west of the Mississippi River and wraps its arms around the Gulf Coast. In the western South states of Louisiana and Texas, race has often eschewed binaries of black and white. The sub-region's complicated racial past includes Spanish and French colonialism, Mexican community building, Anglo-American settlement, and the forced migration of enslaved Africans from the southeast. Beyoncé has frequently posited a Creole racial subjectivity, but one that has been shaped by contact between those diverse groups. The sonic and visual aesthetics crafted by Beyoncé and her collaborators reflect the complex interactions and fusions between people who have shaped the western South.

These explorations of race, ethnicity, and region convey a "jazz impulse" understanding of time and culture. The jazz impulse captures an ongoing dialogue between individuals and their communities, ancestors and their descendants, across space and time.[2] Creole subjectivity necessitates a knowledge and connection with history, yet Creole subjectivity itself is dynamic. The meanings of Creole have been shaped by an African/Iberian/French past in Louisiana, rural-to-urban migration in the twentieth century, and struggles against racial oppression. That heritage is a terrain made up of plantations, shotgun houses, and urban skylines. Orishas live within the sounds of gospel, blues, and country. New Orleans brass and bounce have a dialogue with ethnic Mexican norteño. It is straight and queer. These sights and sounds have been chopped and screwed to create the visual and sonic Borderlands that live in Beyoncé's work.

Roots

The lyrics from "Formation," the first single released in advance of *Lemonade*, confounded some fans. Beyoncé proclaims her specific racial subjectivity by describing herself as a mixture of black and Creole, a combination of her parent's ancestry: "My daddy Alabama/Mama Louisiana/You mix that Negro with that Creole make a Texas Bama." Writing for the popular website Very Smart Brothas, culture critic Damon Young questioned the last line: "Wait, aren't Creole people Black? And wouldn't that make them Negro too?"[3]

The very idea that "Creole" is distinct from "Negro" has been shaped by the history of the western South. Creoles of color are descendants of *gens de couleur libre* (free people of color), a group with roots in colonial Louisiana. Free people of color typically had French or Spanish fathers and enslaved African mothers. Emancipated by their fathers, this mixed-race population formed a separate group in colonial Louisiana. They married one another and formed communities throughout the southern parishes. Some owned land; the wealthier ones even owned slaves. Historically, free people of color considered themselves to be neither white nor black, but a combination of both races. Their descendants, who referred to themselves as Creoles of color after the Civil War, continued to stress their racial and cultural hybridity. Creole subjectivity, then, is rooted in their own history as a group in southern Louisiana.[4]

Beyoncé's maternal family has deep roots in that society. Her first name is derived from her mother's family name, Beyincé. The Beyincé family acknowledges origins in France and Canada, where a French-Canadian ancestor named Jean-Baptiste Marchesseau was born in Quebec in 1782. (The word "Cajun," derived from "Acadian," describes the descendants of those French-Canadians who settled in southwest Louisiana.) Before the Civil War, Louisiana-born members of the Beyincé clan lived in Saint James, Iberia, and Vermilion parishes. In a 2015 interview, Beyoncé's mother, Tina Knowles Lawson (née Beyincé) counted an "enslaved African maternal great-grandmother and paternal grandfather from Bordeaux, France" as part of the family tree.[5]

Like thousands of Creoles of color, the Beyincé family migrated to Texas in the twentieth century. Creoles of color began moving to Houston and surrounding areas after the Mississippi Flood of 1927. The Southern Pacific Railroad also recruited men from Louisiana to move to Houston and work for the company. Approximately one-quarter of the people who migrated to the city between World Wars I and II came from Louisiana. Most Creoles of color settled in a neighborhood that became known as Frenchtown, located in the northern section of the city's Fifth Ward. They spoke French, practiced Catholicism, and brought musical traditions like the accordion-based "la-la." In Frenchtown after World War II, la-la morphed into the style of music known as "zydeco."[6] The Beyincé family relocated to Galveston, the island city southeast of Houston. Tina Beyincé eventually moved to Houston, where she married and raised two daughters.

For many of the Creoles of color who moved to Texas in the twentieth century, "Creole" and "black" referred to two different groups. Indeed, relations between Texans and Louisianans could be tense. Knowles Lawson alleges that black nuns at her Catholic school in Galveston treated her poorly as a girl. Meanwhile, some black Texans claimed that Creoles acted superior. As writer and New Orleans native Yaba Blay asserted, "people who are light skinned, with non-kinky hair and the ability to claim a Creole heritage have had access to educational, occupational, social and political opportunities that darker skinned, kinkier-haired, non-Creole folks have been denied."[7]

By the late twentieth century, many Creoles in Houston acknowledged Catholicism, French surnames, Creole/Cajun cuisine, and zydeco music as markers of Creole subjectivity, regardless of whether their ancestors were free in 1860. Furthermore, generations of Creoles of color lived in or near black communities. In Houston and Galveston, the groups frequently shared neighborhoods and institutions. They also intermarried, as when Tina Beyincé married Alabama-born Matthew Knowles. The "Texas bama" roots mentioned in "Formation" refer to the merging of two black cultures, one from the Anglophone southeast and another from French Louisiana.

Beyoncé Giselle Knowles was born in 1981 and raised with her sister Solange in an affluent section of Third Ward, a historically black neighborhood. She came of age in a rapidly Latinizing city. For most of the twentieth century, the black American population of Houston was larger than the Latinx population. A small Mexican American community had existed since the early twentieth century. Mexican Americans made up 5 percent of the population before World War II. This had changed by 1980. The combination of economic depression in Mexico and the 1970s' oil boom in Houston made the city a destination for Mexican migrants. By 1980, Houston had, for the first time, an equal number of black Americans and people labeled "Hispanic." By the turn of the twenty-first century, Houston had "the largest total Black and Brown population in a southern urban area." In 2000, 742,207 Latinos and 461,584 African American made up 63 percent of Houston.[8] The late twentieth century also saw an increase in the number of migrants from places like Central America, Vietnam, Colombia, India, and Nigeria. Those migrations have made modern Houston one of the most diverse cities in the United States.[9]

As the largest city in the western South, Beyoncé's Houston is a crossroads city, a place that hosts a month-long rodeo and a vibrant slab scene.[10] In the 1990s, deejays at the hip hop radio station 97.9 regularly mixed the sounds of New Orleans bounce into the rotation, and the station also broadcast live from Jamaica Jamaica, a local nightclub that featured dancehall. Beyoncé's experiences in her hometown gave her a cultural heritage that is a result of contact between the diverse Houstonians who have moved to the city. Her work shows an acknowledgment of those traditions, especially in the songs and video that position her as a mixture, a recipient of diverse heritages.

"H-town vicious"

B'Day, Beyoncé's second solo album that debuted in the fall of 2006, offered more explicit nods to her western South roots than her first album or the previous Destiny's Child albums. The alligators and swamps featured on the album art are reminiscent of the murky bayou lands of southern Louisiana and southeastern Texas. The video for the first single, "Déjà Vu," features an early version of the plantation imagery that Beyoncé would incorporate in future work, and Jay-Z's guest verse mentions Houston's slab scene. Daphne Brooks calls the album a "tour of Gulf Coast culture."[11]

Projects related to *B'Day* especially acknowledged the Creole and Mexican heritages of the western South. Rodney "Darkchild" Jerkins worked on an unreleased track, "Back Up," and he recalled that Beyoncé wanted "Creole-type stuff. Zydeco ... We were doing a lot of ideas around that, and the horns, but at the same time, we wanted to give that urban street edge. So we tried to get that combination."[12] "Back Up" did not make the cut for *B'Day*, but Beyoncé did refer to her Creole roots in another song related to that album. Released in the United Kingdom and Japan in deluxe editions of *B'Day*, a track called "Creole" contains one of the first lyrical explorations of her racial subjectivity: "So all my red bones get on the floor ... Then you mix it up and you call it Creole." Over the blare of horns, the lyrics use words historically associated with mixed-race and/or light-skinned black Americans—yellow bone and red bone—and add a reference to brown skin. The song commands dancers of those hues to descend upon the dance floor, creating a seemingly inclusive space (though "black" is noticeably absent from this spectrum). Beyoncé simultaneously associates herself with all of the colors acknowledged in the song. Yellow, red, and brown are invited to the party because the Creole hostess herself is a mixture of all of those shades.

The cultural heritage explored in *B'Day* and related projects also encompasses ethnic Mexican contributions to the regional soundscape. Beyoncé has noted the influence of Spanish-language music on her life, especially the enduring legacy of Selena, the late icon of Tejano music. Selena was born in Lake Jackson, a city 55 miles south of Houston. Beyoncé said in 2006, "I remember listening to Selena all the time." Selena's most iconic live performances took place in Houston's

Astrodome, where she performed at the Livestock Show and Rodeo three years in a row between 1993 and 1995. In her final performance on February 26, 1995, one month before her death, twenty-three-year-old Selena played a medley of disco classics as well as the songs from the Tejano genre that made her famous. As the next superstar from southeastern Texas, Beyoncé has moved just as easily between genres.[13]

The Tejano musical soundscape influenced the creation of an EP containing Spanish-language versions of *B'Day* singles like "Irreplaceable." The project points to Beyoncé's acknowledgement of Spanish-speaking fans in Latin America and the southwest, as well as her own experiences in a city with a growing Latinx population. Producer/songwriter Rudy Perez, who translated the lyrics into Spanish, noted that the singer would sometimes spend six hours at a time trying to master singing the words in a different language. While most of the songs maintain the same arrangement as the originals, with the addition of Spanish lyrics, the album also contains a norteño remix of "Irreplaceable" called "Irreemplazable." The norteño genre originated in northern Mexico, and encompasses styles like corridos, cumbias, and rancheras. Sonically, the genre is most known for its use of accordion and the bajo sexto, a string bass instrument. Those musical elements, when used for the norteño remix, tie Beyoncé to the Mexican aspect of the western South. The venture succeeded, landing on the *Billboard* Latin charts.[14]

If *B'Day* incorporated diverse sounds and landscapes of the western South as a whole, then Beyoncé's 2013 eponymous album focused more on her Houston roots. Songs and videos frequently allude to her hometown. The album opens with the words "Miss Third Ward," and she declares herself "H-Town vicious" on "Flawless."

The video for "No Angel" is a visual love song to black and brown Houston. The clip opens with an image of downtown at dawn, the city's modern skyline illuminated against the jewel-toned, rising sun. This is the vision of Houston seen most frequently on postcards or in publicity shots during sports telecasts. It's an image of a sprawling, oil-rich city, the fourth largest in the nation, home to 4.5 million people. But Beyoncé quickly introduces viewers to a different Houston. "No Angel" takes viewers on a (slab) ride through the oldest and blackest spaces of her hometown.

In the video, the screen quickly fades from the establishing shot of downtown into a series of images depicting Third Ward, as well Fourth Ward, home of Houston's first black neighborhood, Freedman's Town. A young man proudly displays the words "4th Ward" shaved into his fade. Slabs bearing the name of the neighborhood and the words "Dirty South" slowly crawl through city streets. Beyoncé herself struts and poses on the front steps of an ancient shotgun house that looks much like the ones still found in parts of Fourth Ward and Third Ward.[15]

The visual depiction of these structures links the artist to local African American history. Artist John Biggers, who taught in the art department at Texas Southern University, featured shotgun houses in paintings that depict black life in Houston and the South.[16] More recently, artist and activist Rick Lowe transformed dozens of abandoned shotgun homes on Holman Street in Third Ward into a venture called Project Row Houses that offers a public arts program and low- to moderate-income housing to single mothers. Since the days that former slaves constructed their homes in Freedman's Town in 1865, shotgun houses have occupied a central place within the city's black neighborhoods and local memory.

The video blends old Houston with the new. Local rappers make cameos amidst the iconography of shotgun houses. Johnny Dang, a popular local jeweler of Vietnamese descent, makes an appearance. "No Angel" also places Mexican Americans within Houston's black vernacular culture. In one shot, a group of Latinos display a sign that reads, "Dat Mexican Holding." "No Angel" offers a jazz impulse vision of Houston's past and present, showing a spatial, sonic, and visual relationship between the city's modern multiethnic population and the rich black history of Third Ward and Fourth Ward.

"The past and future merge to meet us here"

While *Beyoncé* explored her Houston heritage, *Lemonade* pans out to include the western South in a broader discussion of the African diaspora. The accompanying visual album, which premiered on HBO on the same day as the album's release, mostly takes place in Louisiana, filmed in rural parts of the state as well as New Orleans. But these images take viewers to a western South that remains in dialogue with an African past. The Yoruba orisha Oshun (or Osun), a goddess associated with fertility and love, provides the inspiration for the water imagery and yellow dress in "Hold Up." The Yoruba people of southwestern Nigeria and southern Benin frequently link Oshun to the color yellow and the element of water. Meanwhile, dancers in the "Sorry" video wear Yoruba face markings.[17]

As in "Déjà Vu," *Lemonade* returns us to the plantation South, using Madewood Plantation House in Napoleonville, and Destrehan Plantation in Destrehan, Louisiana, as backdrops to several of the videos.[18] Destrehan, in particular, has a history of slave rebellion and repression. On January 8, 1811, 500 enslaved Africans from that area revolted, burning plantations as they marched down River Road toward New Orleans. U.S. federal troops and a local militia quelled the rebellion. They executed the enslaved rebels and mounted their heads on pikes alongside the river. The bloody visage unfolded for 60 miles.[19]

Yet the plantation South of *Lemonade* is devoid of white people. White people are not absent sonically from the album; most notably, we hear Jack White and Led Zeppelin on "Don't Hurt Yourself." But the removal of white bodies from the plantation scenes remakes those spaces as sites of black female empowerment, without forgetting the history of pain. Little black girls run freely. Black tennis icon Serena Williams twerks exuberantly while Beyoncé watches. This is a plantation South that belongs to the colors of the diaspora, embodied by the black feminine.

Notions of the black feminine in *Lemonade* also draw on queer cultures of the western South, namely the queer performers from the New Orleans bounce scene. Energetic hip hop dance music from New Orleans, bounce songs packed dance floors in that city for decades before breaking into the mainstream with songs like Juvenile's "Back That Azz Up." Beyoncé incorporates the sounds of two queer bounce performers, Messy Mya and Big Freedia, into "Formation." The song uses the late Messy Mya's voice to announce Beyoncé's return in this first single from the album: "Bitch, I'm back by popular demand!" Big Freedia's enthusiastically warns, "I did not come to play with you hoes!"

Yet, as critics have pointed out, the images of these queer performers do not appear in the video. As writer Myles E. Johnson notes, "Big Freedia has been continuously used for her voice, words, and energy, but her body is always abstracted from the visual element of these mainstream moments."[20] Messy Mya's estate filed a $20 million lawsuit in federal court on February 7, 2017 alleging that "Formation" uses the performer's voice without consent.[21] "Formation" incorporates the sounds of two of the region's queer icons, but not their bodies, which tend to blur masculinity and femininity.

The song and video for "Daddy Lessons" offer a sonic and visual representation of the western South through its incorporation of sights and sounds associated with Texas and Louisiana. The song begins with blaring horns, announcing the arrival of NOLA's storied jazz tradition. The saxophones, trumpet, and trombone then greet an acoustic guitar as Beyoncé chants "Texas" several times. The video cuts between scenes of a funeral second-line and pastoral images of cowboys and cowgirls. Beyoncé performed "Daddy Lessons" at the Country Music Association (CMA) Awards in 2016 with a trio of white Texas women, the Dixie Chicks. By merging New Orleans jazz and Texas country, these performances allow us to eavesdrop on a conversation between New Orleans and Texas. That relationship is one that again speaks to Beyoncé's Creole heritage and a history of migration between those places.

When considering Beyoncé's past explorations of norteño music alongside a song like "Daddy Lessons," we see an entertainer who frequently draws on the musical heritage of the western South. It is a jazz impulse soundscape of acoustic guitars, accordions, horns, and 808 drums that have been remixed by a Creole black woman from Houston. "The past and future merge to meet us here," she intones on *Lemonade*'s visual album. In Beyoncé's work, West African, Spanish, French, and Mexican pasts/futures meet to forge a dynamic regional heritage.

Notes

1 Zandria Robinson. "We Slay, Part I." February 7, 2016, http://newsouthnegress.com/southernslayings.
2 Craig Werner has written extensively on the jazz impulse; see *Playing the Changes: From Afro-Modernism to the Jazz Impulse* (Urbana: University of Illinois Press, 1994) and *A Change Is Gonna Come: Music, Race, and the Soul of America* (Ann Arbor: University of Michigan Press, 2006).

3 Damon Young, "Beyoncé Is the New Black: The 10 Blackest Moments in Beyoncé's 'Formation' Video," *Very Smart Brothas* (blog), February 6, 2016, https://verysmartbro thas.theroot.com/beyonce-is-the-new-black-the-10-blackest-mom ents-in-be-1822522588.

4 On Creoles of color in Louisiana, see Gary B. Mills, *The Forgotten People: Cane River's Creoles of Color* (Baton Rouge: Louisiana State University Press, 1977); Arnold R. Hirsch, *Creole New Orleans: Race and Americanization* (Baton Rouge: Louisiana State University Press, 1992); Carl A. Brasseaux, Keith P. Fontenot, and Claude F. Oubre, *Creoles of Color in the Bayou Country* (Jackson: University Press of Mississippi, 1994); George Cable, *The Creoles of Louisiana* (New Orleans: Pelican Publishing, 2000); Sybil Klein, ed., *Creole: The History and Legacy of Louisiana's Free People of Color* (Baton Rouge: Louisiana State University Press 2000); Thomas Brothers, *Louis Armstrong's New Orleans* (New York: W.W. Norton and Company, Inc., 2006); Mary Gehman, *The Free People of Color of New Orleans: An Introduction* (Donaldsonville, LA: Margaret Media, 2009). See also Blair L.M. Kelley's discussion of New Orleans in *Right to Ride: Streetcar Boycotts and African American Citizenship in the Era of Plessy v. Ferguson* (Chapel Hill: University of North Carolina Press, 2010).

5 Information on the Beyincé family accessed through gw.geneanet.org, http://gw.genea net.org/tdowling?lang=en&p=beyonce%2Bgiselle&n=knowles&oc=0 (accessed February 23, 2016); Kierna Mayo, "The Life and Times of Tenie B.," *Ebony* (online), June 15, 2015, https://www.ebony.com/entertainment-culture/cover-story-tina-knowles-la wson-exclusive-987.

6 On Creoles of color in Houston, see Tyina Steptoe, *Houston Bound: Culture and Color in a Jim Crow* (Oakland: University of California Press, 2016).

7 Yaba Blay, "On 'Jackson Five Nostrils,' Creole vs. 'Negro' and Beefing Over Beyoncé's 'Formation,'" *Colorlines*, February 8, 2016, https://www.colorlines.com/articles/ja ckson-five-nostrils-creole-vs-negro-and-beefing-over-beyonces-formation.

8 Tatcho Mindiola, Jr., Yolanda Flores Niemann, and Nestor Rodriguez, *Black-Brown Relations and Stereotypes* (Austin: University of Texas Press, 2002), 4.

9 Brittny Meija, "How Houston Has Become the Most Diverse Place in America, *Los Angeles Times*, May 9, 2017, http://www.latimes.com/nation/la-na-houston-diversi ty-2017-htmlstory.html.

10 Slabs are brightly colored, big-body cars that have become a vital part of Houston's hip hop scene and car culture. See Peter Holley, "The Slab Goes Fab," *Houstonia*, September 30, 2013, https://www.houstoniamag.com/articles/2013/9/30/the-slab-goes-fab-october-2013.

11 Beyoncé, *B'Day*, Sony, 2006; Daphne A. Brooks, "Suga Mama, Politicized," *The Nation*, November 30, 2006.

12 Steven J. Horowitz, "Unreleased Beyoncé Collaborations," *The Fader*, March 3, 2016, http://www.thefader.com/2016/03/03/beyonce-unreleased-songs-formation-album.

13 Joey Guerra, "Late Tejano Singer Selena Remains a RodeoHouston Legend," *Houston Chronicle* (online), February 13, 2015, https://tinyurl.com/yxunvx3qhttps://tinyurl. com/yxunvx3q.

14 Leila Cobo, "The 'Billboard' Q&A: Translation Tricks—Rudy Perez Teaches Beyoncé Spanish," *Billboard* 119, issue 3 (January 20, 2007): 12.

15 Beyoncé, "No Angel," *Beyoncé*, Music Video, Directed by @LILINTERNET, 2013.

16 John Biggers, *Shotgun, Third Ward #1*, 1966, tempera and oil on canvas, 30 × 48 in., Smithsonian Art Museum, Washington, DC.

17 PBS.org, "What Beyoncé Teaches Us about the African Diaspora in 'Lemonade'," April 29, 2016, https://www.pbs.org/newshour/arts/what-beyonce-teaches-us-about-the-a frican-diaspora-in-lemonade; Katie Mettler, "The African, Hindu and Roman Goddesses Who Inspired Beyoncé's Stunning Grammy Performance," *Washington Post*, February 13, 2017, https://waww.washingtonpost.com/news/morning-mix/wp/2017/02/13/these-goddesses-will-help-you-understand-beyonces-grammy-performance/?nor edirect=on&utm_term=.254409e5ed90.

18 Lauren LaBorde, "Mapping the Louisiana Locations in Beyonce's 'Lemonade,'" Nola. com (*Times-Picayune* online), June 3, 2016, https://nola.curbed.com/maps/beyonce-lem onade-louisiana-filming-locations.

19 See Daniel Rasmussen, *American Uprising: The Untold Story of America's Largest Slave Revolt* (New York: Harper Perennial, 2012); LaKisha Michelle Simmons, "Landscapes, Memories, and History in Beyoncé's Lemonade," *UC Press Blog*, April 28, 2016, https:// uncpressblog.com/2016/04/28/lakisha-simmons-beyonces-lemonade/.

20 Myles E. Johnson, "The Ghost of Big Freedia," April 18, 2018, Noisey.com, https:// noisey.vice.com/en_us/article/59j4xn/big-freedia-drake-beyonce-essay.

21 Chelsea Brasted, NOLA.com (*Times-Picayune* online), February 8, 2017.

15

BEYSTHETICS

"Formation" and the politics of style

Tanisha C. Ford

In fall of 2016, I headed to the New Museum in lower Manhattan for *Pipilotti Rist: Pixel Forest*, an exhibition that features work from Swiss visual artist Pipilotti Rist's thirty-year career. I worked my way through the labyrinth, three floors of it, examining Rist's surrealist video and installation art. I paused at a video projection and joined several others splayed out on the comfy pillows, experiencing the sense of intimacy that threads through Rist's work.

In the video, *Ever Over All*, a wiry-framed white woman strolls whimsically down the street of a space that doesn't look like the United States. Dressed in a blue chiffon dress and red slippers, the woman smiles as she playfully handles a metal faux flower with a long stem. Out of nowhere, she swings the flower wildly, busting out the front passenger side window of an older model hatchback. She continues strolling and skipping joyfully down the street, vandalizing cars in her path as a female police officer gives her a nod of approval.

I'd seen this before. I searched my memory, trying to bring the sense of familiarity into focus. Suddenly it came to me—Beyoncé! One of my favorite "videos" from her visual album *Lemonade* is "Hold Up," in which Beyoncé, clad in a yellow Roberto Cavalli gown, slugs out car windows with a baseball bat, singing about an unfaithful lover over a reggae-lite beat. *Lemonade* had only been out a few months at this point and was still fresh in the zeitgeist. I doubt I was the only one experiencing déjà vu. But my triumphant moment of connection went unnoticed in the dark room. I silently asked myself the immediate next question: did Rist copy Beyoncé or did Beyoncé copy Rist? I scanned the description in the exhibition catalogue I was holding to see when *Ever Over All* was made. 1997. The same year Beyoncé and her girl group Destiny's Child released their first single, "No, No, No."

So was Beyoncé copying? Despite the similarities, my gut reaction was "No." And, having unpacked that reaction, I still reach the same conclusion. I believe the key difference is the clearly established aesthetic that grounds *Lemonade*. "Hold

Up" is a distinct work of art, which, especially taken in the context of *Lemonade* as a whole, is an art piece so unique that it is larger and more profound than the many projects, literary, artistic, and spiritual traditions from which it draws inspiration.

To be clear, it's not a minor question. Beyoncé has been accused of stealing multiple times, particularly from avant-garde choreographers. For example, her 2011 video for "Countdown" used choreography and staging that closely mimics Belgian choreographer Anne Teresa de Keersmaeker's experimental pieces *Achterland* (1994) and *Rosas Danst Rosas* (1997).[1] A widely circulated YouTube video shows Beyoncé and her crew of dancers executing moves and wearing slightly updated version of the costumes from de Keersmaeker's work. How intentional were the similarities? De Keersmaeker called it "plagiarism."[2] Beyoncé's co-director for the video, Adria Petty, says that she provided Beyoncé with a variety of contemporary European dance videos, and that Beyoncé selected the clips that inspired her. Her team (hair and makeup, costumes, choreography, and so forth) were all given the same reference clips.[3] I'm not here to jump into the old "Countdown" debate, but as I sank into the cushions in the Rist exhibit, watching her protagonist smash windows with a flower, my mind couldn't help but think about the numerous times people had labeled Beyoncé a thief. "Hold Up" definitely feels like a homage to Rist; but Queen Bey has evolved, and what she's doing with Rist's work is far more sophisticated than the way she used de Keersmaeker's.

One of the key aesthetic differences between Rist's and Beyoncé's works is the color palette. In blue and red, Rist's protagonist looks like she's channeling the *Wizard of Oz*, a grown-up Dorothy wreaking havoc in ruby slippers. The visual signature of "Hold Up" is that of vibrant yellow: the airy dress floats in the wind as Beyoncé moves down the street. The video's director, Jonas Åkerlund, insisted on a yellow dress from the very beginning, and his wife, B. Åkerlund—the stylist for the video—scoured racks around the world to find the right one. And the Roberto Cavalli confection that they decided on actually showed up a day late because it came directly from Cavalli's fall 2016 runway show. But it was the right shade of yellow and had the right amount of flounce, so they scrapped the dress that they had settled on and went with this star.[4]

Jonas Åkerlund wanted to balance the destructive action of the video with an undeniably feminine color, lots of layers and ruffles. In this sense, the yellow dress is the equivalent of Rist's metal flower: a symbol of femininity. And to this extent, you can read the two videos as very similar. But the yellow dress creates so much more meaning than that—meanings that are absent from Rist's video, and key to the message of *Lemonade* specifically.

When *Lemonade* premiered in April 2016, I scrambled to get an HBO Go account so I could watch in real time. I joined the teams of black women live-tweeting *Lemonade* like it was the social event of the year. As a collective audience we saw Oshún, the Yoruba deity: the goddess of water whose signature color is yellow, who is known for being a jealous, vengeful lover, who always has to check her vain, womanizing lover Shangó. It was the perfect visual to communicate an Oshún story: strong, powerful, but vulnerable enough to love and be bruised by its unsavory bits. Tweets like "I see you Bey, channeling Oshún!" ended up forming the core of the body of stories on *Lemonade* that ran in all of the online publications and magazines and blogs for weeks. Åkerlund probably knew nothing of Oshún when he insisted on the yellow dress. But it is the representation of Oshún— deeply rooted in an African diasporic spiritual and cultural vernacular and totally unrelated to contemporary experimental European art—that gives life to "Hold Up," that gives it one of its most significant layers of meaning for an broad audience of black and brown women.

So are all of those women wrong for reading Oshún in the floating yellow dress? I say no. If we recognize the aesthetic scaffolding behind the *Lemonade* project, it's not only possible, but also necessary to read it in layers in order to appreciate the full artistic impact of the work. Oshún and the other orishas are definitely all over *Lemonade*, and as the album becomes part of a visual arts canon, their presence is recorded in the audience reactions from around the world. Moreover, Oshún would say that it was of no consequence that the silly white man directing the video didn't know he was under her influence when he suggested they use a yellow dress but that it was all in her divine plan. This essay is my attempt at making *Lemonade*'s visual architecture legible so that we can understand why it is important to Beyoncé that we see both Rist and Oshún as we watch.

Musicologist Shana Redmond once said, "you have to see Beyoncé to hear her."[5] These days, a lot of the work Beyoncé does goes into curating her own image, building a visual canon through her website and her Instagram. And there is her 2013 documentary, *Life Is But a Dream*, which she directed and executive produced, and, of course, the two visual albums. Managing her own images has become particularly important for Bey since she has all but stopped doing interviews. Visuals are now the medium she uses to speak to the public.

Bey herself coined the term "visual album" to describe a project in which the music and the moving images are equally essential to interpreting the artwork. It isn't just a new marketing trick: it's an art form, one that predates Beyoncé but has now become common parlance when describing similar works. As you *read* Beyoncé's entire catalogue of work, I like to think you can see how her earlier works are evolving toward this point of departure; but there is also a pretty distinct bifurcation between youngin' Bey and *King* Bey. The break point is in 2011 when she fires her father, Matthew Knowles, as her manager and founds her own production company, Parkwood Entertainment. Starting her own company allowed Beyoncé to become one of the few black women to control her own means of production. Before Parkwood, Matthew constructed his daughter as something like a modern-day Diana Ross: demure, polished, glamorous.[6] After Parkwood, Beyoncé begins managing herself. Her music sheds its saccharine quality, taking on new, "edgier" dimensions, and she becomes an unlikely face of the new resurgence in feminist and black protest music.[7] We need a new way of reading King Bey.

Two of her performances give us the language in which to do so. In 2011 at the Billboard Awards she gave a visually arresting performance of her high-energy girl power hit "Who Run the World (Girls)," with digital images projected behind her. In a highly instructive moment, Beyoncé does the signature shoulder shrug choreography that fans worldwide were copying, and, at the same moment, digital Beyoncés appear and multiply on screen behind her, eventually numbering hundreds, moving in sync with *real-life* Beyoncé. The marching Beyoncés—real and augmented—represent the ways that Beyoncé is replicated by her fans and replicates herself by sending out other teams under the Beyoncé label to scour the world for inspiration and new ideas.[8]

The other example comes from the Formation World Tour. Es Devlin, a renowned set designer, was a member of a massive team who created a 360-degree, seven-story LED architectural structure from which videos and images are projected. Its sound system, powered by THX technology, broadcasts Beyoncé's vocals in the large outdoor stadiums she performs in around the world. The structure can even open, allowing Bey and her dancers to come through.[9] Beyond just being a behemoth of modern technology, the cube is also a way to read this era of Beyoncé's performance. Most people in the stadiums holding 50,000+ view a pixilated Beyoncé on the massive screen, while only those concert-goers with pricey floor seat tickets get to see the real Beyoncé, in the flesh. Like the hundreds of marching Beyoncés we saw in the Billboard performance, the Beyoncé of the live tour is many Beyoncés. What we learn from both the augmented reality of the Billboard performance and the stories-high cube is that she (as in Beyoncé the entity, the brand) is an amalgamation of ideas, narratives, and inspirations—both hers and those of others on her creative team. But also, while we may need to *see* Beyoncé to *hear* her, we can't *understand* her (the real-life her) unless we engage her art.

Bey-arts aesthetic

Yes, this is a story about "branding" and the rise of Beyoncé the corporation. But it's also about the rise of a Beyoncé aesthetic that is far more nuanced and grand than it was back in 2011. It is something that I term the "Bey-arts aesthetic," or a language through which we can examine, analyze, and evaluate Beyoncé's artistic and curatorial practice. In French, *beaux arts* means "fine art." And in architecture beaux arts is a specific style that pairs conservative lines with highly ornate, oversized flourishes. Richard Morris Hunt's façade for New York City's Metropolitan Museum of Art—known as The Met (1902)—and Arthur Brown, Jr.'s San Francisco War Memorial Opera House (1932) are examples.[10] I am most interested in the term because it allows me to play with language: if *beaux* equals *fine* then it's an apt descriptor for Beyoncé, who folks consider so alluring and beautiful that they call her *fione* (black vernacular that amplifies just how extremely good-looking one is)! But a beau (drop the "x") is also a *bae* (a loved one or lover, a companion). Saying "s/he/ze is bae" expresses a love for someone in a way that fucks with the boundaries between platonic and romantic/sexual love. And Bey is *bae* to millions of folks. So then, if Bey were to have her own "school of thought" or artistic style and philosophy (akin to that of the École des Beaux-Arts), her style could be described as simultaneously ornate with slick, modern lines; both playful and thoughtful in the way it conjures and signifies; drawing from established fine arts canons while also centering a black diasporic culture and epistemology—or way of knowing. Bey-arts is the scaffolding, the architecture, that undergirds the multiple uses of fine arts and folk culture and cosmologies in *Lemonade*.

Get in "Formation"

We first saw the full expression of the Bey-arts style in the video for "Formation," the lead single for *Lemonade* (though viewers didn't know it at the time). The video was filmed largely at the Fenyes Mansion (a beaux-arts style architectural design) in Pasadena, California, which was redesigned to mimic the southern gothic architecture of New Orleans plantations.[11] The "Formation" set makes visible centuries-old southern black traditions—burial rituals, courtship—while situating Beyoncé within a family lineage. "My Daddy Alabama / Mama Louisiana / You mix that negro with that creole make a Texas 'Bama'," she sings. Beyond the surface layer, creating a public lineage is an undertaking families do when they are building dynastic power. So by making this claim about her bloodline, particularly at this point in her career, Beyoncé (both the individual and the entity) is making a claim about power: she has earned the right to claim her spot among the greats and to elevate her family among the greatest performance families (such as the Jacksons, whom she also references on "Formation"). The lyric is about her personal heritage, a theme of the project as a whole; which is to say, seen the way Beyoncé means us to see it—it (the lyric, the song, the album) —is also about the origins of African-descended people as a whole. Beyoncé does a similar type of lineage-making in "Forward" as she picks up photographs of her descendants, strewn across rolling hills, and places the photos in an ornate trunk of keepsakes. Through both "Formation" and "Forward," it is clear that she is (re)claiming the power of black people across the diaspora, (re)writing our public lineage, (re)centering us in the history of the new world.

FIGURE 15.1 Video still of Beyoncé dancing in a hallway from "Formation." *Lemonade*, Parkwood Entertainment, 2016

She uses the artwork that hangs on the mansion's walls to visually do the work of lineage-making. In the house's long hallway, which is lined with bookcases, hang several portraits of women and families—of a deep chocolate hue. These were not original paintings of aristocratic black folk from the colonial period—this type of art had historically been limited to mostly white people—but were specially created for the video by set designer Ethan Tobman. "This is not a house the slaves are working in," Tobman remembers director Malina Matsoukas saying to him; "this is a house where the slaves are the masters."[12] The way Tobman's crew created this representation of a female-fronted black dynasty was by first selecting portraits of white women and families that fit the time period and aesthetic and then scanning and painting over them, recreating the hair textures and the facial features in kinkier textures and darker skin tones. By remixing that genre of portraiture, by translating an image from canvas to canvas, by layering fresh paint over aged paint, they make something new. Interspersed with these remixed portraits are others—originals, true to the time period—of black people dressed in their Sunday best. Beyoncé and her team essentially visually *rewrite history* so that black people win.

At the same time that Beyoncé stretches us across the diaspora, she presents an aesthetic that is also (hyper)local. By this I mean she is clearly preoccupied with articulating a specific regional culture: that east Texas/western Louisiana connection. It's one with many roots and routes, which became visible to those of us who live outside of the region in the aftermath of Hurricane Katrina, as displaced families found refuge in the homes of their Texas relatives. Even closer still, Beyoncé zeroes in on Houston and the Third Ward. Watching her rep her ward, you get the feeling that you had to live there, in that ward, on that specific block to fully understand the impact of the culture she presents. For example, some of the visuals Beyoncé circulates online during the *Lemonade* promo run include images of she and her hairstylist/seamstress/designer mother Tina Knowles Lawson shopping at a beauty supply store in the 'hood in Houston.

In "Formation," this (hyper)local culture is front and center in her mentions of Creole culinary traditions: "I got hot sauce in my bag, swag!" And even more powerfully in her visuals of the beauty shop, where we see "ratchet," outlandish hairstyles and bright-colored clawed fingernails and slides (flip flops) with socks on. These visuals build upon imagery introduced in videos on her eponymous *Beyoncé*, her first visual album, which can be thought of as an ode to Houston and the Third Ward. In that album's "No Angel," Beyoncé rocks a Houston Rockets jersey, and highlights the city's slab, trap, and strip club cultures. In "Formation" she dons a similar white fur as in the "No Angel" video as she hangs out the window (a similar pose as on "No Angel") of a baby-blue, candy-painted slab— Houston slang for an old school car, sittin' on 4-4s (44-inch rims), with a dope paint job. She dons different fur in "Don't Hurt Yourself," another song/video on the *Lemonade* project. This time it's a collarless, cold shoulder Hood By Air (a label known for the unapologetically black ways it infuses street fashion with haute couture) fur coat atop a flesh-colored bra and leggings set by hip hop giant Kanye West's Yeezy line, as she guts out hardcore rock lyrics, becoming her own version of funk legend Betty Davis. The layering of hip hop, soul, funk, and rock complements the layered textiles of her garments: the heavy fur on the skin-tight body suit on top of her own *café au lait* flesh.[13] Beyoncé's very deliberate repetition of elements—garments, hairstyles, poses, musical genres, and sets—from visual album to visual album allows her to canonize her Bey-arts aesthetic.

Though it is dense with all of the heavier themes that make high art "serious," the Bey-arts style, like its namesake beaux arts, is lavishly ornamented—playful and irreverent even. The pop aspect of the aesthetic is at its most extra in Beyoncé's signature take on the concept of "hood rich." One prime example is in her lyric "When he fuck me good I take his ass to Red Lobster," which has to be one of my favorite lines in "Formation." When I was in college in Atlanta, girls would come back to our dorm bragging about getting "caked" at Red Lobster by some random thug dude. In "Formation," it's King Bey doing the cakin'.

Many people have expressed doubt that Beyoncé would go to Red Lobster when she has access to the finest seafood in the world. I, on the other hand, would be willing to bet she does. That restaurant was the epitome of hood rich for a generation of hip hop folks coming of age in the 1990s. Who, having tasted the buttery, garlicky goodness of a Cheddar Bay biscuit could ever forget Red Lobster? In the 80s, it was nice enough that middle-class families like Beyoncé's would head there after church, still decked out in their Sunday best. It was one of those places where you wouldn't be surprised to find poor and working-class black folk eating next to an IBM executive like Matthew Knowles.

Today, Red Lobster, like many other restaurants from Beyoncé's youth, has become casual. In the major cities of the urban U.S. south, Red Lobster would be packed with black folks on the weekends—particularly around the 1st and 15th, payday. It's also a popular date spot, a bae spot. And working black folk—in the nine to five world and the underground economy—*do* Red Lobster a particular way, transforming the once "fine-dining" space with their gold fronts and ice grills, tattoos and piercings, rainbow-colored hair with matching lipstick and nail lacquer. There is libertory power in Beyoncé's insistence that we see her as a hood chick *and* as a lover and maker of fine arts.

Conclusion: Bey-arts at the Louvre

In the five years between the de Keersmaeker controversy around "Countdown" and the release of *Lemonade*, Beyoncé and her husband, rapper Jay-Z, have made a move toward the world of fine arts. Jay-Z has boasted about how the family has become art investors as a way to accumulate generational wealth. And his more recent rhymes show it: they are peppered with references to Jean-Michel Basquiat, Andy Warhol, Pablo Picasso, Francis Bacon, Kehinde Wiley, and the premiere art show Art Basel. The pair even dressed as Basquiat and Frida Kahlo for Halloween one year.[14]

In October 2014, an image of Bey and Jay in front of the *Mona Lisa* circulated the web. The pair took a 90-minute private tour of the Louvre, snapping social media photos that, to many reporters, seem to be as much about showing off the couple's wealth and stature—the museum is technically closed on Tuesdays, but they were escorted by twenty-five staff for their private tour—as about their burgeoning affinity for fine arts. Of course, wealth, stature, and fine arts all go together, as Beyoncé and Jay-Z are keenly aware, and their representation of the trifecta, however casually published, is historic in its own way. It is no distant past when black folks were only able to access museums if they worked there. German photographer Fritz Henle's stirring photograph *Night at Moma, New York (Cleaning Woman at Left)* (1948) depicts a black woman who is part of the cleaning staff sweeping the floors around some sculptures taller than herself. Artist Fred Wilson's *Guarded View* (1991) and Essex Hemphill's poem "Visiting Hours" (1992) both speak of the museum experience through the lens of the (male) guards—oftentimes black—charged with guarding high-priced artwork in spaces that routinely reject everyone else who looks like them.[15]

The most-circulated picture from the set shows Beyoncé, perhaps mimicking the smile of Mona Lisa, decked out in two braided ponytails, a black brimmed hat, and a rainbow-colored American flag t-shirt, with minimal makeup, looking more like a Brooklyn hipster than the glamazon fans are used to. Jay is beside her, wearing a ball cap that appears to say "Rockstar" and a silver zip-front hoodie. The couple is standing mere inches away from Da Vinci's cherished painting. Beyoncé and Jay-Z know what it means to bring black bodies into this deeply segregated space.

There's another photo from the set that's less common, but it's my favorite. In it, Blue Ivy, then a toddler, runs around the museum, wild and free, with her hair out in an unmanicured Afro (the same Afro her mother would sing of on "Formation"). It's a level of access and freedom that black girls rarely get. The picture is reminiscent of Faith Ringgold's *Dancing at the Louvre* (1991), where black girls—with their black girl plaits and ribbons—dance in the Louvre before the *Mona Lisa*. It is as if Beyoncé knows this work of art and is consciously reproducing it with her smartphone, connecting her family with other black visual artists who have fucked with museum space. The Knowles-Carters enter the fine arts world and transform it with a hip hop ethos rooted in black consciousness. If the portraits in "Formation" re-center history around black women, this Instagram snap re-organizes fine arts around the gravitational pull of black success: it's re-writing history in *real time*.

In summer 2018, Beyoncé and Jay-Z broke the internet with their video for "Apeshit," the lead single to their joint album *Everything Is Love*. In one of the opening scenes, the camera pans down the renovated Salle des Etats, the camera taking in the expanse of the room as Beyoncé and Jay-Z are perched against a table that sits just before the bulletproof glass-encased portrait of Mona Lisa, which instantly places them in the Louvre. In the same positions they were in in 2014 when they took a private tour of the museum. Now, they are clad in pink and green pants suits, respectively, as Beyoncé sings "I can't believe we made it." It's the next step in the evolution of a shared Knowles-Carter vision. And boy is it a black vision! From Beyoncé dripping in MCM (in collaboration with legendary hip hop stylist Misa Hylton) and Versace in the highly ostentatious style of hip hop haute couture, to the dancers in black-girl-nude body suits, which highlight the range of shades of beautiful blackness. To the black woman combing a black man's kinks with an Afro pick in front of the *Mona Lisa*. The message: the future of visual arts is black.

Notes

1 Sanjoy Roy, "Step By Step Guide to Dance: Anne Teresa de Keersmaeker and Rosas," *The Guardian*, September 8, 2009 <https://www.theguardian.com/stage/2009/sep/08/dance-anne-teresa-de-keersmaeker-rosas>.

2 Matt Trueman, "Beyoncé Accused of 'Stealing' Dance Moves in New Video," *The Guardian*, October 10, 2011 <https://www.theguardian.com/stage/2011/oct/10/beyonce-dance-moves-new-video>.

3 Jocelyn Vena, "Beyonce's 'Countdown' Video Shoot Was 'Evolving, Spontaneous'," *MTV News*, October 7, 2011 <http://www.mtv.com/news/1672200/beyonce-countdown-video-shoot>.

4 Carol McColgin, "Beyonce Stylist B. Akerlund on Finding the Perfect Yellow Dress for 'Lemonade'," *Billboard*, April 26, 2016.

5 Shana Redmond, "'You tell me my song is more than a song': Black Music as Protest and (Re)Vision in the Twentieth Century," Lecture, Mt. Holyoke College, Holyoke, Massachusetts, April 11, 2016. Redmond makes this statement on us needing to see Beyoncé in order to hear her in response to a student's question about Beyoncé as a political agent. Redmond asserted that Beyoncé's music fall outside of the black anthem tradition Redmond studies and that Beyoncé's cultural impact is largely made through how she packages and presents herself visually. Redmond delivered this lecture the week before *Lemonade* premiered on HBO.

6 Daphne A. Brooks, "'All That You Can't Leave Behind': Black Female Soul Singing and the Politics of Surrogation in the Age of Catastrophe," *Meridians*, Vol. 8, No. 1 (2008): 180–204.

7 Daphne A. Brooks, "How #BlackLivesMatter Started a Musical Revolution," *The Guardian*, March 13, 2016. For a long history of black protest music see: Shana L. Redmond, *Anthem: Social Movements and the Sound of Solidarity in the African Diaspora* (New York: New York University Press), 2013 and Imani Perry, *May We Forever Stand: A History of the Black National Anthem* (Chapel Hill: University of North Carolina Press), 2018.

8 Beyoncé was accused of stealing the captivating augmented reality visual art show of Italian pop singer Lorella Cuccarini, who had done an eerily similar performance just a year earlier. After seeing a YouTube video of Cuccarini, Beyoncé hired the same graphic designers Cuccarini used to design her Billboard performance. As with the "Countdown" video, Beyoncé is on her way to creating a visual textile or imbricated narrative, something that fashions new and distinct meaning from many pieces—but it's not quite there yet. Her choreography is way more intricate, but it is still too close to Cuccarini's performance, and she uses some of the same imagery in the same graphic black and white. See, Erika Ramirez, "When Beyonce's Inspiration Turns into Imitation," *Billboard*, May 1, 2013 <https://www.billboard.com/articles/columns/the-juice/1560092/op-ed-when-beyonces-inspiration-turns-into-imitation>; Fiorella Ruth Kibongui, "Beyonce vs. Cuccarini," *Vogue Italia*, May 26, 2011 <https://www.vogue.it/en/people-are-talking-about/that-s-too-much/2011/05/beyonce-vs-cuccarini?refresh_ce=>; and Nicole Marie Melton, "Beyonce Responds to Billboard awards Copycat Claim," *Essence*, May 25, 2011 <https://www.essence.com/news/beyonce-lorella-cuccerini-billboard-awards-performance/>.

9 Karen Wong, "How Beyonce's Seven-Story Monolith Sets New Bar of Design Extravagance," *Artnet News*, July 13, 2016 <https://news.artnet.com/art-world/beyonce-formation-tour-art-551048>.

10 For more on race, gender, and modern architecture see, Anne Anlin Cheng, *Second Skin: Josephine Baker and the Modern Surface* (New York: Oxford University Press), 2013.

11 Patrick Sisson, "Beyoncé's 'Formation': How a Historic Pasadena Home Went Southern Gothic for This Year's Biggest Video," Curbed, February 9, 2016 <https://www.curbed.com/2016/2/9/10953432/beyonce-formation-music-video-production-design>.

12 Sisson, "Beyoncé's 'Formation'."

13 Liz Raiss, "Why Beyoncé's Fur Coat in Lemonade is More Than Just a Fashion Statement," *Fader*, April 24, 2016 <http://www.thefader.com/2016/04/24/beyonce-hood-by-air-lemonade-coat>.

14 Frazier Tharp, "Breaking Down the Art References on Jay-Z's 'Magna Carta Holy Grail'," July 8, 2013 <https://www.complex.com/style/2013/07/jay-z-magna-carta-holy-grail-art/the-met>.

15 For more on blackness, protest, and museum spaces see: Susan E. Cahan, *Mounting Frustration: The Art Museum in the Age of Black Power* (Durham, NC: Duke University Press), 2016; Bridget Cooks, *Exhibiting Blackness: African Americans and the American Art Museum* (Amherst: University of Massachusetts Press), 2011; Kellie Jones, *South of Pico: African American Artists in Los Angeles in the 1960s and 1970s* (Durham, NC: Duke University Press), 2017; Catherine Morris and Rujeko Hockley, eds., *We Wanted a Revolution: Black Women 1965–85: New Perspectives* (Durham, NC: Duke University Press), 2018.

16

"I USED TO BE YOUR SWEET MAMA"

Beyoncé at the crossroads of blues and conjure in *Lemonade*

Kinitra D. Brooks and Kameelah L. Martin

The iconic songstress Beyoncé Knowles challenges her audience to think outside the artistic lines in her 2016 audiovisual album, *Lemonade*. Employing a powerful display of black cultural ways of knowing, the album turns away from the artist's popular music roots to gather a score of other black female creatives in a communal bond of artistic hoodoo. Cogently blending the poetry of Warsan Shire, the iconography of African-derived religions such as Ifá and Regla de Ocha, and the beauty of the (black) female form, *Lemonade* offers a narrative of healing and resilience. It has garnered comparisons with the cinematography of Julie Dash and Kasi Lemmons in the ways it targets a decidedly black and female spectatorship. Invoking an undeniable black feminist lexicon, Beyoncé's most recent solo work delves into the machinations of existing at the crossroads of race and gender inciting controversial responses from some of the most prominent black feminist voices in the academy.[1] Here we present a close textual reading of *Lemonade* wherein we argue that the thematic and narrative structure heavily relies upon African diasporic archetypes and vernacular forms.

Our scholarship, more specifically, articulates how and where *Lemonade* converges with blues ideologies and the conjure culture of the American south. We engage Angela Davis' *Blues Legacies and Black Feminism* (1998) as the theoretical foundation for understanding how the blues function as a cultural mediator of gendered consciousness in post-emancipation life, and expand upon Yvonne Chireau's assertion that there is a profound kinship between African-derived spirituality and blues music.[2] Positioning blues as musical genre and social condition that works symbiotically with the conjuring tradition, we argue that Beyoncé's *Lemonade* reflects what we term the "Occult of Black Womanhood"—a bluesy, spiritual matrix in which black women mediate the realities of their twenty-first-century raced and gendered existence.[3] Calling attention to the simultaneous deployment of the blues singer and the conjure woman in the personas of

Lemonade, we contend that the narrative arch that moves from betrayal to catharsis relies upon these communal outcasts with proto-feminist leanings who also privilege communal healing. Reading *Lemonade* as a neo-blues narrative, we demonstrate how Beyoncé's rendition disabuses itself of dichotomies of secular and sacred, engendering a black feminist voodoo aesthetic that generates a space in which blues and spirituality merge.[4]

Lady sings the (Louisiana hoodoo) blues

The historical connection between the blues and conjure stems from the blues' status as a musical form derived from the Negro spirituals of the enslaved. Post-emancipation, the spirituals developed into more formalized gospel music, which converged with the aspirational respectability of the black church.[5] The blues are comprised of the viscera that remains—that which did not survive the spiritual's metamorphosis into the more rigid and appropriate boundaries of gospel music. Angela Davis insists that in the cosmology of enslaved Africans, the secular and the sacred were far more intertwined, "the sacred universe was virtually all-embracing" and refused to account for the concept of such "polar opposites" the post-emancipatory black community attempted to revise.[6] Blues ideals incorporated a focus on the individual—allowing folks to privilege the desires of one above the many. Blues ethics focused on the corporeal, acknowledging the needs of the flesh, the need to dance, to make love, to drink, and to *feel*.

Davis contends that the blues "displace[d] sacred music in the everyday lives of black people" referring to the songs as "secular spirituals," but we wish to push back at this contention.[7] We assert that the blues did not displace the sacred, but rather the blues were simply another form of interacting with the spirit world fulfilling the intrinsic lack of the complex importance of the body found in the "respectable" black church. In the blues, one finds appeals to "da Lawd" to deliver one from a lowly life of oppression, as in "Washwoman's Blues," just as much as one finds "erotic allusions that bespoke a boastful masculine virility or cunning references to a woman's sex appeal."[8] Rather than reifying false divisions between sacred and secular, the blues emerged as a cultural form "open to discourse on every possible subject affecting the people who created it," and thus did "not banish religion."[9] Chireau refers to the blues as "African American theodicity" while insisting that both the "blues *and* spirituals are a form of worship and celebration [emphasis added]." She furthers her argument by referring to blues artists as "musical ministers."[10] Our contentions build upon Chireau's naming the relationship between the blues and African American spirituality as a "paradigm of kinship."[11]

The sacramental nature of the blues exists because of the immense power it initiates in the intimacy between the musician and the audience. This power is perpetuated through conjure, another manifestation of the sacred eschewed by mainstream African American Christian practice. Conjure, often associated with hoodoo, is a set of practices associated with faith and healing but not with one specific religion. In her monograph *Black Magic: Religion and the African American*

Conjuring Tradition (2006), scholar Yvonne P. Chireau defines conjure as "a magical tradition in which spiritual power is invoked for various purposes, such as healing, protection, and self-defense."[12] Conjure is mainly practiced by Black Americans descended from Africans enslaved in the United States. Chireau and other scholars, such as Trudier Harris, have long associated conjure with folklore, terming it a "set of folk beliefs common to slaves" and yet distinct from the formalities of "black church rituals."[13] Scholar Kameelah L. Martin defines conjure as spirit work:

> I mean to suggest an intimacy with both the healing and harming ritual practices of African-derived religious practices that evolved in the New World … [it] also involves, as the term suggests, communication with supernatural entities that in some cultures may be referred to as ghosts, ha'ints, specters, or apparitions but across the African diaspora are known as the Ancestors, loa, orisha, or simply Spirit.[14]

Martin, like many other scholars, also connects the practice of conjure to African American folklore through the figure of the conjure woman. The conjure woman is a figure of power whose presence suffuses the oral narratives of African American folklore and its cultural products. She is a woman of power who possesses the knowledge of medicinal herbs, midwifery, magic, and even counseling through a specific connection to the spirit realm. Conjurers occupied an interstitial position in society that reflected the intersectional role in which they played as midwife, herbalist, fortune-teller, relationship counselor, and spiritual advisor. The gift of power and foresight often occupied the dual role of burden, marking them as outcasts—however revered they may have been. Chireau determines that conjure women were "socially marginalized" women who were depicted as "outsiders, inhabitants of the fringes, dwelling within a cultural demimonde."[15]

Martin insists that there is "a symbiotic relationship between conjure and blues music that originated in post-emancipation cultural production."[16] Blues music contains "songs of power" and often acted as a "vessel through which conjure reached a broad audience."[17] Songs such as Gertrude Ma Rainey's "Louisiana Hoodoo Blues" are ripe with references to the who, what, where, and why of the underground conjure scene. Rainey's lyrics boast "Down in Algiers where the hoodoos live in their den/Their chief occupation is separating women from men" in the second stanza; they then continue with a more instructive tone: "The hoodoo told me to get me a black cat bone/And shake it over their heads, they'll leave your man alone."[18] Not only was conjure culture disseminated through blues music, but the relationship is also reciprocal. Conjure and hoodoo rituals were invoked as the most powerful remedy for the blues—the emotional and psychological condition affiliated with the musical genre.[19] Chireau corroborates the convergence of the two traditions when she notes that, for blues women especially, "charms, conjure, and hoodoo practices provided last-resort antidotes for loneliness, despair, or betrayal. Female blues singers insisted that [African-derived spiritual practices] had the power to 'bring that man home' and 'treat me right.'"[20]

Long associated as a curative for the lonely-heart blues, Zora Neale Hurston collected several conjure spells "To Make a Man Come Home" and another "To Break Up a Love Affair" in *Mules and Men* (1935).[21] Chireau reads blues songs for explicit ingredients for conjure spells such as Lizzie Miles' "Shootin' Star Blues" (1928) even as Davis connects the themes of conjure in the lyrics and titles of blues songs with specific West African cultural practices.[22] We move to demonstrate how this relationship between blues and conjure is transformed in Beyoncé's neo-blues narrative *Lemonade* when she simultaneously performs the roles of the blues singer and the conjure woman.

We assert that the marginalized status of the conjure woman mirrors the simultaneously celebrated and excluded sociocultural status of the legendary blues woman. Blues music is one "vessel through which conjure has reached a broad audience" and blues women purposely "incorporated conjure sensibilities" to become popular ambassadors of the black woman-centered belief.[23] In truth, the blues woman and the conjure woman occupy a similarly complex social status within the African American community. Blues and conjure simultaneously subvert the false binaries of institutionalized black Christianity. Both sets of women were communal outcasts with proto-feminist ideologies who also privileged communal healing. Blues women and conjure women rejected the values of the mainstream African American culture and beliefs. These women existed on the margins of society because they were often associated with practices outside the mores of the black church—a prominent fixture in the larger community. Conjure women, though the majority of their clients were regular church attendees, operated outside of what many considered Christian grace. Their belief in forces connecting back to traditional West African religious practices forced them outside of the cultural milieu. Likewise, blues women were considered immoral and dangerous because of their open celebration of excess and bodily pleasures—sexuality was a prominent theme in blues music.[24] Other themes included:

> advice to other women, alcohol; betrayal or abandonment; broken or failed love affairs; death; departure; dilemma of staying with a man or returning to family; disease and afflictions; erotica; hell; homosexuality; infidelity; injustice; jail and serving time; loss of lover; love; men; mistreatment; murder; other woman; poverty; promiscuity; sadness; sex; suicide; supernatural; trains; traveling; unfaithfulness; vengeance; weariness, depression, and disillusionment; weight loss.[25]

Within such an ideology where black women openly flaunted their agency and executed a self-determination in the face of so-called respectability, a different narrative of black femaleness emerges. The blues are a subversive form for black women as they contradict "mainstream ideological assumptions regarding [black] women and being in love."[26] The blues offer up a mirror to a black female reality that is less glamorized—it reflects the *Occult of True Black Womanhood*. Opposed to the "Cult of True Womanhood" where Barbara Welter first articulates notions of what it meant to be white and female in the nineteenth century, we speak of an *occult* black womanhood that incorporates and valorizes black feminist manifestations of spirituality, the power of the erotic, other ways of knowing, and wherein the authentic selves of black women (in all of her myriad manifestations) lies the source of #blackgirlmagic.[27] It is within this space, where the supernatural world and the blues condition are not estranged, that black women mediate their survival at the crossroads of race and gender. It is in just such a liminal space where we wish to locate *Lemonade* and offer a reading of the film that explores the occult womanhood of Beyoncé as a bluesy conjurer.

Beyoncé as conjure woman

Beyoncé intentionally weaves the audio and visual language of *Lemonade* to revise and reconstruct a contemporary manifestation of the conjure woman that ultimately provides guidance through and past her encounters with the blues while reflecting the Occult of Black Womanhood. Farah Jasmine Griffin posits that the voice of the black woman has the power to cast spells, and Beyoncé uses the magic of her music and her visual mastery to highlight the spiritual potential of contemporary black womanhood as a conjure woman.[28] Beyoncé seems keenly aware of the powerful relationship between African-centered spiritual praxis and the blues condition, pushing her to reject a simplistic rendering of black Christianity in ways that privilege the spirit work necessary to heal and renegotiate healthy boundaries for moving forward. Scholar Janell Hobson sees Beyoncé's spirit work as a reclamation of "all the aspects of black life that have been rendered as deviant, as waste, as toxic, as destructive"; and we further posit that she embodies the conjure woman as a literal manifestation of what Omise'eke Natasha Tinsley deems "grown ass black woman magic."[29]

The worrying of the falsely constructed lines between black Christian practice and African-centered spiritualities is introduced in the second chapter of *Lemonade*, titled "Denial," in the crucial privileging of black feminist manifestations of spirituality. The Beyoncé character begins to seriously contemplate the possible infidelities of her partner after diving into a bedroom filled with water and various floating religious objects:

> I tried to change. Closed my mouth more, tried to be softer, prettier, less awake. Fasted for 60 days, wore white, abstained from mirrors, abstained from sex, slowly did not speak another word. In that time, my hair, I grew past my ankles. I slept on a mat on the floor. I swallowed a sword. I levitated. Went to the basement, confessed my sins, and was baptized in a river. I got on my knees and said "amen" and said "I mean." I whipped my own back and asked for dominion at your feet. I threw myself into a volcano. I drank the blood and drank the wine. I sat alone and begged and bent at the waist for God. I crossed myself and thought I saw the devil. I grew thickened skin on my feet, I bathed in bleach, and plugged my menses with pages from the holy book,

but still inside me, coiled deep, was the need to know … Are you cheating on me? Cheating? Are you cheating on me?[30]

This passage in particular—teamed with the images of the Beyoncé character awakening from slumber and floating in various poses of prayer, circular movements, and literal self-reflection as she silently stares at a doppelganger of herself—conflates and explodes European notions of the divine. We proffer the language of Daphne Brooks to discuss the theoretically revolutionary and politically savvy ways in which Beyoncé uses the conjure woman characterization to "conflate and pervert the boundaries of" mainstream Southern Christian black womanhood.[31] In this passage, she brings in classic methods of black Evangelical worship—fasting from food, sex, vanity as she confesses her sins and goes down to the river to be baptized; and yet in each act of Christian piety, something is clearly … *different.* In her fasting, she wears white for sixty days. She confesses her sins, but goes down to her basement, not a church, to offer confession. She privileges baptism at a river—again eschewing the formalities of the church. She obediently falls to her knees to proclaim "Amen" but quickly equivocates the blessing with the self-articulation of "I mean." And it is here, in these disjunctures of growing subversion that the power of Beyoncé's conjuring comes to the fore.

The conjure woman of Southern folk culture is marked by the distinct West African spiritual influences in her practice and these themes that suffuse the narrative of "Denial." Specifically, the narrative is inundated with multiple references to the process of becoming an *Iyawo*, the Yoruba word for "bride." In Vodou, an advanced practitioner literally marries their personal loa, hence becoming a bride. In Santería, or Regla de Ocha, advanced practitioners who have received their "head" or "ori" and are chosen as priests/priestesses wear white during the first year of their initiation, for they have become newly born in their relationship with their tutelary orisha.[32] The conjuring of Beyoncé's character adopts the spiritual mandates of the *Iyawo* who is expected to "observe a year dressed entirely in white with strict behavioral restrictions including not being out at night, not taking things from other people's hands and not cutting their hair."[33] Hence we see her privileging the presence and journey to the African diasporic spiritual feminine—via conjuring—in one's time of doubt and need.

It is necessary to highlight Beyoncé's intentional complication of black women's modes of worship in the black Evangelical tradition—of service, silence, and suffering for the collective good of the patriarchy that suffuses the institution. It is the Beyoncé character's very battle with the symptom of patriarchy known as marital infidelity—a sin often ignored and perpetuated in the church structure when committed by its men—that causes her to cry out to older traditions that celebrate the black spiritual feminine. Her realization of this glaring lack of the institutional black church to provide answers is seen as she "drank the blood and drank the wine," embracing the gospel and the secular; the Christian symbolism of the wine for Christ's blood as well as the *ajé,* or life force, offered by the blood sacrifice of animals to the West African pantheon. The Beyoncé character finds herself alone begging for God—but when she performs the familiar Christian genuflection, she is threatened with the presence of the devil. Again, this is not a rejection of black Christian dialectics, but a recognition that it is not sufficient, that a lack remains. Further, we insist that this lack remains ostensibly because of the church's continued commitment to patriarchy over the spiritual, emotional, and psychological health of its largest demographic, black women. The final reinforcement of the black church's problematic lack of multi-faceted solutions for black women's uniquely complex spiritual needs is the visual presentation of the Holy Bible floating away in the water as the Beyoncé character declares how she "plugged [her] menses with pages from the holy book." The static Christianity translated from dead languages is of little use to her—unless it has been flooded, literally, with her womanly essence.

The visual presentations in "Denial" undergird the narrative read by the Beyoncé character, further inscribing on our psyche the powerful conjuring to which viewers are bearing witness. Beyoncé proves herself a conjure woman fluent in African-centered spiritual cosmologies as she embodies two major and one minor orisha figures in this short preface to "Hold Up." The minor orishas, the Ibeji (previously alluded to as the doppelgänger of self-reflection), are the divine twins and children of Shangó and Oshún.[34] The deliberate act of twinning renders the blues and spirit work as two working parts of one healing whole—solidifying them as Ibeji born of the same womb, in this instance Louisiana. The presence of the Ibeji further makes sense because of the overarching presence of the orisha Yemaya, who took in the Ibeji after Oshún abandoned them as children.[35]

The entire sequence takes place underwater as the Beyoncé character conjures one of the most powerful orisha, Yemaya:

> She is the mother of all living things, rules over motherhood and owns all the waters of the Earth. She gave birth to the stars, the moon, the sun and most of the orishas. Yemaya makes her residence in life-giving portion of the ocean.[36]

It is Yemaya who nurtures the Beyoncé character as she struggles with the deficiencies of the black church. Most importantly, it is Yemaya who initiates Beyoncé's *Iyawo* journey. Though the journey as *Iyawo* is usually to one singular orisha or loa—we posit that it is in "Denial" that the Beyoncé character acts as a conjure woman, for she is *Iyawo* to multiple orishas and loas across the many African-centered spiritual traditions. She has become *Iyawo* to divine black feminine spirituality as a whole. This gives her the maneuverability to end the segment as Oshún, opening the double doors to a deluge of water as she saunters down the steps filled with dangerous laughter.

Beyoncé's blues as feminism

Angela Davis renders visible the "hints of feminist attitudes" that suffuse the performances of blues women as she demonstrates their participation in the construction of oral feminist traditions. Blues women could be economic powerhouses, at times experiencing a financial independence so often denied post-emancipatory black women; but the highlight of the blues woman's black feminist tradition remains her sexual freedom. "6 Inch," for example, is a rhapsody on the financial security and self-fulfillment the protagonist finds when she "grinds from Monday to Friday/Work from Friday to Sunday."[37] And although she is a married woman, Beyoncé seemingly reserves the right to her sexual freedom as she asserts, "Who the Fuck do you think I is?/You ain't married to no average bitch, boy/You can watch my fat ass twist, boy/As I bounce to the next dick, boy."[38] Beyoncé's blues performance in *Lemonade* falls in line with the conventions of blues women that Davis articulates. Many of the songs included in the visual album address the themes of infidelity, betrayal, social injustice, heartache, and sadness. The themes of motherhood and marriage are not completely absent, but they appear subordinate to the identity the blues woman worked hardest to shape. Blue Ivy, Beyoncé's daughter, is mentioned once, though not by name, and she appears in the visual; but it seems that Beyoncé's focus is not on motherhood as her sole identity. Rather, she focuses on her career, her relationship, her creativity, her bond to other women, and her ambition—these are just as much a part of her identity as motherhood. In fact, she had these before she was a mother.

According to Davis and others, these blues women eschewed marriage and husbands and reveled in bragging about the prowess of their many lovers, some of whom were female. Blues women also displayed a proto-feminist independence of spirit by living life in the fast lane: "All of them women who'd sing the blues would curse, be drunk, just sit up and talk a lot of shit, man. What foul language!"[39] *Lemonade* is the first album in which Beyoncé openly and unapologetically engages in profanity, tossing aside the respectability politics of her public persona and digging deep into the roots of the blues aesthetic. Her lyrics are raw, unfiltered, and raunchy at times; Beyoncé engages in male posturing/gender bending like many of the classic blues women performers such as Gertrude "Ma" Rainey, Mamie Smith, and others. She proclaims, "I don't give a Fuck, chunking my deuces up/Suck on my balls pause/I had enough/I ain't thinking 'bout you" in "Sorry," which is the absolute antithesis of an apology.[40]

Another way that Beyoncé's blues performance rings authentic is the way in which she responds to the wayward heart of her lover. Travel was often a means for the blues man (or man with the blues) to escape his present situation and reinvent himself in a world where the blues were not chasing so closely on his tail. The itineracy that became synonymous with blues men is just one of the reasons why the train, the major source of cross-continental travel during the early twentieth century, is a recurring symbol in blues music. The gendered symbolism has taken on a life of its own; while the women folk were less likely to "flag a freight train and ride" due to familial obligations, not every woman "hangs her head and cries" either.[41] Women who identified with a blues aesthetic and lifestyle

> did not acquiesce to the idea … that men take to the road and women resort to tears. The women who sang the blues did not typically affirm female

resignation and powerlessness, nor did they accept the relegation of women to private and interior spaces.[42]

Visually, *Lemonade* illustrates that one of the first things the lead character does is leave the urban sprawl and return to Louisiana—perhaps a sly riff on the classic "Louisiana Hoodoo Blues" in which the performer ventures to the land of creoles and conjure to secure a mojo hand to resolve the problem of an unfaithful lover.[43]

Beyoncé is not bereft of agency in response to her lover's infidelity; the entire cinematic album demonstrates this in words and deeds. Beyoncé as blues woman does not falter or crumble in asserting her fiery independence as she belts out, "And keep your money/I got my own/Keep a bigger smile on my face/Being alone" in "Don't Hurt Yourself." And if there is any question about her hanging her head and crying, she clarifies that she would rather commit "suicide before you see this tear fall down my eyes."[44] Neither does she shy away from the violence, antagonism, and female rivalry that often erupts when bluesy women take a liberated and assertive stance to being "done wrong" by a lover.[45] The refrain of the opening song, "Pray to catch you whispering/I Pray you catch me listening," signifies a desire for confrontation even with the tone of humility and gentility with which Beyoncé sings. Culturally fluent listeners recognize that being caught eavesdropping on an impropriety gives a black woman license to "act a fool." Though her voice is accompanied by melodies and rhythms that call to mind a Caribbean steel pan drum band in "Hold Up," the singer concedes, "I don't want to lose my pride but I'ma Fuck me up a Bitch."[46] The violence that she intones in the poetic interlude "Anger" easily exposes the thin differential line between a rough and tumble blues aesthetic and the otherworldly harm that can be conjured upon a soul. The blues woman moves from a figurative performance of violence in song to a sinister mutilation, promising to use her rival's "teeth as confetti" and "sternum [as her] ... bedazzled cane"—a thinly coded hint of her conjuring prowess.

Beyoncé tosses aside respectability politics to engage in the raw realism of the blues milieu, as demonstrated in her language and attitude toward "Becky with the good hair."[47] By engaging in this blues aesthetic, Beyoncé consciously connects to the working class, women folk rather than the upper-middle class, club women with unbreakable ties to the black church. Beyoncé's identification with Houston's Third Ward—known for its black working-class sensibilities—is most evident in her performance of "Formation," which was touted as unapologetically black and southern and "hood." Billboard columnist Kris Ex described the iconography as being:

> centered around the legacy of pre- and post-diluvial New Orleans; full of allusions to Trayvon Martin, Tamir Rice and Mike Brown; highlighted by around the way girls, echoes of Dapper Dan, Southern belles reimagined; lots of cornbread and collard greens and not a white person in sight.[48]

The most impressive element that draws parallels between blues women and conjure women, however, is their belief and participation in the healing powers of their gifts to build community. There exists more clarity in how conjure women were often read as healers "who viewed healing as a sacred duty."[49] Some were midwives and were often more affordable options to medical doctors for minor ailments given their talent for herbs and tonics. Conjure women were also spiritual counselors providing mental and emotional healing to their customers as well. Blues women were healers that focused "on the fixing of relationships gone awry and the resolution of oppressive romantic entanglements."[50] Blues women's performances were conceived as "preachin' the blues" as their sermons on love—of the self as well as others—demonstrated the healing potential in connecting "spiritual and sexual joy."[51] Ultimately, blues women privileged the psychological and spiritual wellness of their audience by expelling their blues by naming it, singing it, and taking away its power. And it is through evoking the power of *nommo*, the power to name black female experience, that healing becomes possible through the blues:

> Indeed, the musical genre is called the "blues" not only because it employs a musical scale containing "blue notes" but also because it names, in myriad ways, the social and psychic afflictions and aspirations of African Americans. The blues preserve and transform the West African philosophical centrality of the naming process. In the Dogon, Yoruba, and other West African cultural traditions, the process of nommo—naming things, forces, and modes—is a means of establishing magical (or, in the case of the blues, aesthetic) control over the object of the naming process.[52]

By naming (through creative processes) her experiences with the two major men in her life (her father and her husband), Beyoncé exudes both spiritual and aesthetic control over her narrative of healing. She takes ownership and control through the power of *nommo*, taking care to speak and name not just her own personal trajectory of healing, but also the universal experiences of her black female audience so that they might heal alongside her. Davis asserts that:

> One of the principal modes of community-building in women's blues is that of sharing experiences for the purpose of instructing women how to conduct their lives. Many of the songs that describe the difficulties of romantic partnerships are pedagogical in character.[53]

It is through the act of naming and including that *Lemonade* builds community within the frames and among the black female spectators who watch. *Lemonade* is a safe space (sonically as well as visually) for black women to gather and be anointed with the healing balm of the blues and conjure. The narrative arc of *Lemonade* moves from betrayal to healing, and invokes the wisdom of black female Ancestors to impart to the audience a lesson of survival—not just in romantic relationships— and preaches how to "[spin] gold out of this hard life" and "[conjure] beauty from the things left behind."[54] This is the epitome of the Occult of Black

Womanhood—a space engendered with spiritual dexterity and vernacular forms of bearing witness. Black women instruct other black women to take the lemons (bitterness) that life serves them due to race, class, and gender oppression and make lemonade. Beyoncé's blues performance, rife with the calling card of conjuration, imparts the lesson that life can be made sweet again (a common message of the orisha Oshún) through a creative laying-on of black female hands upon black female bodies—this is what blues and hoodoo have always done for those who know how to invoke them. As one critic called it, *Lemonade* is Beyoncé's love letter to black women, and it seems to have been received overwhelmingly.[55]

Notes

1 See, for example, bell hooks' blog post "Moving Beyond Pain." Bell Hooks Institute. May 9, 2016. http://www.bellhooksinstitute.com/blog/2016/5/9/moving-beyond-pain.

2 Davis, Angela Y. 1998. *Blues Legacies and Black Feminism: Gertrude "Ma" Rainey, Bessie Smith, and Billie Holiday*. New York: Vintage Books. Chireau discusses the relationship between conjure and blues in the final chapter of her monograph *Black Magic: Religion and The African American Conjuring Tradition*, 144–149.

3 Here we acknowledge Ann DuCille's coining of the phrase "occult of true black womanhood" in her 1994 article "The Occult of True Black Womanhood: Critical Demeanor and Black Feminist Studies" in *Signs*. While similar in lexicon, our terminology differs from DuCille's by focusing on the liminal space wherein black womanhood negotiates the blues condition and one's spiritual agency by virtue of her race and gender rather than posing a question of how to navigate the growing hazards that "our once isolated and isolating intellectual labors have attracted to the magnetic field of black feminist studies" (DuCille 1994, 593).

4 In *Envisioning Black Feminist Voodoo Aesthetics*, Kameelah Martin defines black feminist voodoo aesthetics as a specifically black female ethos wherein "Voodoo aesthetics become manifest in the performance of ceremony, the inclusion of sacred objects or accoutrements on the body, the use of the body as a vessel for Spirit, and various other associations between persons of African descent and African religious iconography" (2016, xvi–xvii).

5 Davis, 5.

6 Ibid., 6.

7 Ibid., 6; 8.

8 For a transcription of "Washwoman's Blues," see ibid., 349; Chireau, 146.

9 Davis, 133.

10 Chireau, 150; 147; 148.

11 Ibid., 148.

12 Chireau, 12.

13 Harris, Trudier. 1991. *Fiction and Folklore: The Novels of Toni Morrison*. Knoxville: University of Tennessee Press, 2–3.

14 Martin, Kameelah L. 2012. *Conjuring Moments in African American Literature: Women, Spirit Work, and Other Such Hoodoo*. New York: Palgrave Macmillan, 1–2.

15 Chireau, 24; 23.

16 Martin, *Conjuring Moments in African American Literature*, 128.

17 Ibid.

18 For complete lyrics, see Davis, 229.

19 Cone, James. 1992. *The Spirituals and the Blues: An Interpretation*. Maryknoll, NY: Orbis Books, 102.

20 Chireau, 147.

21 Hurston, Zora Neale. 1935. *Mules and Men*. New York: Perennial, 276.

22 Chireau, 145; Davis, 128.

23 Martin, *Conjuring Moments in African American Literature*, 128.

24 Davis, 11.

25 Ibid., 13.

26 Ibid., 11.

27 Welter, Barbara. "The Cult of True Womanhood: 1820–1860." *American Quarterly*, vol. 18, no. 2, 1966, pp. 151–174.

28 Griffin, Farah Jasmine. 2004. "When Malindy Sings: A Meditation on Black Women's Vocality." Ed. O'Meally, Robert, Edwards, Brent Hayes, and Griffin, Farah Jasmine. *Uptown Conversation: The New Jazz Studies*. New York: Columbia University Press, 110.

29 Hobson, Janell. "Beyonce as Conjure Woman: Reclaiming the Magic of Black Lives that Matter." *Ms. Magazine.com*. Feb. 8, 2016. http://msmagazine.com/blog/2016/02/08/beyonce-as-conjure-woman-reclaiming-the-magic-of-black-lives-that-matter/ and Tinsley, Omise'eke Natasha. "Beyonce's Lemonade is Black Woman Magic." *Time.com*. April 25, 2016. http://time.com/4306316/beyonce-lemonade-black-woman-magic/.

30 Toglia, Michelle. "Transcript of Beyonce's Lemonade because the Words are just as Important as the Music." https://www.bustle.com/articles/156559-transcript-of-beyonces-lemonade-because-the-words-are-just-as-important-as-the-music.

31 Brooks, Daphne. 2006. *Bodies in Dissent: Spectacular Performances of Race and Freedom, 1850–1910*. Durham, NC: Duke University Press.

32 Interview with Arek Samuels, practitioner. June 11, 2016.

33 http://santeriachurch.org/our-services/santeria-initiations/.

34 http://santeriachurch.org/the-orishas/ibeji/.

35 Ibid.

36 http://santeriachurch.org/the-orishas/yemaya/.

37 All lyrics from *Lemonade* are quoted from Beyoncé's official website http://www.beyonce.com/album/lemonade-visual-album/?media_view=songs.

38 See lyrics for "Don't Hurt Yourself," ibid.

39 Garon, Paul and Beth Garon. 1992. *Woman with Guitar: Memphis Minnie's Blues*. New York: Da Capo Press, 45.

40 For full lyrics, see http://www.beyonce.com/album/lemonade-visual-album/?media_view=songs.

41 These lyrics are taken from "C. & A. Blues" performed by Peetie Wheatstraw.

42 Davis, 20.

43 "Louisiana Hoodoo Blues" was written and performed by Gertrude "Ma" Rainey, and is one of the most well-known and improvised blues songs. Renditions by Victoria Spivey, Lightin' Hopkins, and Muddy Waters were also recorded.

44 See lyrics for "Sorry."

45 Davis, 21.

46 See lyrics to "Hold Up."

47 See lyrics to "Sorry."

48 Ex, Kris. "Why are People Suddenly Afraid of Beyoncé's Black Pride?" Billboard.com. Feb. 10, 2016. http://www.billboard.com/articles/columns/pop/6873899/beyonce-formation-essay.

49 Chireau, 140.

50 Ibid., 147.

51 Davis, 130.

52 Ibid., 33.

53 Ibid., 53.

54 *Lemonade: A Visual Album*. Dir. Khalil Joseph, Beyoncé Knowles-Carter, et al. Perf. Beyoncé. Parkwood Entertainment, 2016.

55 Tulesma, Blue. "Beyoncé's 'Lemonade' Is the Love Letter to Black Women We've Been Thirsting For." *The Griot.com*. 24 April, 2016. http://thegrio.com/2016/04/24/beyonces-lemonade-is-the-love-letter-to-black-women-weve-been-thirsting-for/.

Bibliography

Lemonade: A Visual Album. Directed by Khalil Joseph, Beyoncé Knowles-Carter, et al. Performed by Beyoncé.

Brooks, Daphne. 2006. *Bodies in Dissent: Spectacular Performances of Race and Freedom, 1850–1910*. Durham, NC: Duke University Press.

Chireau, Yvonne. 2003. *Black Magic: Religion and the African American Conjuring Tradition*. Berkeley: University of California Press.

Cone, James. 2004. *The Spirituals and the Blues: An Interpretation*. 1972. Maryknoll, NY: Orbis Books.

Davis, Angela. 1998. *Blues Legacies and Black Feminism: Gertrude "Ma" Rainey, Bessie Smith, and Billie Holiday*. New York: Vintage Books.

DuCille, Ann. "The Occult of True Black Womanhood: Critical Demeanor and Black Feminist Studies." *Signs* 19, no. 3(1994): 591–629.

Ex, Kris. 2016. "Why Are People Suddenly Afraid of Beyoncé's Black Pride?" *Billboard.com*. February 10. Accessed December 15, 2016. http://www.billboard.com/articles/colum ns/pop/6873899/beyonce-formation-essay.

Garon, Paul, and Beth Garon. 1992. *Woman with Guitar: Memphis Minnie's Blues*. New York: Da Capo Press.

Griffin, Farah Jasmine. 2004. "When Malindy Sings: A Meditation on Black Women's Vocality." In *Uptown Conversation: The New Jazz Stuides*, edited by Robert O'Meally, Brent Hayes Edwards, and Farah Jasmine Griffin, 102–125. New York: Columbia University Press.

Harris, Trudier. 1991. *Fiction and Folkore: The Novels of Toni Morrison*. Knoxville: University of Tennessee Press.

Hobson, Janell. 2016. "Beyonce as Conjure Woman: Reclaiming the Magic of Black Lives that Matter." *Ms. Magazine.com*. February 8. Accessed December 20, 2016. http://msma gazine.com/blog/2016/02/08/beyonce-as-conjure-woman-reclaiming-the-magic-of-bla ck-lives-that-matter.

hooks, bell. 2016. "Moving Beyond Pain." Bell Hooks Institute. May 9. Accessed December 20, 2016. http://bellhooksinstitute.com/blog/2016/5/9/moving-beyon-pain.

Hurston, Zora Neale. 1935. *Mules and Men*. New York: Perennial.

Martin, Kameelah L. 2012. *Conjuring Moments in African American Literature: Women, Spirit Work, and Other Such Hoodoo*. New York: Palgrave Macmillan.

Martin, Kameelah L. 2016. *Envisioning Black Feminist Voodoo Aesthetics: African Spirituality in American Cinema*. Lanham, MD: Lexington Books.

Tinsley, Omise'eke Natasha. 2016. "Beyonce's Lemonade is Black Woman Magic." *Time. com*. April 25. Accessed December 21, 2016. http://time.com/4306316/beyonce-lemona de-black-woman-magic/.

Toglia, Michelle. 2016. "Transcript of Beyonce's Lemonade Because the Words Are Just as Important as the Music." *Bustle.com*. April 24. Accessed December 30, 2016. https:// www.bustle.com/articles/156559-transcript-of-beyonces-lemonade-because-the-words-a re-just-as-important-as-the-music.

Tulesma, Blue. 2016. "Beyonce's Lemonade Is the Love Letter to Black Women We've Been Thirsting For." *The Griot.com*. April 24. Accessed December 21, 2016. http:// thegrio.com/2016/04/24/beyonces-lemonade-is-the-love-letter-to-black-women-we ve-been-thirsting-for/.

Welter, Barbara. 1966. "The Cult of True Womanhood: 1820–1860." *American Quarterly* 18 (2 Part i): 151–174.

17

BEYONCÉ'S *LEMONADE* AND THE BLACK SWAN EFFECT

Kyra D. Gaunt

Introduction: rethinking the improbable impact of black women

Stories remain powerful ways to re-present and disrupt the hegemonic assumptions that rob us of other truths. The smashing shared storyworld of Beyoncé's *Lemonade* is a prodigious feminist manifesto, embodied in spoken word, music, and moving images. It explores the ways we squeeze ourselves and each other into prisons of emotional, racialized, and gendered oppression—and insists that it's high time we broke the spell. No longer will the erotic sexuality of women be threatened. And while *Lemonade* was nectar for female and male feminists alike, it is Black women who occupy its center. Beyoncé notably declares, "Until there is a mosaic of perspectives coming from different ethnicities behind the lens, we will continue to have a narrow approach and view of what the world actually looks like."[1] It is as if Beyoncé was out to free pop culture of its racialized patriarchy, inviting viewers to imagine a womanist world of magical realism through Southern Gothic, antebellum scenes set to an Afrofuturistic song cycle.

Lemonade recollects—and tackles—male domination and female oppression of wives, daughters, and mothers. Emotional stories like *Lemonade*, particularly in the age of networked publics and digital social media, can frame and refocus, and, conversely, sustain and perpetuate perceived realities to others as well as ourselves. The quote attributed to Plato, "Those who tell stories rule society,"[2] reminds us that the stories we tell, and those we don't, reveal whose subjectivities matter, and to whom.

Centuries ago, a story shared among the English had it that black swans did not exist. But they *did* exist. Non-white swans turned up after British naval Captain James Hook "discovered" Australia in 1770, which (surprise, surprise) led to the dispossession of Indigenous peoples from their land. The English amplified their false worldview in a tidy figure of speech: "You'd sooner see a black swan than ..." let's say for the purposes of thinking about *Lemonade*, equal rights for women of African descent. The idiom encapsulated highly improbable events as if they were impossibilities. In his 2007 book *The Black Swan: The Impact of the Highly Improbable* Nassim Nicholas Taleb called the phenomenon where "wildly unexpected events and processes [reach] far beyond their initial apparent import" the *black swan effect*. [3] The effect is distinguished by three characteristics: 1) it is unpredictable, defying presumed expectations; 2) it has wide-ranging consequences; and 3) its impact seems only plausible *after* the fact. Since then, the effect has become a catch-all for "outliers" of any kind. The fact that black swans were and are real did not undo the colonializing thinking that accompanied the initial figure of speech.

> If a Lie be believ'd only for an Hour, it has done its Work ... Falsehood flies, and the Truth comes limping after it
>
> *Anglo-Irish political satirist Jonathan Swift (1710)*[4]

Such surprising effects are more likely a consequence of the structural logic behind oppression and intersectionality that often hides what George W. Bush once referred to as "soft bigotry of low expectations."[5] The undoing of such lies about Black women brings to mind Moya Bailey's queer feminist work as she described the compelling sounds of "rampant misogyny and sexism" in rap music, coining the term "misogynoir."[6] This chapter explores the counter-hegemonic work of Beyoncé Knowles-Carter—a self-made millionaire ranked among the wealthiest women in the entertainment industry (alongside Madonna, Celine Dion, Barbra Streisand, and Taylor Swift)—as she meets and dismantles the patriarchy in the business of music and marriage in subtle and substantive ways.

In both social and business relationships, people use contracts to ensure security or certainty in human affairs, particularly among unknown others or strangers. In music as in marriage, contracts often reflect gender stratification and if executed well can even disrupt gender inequalities. This chapter also teases out how Beyoncé as CEO of Parkwood Entertainment utilizes the shared emotional world of "transmedia storytelling" to tackle issues of racialized patriarchy and gender oppression in *Lemonade*. It also explores how work that seems "highly improbable" when it comes to Black women in the business of music has historically had a significant but often forgotten impact on the recording industry for over a century: a phenomenon that might be called the "white swan effect" of racialized patriarchy and white superiority.

Queering the pitch of cis-gender normativity

In "Don't Hurt Yourself," Beyoncé declared to the imagined marital partner in her audience, "Motivate your ass / Call me Malcolm X," simultaneously queering cis-gender heteronormativity and revolutionary blackness. The audio heard immediately after this is an unaccompanied sample: a speech Malcolm X gave on May 22, 1962 to a Los Angeles crowd of Black Muslims that converges like a percussive break into a powerful audio-visual sequence. The convergence twists the gender ideology of the iconic voice of male dominance and positionality over women in black power's resistance to white supremacy ...

> *The most disrespected person in America is the Black woman.*
> *The most unprotected person in America is the Black woman.*
> *The most neglected person in America is the Black woman.*

... to set our eyes and attention on Black women—and Beyoncé's authorial voice and filmic direction. Our gaze shifts from music video to documentary film as we peer at the faces of everyday Southern-rooted Black women posing and presenting themselves, smiling without artifice or much affect, letting themselves be seen by a friendly and familiar eye.

In true fashion of the hip-hop sampling aesthetic, the iconic voice and percussive articulation re-members us to Malcolm, but when the beat drops back in, Beyoncé wrecks that ideology and reclaims her time: "I am the dragon breathing fire. Beautiful man [or "mane"—reduced to an objectifying part], I'm the lion ... I am not broken, I'm not crying." The histories and memories of Black women, individually and collectively, in the music entertainment industry (no different than those of everyday women) have been symbolically annihilated or are ecologically threatened, not unlike black swans in their existing habitats today. A general viewer of *Lemonade* is liable to be miseducated about the role of Black women as cultural producers. They live with a preponderance of evidence that Black women in the audio-visual texts of popular music are mute, sexually-objectified dancers serving primarily as background decoration with a few stars as exceptions.

Long before hip-hop, lyrics and images in mass popular music culture contributed to the normalization of derogatory language and stigmas about Black women that persist in the present-day content and language expressed by both men and women, girls and boys. Self-objectifying, sexploitative, and patriarchal discourse contributes to the improbability of recognizing the significant role Black woman, including Beyoncé, have played as composers, producers, video directors, production managers, and CEOs in the music entertainment industry.

The sounds of "black swans" in the early business of records (1853–1921)

You now know it would be a lie to say *you'd sooner see a black swan than* a Black woman in the record business wielding power, prestige, and wealth a century before Beyoncé accomplished her feats. The history of Black women in music and entertainment dates back a century before *Lemonade* to the operatic performances of Elizabeth Taylor Greenfield (c. 1819–1876) and the pioneering firsts in the career of singer-actor Ethel Waters (1896–1977). Born into slavery on a Mississippi plantation, Elizabeth eventually won acclaim and sailed to England in 1853 to perform arias and other songs before Queen Victoria, the Duchess of Sutherland, and other dignitaries as part of the abolitionist movement in the U.K. Greenfield was immediately compared to her contemporary—soprano and diva Jenny Lind, who was known as the "Swedish Nightingale"—and thereafter she was branded "The Black Swan." It was *highly improbable* that European audiences would have seen or imagined a former enslaved African woman or an African of any status singing the high-prestige arias of grand opera.

Greenfield's operatic appearance in England took place only twenty years after the Slavery Abolition Act of 1833 in the British Empire.[7] Opera remains one of the whitest genres of performance more than a century after the 1863 signing of the U.S. *Emancipation Proclamation*. For example, the Metropolitan Opera did not cast a Black woman on its stage until 1955, the same year Rosa Parks also made history, and it finally banned blackface on its stage in 2005.

Elizabeth Taylor Greenfield was not alone in her nineteenth-century performance. In James Monroe Trotter's compendium *Music and Some Highly Musical People: Containing … Sketches of the Lives of Remarkable Musicians of the Colored Race*, published in Boston in 1878, many other Afro-classical musicians, female and male, were represented in drawings and biographies depicting the era. The falsehoods of the non-existent black swan would follow an emerging star, vaudeville blues singer Ethel Waters, when she signed on with the first "colored-owned" record label.

Black Swan Records—a name adopted by owner Harry Pace and associated with the operatic singing of Greenfield, even though swans are mute—made headlines in the *Chicago Defender* on December 24, 1921 with a record label contract that forbade the incumbent superstar to marry: "ETHEL MUST NOT MARRY–SIGNS CONTRACT FOR BIG SALARY."[8] A year earlier the 19th Amendment to the Constitution was ratified, guaranteeing mostly white women the right to vote. That same year the first blues record and the first recording with a blues title by a black artist was recorded by African American Mamie Smith on Okeh Records. Female vaudeville blues singers like Waters and Smith came to be called *blues queens* following the blues record "craze" that ensued with the new buying public. The white A&R representative and music publisher Ralph Peer, credited with recording Mamie Smith, coined the term "race record," which came to denote phonograph recordings made in the U.S. that were marketed to segregated Negro listeners between 1921 and 1942.[9] Blues expert scholar-guitarist Elijah Wald wrote that blues queens "established a dynasty so pervasive that the most popular black male singer to record the blues in the early 1920s, Charles Anderson, was a female impersonator."[10]

The Black Swan Record Company was short-lived, but Ethel Waters' career kept rising. She became the highest-paid recording artist of her "race,"[11] and went on to become a millionaire[12] recording more than 100 sides with various record labels, including Columbia Records. She led her own ensembles and was accompanied by the leading male jazz artists of her day, including Fletcher Henderson, Coleman Hawkins, James P. Johnson, Duke Ellington, Jack Teagarden, Benny Goodman, and Tommy Dorsey. She was first in nearly every category of mass-mediated entertainment and technology, from records and radio to film and television, from the 1920s to the 1950s. She was the first African American to perform live on radio during a Southern tour with Black Swan Records that was heard in five states as well as Mexico in April of 1922. Even Duke Ellington, who had been famous long before her, did not appear on radio until 1923. Waters was the first to co-star with an all-white cast on Broadway in *As Thousands Cheer* with music by Ira Gershwin (1933); she performed in the South with white co-stars.[13] Waters was also the first black actor to host her own television show; airing on June 14, 1939. NBC's *The Ethel Waters Show* was a one-off variety show,[14] perhaps broadcast too soon for its white audiences, but happened twenty years before *The Hazel Scott Show* (1950)[15] or *The Nat King Cole Show* (1956), both of which are erroneously cited in various sources as the first television show hosted by an African American female or male.[16]

Why does this matter in a discussion of *Lemonade*? Ethel Waters was the "Beyoncé" not the "black swan" of the early twentieth century, and I assert that this demonstrates how patriarchy and white supremacy orientalizes public recognition away from the accomplishments of Black women. Ethel Waters' televised variety show featured a dramatic sequence from the Broadway play *Mamba's Daughters*, scripted specifically for her by the husband and wife team of DuBose and Dorothy Heyward, who co-wrote the opera *Porgy & Bess*, and set like the Gullah-Geechee film *Daughters of the Dust*, the first full-length feature film by Julie Dash that inspired *Lemonade*, in the African-rooted region of the sea islands off the coast of South Carolina.[17] The plot of *Lemonade* has been linked to *Daughters of the Dust* and should also be linked to *Mamba's Daughters*. All three productions were the driven by the passion of a Black woman telling stories and lessons of survival, courage, loss, and redemption through the lives of strong Black women across multiple generations. All received critical acclaim. The former two are easily forgotten.

Ethel Waters' 1921 recording of "Oh Daddy" (#2010-A) reportedly made over $104,000 from its sales and a Southern vaudeville tour for Black Swan Records. The song has similar themes of betrayal and anger echoed in the sophisticated storytelling of *Lemonade*:

> Oh, Daddy! / You with you fooling / Think what you're losing /
> Oh, all the little lovings that I gave for you / It's going to make you feel awfully blue/
> When you miss me and long to kiss me / You'll regret the day that you ever quit me.

Before the label went belly-up less than two years later, Ethel penned and recorded "Ain't Gonna Marry / (Ain't Goin' Settle Down)."

> Just when you think that your lovin' man is true /
> He's my man, your man, somebody else's too.
> *Ethel Waters (#14145-B, Black Swan Records)*

On record, its lyrics defied or queered heteronormativity (akin to "Don't Hurt Yourself"), hiding Waters' private life despite the publicity associated with her marriage-restricted fame. "Ain't Gonna Marry" pitches Waters' talent against the patriarchal contract that attempted to govern her right to choose whom to marry while signed with Black Swan Records while off record, Ethel lived a lesbian and/ or bisexual life among friends in Harlem. Her last recording with Black Swan seemed to signal some awareness on her part that the Black Swan label was on its last legs. Waters, like Beyoncé, uses song to signify on the limiting social contracts and institutions that prohibit their full humanity and freedom.

Over a century ago, the voices of Black women amplified race and sexuality to a new mass audience of Americans. Meanwhile, many were disenfranchised throughout the Jim Crow South. Black women would be the last group to gain the right to vote. In Southern states, misogynoir would continue to disenfranchise Black women in the democratic election process, for some as late as the 1960s.[18] *Lemonade* lives inside that legacy of the public and domestic forms of disenfranchisement and alienation of rights and voice. With it, Beyoncé as CEO and President of Parkwood Entertainment snatches back the dignity of Black women as cultural producers with a unique style of storytelling in the digital age of the music and recording business a century later.

A bevy of black swan effects: *Lemonade* as transmedia storytelling

The surprise release of Beyoncé's Emmy-nominated film/visual album *Lemonade* is a superb example of the "black swan effect," while the text itself defies the deficit ideology that pervades contemporary music media and its storytelling. It also does digital counter-hegemonic work; the shared digital storyworld Beyoncé crafted with *Lemonade* also needed to confront the online clicks, swipes, likes, and dislikes of a new dimension: Black girls' and women's algorithmic oppression.[19] The episodic storyworld of *Lemonade* recalls not only music video, but also long-form poetry, cinematic film, the grand spectacle of opera, and the acrobatics of Cirque du Soleil with the help of sophisticated staging, video direction, technology and editing, and more. If the medium is the message, *transmedia storytelling* is Beyoncé's method in *Lemonade*.

Lemonade won a prestigious Peabody Award, akin to a Pulitzer, recognizing the best storytelling in radio, television, and digital media. The 2016 Peabody prize committee described the breadth and impact of the work:

> The innovative and stunningly beautiful masterpiece challenges us to readjust our visual and sonic antennae and invites a reckoning with taken for granted ideas about who we are. [The award is given] For the audacity of its reach and the fierceness of its vision in challenging our cultural imagination about the intimacies and complexities of women of color.[20]

Transmedia storytelling, a concept coined by digital ethnographer and social media expert Henry Jenkins, is distinguished by its "shared storyworld" and how its participatory engagement operates across multiple platforms.[21] For example, *Lemonade* was released as an HBO film, which was nominated for an Emmy. It was a collection of separately shot music videos and recorded tracks. It was a visual album interspersed with poetic interludes, featuring amazing cinematography, and shaped by an over-arching film narrative of betrayal, anger, recovery, love, and redemption. It was accessed as a digital download as well as the asynchronous always-available streaming of digital video available exclusively via HBO and HBO Go for one week starting April 23, 2016. It was distributed exclusively via various channels, including iTunes and Tidal—the first artist-owned music streaming service in the world, owned by Jay-Z, in which Beyoncé is one of its artist-owner investors.

London-based, transmedia consultant Robert Pratten explained, "A traditional definition of transmedia storytelling would be: telling a story across multiple platforms, preferably allowing audience participation, such that each successive platform heightens the audience's enjoyment." It should produce a "synergy between the content and a focus on an emotional, participatory experience for the audience."[22] *Lemonade* broke the Internet holding viewers' undivided attention for over thirty minutes in an age of constant notifications and mobile multi-tasking, which is a wildly unpredictable feat organized by Parkwood Entertainment. *Lemonade* allowed new fans and ride-or-die members of the Beyhive to self-organize as an imagined community of Black women and women in general, sharing our conviviality and digital connection for months across the nation.

Two weeks after the release of *Lemonade*, I remember sitting next to a sista on my morning subway commute between central Brooklyn and midtown Manhattan. Our skin and hair are not what made it obvious; yes, we shared a certain group identity, but nothing else could have signaled what was happening between our headphones. Perhaps it was that we both were so deeply immersed in our devices. I did not notice a yellow dress on her screen or a baseball bat named "Hot Sauce" swinging. And given what happened, I doubt she saw my screen; but suddenly when our eyes met, she uttered one quizzical word: "Lemonade?!?" I nodded and we both went back to the secret society made possible by our screens. We were part of some secret society building itself and stitching ourselves into a larger imagined community of Black women and other fans through *Lemonade*. For weeks many of us lived for the rare beauty of the emotion published for the world to see what we felt was ours. That is/was the shared antebellum/afro-futurist imaginary of *Lemonade* and its transmedia storyworld.

In the following sub-sections, I explore various mediums evoked throughout the text of *Lemonade* that also highlight its transmedia storytelling.

Lemonade *as feminist picaresque*

Asian American author and queer lit writer Alexander Chee published his novel *The Queen of the Night* in 2016 months before *Lemonade* dropped. Chee sought to uncover and reclaim the feminist imaginary of women in fiction by composing, "a nineteenth-century tall tale autobiography—the confessions of a celebrity … that becomes a picaresque with a woman in the place where a man usually is" throughout most of the history of novels.[23] He added, "I wanted to forget the weak cinema courtesans I had seen to try and imagine the women I was sure had existed, had found in my sources—confident, bold, hilarious and sexy."[24] An imaginary lost to the patriarchal masculinity that marked the early formation of the novel that couldn't see Asians or queer figures. Chee's description of his own work could eloquently be transferred to the Southern Gothic, time-traveling, collective biography of Black women voiced by Beyoncé through the words of British-Somali poet-activist Warsan Shire, thirty-six creative designers, and the songwriting of over a dozen collaborators in *Lemonade*.

The Guardian invited Chee to make a literary mixtape devoted to his own novel.[25] It began with Beyoncé's "Check On It" (2005); co-written with her cousin and frequent collaborator Angela Beyince, who at one time served as VP of Operations at Parkwood Entertainment. A decade before *Lemonade* this song was one of the two longest-running number-one singles in 2006 as well as Beyoncé's third U.S. number-one single as a solo artist. The *picaresque* was an early, episodic form of the novel traditionally associated with unhindered male protagonists. It involved the classic quest of masculine identity: a lone hero's journey to manhood improvising as he goes marked by itinerant sexploits. One literary critic described it as "the adventures of a rogue held together only by the personality of its hero, with no unifying structure or situation."[26] *Lemonade* fits the description, but it is a black feminist rebellion pitching to viewers and listeners Beyoncé's version of a 21st-century *picaresque* whose exploits in song, poetry, cinematography, and choreography expose the misogynoir facing the lone black heroine of *Lemonade* who is not alone by the end of the film. She finds herself among her sisters and in her roots in the deep South.

Beyoncé as impresaria

To understand why I found *Lemonade* so compelling as an art form, I started to resituate the Beyoncé I knew as recording artist to Beyoncé Knowles-Carter the CEO whose fame is not her only talent. As a former graduate student of the history of grand opera, her role as an artist-executive reminded me of an 18th-century impresario as well as a film director or auteur. I began speculating about her executive role as if she were an impresario/a rather than a pop star.

The noun "impresario" is defined in Merriam-Webster's as: "one who organizes public entertainments, 1746, from Italian impresario 'operatic manager,' literally 'undertaker (of a business),' from *impresa* 'undertaking, enterprise, attempt'." An 18th-century impresario in opera often cited for mounting light opera was French composer Jacques Offenbach (1819–1880). His operettas were intended to counter the inaccessibility of nineteenth-century grand opera in scale and libretto.[27] Then there was promoter and businessman P.T. Barnum (1810–1891).[28] Considered the greatest showman on earth, he produced "theatrical matinées, blackface minstrelsy, melodramas, circus tours (the first to own private trains), farces, baby and beauty contests, and temperance lectures"—though he is more commonly known as the founder of the Ringling Bros. and Barnum & Bailey Circus.

Contemporary titans of the entertainment industry could also be recognized for the impact on public entertainment at a massive level, including Quincy Jones, Oprah, or recent filmmakers Ava DuVernay or Ryan Coogler. An impresarix must develop and leverage their professional fame as well as economic and social capital to entice large private investors to bank on their vision and support their projects. The most stable titans with longevity and social proof get to set their own terms. The same is true whether in opera or film. In film studies, the director who commands such presence is referred to as an *auteur*.

Artist-executive CEO as auteur

If a filmmaker has such great influence and artistic control over a movie that they are regarded the author of the movie or film, *auteur* is applied: a term that arose in film theory to register and recognize the coordination effort exhibited as "a combination of talent, financial, and labor factors."[29] Prior to the term, the vision of a filmmaker or director was often subject to the whims and desires of the film's financial backers: "Auteur critic Jean-Louis Comolli notes even 'independent' films [were] subject to these influences … If financiers [didn't] like a movie's story, they [would] not fund it. [It was] inescapable."[30]

As filmic storytelling grew, with Alfred Hitchcock serving as a prime example, filmmakers began experimenting with conventions, scoring and detailed storyboarding of shots. Film theorist David Tregde wrote that Hitchcock set the standard for the "combination of high technical skill and artistry that makes an auteur."[31] The convergence of emerging technologies, star power, and capital can forge the conditions that change the game throughout a category.

With *Lemonade*, Beyoncé ascends to the role of impresaria with her expansive artistic vision, production and management, her partnership with HBO and iTunes, and the grand scale depicted in the work as transmedia storytelling. Though many fans witnessed *Lemonade* on a small screen like a desktop, an iPad, or a mobile phone as much as on a big TV screen, the scale we get is tantamount to grand opera. Our intimate, always-on and on-demand connections to mobile dreamworlds of our phones and devices transforms the reach and the connection to and from musical blackness and Black women arguably due to the convergences of new and old medias found in transmedia storytelling.

Songwriting executive

Before *Lemonade*, Beyoncé had established a critical career identity as a mega-artist. She was the second most-awarded recording artist of all time, with twenty-two Grammys awards and sixty-three nominations. She remains the most-nominated artist in Grammy history as of November 2018, despite the fact that *Lemonade* did not win the coveted Grammy for Album of the Year. In the fifty-one-year history of the Billboard Hot 100, she was the only performer to top the chart for ten weeks or more with a group and as a solo artist. Before the 2016 release of

Lemonade, Taylor Swift held the record for most songs on Billboard's Hot 100 simultaneously with eleven songs, set November 13, 2010.[32] With the unprecedented release of twelve tracks (and twelve videos coordinated within a unique visual narrative that contributed to a genre and convention defying magnus opus), Beyoncé became the first female act to chart twelve or more songs on the Hot 100 in the same week. Drake holds the record for male acts, debuting twenty-four tracks at once in the same week. [33]

Beyoncé was the first Black woman to win the American Society of Composers, Authors, and Publishers (ASCAP's) coveted Songwriter of the Year award for "Independent Women Part I," "Jumpin Jumpin," and "Survivor" in 2002. She has been recognized as Woman of the Year by *Glamour Magazine* in 2007 and *Billboard* in 2009, and in 2017 she was recognized by *Forbes* as the fourth wealthiest female musician and the sixth richest self-made female millionaire, with a net worth of $350 million at age thirty-six. Zack O'Malley Greenburg wrote in *Forbes*:

> Last year's *Lemonade* was her sixth solo No. 1 album—and spawned the Formation World Tour, which grossed a quarter of a billion dollars. Expecting twins with her husband, Jay-Z, Beyoncé is taking a break from the stage, but has still taken time to voice support for causes like Black Lives Matter.[34]

Her accomplishments be damned. YouTube is abuzz with content creators and celebrity trolls who suggest Beyoncé is a copycat, a cheat, a stealer of choreography, and a plagiarizer rather than a curator of trends in her industry and collaborator in her artistic vision.[35] The notion that an acclaimed songwriter and executive producer cannot collaborate with others or mount public entertainment that involves others' ideas or talents, even when credited, seems absurd. The do-it-yourself mentality forced into such arguments are also absurd. James S. Murphy wrote in *Vanity Fair*, "Art has rarely, if ever, been the product of the isolated genius."[36] Beyoncé's genius is about a dialogue with its references to earlier works and genres both in black cultural contexts and in the wider/whiter realms of culture and knowledge from Africa and its diaspora to high art and Westernized culture. *Lemonade* represents anything but business as usual in the record industry.

Executive producer

After the rise of Napster in 1999, the internet changed the business of music in every way, for better or worse. The entire industry has been trying to figure a new model that incorporates digital media and audio and video streaming to maintain its profits. Beyoncé's first self-titled visual album became the subject of a Harvard Business School case study. The case study revealed the mechanics behind the black swan effect of producing twelve music videos in about six months with twelve different directors defying business-as-usual marketing strategies with Sony and iTunes. Beyoncé's former general manager, Lee Ann Callahan-Longo, was quoted and began to articulate what she felt set Parkwood Entertainment apart from its predecessors. She said, it was a "management, music, and production company ... owned and operated at the highest level by an artist."

The cooperative power required to produce *Lemonade*, a semi-autobiographical tale of infidelity and a product that sells the renewal of her nuptials to Jay-Z and marks her towering presence in the industry at the same time defies expectation. *Lemonade* challenged not only popular culture's norm of sex, drugs, and youth-oriented music videos as profitable but also let us know that black music, the hip-hop aesthetic, and pop culture could also be turned around to make feminism sexy or make grown folks talk of marriage as imperative as mass communication and culture in an age where marriage has declining significance for millennials. It would be another lie to say *you'd sooner see a black swan* than think of Black women as pioneers in the emerging technologies and practices of the music and recording industry. *Fast Company* magazine named Parkwood Entertainment the most innovative company of 2017. *Lemonade* netted nine Grammy nominations and "Formation" was the second-highest grossing tour of 2016, earning $256 million. As a record label, Parkwood also brought its first new artists—Chloe x Halle, Ingrid, and Sophie Beem—onto its roster.

Beyoncé insists that her distributors, producers, creative artists, and songwriters work together in much the same way. This strategy is not unlike the collaborative alliances between sheet music composers and publishers, song-pluggers and Victrola owners of Tin Pan Alley—referring to the business of printing and promoting sheet music for the first time to the general public between 1903 and 1930—but led by new money not old business. Parkwood Entertainment hired dozens of songwriters, bringing some together under one roof in the Hamptons for the self-titled visual album in order to craft the best songs with one other. Tin Pan Alley used a similar practice that contributed to the expansion of the record business and music industry in the early twentieth century. As CEO, Beyoncé also devises marketing plans that require the cooperation and divergent industry practices of corporations like iTunes and Sony Records. Also, she gives writing and producer credits to well over seventy artists, including those whose music and/or lyrics she incorporates into her vision, whether recognizable or not, in *Lemonade*, from Led Zeppelin and Burt Bacharach to Souljah Boy and new artist Ingrid Burley.[37]

In a Billboard interview, Native Houston rapper and now Parkwood label artist Ingrid Burley, who wrote for Beyoncé's first visual album and co-wrote "Love Drought" (which is not about Jay-Z) with Beyoncé producer Mike Dean for *Lemonade*, shared her reflections on being mentored by Beyoncé: "Every song I write, she gives me feedback on. ... There were songs I had to rewrite 10 times—she challenged me."[38] Beyoncé as CEO is hands-on; she mentors as well as collaborates to disrupt industry practices and genres, shaking up the way people co-create music and products, including the ways their personal narratives drive the attention to both her artist–husband relationship and the role of Black women as producers of major public content. Despite the fact that she digitally records and archives every aspect of her life, it is remarkable how she has been able to maintain the scarcest commodity of the digital age—secrecy—in the contracts that maintained the surprise of *Lemonade* to even industry insiders.

Sampling the emotional sounds of black life

Paying attention to the unexpected audio dimensions of *Lemonade*, while the anthem "Freedom" (featuring Kendrick Lamar) trains our eyes and ethical sensibilities towards the Black Lives Matter movement with the emotional appearance of the mothers of the most notable victims of police brutality, it also trains our ears with the sediments of historical samples: field recordings originally recorded and pioneered by white ethnomusicologist Alan Lomax back in the 1940s and 50s of sacred and secular black life.

Lomax crossed the color lines of Southern segregation to record a mélange of Negro (*sic*) folk culture, including children's musical play, music of workers and prison gangs, and singing preachers with their homolectic moaning in prayer and praise edifying the spirit and raising up a song with their congregations. *Lemonade* sampled a recording of an unidentified lining hymn from the Reverend R.C. Crenshaw Collection Speech and a prison song recorded around 1947–48 at Parchman Farm in Mississippi, all sounds that are accessible to the public via the national archives housed as Smithsonian Folkways Records. "Hold Up" includes samples that remix diverse styles and genres of popular and dance music. It includes the artistry of international DJ and producer Diplo and the rock group Vampire Weekend's Ezra Koenig, who co-produced the track. There's a subtle lyrical reference to Soulja Boy's "Turn My Swag On" (2008) and "Maps" (2003) by The Yeah Yeah Yeahs; both are given writing credits.[39]

"Hold Up" is an exemplary model of the coordination and creativity of Beyoncé as a big thinker about mass-public entertainment in the age of the attention economy where emotion rules the day. She's more than co-producer and co-writer credited along with the fourteen other songwriters of the track. She inhabits the inimitable poetry of Warsan Shire as if it is her autobiographical story, which adds to the sense that *Lemonade* is a collective biography not merely about Beyoncé's marriage and life. This reflects what can be done with and from a woman's power. A queen embraces her family, her community, and the world. She uses that power to level all boats up.

Conclusion

Lemonade's rebellion is visually episodic, beginning with a dramatic proscenium stage reminiscent of vaudeville, a suicidal precipice evoking *The Matrix*, an underwater sequence, and other-worldly realms defined by angry delight recalling the dramatic arias of grand opera or the dying swans of classic ballet. This kind of dramatic entertainment cannot be captured in a three- to five-minute music video. The storytelling in *Lemonade* reinvents and explodes the conventions of music television and video. Not unlike the women in opera plots I introduced in my blog post, the majority of popular music videos where women's work intersects with advertising as if a sanitized form of sex-work, second-generation gender bias abounds. Perhaps this explains the problem for which *Lemonade* was the perfect solution; the most popular genres and mediums of black musical entertainment are primarily under the eye, direction, and control of men.

Galvanized by the convergence of old and new media, the visual album does not merely expand the genre of music video. *Lemonade* reframes ideologies with a mixture of existing music video techniques, storytelling associated with blogs, vlogs, and podcasts, *vidding*—a thirty-year-old white feminist film-making collective dating back to VHS and reel-to-reel tape splicing, black feminist choreopoems—RIP ancestor Ntozake Shange, and slam poetry and spoken word artists like Jessica Care Moore and Jill Scott, that when combined bring multiple diverse audiences and demographics together around one amazing storyworld. *Lemonade* operates at the level of major mainstream film art made for the big screen accessed by millions of mobile screens instead.

The sophisticated digital storytelling of *Lemonade* contributes to the black swan effect again and again. It defies the improbability held in too many minds that a Black woman can be a wealthy, working, happily-married woman … with or without kids, not to mention with a Black husband. Unfortunately, the cheating part is perhaps expected; but the feminist resistance that runs through *Lemonade* is not what was expected in an industry still dominated by patriarchal gender performance.

> *Lemonade* acts as a resistance … it has the ability to include the roots of its cultural conception into both a capitalistic product for consumption and a narrative for women who have been made to feel as if their entire existence depends on the emotional and financial capital of a man.[40]

Lemonade does the work of defying probabilities through a process of *transmedia storytelling*, an elaborate, emotional, and dialectical production that utilizes racialized and gendered tropes to challenge social contracts—contracts that have contributed to creating inequality where women are simultaneously at work in the public-business domain of the music industry and the private-domestic domains of marriage. It tackles issues of consumption and sexploitation of girls and women of color found throughout mass and digital media.

The notion of collaboration is a big deal in my view. The reciprocal exchange of value with others who share your values is constantly belittled in an age where the old values of America's rugged individualism, and the new disconnected yet networked individualism of our personal devices is, I would assert, leading to a severe loss of social power and community. Zoologist and science writer Matt Ridley asserts that our need for reciprocal exchange of ideas and talents is a biological imperative. In a popular TED talk he says, "self-sufficiency is the new poverty … exchange is to cultural evolution as sex is to biological evolution."[41]

While Black women in the music and entertainment industry have played pivotal roles in establishing the record and music industry, their feminist legacies have not always remembered. This erasure is patriarchy's falsehoods. As an ethnomusicologist who studies music between the sexes as well as online music content and the consequences of gender, race, and technology, the pioneering production of Parkwood Entertainment's *Lemonade* as transmedia storytelling gave me an opportunity to explore and combine twelve years of operatic study and art song training, a doctorate in historical and cultural musicology including the study of feminist musicology in Western art music, and my current research on interactivity and YouTube music videos.

While writing about *Lemonade* allowed me to touch and use every dimension of my career identity, I cannot lie. I have never called myself a Beyoncé fan. I'm not a member of the BeyHive. I've never purchased any of her music; in the past I have declined invitations to write about Queen Bey. But the tour de force that is Beyoncé's sixty-minute visual album, I drank her *Lemonade* in a post for the TED Fellows blog,[42] which follows with subtle changes here and there.

The struggle to free women in performance cultures is real. For centuries, female characters in opera and ballet were murdered or driven to suicide by men, forced to give up their identity or status with no hope for happiness, or dragged into marriages they never desired, or gave their consent. The death songs sung by divas in the sixteenth, seventeenth, and eighteenth centuries created theatrical dramas where female characters—Cio-Cio-San (a Japanese geisha), Carmen (a factory-working gypsy), Isolde (a princess betrothed without choice), Tosca (a celebrated, jealous singer), and Desdemona (miscegnating a Moor)—never survived to threaten the structures of patriarchy.

In more contemporary times, in the cultural figures of Disney princesses, Hannah Montana, and plastic Barbies, women have been expected to sacrifice their voices, lucidity, and bodies in the name of keeping a man. If she didn't lose her voice, she was deemed mad—and Black women are the maddest. Meanwhile, we witness the state's brutality against our sons and daughters as well as the sexual abuse-to-prison pipeline, online sexploitation, slut

FIGURE 17.1 Video still of Beyoncé walking down a street with both hands held high in a yellow dress from "Hold Up." *Lemonade*, Parkwood Entertainment, 2016

shaming, beatings and suicides, all ravaging what we see and think about black girls' and women's bodies.

Not so in Lemonade. *Visually, water breaks in slow motion from within a catacomb of denial as a bright musical ostinato of pizzicato strings in the key of C alternates with a bombastic bassline. Beyoncé emerges sassy and sophisticated in "Hold Up."* Dressed in saffron, she is Bizet's gypsy, Carmen, skipping like a schoolgirl down the street in a seductive tango with the patriarchal gaze that plagues pop music television and Black women walking down their own streets. She smashes men's toys with her monster truck, decapitates hydrants controlled by the State, breaks windows of consumption—clubbing the constant surveillance of the black female body as though they were pumpkins. And in this world, there will be no arrest.

In the transition between "Don't Hurt Yourself" and "Sorry," a familiar 16-bar melody is heard from some tiny, wind-up music box. It repeats again and again as a lone female drummer recovers from fury in an empty parking garage. The music of its metallic combs? A sample of the principal theme from the 2nd act of Swan Lake. In the nineteenth-century libretto, the ingénue was always a beautiful, usually Caucasian, victim in a white tutu. The white swan stands as a metaphor, as the epitome of European ideals. Enslaved in her music box, the symbolic white figurine of the ballerina pops up when the jewelry box is opened to float mechanically above cheap, mass-produced metalwork. She pops up in her mechanical role the same unchanging way, conforming to convention every time.

In Tchaikovsky's ballet, Odette is a beautiful but cursed maiden—like Beyoncé cursed by a cheating husband. Odette must live as a swan beside an enchanted lake created from her mother's tears—in Lemonade, the tears of Beyoncé's black female ancestors—and only at night may she return to human form. In the ballet, the princess can only be freed by a man

FIGURE 17.2 Video still of Beyoncé opening double doors as water rushes from behind her from "Hold Up." *Lemonade*, Parkwood Entertainment, 2016

who loves none but her. Beyoncé's film is her attempt at restoring Black women to their human form.

Beyoncé's representation of freedom—culminating with a song of the same name in this astonishing filmic narrative—had me break down and weep alone in my living room. Throughout the twentieth century, popular artists from Josephine Baker to Ethel Waters to Nona Hendryx to Meshell Ndegeocello have attempted, in their own ways, to flip the asymmetrical positions of masculinity and femininity through song and image.

Beyoncé's album organizes a whole new and public vision of the task, and makes "women" and "winner"—nearly homonyms in the anthem "Freedom"—ever more synonymous. Just listen to it.

Lemonade is about more than infidelity in marriage. I see it as one of the boldest statements a black female artist of the twenty-first century has offered through song, calling for an examination of how pop culture hides the social suffering of black girls and women while simultaneously objectifying us. But we must not make a home out of Beyoncé's voice. Nor can popular music or culture house our politics (cf. Stuart Hall)—though it sure could ignite a revolution with its symbolic images, memes, and gestures—what I call "kinetic orality." Beyoncé's vision of crisis in our patriarchy is framed within a dramatic and elaborate album of musical theatre, but we must remember that this story is hers—not ours—to overanalyze.

Lemonade instead puts everyone on notice and reminds us that pop culture can carry the gutbucket politics of a re-imagined justice—one that deals simultaneously with race, gender, and sexuality while confronting multiple oppressions. Beyoncé's opus speaks to inequalities that we all must demand be overcome. [43]

The intent of ambulatory writing around the stories of black swans and the black swan effect and the power of storytelling in *Lemonade* was to try to tease out the transactional consequences between hegemonic stories of dominance that exclude Black women (like the remains of an archaic figure of speech about black swans) and the bevy of black swan effects that actually lead us to Beyoncé's incredible curatorial vision and power within her own career and as a legacy of those like Elizabeth Taylor Greenfield and Ethel Waters.

The amount of work and action, the amount of labor it took to design the required secrecy and maintain it in an industry plagued by leaks and gossip, and the forces necessary to mount a collaborative feat of mass-public entertainment is as unbelievable, to some, as the structural system that maintains patriarchy itself. There is nothing easy about constructing a sophisticated offer that doesn't fail in the music business. But Beyoncé not only achieves her aims; she was also able to enact its popular and political intentions while hiding all its elaborator coordination, work, and labor. By introducing the frames of *impresaria* and *auteur* while unpacking its transmedia storytelling, I hope readers more fully appreciate both the mastery of Beyoncé Knowles-Carter as a business executive and creative and the powerful role stories have played in making the representation of Black women invisible or retrieving the memories of Black women as cultural producers that are constantly lost.

Notes

1 Beyoncé. 2018. "Beyoncé September Issue in Her Own Words: Her Life, Her Body, Her Heritage." *Vogue*, August 6, 2018. https://www.vogue.com/article/beyonce-september-issue-2018.

2 Hartley, John. 2013. "Use of YouTube: Digital Literacy and the Growth of Knowledge." In *YouTube: Online Video and Participatory Culture*. Eds. Burgess, Jean, and Joshua Green. New York: John Wiley & Sons, 141.

3 Foden, Giles. 2007. "Review: Stuck in Mediocristan: The Black Swan: The Impact of the Highly Improbable by Nassim Nicholas Taleb." *The Guardian*, May 12, 2007.

4 Swift, Jonathan. 1710. November 2 to November 9, *The Examiner*, No. 15, Quote Page 2, Column 1, Printed for John Morphew, near Stationers-Hall, London (Google Books Full View).

5 In his 1999 speech "Improving Education," George W Bush discussed Black and Latino low reading scores at a meeting with the Latin Business Association: "No child in America should be segregated by low expectations, imprisoned by illiteracy, abandoned to frustration and the darkness of self-doubt … Now some say it is unfair to hold disadvantaged children to rigorous standards. I say it is discrimination to require anything less—the soft bigotry of low expectations … Children who never master reading will never master learning. They will face a life of frustration on the fringes of society." This was published in the *New York Times* on September 3, 1999. But Bush makes no mention of the long-term structural consequences of institutional oppression against Black and Latino schools, curricula, and educational funding.

6 Bailey, Moya [moyazb]. 2010. "They Aren't Talking about Me … [Blog Post Introducing Misogynoir Critique of Hip-Hop]." *Crunk Feminist Collective* (blog). March 15, 2010. http://www.crunkfeministcollective.com/2010/03/14/they-arent-talking-about-me/.

7 Inks, Peter P. et al. 2007. *Encyclopedia of Antislavery and Abolition*. Westport, CT: Greenwood Press, 643.

8 Suisman, David. 2004. "Co-Workers in the Kingdom of Culture: Black Swan Records and the Political Economy of African American Music." *Journal of American History* 90 (4): 1295–1324. https://doi.org/10.2307/3660349.

9 Oliver, Paul. 2001. "Race Record." *Grove Music Online*. http://www.oxfordmusiconline.com/view/10.1093/gmo/9781561592630.001.0001/omo-9781561592630-e-0000022778.

10 Wald, Elijah. 2010. *The Blues: A Very Short Introduction*. Oxford, New York: Oxford University Press, 22.

11 De Loo, Ivo, and David Davis. 2003. "Black Swan Records 1921–1924: From a Swanky Swan to a Dead Duck." SSRN Scholarly Paper ID 476943. Rochester, NY: Social Science Research Network. https://papers.ssrn.com/abstract=476943.

12 Fraser, C. Gerald. 1977. "Ethel Waters Is Dead at 80." *New York Times*, September 2, 1977. https://www.nytimes.com/1977/09/02/archives/ethel-waters-is-dead-at-80-ethel-waters-singer-and-actress-on-stage.html.

13 Pleasants, Henry. 2001. "Waters [Née Howard], Ethel." *Grove Music Online*. https://doi.org/10.1093/gmo/9781561592630.article.29946.

14 Bourne, Stephen. n.d. "Waters, Ethel." In *Museum of Broadcast Communications: Encyclopedia of Television*. Accessed November 17, 2018. http://www.museum.tv/eotv/watersethel.htm; Robertson, Patrick. 2011. *Robertson's Book of Firsts: Who Did What for the First Time*. Bloomsbury Publishing USA.

15 *The Hazel Scott Show*. n.d. Accessed November 16, 2018. http://www.imdb.com/title/tt0324844/.

16 Watson, Mary Ann. n.d. "Nat 'King' Cole Show, The." In *Museum of Broadcast Communications: Encyclopedia of Television*. Accessed November 16, 2018. http://www.museum.tv/eotv/natkingcole.htm.

17 Wallace, Carvell. 2017. "Daughters of the Dust: Julie Dash's Lush Drama Remains a Vital Portrait of Black Life." *The Guardian*, April 12, 2017. https://www.theguardian. com/film/2017/apr/12/daughters-of-the-dust-julie-dash-beyonce.

18 Norman, Martha Prescod. 1997. "Shining in the Dark: Black Women and the Struggle for the Vote, 1955–1965." In *African American Women and the Vote, 1837–1965*, edited by Ann D. Gordon. Amherst: University of Massachusetts Press. http://www.umass. edu/umpress/title/african-american-women-and-vote-1837%E2%80%931965.

19 Noble, Safiya Umoja. 2013. "Google Search: Hyper-Visibility as a Means of Rendering Black Women and Girls." *Invisible—InVisible Culture: Journal of Visual Culture*, no. 19 (October). http://ivc.lib.rochester.edu/google-search-hyper-visibility-as-a-mea ns-of-rendering-black-women-and-girls-invisible/.

20 "Lemonade." n.d. Peabody Awards. Accessed April 3, 2018. http://www.peabodyawa rds.com/award-profile/lemonade.

21 Jenkins, Henry. 2010. "Transmedia Storytelling and Entertainment: An Annotated Syllabus." Continuum: Journal of Media & Cultural Studies 24 (6): 943–58. https://doi. org/10.1080/10304312.2010.510599.

22 Pratten, Robert. 2015. *Getting Started with Transmedia Storytelling: A Practical Guide for Beginners*, 2nd ed. https://talkingobjects.files.wordpress.com/2011/08/book-2-robert-p ratten.pdf.

23 Chee, Alexander. 2016. "Literary Mixtape: Alexander Chee Finds a Heroine—with Beyoncé's Help." *The Guardian*, February 3, 2016. http://www.theguardian.com/ books/literary-mixtapes-by-electric-literature/2016/feb/03/literary-mixtape-alexa nder-chee-queen-of-the-night-beyonce.

24 Ibid.

25 Ibid.

26 Fortini, Amanda. 2016. "Why Can't You Be Sweet?" *Los Angeles Review of Books*. April 29, 2016. https://lareviewofbooks.org/article/why-cant-you-be-sweet/.

27 Lamb, Andrew. 2001. "Offenbach, Jacques." *Grove Music Online*. January 20, 2001. http s://doi.org/10.1093/gmo/9781561592630.article.20271.

28 Brooks, William, and Deniz Ertan. 2012. "Barnum, P(hineas) T(aylor)." *Grove Music Online*. October 4, 2012. http://www.oxfordmusiconline.com/view/10.1093/gmo/ 9781561592630.001.0001/omo-9781561592630-e-1002227705.

29 Tregde, David. 2013. "A Case Study on Film Authorship: Exploring the Theoretical and Practical Sides in Film Production." *Elon Journal of Undergraduate Research in Communications* 4 (2). http://www.inquiriesjournal.com/articles/1700/a-case-study-on-film -authorship-exploring-the-theoretical-and-practical-sides-in-film-production.

30 Ibid. (internal citations omitted).

31 Ibid.

32 Concepcion, Mariel. 2009. "Beyonce Is Billboard's Woman of the Year." *Billboard*. August 25, 2009. https://www.billboard.com/articles/news/267596/beyonce-is-billboa rds-woman-of-the-year.

33 "Drake Breaks Hot 100 Records: Most Hits Among Solo Artists & Most Simultaneously Charted Songs." *Billboard*. Accessed April 2, 2018. https://www.billboard.com/articles/ columns/chart-beat/7736706/drake-breaks-hot-100-records-most-hits-solo-artists-m ore-life-songs.

34 Greenburg, Zack O'Malley. 2017. "America's Wealthiest Female Musicians 2017." *Forbes*. May 17, 2017. https://www.forbes.com/sites/zackomalleygreenburg/2017/05/ 17/americas-wealthiest-female-musicians-2017/.

35 Magrath, Andrea. 2011. "Did Beyoncé Steal the Idea for Her Billboard Awards Performance?" *Mail Online*. May 24, 2011. http://www.dailymail.co.uk/tvshowbiz/a rticle-1390490/Did-Beyonce-steal-idea-Billboard-Awards-performance.html.

36 Murphy, James S. 2016. "Here's Why Criticizing Beyoncé for Working with Songwriters Is Ignorant." *Vanity Fair*. April 25, 2016. https://www.vanityfair.com/holly wood/2016/04/beyonce-songwriters.

37 "Breaking Down Beyoncé's Lemonade Samples." n.d. Pitchfork. Accessed March 6, 2018.
    https://pitchfork.com/thepitch/1116-breaking-down-beyonces-lemonade-samples/.

38 Platon, Adelle. 2016. "Beyoncé Protege Ingrid on Being Mentored by the Superstar:
    'She Challenged Me.'" *Billboard*. May 26, 2016. https://www.billboard.com/articles/
    news/magazine-feature/7378253/beyonce-protege-ingrid-on-being-mentor
    ed-by-the-superstar.

39 Cooper, Duncan, and Miles Tanzer. 2016. "Here Are the Full Album Credits for
    Beyoncé's LEMONADE." *FADER*. April 23, 2016. http://www.thefader.com/2016/
    04/23/full-album-credits-beyonce-lemonade.

40 Magavin, Liam. 2016. "Beyoncé and the Sexual Objectification of Lemonade." *Public
    Seminar* (blog). May 25, 2016. http://www.publicseminar.org/2016/05/beyonce-a
    nd-the-sexual-objectification-of-lemonade/.

41 Cited in Shermer, Michael. 2010. "When Ideas Have Sex." *Scientific American*. June 1,
    2010. https://doi.org/10.1038/scientificamerican0610-32.

42 Gaunt, Kyra. 2016. "Beyoncé's Lemonade Is Smashing." *TED Fellows* (blog). May 12, 2016.
    https://fellowsblog.ted.com/beyonc%C3%A9s-lemonade-is-smashing-1cc70bda2197.

43 This blog post was included in *#Lemonade: A Black Feminist Resource List* curated by
    Janell Hobson and Jessica Martin Johnson published by the African American Intellectual
    History Society (2016), for which I offer my gratitude. I also want to acknowledge the
    editorial assistance of TED Fellows staff members Karen Eng and Patrick D'Arcy who
    helped me revise my original post.

18

SHE GAVE YOU *LEMONADE*, STOP TRYING TO SAY IT'S TANG

Calling out how race-gender bias obscures Black women's achievements in pop music

Birgitta J. Johnson

It is quite fortuitous that *Lemonade* premiered in the same news cycle as the sudden passing one of the late twentieth century's biggest musical icons. Prince died in his home on April 21, 2016, alone in a private elevator—exacerbating the loss to the music world on a poetic level.[1] At this moment, in the wake of the world grappling with the loss of Prince and his enigmatic musical genius and influence across popular music genres, a younger icon in the making—one who was three years old when "Let's Go Crazy" made its debut—released what may now be considered the "masterwork" of her career. However, unlike the rave reviews and lightning bolt acclaim that occurred when Prince and the Revolution burst onto the mainstream pop scene to join the highest ranks of 80s' music giants like Michael Jackson and later Madonna, Beyoncé's *Lemonade* and the mixed and gendered receptions of it exposed a generational bitter pill that Black women in popular music in America have been forced to swallow for most of the twentieth century.

Though Beyoncé had "broken the internet" a second time in her career with another surprise release and executed self-one-upmanship by supercharging the cinematic and thematic scope of her second visual album, at this moment, probably more than ever, we got to see the very gendered ways in which artistic genius is measured and bestowed (or withheld) when the star in question is a Black woman. We got to see how gender as well as racial bias still colors how audiences view artistic achievements and cultural production in today's society. We saw through some music critics' skepticism, anti-fans' enthusiastically feigned disinterest in the visual album, and through the predictable misogynistic rants on social media the ways in which society still traffics in language that easily assigns greatness to male and white female artists but, conversely, finds very convenient ways to discount, question, flatten, disperse credit, and challenge the authenticity and agency of Black female artists. Furthermore, and not since feminist icon bell hooks declared Beyoncé to be terrorist in a discussion at The New School in May of 2014, we even saw exposed schisms among feminist thought leaders on just how to engage and read Beyoncé's latest multi-media endeavor.[2]

As *Lemonade* premiered on HBO and Tidal on April 23rd, and a weekend of mourning Prince was greatly augmented by audiences trying to get a handle on the black female-centered world that Beyoncé had created in *Lemonade*, many of us braced for the predictable biased challenges to her latest work. Just as the blues mothers of the 1920s, the mothers of rock and roll of the 1940s, and the soul sisters of the 1960s had indelibly changed American music and the music industry—only to have their contributions overlooked and understudied, and their legacies lauded far too late—some of us observed how the magnitude of *Lemonade* as an artistic tribute to the lives of Black women and girls was being thwarted in the first days of its release and Beyoncé given the "presumed incompetent" treatment.[3] While Beyoncé, true to form of most of her professional career, demonstrated that she has just as much (if not more) intense drive, discipline, commitment, and care regarding her craft as her white female and male peers, some viewers had trouble conceiving *Lemonade* as anything more than Beyoncé airing the dirty laundry of her marriage like any other female pop star. Beyoncé was serving freshly squeezed, premium, organic lemonade on behalf of Black womanhood worldwide, but many were intellectually engaging her 2016 visual album like a plastic cup of artificially flavored Tang.

Even though the impact and deeper influence of *Lemonade* would eventually prevail in the weeks and months after its premiere and its critical acclaim across a variety of mediums would become poignantly obvious, the initial responses by music critics and average listeners alike sounded a familiar set of biased tunes. Similar to Beyoncé's last surprise album, *Beyoncé* from 2013, one could observe a type of communal "crooked room"[4] many audiences were prescribing not only for Beyoncé but also for so many other Black women artists that came before her. Some of the conversations, reviews, and critiques had a penchant for subtly re-inscribing race-gender bias into how Beyoncé, specifically, was being read and how Black women artists in general are often read. In the same ways in which some hip-hop gate keepers questioned Lauryn Hill's fitness as a hip-hop artist after the release of her groundbreaking album *The Miseducation of Lauryn Hill* in 1998 because the album canvased hip-hop *and* soul and often opted for live instrumentation over the heavy use of samples, some audiences couldn't reconcile a Beyoncé who on *Lemonade* traversed genres outside of the expected pop or hip-hop tinged R&B of most of her previous works—daring to reclaim black genres such as rock ("Don't Hurt Yourself" and "Freedom") and country music ("Daddy Lessons") as the visual album cyphered through its revolutionary Black female community-centered ethos.

While Beyoncé had proven herself to be a bona fide superstar and hit maker for over a decade as a member of Destiny's Child during the late 1990s and a solo artist in the 2000s, and amassed enough wealth and cultural currency to make more radical moves in music content and her visual presence by the 2010s, the push back against her most political and intentionally Black female-oriented album project to date is particularly reminiscent of another now legendary album by a Black female pop icon. The ways in which some questioned whether Beyoncé was alienating her white audiences or becoming too political—especially after her tribute to the Black Panther Party at Super Bowl 50 in 2016—mirror the initial push back received by none other than the most controversial Super Bowl guest artist of all time, Janet Jackson. Even though Ms. Jackson hailed from American music royalty, broke album sales, chart, and award records with her 1986 breakout album *Control*, and helped to propel MTV into the 1990s with innovative dance music videos, she received push back from her record label before the release of her follow-up album, *Janet Jackson's Rhythm Nation 1814* in 1989. After its release, some critics took no time doubting Jackson's decision to produce a more socially conscious and politically oriented album in lieu of a *Control* part two, filled with dance club hits and love ballads. *New York Times* writer Jon Pareles noted, "Over the last three years, Ms. Jackson may have begun worrying about social problems, and perhaps she decided to use her popularity as a pulpit. Her motives may be sincere; the results are unconvincing."[5] While Pareles and others praised the musicality of the album and agreed that it would be a successful project for Jackson, their doubt about her concern for social issues and disregard of her real-world engagement in political issues such as racism, prejudice, and injustice demonstrated the same kind of doubts and naysaying that Beyoncé would face in the first weeks of *Lemonade*'s release. Even though Janet Jackson as a Black platinum-selling pop star was joining other Black artists of the time who were addressing these issues in their music— NWA's "Fuck tha Police" was released a year earlier to critical acclaim and con- troversy—some critics questioned her authenticity or painted the album as "a cause without a rebellion" (Pareles 1989). However, these initial doubts and devaluing of the cultural impact of *Rhythm Nation* faded into the background in similar ways that similar negations of *Lemonade* would by the end of 2016.[6]

In the weeks and months after *Lemonade*'s debut, it had become a global phe-nomenon. In addition to fan-inspired cover songs, parodies, memes, and humorous vamping of the album and its imagery by professional comedians and average lis-teners alike, at least three reading lists and *Lemonade* resource syllabi were compiled and distributed on the Internet; public libraries and church groups hosted *Lemonade* reading groups; community groups hosted screenings; and several fall semester college courses were developed to capture and examine the themes of woman-hood, empowerment, healing, and survival from the album.[7] Over 2 million people saw the Formation World Tour in stadiums in North America and Europe, and helped solidify Beyoncé's global icon status. Grossing $256 million in sales, the Formation World Tour is among the top twenty highest-grossing concert tours of all time with only forty-nine concert dates. By the end of 2016, *Lemonade* was at the top of most critics' "best of the year list," hands down and without equivoca-tion—often being referenced as Beyoncé's most critically acclaimed album of her career. At the 59th Annual Grammy Awards in February of 2017, *Lemonade* led award nominations with nine bids and ahead of British pop singer Adele and another juggernaut album project, *25*. By April of 2018, over a year after

Lemonade's debut, "Freedom" was among several songs from *Lemonade* and other Beyoncé albums used to set the first "Beyoncé Mass" at Grace Cathedral in San Francisco, California. The mass was also inspired by a seminary class developed by Assistant Professor and Reverend Yolanda Norton titled, "Beyoncé and the Hebrew Bible" and offered at San Francisco Theological Seminary. The Beyoncé Mass drew nearly a thousand people and was the subject of an episode of *VICE Selects*, an online video platform for the Canadian-based media company VICE. The episode, "Finding God at a Beyoncé Mass," has been viewed nearly 20 million times on the *VICE Selects* website alone.[8]

Looking back at what *Lemonade* would become and the expected elevation of Beyoncé to global icon status as an artist, influential cultural figure, Black business woman, and philanthropist, one may ask: How could the visual album and artistic talents of Beyoncé be snubbed or disparaged? How were some initial critiques and responses to *Lemonade* engaging in more subtle forms of biased readings, or even what feminist philosopher Robin James and others call "epistemic violence"?[9] How were some viewers reading *Lemonade* through perspectives and opinions that downgraded or underscored its cultural value—even in some instances of reluctant praise for the visual album and Beyoncé as an artist? Seeing a familiar pattern around tinted readings of Beyoncé and other Black female popular music figures from previous eras, I opted to form a checklist that addresses the tradition of double standards and biased reads by music journalists, some scholars, and even casual listeners who today often share their thoughts on various social media platforms and blog spaces. These distorted ways of engaging Black female artists even at the height of their creative, social, and economic powers do work to downgrade their artistic contributions, flatten the scope of their long-term influence, and place them in spaces where the goal posts of legacy and long-term success are constantly being moved back, out of reach. It also socially models what queer black feminist Moya Bailey describes as *misogynoir* [10] in that, regardless of which economic or social class Beyoncé occupies, her artistic *oeuvre* will still be viewed through an anti-black female lens, whether it be overtly through outright denouncements or subtly through backhanded compliments. This, in turn, reinforces the same anti-black female marginalization of other assertive, successful, and unapologetically self-possessed Black women and girls in the broader society and within Black communities worldwide. In compiling this brief (and not all-encompassing) checklist, the goal of the remainder of this piece is to call out and acknowledge at least three ways that biases rooted in race, gender, and even class reflect slanted and even discordant readings of Black women's artistic and professional achievements in popular culture in ways not always applied to male and white female artists.

I'm not a fan but …

When one considers the top music artists and genres of the first decades of the twenty-first century, it may be safe to say the disclaimer of "I'm not a fan but …" is most heard when people are discussing hip-hop music and Beyoncé. The musical output of both frequently cast them into the public conversations about music and commercial music making in America. And while hip-hop music in its vast coverage of artists, topics, regions, and controversial expressive tradition often seems to require such disclaimer, at the end of the day it is unnecessary—for hip-hop just as it is for Beyoncé. In order to positively regard or favorably analyze an artist or their work, fandom is just not a requirement. The inherent value and merit of an artwork or artist is not wholly contingent upon that work or person's current popularity or favorable regard by those analyzing the work. A person can legitimately hate classical music and at the same time regard Beethoven's Ninth Symphony as a great artistic achievement just based on the aesthetics of the genre alone and what that work did to propel the symphonic form in classical music.

When one says, "I'm not a fan but ..." it communicates the belief that genius or worth is predicated on fandom, adoration, or popularity. On the contrary, some great works aren't recognized as such until after an artist is dead. Much of the classical music we think is the gold standard today was summarily a flop or received mixed reviews when it was first performed hundreds of years ago. For example, musicians and audiences bristled at the one hour and five-minute running time of the Beethoven's Ninth at its London premier in 1825.[11] The need to align oneself with or disassociate oneself from fandom in order to grant approval or recognition of an artist's genius is something that we rarely do for male musical achievement and genius. There was no, "I'm not an Earth, Wind and Fire fan but ..." statement made when Maurice White passed in 2016—neither was it done for David Bowie who also died that year. However, when the legendary Donna Summer passed in 2012, "I'm not a fan of disco but ..." was a common backhanded compliment. Considering her longevity beyond the disco decade, and in spite of the racist and homophobic-tinged "disco sucks" movement, the time of Summer's passing should have been met with unequivocal praise and respect of her career considering her iconic status in disco and beyond it as a musical model for feminism during the 1970s and 1980s. When *Lemonade* topped the artistic and social relevance of her last albums, one way in which listeners navigated their personal disinterest or disdain for Beyoncé in the face of a very compelling multi-media spectacle was to take cover behind their orientation around fandom instead of just offering favorable or positive assessments of what would become obvious to millions by the end of the year. What would public critical discourse look like if successful Black women in all spheres of life could have their achievements regarded on their own merits and the aesthetic values of their craft without concern about how popular or likeable we deem them to be through a gender-biased gaze?

When the men are disciplined geniuses but the women are controlled by machines ...

In the realm of pop stardom, the push to negate and diminish Black female artistic achievements and genius is very common, but also tied to how we read them in the context of retractable fences that are often placed around how we define "what" actually "makes" a pop star. The works of Black female artists are often comfortably negated, valued less, or not given full acknowledgment because often all or most of the credit is assigned to some mythical "machine" of the music industry and the entertainment industry's allegedly magical "packaging" of female artists. The discipline, planning, strategy, and preparation female artists put into their total creative offerings are regularly graded and judged as sanitized, calculating, controlled, and mediated by outside forces. This is even in spite of it being known that some of the most controlling icons in popular music have been Michael Jackson, Prince, James Brown, and a host of male artists upon which we've bestowed the labels genius and innovator. The teams, entourages, assistants, and crews that upheld their successes were rarely referred to as "machines," if they were referenced at all when speaking of the magnitudes of their greatness across the span of their careers. James Brown fined musicians for playing wrong notes or missing cues. Jackson often demanded that musicians in his band performed songs exactly like the recordings, almost note for note, for live performances in giant arenas. Prince was known for holding ten or more hour rehearsals of concert song sets, and at a moment's notice would change the entire set the next day. How are those things not considered packaging or controlled?

Over the decades, critics have accused Madonna, Janet Jackson, Beyoncé, Taylor Swift, and other female artists as being packaged; but did not Marvin Gaye and Michael Jackson come out of the most successful "machines" in music industry history, Motown Records? Berry Gordy literally built Motown's music production ethos from the assembly line concept that galvanized the Detroit car manufacturing industry. Today, however, the precision or strive for high production value performances and presentations often can mean Black pop artists like Beyoncé, Rihanna, and Nicki Minaj are accused of being "robots" or under the control of a record company's desires not their own agency. In the panel discussion just before bell hooks labeled Beyoncé a terrorist back in 2014, months after Beyoncé's self-orchestrated first surprise visual album was released, the feminist scholarship icon noticeably stripped any semblance of agency and control Beyoncé had over her own career and placed the choices for her *Time* magazine cover photo in the hands of others. She opines, "Let's take the image of this super rich, very powerful Black female and let's use it in the service of imperialist, white supremacist capitalist patriarchy because she probably had very little control over that cover—that image."[12] Even when other feminist panelists like Janet Mock pushed back on the assertion that Beyoncé had little or no control over the cover image, hooks turned the conversation towards collusion rather than to concede that the power, wealth, access, and influence Beyoncé had built up to that point in her career could actually be used to weigh in on a magazine cover image.

While many female artists in the industry are indeed beholden to the ideas and plans of mostly white male record executives, producers, and managers, artists that have reached the rarefied air of top-tier pop stardom and wealth such, as Beyoncé, Madonna, the late Whitney Houston, Barbara Streisand, and even Britney Spears, are often more able to steer aspects of their own career in more intentional ways that benefit their own visions for themselves in the industry—whether they actually opt to do so or not. In the case of Beyoncé, the *Lemonade* era of her career confirmed that she had once again reached into the highest echelons of access and agency, and at levels rarely experienced by most Black female pop stars. Prior to the release of *Lemonade*, Beyoncé executed several business moves that signaled that she was no longer a mere product of the music business; nor was she haplessly at the whim of some nebulous industry machine. About three months before *Lemonade* debuted, and just before her controversial and show-stealing appearance at Super Bowl 50 as a special guest of the British band Coldplay, *Page Six* reported that not only had Beyoncé parted with her longtime business manager, Lee Anne Callahan-Longo, but she had also restructured several departments and hired a new promotional and management team for herself and her growing Parkwood Entertainment empire.[13] In essence, Beyoncé cleaned house in her own house on the eve of releasing her most ambitious and significant art project of her solo career. If there is a machine running Beyoncé's career, she is dually the engine and the engineer running the show at this point of her journey.

The collaboration tax

One of the biggest ways that audiences negate or diminish the artistic value or creative contributions of women in music is to assert that their talent or worth as an artist is predicated on "needing help" or not being able to independently create or write their own music. Over the course of Beyoncé's last two album projects, a common response of some individuals online is to ridicule the number of songwriters credited on her album projects and openly suggest that Beyoncé in fact is not talented or a creative genius as many may claim. Even though collaboration is a key practice in the making of most Black musical genres historically speaking, Black women in particular often face a collaboration tax that often ends up not only dispersing how we read their agency in their art works but also distorts how some frame their creative impact on popular culture. Much like female hip-hop MCs, Beyoncé is often taxed for employing collaboration to make music.

Every top female hip-hop artist from every hip-hop era—from MC Lyte and Queen Latifah to Nicki Minaj and Cardi B—has been accused of having ghost writers and not "really" being the author of their own lyrics if they engaged in any form of lyrical collaboration with a male MC or producer. The legacy of *The Miseducation of Lauryn Hill* album is slightly marred by the lawsuit that came along with its meteoric and historic success. On the heels of being acknowledged for penning the first hip-hop album to win the "Album of the Year" Grammy Award, Lauryn Hill was being sued by musicians who worked on the album who claimed that they did not receive writing credit for music on the project. While Hill had already proven her worth as an MC and singer as a member of the Fugees, and had demonstrated command of a stage and *Billboard* charts as a solo artist, the two-year lawsuit around who actually "wrote" the critically acclaimed album became a subtle way to diminish or at least question the true creative talents of Ms. Hill, away from the male collaborators of her past.

In Beyoncé's case, collaboration or the mere practice of fully giving credit to every contributing creator who is involved in her music making process is often portrayed as Beyoncé "needing help" to make chart-topping music or her needing "a team" of writers to make music that is popular to the masses due to some lack of talent or ability on her part. Even though musical collaboration is and has been the main mode through which most popular music is written and produced in the industry, ridiculing the number of song writers "listed"[14] on Beyoncé's albums has become a trend online and through online comments and memes since her first visual album, *Beyoncé*, went head to head with Beck's *Morning Phase* album at the 2015 Grammy Awards in the category of Album of the Year. While *Beyoncé* was easily the most recognizable album and had received the most mainstream praise and cultural acclaim that year, the award went to *Morning Phase*. In the immediate shock and aftermath of such a curious and controversial snub, male commenters in particular took time to point out that Beck wrote and performed all the music on his album, while ridiculing the number of song writers listed on *Beyoncé*. Either by posting screen captures of the song-writing credits of *Beyoncé* and *Morning Phase* side by side in memes or listing the number, the trend of questioning Beyoncé's song-writing talents or ability to create her own music continued years later and immediately after *Lemonade* was released. Even though in previous years, song writers and producers would attest that songs sent to Beyoncé or songs reworked by her were significantly transformed or rearranged by the singer herself, the practice of lambasting song credit lists had become a regular reaction in ways that until recently wasn't discussed when it came to other top popular music acts. However, in 2016 when online trolls thought to ridicule the seventy-two writers credited on *Lemonade*, a few writers explored not only their angst against Beyoncé but also highlighted the myths around the sole creative genius trope that is often an outlier in popular music in general, but especially in today's pop music scene. In "Beyoncé's 'Lemonade': How the Writing Credits Reveal Her Genius," Kelsey McKinney not only provides perspective about the range of song-writing credits on *Lemonade*—for example, "Hold Up" lists fifteen writers and "Formation" lists two writers—she also provided a historical canvas of art and creative culture that called into question the myth of sole authorship as being "the" hallmark of "true genius." McKinney pokes at the myth-making around the sole creative genius trope, taking on narratives about Steve Jobs and the creation of his Apple empire, or even highlighting the thirteen assistants who helped Michelangelo paint the ceiling of the Sistine Chapel hundreds of years ago. By addressing how reductive "single-author" or "lone-creator" myths are, McKinney's approach can also be used to highlight how these myths elevate male creative geniuses but inversely are used to discount female creative genius that involves collaboration. She goes on to normalize or recognize how collaboration occurs in all forms of creative endeavors, be it music, film production, or even aviation. She notes, "throughout the history of art, innovation has rarely come about in a vacuum … Collaboration breeds creativity, and no one can claim that *Lemonade* isn't a creative album."[15] Lastly, McKinney makes the full circle step to connect Beyoncé's use of collaboration on

Lemonade to the overall intent and inspiration of the project, an ode to Black women. She notes:

> *Lemonade* isn't just an album for Beyoncé. *Lemonade* is an album that is undeniably written for, marketed to, and—most importantly—inspired by black American women. It is saturated with their stories, their lore, and their faces.

The use of a variety of song writers in the making of *Lemonade* the musical album as a sonic artwork that grounds the cinematic work of *Lemonade* the visual album—which also features Black women in various scenes of collaborative work, healing, and celebration—exalts a type of black feminist praxis that overrides reductive and sexist accusations around the creative genius or talents of the chief song writer/producer of *Lemonade*. Thus, by the release of *Lemonade* some pop culture writers started to push back against social media memes and debates about the number of song writers associated with Beyoncé's album projects—some calling out the sexism implied in the arguments, but most citing that collaboration and using many writers to make songs and albums is actually the norm in popular music today. In McKinney's article as well as Kevin Fallon's "Does Beyoncé Write Her Own Music? And Does it Really Matter?" for the *Daily Beast*, both authors compare the seventy-two writers listed in *Lemonade*'s credits alongside the more than thirty writers for Rihanna's *ANTI* and the Weeknd's *Beauty in the Madness,* the over forty writers listed on Drake's *Views*, and the over one hundred writers listed on Kanye West's *The Life of Pablo*. [16] Even marketed and lauded pop music singer-song writers Taylor Swift and Adele employ a team of writers on the album projects that have dominated the music industry alongside the R&B, pop, and hip-hop projects listed above. In the midst of the real-time shock around Adele's *25* winning three of the big four Grammy categories (Album of the Year, Song of the Year, and Record of the Year) over *Lemonade* and its chart-topping music, many people may remember Adele paying tribute to Beyoncé and the global impact of *Lemonade* during her acceptance speech; but most people and a few commentators noted the eleven, mostly male and white song writers from *25* standing behind Adele onstage as she accepted her awards. And she certainly was not castigated for working with them on an album that sold nearly ten times more records than *Lemonade*.

The ways in which the collaboration tax is levied against Beyoncé also reveals the race–gender double standard once one considers how other Black male artists around the time of *Lemonade*'s release and over the arch of Black popular music over the last thirty years have not been chided for working with multiple song writers and contributing voices on their projects. A year earlier in 2015, hip-hop artist Kendrick Lamar released *To Pimp a Butterfly*, a genre-crossing album that employed few samples and a lot of live instrumentation to produce a hip-hop album that dug from the wells of funk, acid jazz, neo-soul, and contemporary West Coast jazz in addition to the banging beats and percussive tracks common in hip-hop production. The album project was expansive and an immediate critically acclaimed success even as listeners waded through the often dense sound textures to decipher the album's lyrics. The sonic richness of the album even led some to research who produced and participated in the album; but not once did they suggest that Kendrick Lamar "needed help" or had to "hire a team" of writers to pull off his break-out masterpiece. When Lucas Garrison of *DJBOOTH* wrote, "All 71 People on Kendrick Lamar's 'To Pimp a Butterfly' Album," at no point did he suggest that Lamar was less of an artist or a less than capable talent because seventy-one people had a hand in writing and/or performing on his album. On the contrary, the expansive scope of *To Pimp a Butterfly* actually inspired Garrison's nostalgia around the liner notes era of commercial music when one could see all of an album's players and producers listed along with the physical copy of the record after you bought it. Before he took time in the article to note the contributions of all seventy-one people listed on the album, he noted:

> Call me old-fashioned, but liner notes fascinate me. However, in this day and age, where labels send whole albums through a series of interconnected computers that spans the entire world, uploading them (by accident?) to a virtual store where people can then buy it while sitting on the toilet, they have become a lost art. If ever there was an album that needed liner notes, this is it.[17]

Garrison also referenced an earlier article where he explored the ninety-three people named on J. Cole's *Note to Self* album project; but it is also in the vein of interest in the participants and collaborators on that album not to deride or undermine J. Cole's artistic talents. It is particularly telling that at the same time Black male artists are employing the same number of song writers and collaborators (or more) for their successful and critically acclaimed album projects and no one is questioning their use of collaboration or creating memes about their lack of talent or genius. However, when *Lemonade* arrives months later, Beyoncé's fitness as a creative talent was called into question due to her use of collaboration and her abiding by the standard legal practice of crediting each contributor on every musical aspect of her visual album.[18]

Notes

1 In the pre-chorus of Prince's second number one song, "Let's Go Crazy," the lyrics ask, "Are we gonna let the elevator bring us down? Oh, no let's go." In addition to other religious and existential references in the song, much of the song's call for rebellion and uplift was cast against a symbolic representation of "the elevator" as life or the world's challenges that people should fight to overcome by any means necessary. Fans noted the irony of Prince dying alone in an elevator days after the details of his last hours were revealed.

2 Feminist scholar, Roxane Gay assessed and summarized hooks' problematic reading of Beyoncé as an artist in a piece for *The Guardian* in May of 2014. It was one of many response writings to bell hooks' conversation at The New School as a co-panelist along with Janet Mock, Shola Lynch, and Marci Blackman on May 6th. On May 5th, Beyoncé made the cover of *Time* magazine's "100 Most Influential People" double issue. See "Beyoncé's Control of Her Own Image Belies the bell hooks 'Slave Critique" at https://www.theguardian.com/commentisfree/2014/may/12/Beyoncé-bell-hooks-sla

ve-terrrorist To see bell hooks' conversation from The New School, "Are You Still a Slave?" see https://livestream.com/TheNewSchool/Slave.

3 See *Presumed Incompetent: The Intersections of Race and Class for Women in Academia*, edited by Gabriella Gutiérrez y Muhs, Yolanda Flores Niemann, Carmen G. González, and Angela P. Harris (Utah State University Press, 2012).

4 In her 2011 book *Sister Citizen: Shame, Stereotypes, and Black Women in America* (Yale University Press), political science scholar Melissa V. Harris-Perry notes that often Black women are so defined by racist and sexist stereotypes in wider society that it difficult for them to navigate and orient themselves in political discourse and spaces inside and outside their communities. She suggests that Black women and girls face extreme challenges to "stand up straight" in ways that are empowering and liberating when their surroundings are tilted by external perceptions and stereotypes about them, i.e., a "crooked room."

5 From "Janet Jackson Adopts a New Attitude: Concern," by Jon Pareles in the *New York Times*, September 17, 1989.

6 *Janet Jackson's Rhythm Nation 1814* reached the number one slot on the Billboard 200 and Top R&B/Hip-Hop albums charts.★ It was the best-selling album of 1990 in the US, selling 2 million copies by the end of the year; it is the only album in history to produce seven top-five hits; it is the only album to have number one hits in three separate calendar years; and it set several other sales records in other countries. Janet Jackson also became the first woman nominated for a "Producer of the Year (Non-Classical)" Grammy award for her work on the album. The Rhythm Nation World Tour filled arenas, broke sales records, and is considered the most successful debut concert tour in history due to the estimated over 2 million attendees. The success of *Rhythm Nation* propelled Jackson's star power on par with and some say surpassing her own brother, Michael Jackson. When her contracted ended with A&M Records in the following year in the midst of *Rhythm Nation*'s sustained success, Janet Jackson signed a new album deal with Virgin Records for $40 million, making her the highest-paid musician—male or female—until Michael Jackson signed with Sony several months later for $65 million and Madonna was able to ride the wave for $60 million in April of the same year. ★*These are the current-day Billboard chart names.*

7 *Lemonade*-inspired college courses were offered in the fall of 2016 at the University of Texas, San Antonio (ENGL 3613/AAS 4013/WS 4952 "Black Women, Beyoncé, & Popular Culture" by Dr. Kinitra Brooks), the University of South Carolina (AFAM 202.2 "Lemonade: A Survey of Black Women's Agency and Community Building Through Music and Performance" by Dr. Birgitta Johnson), and Arizona State University ("*Lemonade:* Beyoncé and Black Feminism" by Dr. Rachel Fedock). While these were not the first college courses related to Beyoncé or a black feminist reading of her works, they represent the fast-paced engagement of black feminist scholars in bringing contemporary pop culture into university campuses and curriculum spaces.

8 To view "Finding God at a Beyoncé Mass," see https://www.facebook.com/VICE/videos/867076020147056/.

9 "How Not to Listen to Lemonade: Music Criticism and Epistemic Violence" by Robin James in *Sounding Out!* May 16, 2016 at https://soundstudiesblog.com/2016/05/16/how-not-to-listen-to-lemonade-music-criticism-and-epistemic-violence/.

10 Moya Bailey coined the term "misogynoir" in 2010 while a graduate student at Emory University. Even though Bailey included the concept in her thesis and scholarship years later, its first public appearance occurred on *The Crunk Feminist Collection* blog on March 14, 2010 in a piece titled, "They Aren't Talking about Me … ." See http://www.crunkfeministcollective.com/2010/03/14/they-arent-talking-about-me/.

11 For more nineteenth-century salt thrown at Beethoven's 9th Symphony see *Lexicon of Musical Invective: Critical Assaults on Composers Since Beethoven's Time* by Nicolas Slonimsky (New York: W.W. Norton & Company), 2000.

12 "Are You Still a Slave?" bell hooks at The New School. May 6, 2014. https://livestream.com/TheNewSchool/Slave.

13 Emily Smith and Carlos Greer, "Beyoncé Shakes Up Her Management Team," in *Page Six*. February 3, 2016. https://pagesix.com/2016/02/03/Beyoncé-shakes-up-her-management-team/.

14 Due to several copyright lawsuits of the last fifteen years, it is common for every contributing writer present in a song to be included in the song credits—even if they were not actively a part of the song-writing process. This includes the song writers of sampled material. Thus, songs which include samples or covers, like hip-hop songs or hip-hop influenced R&B/pop, tend to have longer song writer credit lists than other genres due to every song writer on every sample used—no matter how short the sample is—being listed. Thus, "Hold Up" from *Lemonade* has fifteen song writers listed for the one song.

15 McKinney, Kelsey. "Beyoncé's 'Lemonade': How the Writing Credits Reveal Her Genius," *Splinter*, April 25, 2016 at https://splinternews.com/Beyoncé-s-lemonade-how-the-writing-credits-reveal-her-1793856448.

16 Fallon, Kevin. "Does Beyoncé Write Her Own Music? And Does It Really Matter?" *Daily Beast*. April 30, 2016. See at https://www.thedailybeast.com/does-Beyoncé-write-her-own-music-and-does-it-really-matter?ref=scroll.

17 Garrison, Lucas. "All 71 People on Kendrick Lamar's 'To Pimp A Butterfly' Album," *DJBOOTH*. March 18, 2015. At https://djbooth.net/features/2015-03-18-kendrick-lamar-to-pimp-a-butterfly-album-credits

18 In light of Beyoncé and company's thorough attention paid to giving song-writing credit on these last album projects, it is ironic or possibly erroneous understanding of fair use laws that led to one of the most controversial lawsuits related to *Lemonade*. The estate of Anthony Barré (aka Messy Mya) sued Beyoncé and Parkwood Entertainment for infringement for using the black queer YouTube star's voice in "Formation" and not giving any credit or paying any fees or royalties for the use of Barré's voice to his surviving family (Barré was murdered in 2010).

INTERLUDE G: ERASING SHAME

Beyoncé's *Lemonade* and the Black woman's narrative in cinema

Aramide Tinubu

For Black women, filmmaking is a revolutionary act. Since the birth of the medium, Black women have worked tirelessly behind the scenes with little credit or ability to control narratives in cinema. Beyoncé Knowles Carter is a world-renowned creator who has been both bold and forceful as she's matured in her career. It makes sense then that she chose cinema as the vessel in which to bare her soul to the world with her 2016 cinematic marvel, *Lemonade*.

From its origins at the turn of the twentieth century and into the digital age, film has been an elite art form. Though it is expansive in its reach, the hefty cost of equipment coupled with systemic racial barriers barred Black women from telling their stories on film for decades. Instead, the cinematic work of brown-hued sistas like the 1938 film *Children's Games* by Zora Neale Hurston were buried and forgotten. In the event that Black women were seen on screen, they were cast as stereotypes. This trend continued into the 1960s. Even as Black women began to secure broader roles, there were still issues concerning respectability politics and what Black women were "allowed" to do on screen. Black actresses took roles in films like *Imitation of Life* (1959) and *For Love of Ivy* (1968) that depicted long-suffering women who never spoke of their wounds, and who remained at the beck and call of their Black husbands and white men. Luckily, by the 1970s those archetypes were unraveling.

As Blaxploitation rippled through Hollywood, films like 1974's *Claudine* began to trickle through. In contrast to their successors, these films depicted the pain and perseverance of Black women in all of their afro-haired no-nonsense glory. The tide truly began to turn with the dawn of the LA Rebellion, which produced films like Alile Sharon Larkin's *A Different Image* and Kathleen Collins's 1982 drama, *Losing Ground*. For the first time in cinematic history, Black women were able to turn the lens inward, peeling back the curtains that had hidden away their deepest insecurities, pains, and desires. For Larkin, it was examining the commodification of the Black female body in comparison to Eurocentric standards of beauty. For Collins, it was investigating the universal tropes of love, lust, relationships, and sex.

These radical films ushered in a new era of Black female directors, creating a path for Julie Dash, Kasi Lemmons, and more recently Ava DuVernay. Though it stands outside of the confines of a traditional narrative feature, one of the more astonishing films to debut from the lens of a Black woman is Beyoncé Knowles-Carter's 2016 work, *Lemonade*. With unprecedented vulnerability from one of the most prominent and notoriously private entertainers of our time, the songstress dragged her personal stories of Black girlhood, miscarriages, infidelities, and insecurities into the forefront of cinema, turning the lens on herself while unveiling the truths that many Black women face on a daily basis. Lush and poignant with cinematography that drapes the singer in a variety of washes, costumes, and time periods, *Lemonade* is heavily influenced by Dash's astounding 1991 work, *Daughters of the Dust*. The 58-minute work is sliced into several sections labeled "Intuition," Denial," "Anger," "Apathy," "Emptiness," "Loss," "Accountability," "Reformation," "Forgiveness," "Resurrection," "Hope," and "Redemption." Using Beyoncé's stunning vocals and the glittering poetry of British-Somali poet Warsan Shire, *Lemonade* is as much a cinematic journey as it is a spiritual and musical one. The film begins with a shot from the "Anger" vignette. Knowles-Carter's head is bowed and her face remains hidden until the next clip, where she sits cross-legged on a vaudeville-style stage, evocative of the origin of cinema.

Lemonade opens with "Intuition"; Knowles-Carter speaks softly as the melody from "Pray You Can Catch Me" arises eerily in the background. She says, "I tried to make a home out of you, but doors lead to trap doors, a stairway leads to nothing. Unknown women wander the hallways at night. Where do you go when you go quiet?" Barefaced and surrounded by dilapidated bricks and billowy grasses, the "Formation" singer uses cinema to unpack her warring emotions, including all of the personal struggles she and most Black women are told to be embarrassed about. Swaying into different segments of the film and different songs from the *Lemonade* album, Knowles-Carter transports us into various time periods. Initially, the lush trees and plantation cabins of the Deep South surround her, in a setting reminiscent of the antebellum period. Moving into "Denial," the songstress thrusts herself off a building and is next seen drowning underwater, suffocating beneath the weight and the desire for perfection. Yet, her magic does not allow her to stay submerged. As the pummeling beats of "Hold Up" begin to chime out, Knowles-Carter reemerges in a canary-yellow dress and platform heels, paying homage to the assertiveness and boldness of the legendary Pam Grier in the 1970s. A superhero of sorts, she charges down the street swinging a baseball bat as vintage cars zip past her. The Destiny's Child alum seems off-kilter at first, but it soon becomes clear that she's simply reveling in her pain. Speaking directly into the camera, she dares the viewer to look away or to mark her anger as invalid.

Lemonade moves forward full throttle with Knowles-Carter throwing her wedding ring to the ground during "Don't Hurt Yourself" as the camera pans, capturing a mystical séance of Black women in prayer. Later, in the section labeled

"Accountability," she reflects on Black girlhood, and the parallels Black women can often find between their husbands and fathers as she croons out the bluesy "Daddy Lessons." It all leads to *Lemonade*'s final segment, "Redemption," where the vocalist spins out the dizzying bars of "All Night" over a montage of home videos of her daughter, Blue Ivy, and rapper husband Jay-Z, interlaced with footage of lovers walking the streets of present-day New Orleans.

It is no accident that a quarter of the way through the film the voice of the late legendary Malcolm X rings out declaring, "The most disrespected person in America is the Black woman." Blistering words from the civil rights activist's May 22, 1962 speech in Los Angeles make it very clear that Knowles-Carter is chronicling the journey of Black women, not just in cinema but also as citizens in a country that has continually conspired against them.

The images used in *Lemonade* are feminine and deliberate—men are utilized as mere props that appear intermittently and vanish just as quickly. *Lemonade* might be Knowles-Carter's personal story, but a slew of Black women are on hand to help her tell it. Their presence assures Knowles-Carter that her vulnerability will not shatter her crown. From tennis legend Serena Williams, who twerks with the *Dangerously in Love* singer during "Sorry," to the heartbroken mothers of Trayvon Martin, Eric Garner, and Michael Brown, who clutch their dead sons' photos in worship, multiple generations of Black women are represented. Knowles-Carter's grandmother, mother, and daughter also make appearances, each of them with their own stories to tell and burdens to cast aside.

Part video (using everything from Super 8 to digital and B&W), part narrative film and art isolation, Knowles-Carter, along with six directors—including Melina Matsoukas, Kahlil Joseph, Todd Tourso, Mark Romanek, Dikayl Rimmasch, and

FIGURE G.1 Beyoncé Knowles-Carter sits pensively in a tub. Her face is turned downward and she's cast in hues of blue and green

Jonas Åkerlund—takes the viewer through *Lemonade*. No single director acts as an auteur here, except perhaps Knowles-Carter herself. Instead, the cinematographers and filmmakers operate as members of the singer's chorus, wielding their lenses towards her so that she literally vibrates off the screen. There are obvious film influences in *Lemonade*. Along with *Daughters of the Dust*, the fiery explosions in "Hold Up" heavily echoes Angela Bassett's infamous car burning scene in 1995's *Waiting to Exhale*. Whispers of David Lynch's *Mulholland Drive* (2001) paint the background of the film's opening sequences—the bright red of the vaudeville stage curtain acts as a beacon into Knowles-Carter's world. Even the sharp corridors in the segment labeled "Emptiness" are oddly similar to scenes found in Stanley Kubrick's *The Shining* (1980). Still, just like the directors who contributed to *Lemonade*, the genres and various images melt into one cohesive piece—one that allows a Black woman to speak for herself.

Lemonade is stunning, but it is not glamorous. Knowles-Carter and the numerous women around her stand tall as time, and space shifts and bends behind them, whispering of the unbearable oppression of the nineteenth century to the freedom cries of the 1960s, and onto our twenty-first-century streets. In the midst of all, perhaps the most compelling aspect of this cinematic feat is Knowles-Carter's ability to connect with everyday women. Tapping into the pain and history of Black women who have loved and lost, the *Everything Is Love* singer speaks her truth and refuses to apologize for it. When *Lemonade* begins it seems at first that Knowles-Carter is a victim, but it is soon made quite clear that she is a survivor.

In the end, *Lemonade* is not just about the pain of Black womanhood, or the exhaustion that comes with proving oneself in a world that seeks to erase you. It is about the joys and the magnificence of sisterhood. More than that, it is about a Black woman reclaiming her story without the red tape and the marginalization of Hollywood. In the digital age, cinema has become an accessible medium to almost everyone, and Knowles-Carter used that to her every advantage. By revealing the aspects of Black womanhood that she was told to keep hidden away, *Lemonade* shattered the illusion of shame, and Knowles-Carter proved just how beautiful, strange, and terrifying Black women are.

AFTERWORD

I watched *Lemonade* when it first aired on HBO back in April 2016. I started off watching the visual album with my husband, Roy, and finished watching it alone on the edge of my seat; Roy having retreated upstairs to watch television in our bedroom. *Lemonade* presents Beyoncé as conjurer, griot, wailer, and reckoner. Like so many other Black women who watched, *Lemonade* left me in a gamut of my own feelings—clapping at the television in anger, talking back to Beyoncé through a series of sighs and hollers, and the well-worn but forever astute southern collo-quialism, "chiiiiiile!"

And chile, above all else *Lemonade* let me be seen as a contemporary southern Black woman. When I talked to Dream Hampton about the album the next day, I said *Lemonade* was a love letter from a southern Black woman to other southern Black women. She is in conversation with other love letters from southern Black women like Anna Julia Cooper's plea for Black women and girls in *A Voice from the South*, Zora Neale Hurston's *Their Eyes Were Watching God*, and Alice Walker's *The Color Purple*. *Lemonade* is a no bullshit reminder that Beyoncé is a superstar with unapologetic "ruts"—roots for the uninitiated tongue—across the American Deep South. It was her presentation of southernness more so than her Blackness that tripped folks up. Beyoncé built *Lemonade* upon the illegibility of a South that decenters both white folks and Black men. *Lemonade* thrives in the interstices of Beyoncé's southern sensibilities, amplifying the unknown and unacknowledged experiences in the South that her larger fan base is unable to translate. With *Lemonade*, southern Black women are the epicenter of her storytelling, conjuring up the past to talk about the present and the future. Beyoncé literally and figuratively sets the table for Black women and their ancestors to engage each other. Beyoncé, along with other Black women, gather—and dare I say worship—through numerous acts of dance, laughter, and quiet sojourner while barefoot on a front porch. They hold space and love for each other, not shying away from the trauma of southern Black womanhood but welcoming it into conversation with other narratives that contextualize Black women. It is important to note here that Beyoncé's rendering of trauma is not blatantly overwhelming. Rather, trauma in *Lemonade* registers quietly in some places and demanding in others; never the centerpiece of Beyoncé's storytelling, only a part of it. And, perhaps most importantly, trauma is presented as an overlap of the spiritual and sacred, which is undeniably rendered feminine. In addition to re-posturing Black women in the south, Beyoncé reshapes the southern social-cultural landscape by offering up alternative lenses of a southern Black experience that is pushed to the margins in favor of a more easily digestible southern narrative.

From this perspective, *Lemonade* functions as an audio-visual space that enables the audience to become aware of not only Beyoncé's complicated performance narrative, but also the equally complex influences that dictate her performances. Guthrie Ramsey's discussion of music as cultural site of memory in *Race Music* (2003) is particularly useful for understanding *Lemonade* as a working site of southern Black women's cultural memories. Ramsey writes:

> Cultural forms such as tales, stories, and music (especially the *performative* aspects of such) function as reservoirs in which cultural memories reside. These memories allow social identities to be knowable, teachable, and learnable. And most important, the cultural, communal, and family memories associated with forms like music ... often become standards against which many explore and create alternative and highly personal identities for themselves.[1]

Beyoncé pulls from the south's hidden-in-plain-sight truths and uses them to speak to the power of Black women. Using aural and visual storytelling, *Lemonade* does labor that introduces a wider audience to the secrets of the bayou, the plantation, and the wildness and unpredictability of spirituality engrained in the lore of forgotten ancestors and souls demanding to be remembered. *Lemonade* intentionally exists outside of a strictly white, Christian, heteronormative space. Building upon Ramsey's observation of music as a working space where the "invisible function" of ethnic performance is panned out, *Lemonade* challenges the listener to reconsider how Beyoncé's identity politics and gender performances intersect with racial performance. In other words, how we listen and view *Lemonade* speaks to how we listen not only to Beyoncé, but also how society views and listens to Black women in general. Beyoncé's performances of gender and varying registers of southernness speak to the need to incorporate alternative frameworks of analysis and discussion that are able to negotiate the complexities of a post-Civil Rights African American (women's) experience.

It is from this need that *The Lemonade Reader* enters as a daring and vigorous interdisciplinary analysis of the many layers of Beyoncé's masterwork, refusing to shy away from the sharp edges and less-than-savory elements of Beyoncé's explication of southern Black womanhood(s). Resulting from a weekend-long Black Feminism think tank at the University of Michigan, *The Lemonade Reader* showcases some of the sharpest thinkers in cultural studies, ethnomusicology, history, and women's studies. The cutting-edge scholarship presented in this volume intricately engages each other in the same vein that Beyoncé intersects performance, history, and cultural legacies in the visual album. *The Lemonade Reader* is a manual on how to fruitfully engage Beyoncé's work as a critical framework for reckoning with the contemporary Black American South.

Regina N. Bradley

Note

1 Guthrie Ramsey, *Race Music: Black Cultures from Bebop to Hip-Hop* (Berkeley: University of California Press, 2003), 33.

INDEX

Page numbers in *italics* refer to figures.

"Accountability" 77, 119, 248
Adichie, Chimamanda Ngozi 6, 134, 150, 173–4
aesthetics: Black feminist voodoo 3, 24–5; supernatural 175–6; *see also* Beysthetics
African American Language (AAL) 56–7, 66
African American women's language (AAWL) *see* language (AAWL)
African cosmologies/diasporic religions *see* black spiritual traditions; blues and conjure; diaspora heritage and ancestry; orishas; Oshún; *entries beginning* spiritual
African Sande initiation rituals 137, 138–9
Afro-Cuban Lukumí religion 88–95, 128
"All Night" 155, 183, 248
ancestors 49, 52, 86, 87, 92–3, 171–2; *see also* diaspora heritage and ancestry
"Anger" 80, 94, 117–18, 119, 210
anger/rage: Black fat femmes 11, 12; "eroticized rage" 35–6; female 24
"Apathy" 46–7, 80, 94–5, 118, 119, 136–7
Apeshit 41, 155, 199–200
art *see* Beysthetics
artist-executive CEO as auteur 223
Atlantic World/Ocean 88, 116–17; Oshún 126, 129, 131

B-Day 174, 186–7
Badejo, Diedre 125, 130
Baker, Josephine 106
BaKongo/Kongo cosmology 135, 138–9

Baldwin, James 78–9
Barber, Karin 129–30
beauty: and Black fat femmes and women 9–14; light skin 31, 34, 35, 36, 127–8, 186; Oshún 18; and politics 7, 17; *see also* "Becky with the good hair"
"Becky with the good hair" 12–13, 31–3, 40–1; calling out 33–4; hair journeys 35–7; up(braiding) 37–40
Beier, Ulli 127–9
Belafonte, Harry 150–1
Bell, Christa and Ward, Mako Fitts 134
Beloved (Morrison) 42, 116
Beyisms: sociolinguistic analysis 63–7
Beyoncé: diverse responses to 5–7; Louvre tour 198–200; and Obamas 36, 37; Oprah Winfrey interview 43, 45; Parkwood Entertainment 220, 222–6, 240; wealth 155–7, 224, 225
Beyoncé (awards and performances) 224; Billboard (2011) 194–5; Country Music Association (CMA) (2016) 189; Grammy 99, 223–4, 241, 242; Grammy (2017) 17, 40, 52–3, 86, 88, 98, 99–101, 106–7, 146, 236; Peabody (2016) 220; Songwriter of the Year (ASCAP) 225; Super Bowl, New Orleans 120–1, 137–8, 139–40, 152, 157, 236
Beyoncé (family): daughter *see* Carter, Blue Ivy; and early life 147–8, 185–6; father *see* Knowles, Mathew; grandmother

112–13, 115, 161; husband *see* Jay-Z;
mother *see* Knowles Lawson, Tina; sister
see Knowles, Solange; twins (Rumi and
Sir) 52–3, 80
Beyoncé (media acclaim): *Fast Company*
magazine 225; *Glamour Magazine* 224;
Ms. magazine 34; *Time* magazine cover
(2014) 31, 239
Beysthetics: art aesthetics 195–6;
"Formation" 196–8; imitation/
plagiarism192–4; Louvre tour 198–200
Big Freedia 189
Billboard charts/Awards 187, 194–5,
223–4, 240
black church tradition *see* Christianity
Black fat femmes and women 9–14
Black Feminine Divine 98–9; Beyoncé as
Holy Grail 99–101; God and Goddess
theology 102–5; *slay* factor 105–7
Black feminist scholarship 1–4
Black Feminist Triune Divine 86
Black feminist voodoo aesthetics 3, 24–5
Black Lives Matter movement 38, 40, 49,
61, 141, 157
Black Madonna 86, 98, 101
Black Panther Party 120–1, 152, 236; and
Black Power 157
black sociality 172–3
black spiritual traditions 20, 21; conjure
women 204; feminist voodoo aesthetics
3, 24–5; and folk-heroes 20–2, 25; and
sexuality/sexual love 19, 22–3; *see also*
orishas
black swan effect 164; early music business
(1853–1921) 217–20; queering cis-gender
normativity and revolutionary blackness
216–17; rethinking impact of black
women 215–16; and transmedia
storytelling 220–30
Black Swan Record Company 218–20
Black women: economic and social trends
145–6
#BlackGirlMagic 146, 152, 206
blogs 1, 2, 43, 228–9
blues and conjure 203–4; Beyoncé blues as
feminism 208–12; Beyoncé as conjure
woman 206–8; Louisiana hoodoo 203–6;
marginalized status of women 204, 205
blues queens 218
The Bluest Eye (Morrison) 34
Boo Hag/Soucouyant 117–18
bottom bitch to candid convert 133–5
Bradley, Regina 61, 62, 72
Brooks, Daphne 169, 174–5, 186, 207
Brown, James 239

Burley, Ingrid 225
Burrell, Colleen 43

capitalism 155–7; white supremacist
patriarchy 31–2, 145, 147–8, 239
Carpenter, Les 140
Carter, Blue Ivy (daughter) 17, 37, 38, 43,
101, 120, 141, 199, 209
Cervenak, Sarah Jane 176–7
"Check On It" 222
Chee, Alexander 221–2
Chenfield, Dylan 105
Chireau, Yvonne P. 203–4, 205
Christ, Carol P. 105
Christianity/black church tradition 85, 86,
100; "Beyoncé Mass" 237; black and
womanist theology 104–5; blues and
conjure 203, 205, 206–8, 210; Emmanuel
A.M.E. church massacre 176; gospel
music 99, 167, 203
cinema *see* film
Coachella 152–3
collaboration: race-gender bias 240–3; as
spiritual praxis 170–3
Collins, Patricia Hill 24, 25
The Color Purple (Walker) 104
A Colored Woman in a White World
(Terrell) 44
Combahee River Collective 60, 163
community/ies: blues and conjure 211–12;
and collaboration 172–3; discursive
59–60; imagined 221; music genres 235
conjure 206–8; *see also* blues and conjure
Cooper, Brittney 6, 32, 34
"Countdown" 193
"Creole" 186
Creole: Louisiana culture 111–12;
subjectivities and roots 183–5, 186;
women 35, 38
Cuba: Afro-Cuban Lukumí religion 88–95,
128; tours 130–1
curses 92–3, 119–20

"Daddy Lessons" 40, 77, 189, 248; verbal
and non-verbal analysis 57, 58, 62, 63–6
Daly, Mary 102–4
Dangerously in Love 148, 248
Darling, Martha J. 42
Dash, Julie: *Daughters of the Dust* 3, 49, 171,
175, 219, 247
Davis, Angela 20, 27, 70–1, 203, 205,
208–9, 211
Dawes, Kwame 81
de Conquer, John 21–2
"Déjà Vu" 174, 186

"Denial" 79, 93–4, 116–17, 135–6, 206–8, 247
DePrince, Michaela 40, 175
Destiny's Child 34, 35, 36, 146, 147, 148–9, 153
Destrehan Plantation rebellion and executions 118, 188
diaspora heritage and ancestry 111–12; New Orleans 115–20; public and private life 111, 112–15, 121
Diplo 71, 226
Divine Mother 86
"Dollbaby Standing in the Orchard at Midday" (Hamilton) 178–9
"Don't Hurt Yourself" 39, 94, 100, 117, 118, 188, 197, 210, 216–17, 247–8; scream 60–1
"Drunk in Love" 134
Duan, Noel Siqi 106
Duparc, Nanette Prud'homme 49

economic and social trends 145–6
"Emptiness" 47, 80, 95, 119, 209, 249
epistemic violence 74–5, 237
"eroticized rage" 35–6
Etter-Lewis, Gwendolyn 62
Everything is Love 153, 199
executive producer role 224–5

Fallon, Kevin 69–70, 71–2, 74, 75
feminist picaresque 221–2
Fennell, Christopher C. 139
film: Black woman's narrative in 246–9; collaboration as spiritual praxis 170–3; hair styles 36; representations of Blackness 78–9
"Flawless" 134, 150, 173, 187
folk-heroes 20–2, 25
folklore see black spiritual traditions; orishas
"For Women Who Are Difficult to Love" (Shire) 77–8, 79
"Forgiveness" 119–20
forgiveness 133, 138–9
"Formation" 5, 33, 37–8, 59, 69, 111, 152, 210; arts and culture 196–8; and capitalism 155–7; performing the ancestor 120–1; queer performers 189; "slay" 106; "Texas bama" 86, 111, 184, 185, 196; world tour 152–3, 195, 236; and Yemayá iconography 26–8
"Forward" 91, 196–7
Franklin, Aretha 166–8, 169–70
"Freedom" 7, 40, 59, 85, 141, 156, 226
freedom and sexual love 19, 22–3, 25, 27–8, 71

Garrison, Lucas 243
genealogies: of loss 49, 50, 120; see also Western South
"Girl Power" 149
Gleason, Judith 130
goddesses: God and Goddess theology 102–5; Kali 86, 98, 106–7; symbol 105–6; Yemayá 26–8, 94, 125, 208; see also Oshún
"good girl" image 149–50, 151
gospel music 99, 167, 203
Grammy Awards see under Beyoncé (awards and performances)
grandmother's lemonade recipe 112–13, 115, 161
Greenfield, Elizabeth Taylor 217–18
"Grief Has Its Blue Hands in Her Hair" (Shire) 80
Griffin, Farah Jasmin 112, 206
Gyn/Ecology (Daly) 102–4

hair styles see "Becky with the good hair"
Hamilton, Allison Janae 176, 178–9
Harding, Rachel Elizabeth 131
Harlow, Winnie 40
Harvard Business School case study 224–5
HBO 43, 133, 220–1, 223, 235
healing: blueprint for 3; family and ancestral heritage 119–20; grandmother's lemonade recipe 112–13, 115, 161; maternal loss and 49, 50, 120; music (blues and conjure) 203–4, 210–12; "Redemption" 112–13, 115
Hebrew Bible 85–6, 237
Henderson, Cinque 167
Henry, John 20–1
Higginbotham, Evelyn Brooks 58
"High John de Conquer" (Hurston) 21–2
Hill, Lauryn 107, 235, 240
Hine, Darlene Clark 44
hip-hop 217, 235, 237–8, 240, 242–3
Hobson, Janell 2, 34, 120
"Hold Up" 11, 24, 25–6, 39, 93–4, 100, 127, 135, 188, 192–3, 208, 210, 226, 228, 229, 247, 249; verbal and non-verbal analysis 57, 60–1, 63–6
Holland, Sharon 42
hoodoo 203–6
hooks, bell 1, 6, 19–20, 23–4, 25–6, 27, 31, 32, 33, 72, 150, 155–6, 234–5, 239
"Hope" 80, 140–1
Houston 185–7, 187–8, 197, 210; "H-town vicious" 186–9
Houston, Whitney 151, 239–40

"How to Wear Your Mother's Lipstick" (Shire) 77
Hurricane Katrina 26, 27, 140, 141–2, 172, 197
Hurston, Zora Neale 19–20, 117, 145, 205, 246
"hush harbors" 57, 61–2

Ibú (tributaries) of Oshún 128–9
Ifá divination 90, 93–4
Igba iwa-odu 92
Igbo ontology 114
imitation/"plagiarism" 192–4
implicit knowledges 73–5
impressaria, Beyoncé as 222–6
infertility and miscarriage see motherhood and mourning
infidelity 32–3, 39, 70–1, 111, 112, 134–5, 152, 153; and spiritual rebirth 133–42
initiation rituals 137, 138–9
Internet 234, 236, 237; see also transmedia storytelling
intersectional strategies of language (AAWL) 59–60
"Intuition" 79, 92–3, 113–14, 115, 116–17, 121, 178, 247
"Irreplaceable" 187
itán (legends) and oríkì (orature) 123–4, 126, 128–31
iTunes 221, 223, 224, 225
Iyawo (bride) 207, 208

Jackson, Janet 236, 239
Jackson, Michael 239
Jacobs, Harriet 19
Jafa, Arthur 166–7, 173
Jay-32 33, 35–6, 41, 50, 53, 89
Jay-Z: Apeshit 41, 155, 199–200; art collection and Louvre tour 198–200; cheating/infidelity 32–3, 39, 70–1, 111, 112, 134–5, 152, 153; "Déjà Vu" 174–5; grandmother (Hattie) 112, 161; marriage and respectability 149, 149–50; performances 134; Tidal 221
jazz 219–20
jazz impulse 183–4, 188, 189
jealousy 34; betrayal and reconciliation 70–1
Jones, Gayl 176–7
Jones, Melanie 86
Jordan, June 21
Joseph, Kahlil 77–8, 79, 170–1, 172

Kali (Hindu goddess) 86, 98, 106–7
Kalunga line 135, 137–8

Kayode, Afolabi 125–6
King, Carol and Goffin, Gerry 166
knowledges, implicit 73–5
Knowles, Mathew 35, 119, 147, 148, 150, 152, 185, 194
Knowles, Solange 37, 147–8, 163
Knowles Lawson, Tina 17, 35, 99–100, 101, 119, 147, 152, 184–5
Kongo/BaKongo cosmology 135, 138–9

Lamar, Kendrick 242–3
Lanehart, Sonja 57
language (AAWL) 55–6; Beyisms 63–7; defining foundational terms 56–9; feature frequency 64–5; intersectional strategies 59–60; rhetorical functions 60–2
Laughlin, Charles 113
legacy 161–4
"Letter to Mary Daly" (Lorde) 103–4
Levine, Lawrence 21
Life is But a Dream 43–4, 45, 50, 149
light skin 31, 34, 35, 36, 127–8, 186
Lomax, Alan 226
Lorde, Audre 103–4, 106
loss see motherhood and mourning
"Loss" 48
Louisiana 111–12, 184–5, 188, 189; hoodoo 203–6
"Louisiana Hoodoo Blues" (Ma Rainey) 204
love 17, 18; freedom and sexual love 19, 22–3, 25, 27–8, 71; self- 24, 61, 119, 120, 133–4, 138
Love, Velma 136
"Love Drought" 88, 100, 119, 137–8, 141, 225
Lukumí religion 88–95, 128
Lumet, Jenny 7

Ma Rainey, Gertrude 204, 209
McKinney, Kelsey 241–2
McKittrick, Katherine 118, 176
McSpadden, Lesley 49, 50
Malcolm X 80, 117, 121, 153, 216–17, 248
Mamba's Daughters (play) 219
mammification 10–11
Maner, Sequoia 77
Martin, Kameelah 3, 24–5, 80, 204
Matibag, Eugenio 90
memory 113–14, 251; and rememory 116
Mercer, Kobena 32
Messy Mya 189
Mexican migration and musical influences 185, 186–7
minkisi 139

Miranda, Carolina 78
miscarriage and infertility *see* motherhood and mourning
misogynoir 216, 220, 222, 237
Mock, Janet 6, 31, 150, 239
Mona Lisa 198–200
Montejo, Esteban 90–1
Moore, Madison 27
Morgan, Marcyliena 58, 59–60, 61, 66
Morrison, Toni 22, 34, 50, 111, 113–14, 114, 121; *Beloved* 42, 116; Portland State University speech 144–5, 153–4
Moten, Fred 167–8, 172
motherhood 17–18, 80, 86, 101, 209
motherhood and mourning 42, 80; Black Lives Matter movement 49, *50*, 141; blood, pain, and miscarriage 45–8; genealogies of loss 49, *50*, 120; monstrous mothers and fertility 52–3; personal reflections on blood 50–2; silence, dissemblance and personal narratives 43–5
The Mrs. Carter Show World Tour 150
music criticism 70–4; and epistemic violence 74–5, 237
music and entertainment industry *see* black swan effect; race-gender bias in pop music; transmedia storytelling

"Nail Technician as Palm Reader" 80, 140–1
Nash, Jennifer 75
"Nasty Girl" 148
National Association of Colored Women (NACW) 44
"natural woman" 166–8; archive 169–70; collaboration as spiritual praxis 170–3; politics 173–5; spiritual practice of wandering outdoors 176–9; and supernatural aesthetics 175–6
New Orleans 38; as city of the ancestor 115–20; Hurricane Katrina 26, 27, 140, 141–2, 172, 197; music 186, 189; Super Bowl performances 120–1, 137–8, 139–40, 152, 157, 236; *see also* Western South
Newsome, Bree 176
Nigeria: Oshogbo River 125–6, 127–9, 130
"No Angel" 187–8, 197
nommo (naming) 211
Norton, Yolanda 85–6, 237
Nunley, Vorris 61–2
Nwafor, Matthew Ikechukwu 114, 119

Obama, Barack 166; and Michelle 36, 37, 145

Obba Nani 89
Obsessed (film) 36
occult black womanhood 205–6, 211–12
odú 91–2
"Oh Daddy" (Waters) 219–20
opera 217–18
oríki (orature) 123, 129–30
orishas 25–8, 89–91, 94, 207; and *odú* 91–2; and Olodumare 89–90; Yemayá 26–8, 94, 125, 208; *see also* Oshún
Ortega, Mariana 74–5
Oshogbo River, Nigeria 125–6, 127–9, 130
Oshún 17–18, 26, 38–9, 40, 87, 88, 93–5, 98, 100–1, *124*; embodiment, spiritual possession and conversion 135–6; goddess of living, moving waters 123–6; "Hold Up" 188, 208; *itan* and *oríki*: stories and orature 123–4, 128–31; "Love Drought" 138, 141; as mermaid 116; water and fire: music and motion 126–8; yellow dress 100–1, 136, 170, 188, 192, 193–4, *228*
Otero, Solimar 26
"Other Woman" 32–3, 35, 39, 40

"paper" 155, *156*, 157
Parker, Alison 44
"past and future merge to meet us here" 93, 113–14, 161, 188–9
patakís (myths) 90–1
patriarchy: of Christian church 207–8; of music and entertainment industry 219–20, 227–8; white supremacist capitalist 31–2, 145, 147–8, 239
Pérez, Elizabeth 26, 27
Pierce, Yolanda 100
"plagiarism"/imitation 192–4
plantations *see under* slavery
poetry 75; Warsan Shire 77–81, 101, 113, 119–20, 152, 161, 173, 226
police violence 49, 157
political agency 27–8; folk-heroes 20–2, 25; narrow concept of 23–4; and other modes of agency 22, 25; sexual love and freedom 19, 22–3, 25–6, 27–8, 71
political and personal 5–6, 71
politics: and beauty 7, 17 (*see also* "Becky with the good hair"); of joy 22; "natural woman" 173–5; public and private life 121; respectability 144–54; and socio-historical vision 164; and sound/musical performance 71, 72–4, 75; *see also* social activism/resistance
Pough, Gwendolyn 55
Pratten, Robert 221
"Pray You Catch Me" 59, 92–3, *178*, 247

"Pretty Hurts" 37
Prince 48, 99, 234, 235, 239
public and private discourses *see* language (AAWL)
public and private life 111, 112–15, 121

Queen Nefertiti 94–5; and regal line 101
The Queen of the Night (Chee) 221–2
Queen Ya Ya of Washitaw Nation Mardi Gras Indians 49, 162
queer/queering 26, 27, 189, 216–17
Quevedo, Marysol 130–1

"Race Champions" 22
race-gender bias in pop music 234–7; collaboration tax 240–3; conceptions of men and women artists 238–40; I'm not a fan but ... 237–8
race-gender double standards 71–2
racism 144–5, 176
Ramsey, Guthrie 251
Rasmus, Rudy 85
Red Lobster restaurant 198
"Redemption" 112–13, 115, 177–8, 248
"Reformation" 119, 137–40
rememory 116
reproduction and loss *see* motherhood and mourning
respectability politics 144–54
"Resurrection" 79, 91, 120
rhetorical functions of language (AAWL) 60–2
Roach, Joseph 115, 120, 121
Roberts, Kamaria and Downs, Kenya 114, 116, 118
Robinson, Zandria 27, 114–15, 183
roots: rootedness and up-rootedness 175–6; western South 184–6; *see also* diaspora heritage and ancestry
Rowe, Bruce M. and Levine, Diane P. 59
Ryan, Judylyn 171

sampling 226
"Sandcastles" 57–8, *73*, 91, 100
Sande initiation rituals 137, 138–9
"Say My Name" 35
Selena 186–7
self-definition 22–3, 26, 27
self-love 24, 61, 119, 120, 133–4, 138
Senbanjo, Laolu 171–2
sexuality: blues music 205, 208–10; and desexualized/non-sexual black women 9, 10, 11; hypersexualized display 31–2, 174–5; love and freedom 19, 22–3, 25–6, 27–8, 71; symbolism 21; *see also* infidelity

Sharpe, Christina 47, 161, 162, 168
Shire, Warsan 77–81, 101, 113, 119–20, 152, 161, 173, 226
shotgun houses 187–8
Shriver Report 35
silence: "hush harbors" 57, 61–2; miscarriage and infertility 43–5
Simmons, LaKisha Michelle 115, 118–19
Sir Mix-a-lot 33–4
"6 Inch" 47–8, 62, 95, 119, 209
slavery 19, 22, 23, 39, 40; blues and conjure 203, 204; and emancipation 71, 203; genealogies of loss 49, 120; opera 217–18; orisha and patakís myths 90–1; plantations 118, 162, 174, 186, 188; shotgun houses 187–8; "white supremacist capitalist patriarchy" 31
"slay" 26, 27, 38; Black and feminist future 105–7; Kali (Hindu goddess) 86, 106–7
Smitherman, Geneva 56–7
social activism/resistance 141–2, 150–1, 157, 162, 236; Super Bowl performances, New Orleans 120–1, 137–8, 139–40, 152, 157, 236
social and economic trends 145–6
sociolinguistic analysis *see* language (AAWL)
songwriting executive role 223–4
"Sorry" 11–13, 39, *46*, 63, *78*, 94–5, 100, 188, 209, 248
Soucouyant/Boo Hag 117–18
South: Afro-Cuban religion 88–9; Black fat femmes and women 10–11; Black women 250–2; folk archives 226; misogynoir 220; spiritual practice of wandering outdoors 176–9; *see also* blues and conjure; Western South
"spiritual ecology" 168
spiritual longing 85–7
spiritual practices 170–3, 176–9; *see also* black spiritual traditions; blues and conjure
spiritual rebirth 133–42
Stoever-Ackerman, Jennifer 75
storytelling 215; *itán* (legends) and *oríkì* (orature) 123–4, 126, 128–31; *patakís* (myths) 90–1;
transmedia 220–30
Super Bowl performances, New Orleans 120–1, 137–8, 139–40, 152, 157, 236
supernatural aesthetics 175–6
Survivor 148
Swift, Jonathan 216
Swift, Taylor 36–7, 224, 239, 242

"Take My Hand, Precious Lord" 99

Taleb, Nassim Nicholas 216
TED Fellows blog 228–9
Tejano music 186–7
Terrell, Mary Church 44
"terrorist" accusation 6, 31, 32, 234–5, 239
Texas 189, 197; *see also* Houston
"Texas bama" 86, 111, 184, 185, 196
Their Eyes Were Watching God (Hurston)
 19–20, 22–3
Thomas, Erik R. and Bailey, Guy 66
Tidal 221, 235
To Pimp a Butterfly (Lamar) 242–3
Tobman, Ethan 197
transmedia storytelling 220–30

Union, Gabrielle 45

Valdés, Vanessa K. 25–6
verbal and non-verbal analysis *see* language
 (AAWL)
Vermallis, Carol 172
violence: against Black fat women and
 femmes 11, 12, 13, 14; epistemic 74–5,
 237; female 24; and fierceness in orisha
 worship 26–7; police 49, 157; racist 176
"voiced breaths" 59
Voodoo aesthetics 3, 24

"wake work" 168
Walker, Alice 104–5
Wallis, Quvenzhané 141
wandering outdoors, spiritual practice of
 176–9
water imagery/symbolism: Anger and
 Reformation 119; Denial 116–17, 135;
 initiation ritual 139; Intuition 113–14,

116–17; orishas 89, 94, 100, 188, 208;
 spirituality and Christianity 206–7; *see also*
 Oshún
Waters, Ethel 218–20
Wenger, Susanne and Chesi, Gert 126, 129
We're Going to Need More Wine (Union) 45
West, Kayne 36, 242
Western South 164, 183–4, 189; music and
 cultural heritage 186–8; "past and future
 merge to meet us here" 188–9; roots
 184–6
White, Deborah Gray 44–5
white clay/chalk face painting 94, 137,
 139, 140
white dresses/clothing 138–9, 141, 207
"white male gaze" 150
white male music critics *see* music criticism
white supremacism 9, 10, 11, 12, 13;
 capitalist patriarchy 31–2, 145, 147–8,
 239; film 79
white women *see* "Becky with the good
 hair"
"Who Run the World (Girls)" 194–5
Williams, Serena 11–12, 39, 118–19, 175,
 188, 248
Wilson, Carl 69–70, 71–2,
 74, 75
Winfrey, Oprah 43, 45
womanist theology 104–5
Wright, Richard 19–20, 21

Yeboah, Amy 114, 116, 118
yellow dress 100–1, 136, 170, 188, 192,
 193–4, *228*
Yemayá 26–8, 94, 125, 208
Yoruba religion *see* orishas; Oshún

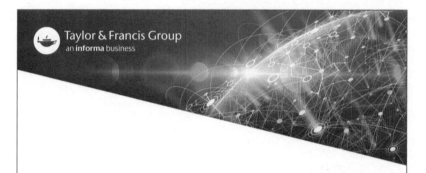